D1608472

KJV Commentary
BIBLE

Presented to

_____

On this _____ day of _____

Occasion

_____

By

_____

KJV
Commentary
BIBLE
King James Version

Red-Letter Edition

world
PUBLISHING
SINCE 1928

KJV Commentary Bible
King James Version

Printed in the United States of America
1 2 3 4 5 6 7 8 9 — 14 13 12 11 10 09 08 07 06

Table of Contents

Where to Find It in the *KJV Commentary Bible*

A. Charts appear at various places in the Bible text. They are listed on the Table of Contents Page and in the Index to Major Notes and Charts.

B. Each book of the Bible has an introduction that always includes Author, Key Verse, Time, and Theme.

A.

	Ma	Mk	Lk	Jo
FROM THE RESURRECTION TO THE ASCENSION—*Cont'd*				
2. The report of the guard	28:11-15			
3. The walk to Emmaus		16:12-13	24:13-35	
4. Appearances				
To the disciples in Jerusalem, Thomas not present		16:14	24:36-43	20:19-25
To Thomas with the others				20:26-29
To seven disciples by the sea of Galilee				21:1-24
To the Eleven in Galilee	28:16-20	16:15-18		
Final appearance and ascension		16:19-20	24:44-53	

B.

AUTHOR: Jesus nicknamed John and his brother, James, "sons of thunder" (Mk 3:17). John was evidently among the Galileans who followed John the Baptist until they were called to follow Jesus at the outset of His public ministry. These Galileans were later called to become full-time disciples of the Lord (Lk 5:1–11), and John was among the twelve men who were selected to be apostles (Lk 6:12–16). The author of this Gospel is identified only as the disciple "whom Jesus loved" (Jo 13:23; 19:26; 21:7), but attention to detail concerning geography and Jewish culture in the Gospel lend credibility to the author's claim to be an eyewitness. The strong testimony of the early church relates this eyewitness to the apostle John.

KEY VERSE: Jo 20:30-31

TIME: C. A.D. 29–33

THEME: John is a great book for new or young Christians because it intentionally helps the reader understand the significance of Jesus. What becomes increasingly clear as you read the Gospel of John is that Jesus does not fit the image of someone who is simply a nice moral teacher. Only a lunatic would make the claims he makes for himself unless he was who he said he was. John leaves no room for indecision. Like the many people Jesus encounters in the book, as you read, you must either reject him or accept him, and say in the end like Thomas: "My Lord and my God" (20:28). This Gospel is an incredibly powerful presentation of Jesus.

IN the beginning was the Word, and the Word was with God, and the Word was God. 2 ᴿThe same was in the beginning with God. Ge 1:1 3 ᴿAll things were made by him; and without him was not any thing made that was made. Ps 33:6 4 ᴿIn him was life; and the life was the light of men. [1 Jo 5:11]

1:1–4

C. The World's Visual Reference System™ notes the prophecies of the first coming of Christ with a ✝ in the text and a footnote indicates the verse of the reference and the passage in which the prophecy is fulfilled.

8   And they heard ᴿthe voice of the LORD God walking in the garden in the cool of the day: and Adam and his wife ᴿhid themselves from the presence of the LORD God amongst the trees of the garden.   Job 38:1 · Je 23:24
9   And the LORD God called unto Adam, and said unto him, Where *art* thou?

this, thou *art* cursed above all cattle, and above every beast of the field; upon thy belly shalt thou go, and ᴿdust shalt thou eat all the days of thy life: Is 65:25; Mi 7:17
✝ 15   And I will put enmity between thee and the woman, and between thy seed and her seed; it

✝ 3:15—Ga 4:4   **C.**

D.

3:5 *ye shall be as gods.* God's fullness of knowledge was only one of the superiorities that set Him apart from the woman. But the serpent combined all of God's superiority over the woman into this one audacious appeal to her pride. **3:6–7 Sin's Consequences**—At first Adam's sin does not appear to be all that significant. All he did was take a bite of some fruit. But Scripture takes it very seriously. Adam's sin was one of disobedience and rebellion. God told Adam not to eat the fruit of the "tree of the knowledge of good and evil" under penalty of death (2:17). That action of eating the fruit changed Adam's whole nature as well as his relationship with God. Adam became a sinner and as such he died. His spiritual death was immediate, the physical death progressive. Adam, who began the human race, then became the source of sin for the world. We are all sinners by nature because Adam sinned (Ro 5:12–14). We inherit sin from Adam in our natures in the same way we inherit many of our physical characteristics from our parents. Sin is a universal part of our spiritual inheritance. **3:14–21 The Covenant with Adam**—The Adamic Covenant is the second covenant God made with man. It sets forth conditions that will be in effect until the curse of death is lifted (Is 11:6–10; Ro 8:18–23). In Christ's death and resurrection we have the beginning (firstfruits) of the lifting of the curse. The ultimate lifting of the curse will happen as Christ establishes his final reign on earth. **3:14 *unto the serpent.*** The Lord turned first to the serpent and brought judgment upon him. God did not excuse the woman because she was deceived, but He did bring the harsher judgment on the one who had deceived her.

D. Comprehensive commentary footnotes are found on almost every page of the *KJV Commentary Bible*. Notes such as **3:5 *ye shall be as gods*** and **3:14 *unto the serpent*** are exegetical in nature and reveal information that comes from a detailed study of the text. Notes such as **3:6–7 Sin's Consequences** and **3:14–21 The Covenant with Adam** are more theological in nature and when linked together give a systematic overview of Scripture. An index topical to the major commentary footnotes is found on pages ix–xii in the front matter of this volume.

E. Throughout the text the World's Visual Reference System™ notes all of the promises God has given us and the miracles of the Bible. These are noted by a 🕊 in the text for the promises and a 🔥 for the miracles. With each promise or miracle a footnote is found at the bottom right of the text indicating the verses that are part of the promise or miracle.

A system of cross-references are included at the end of verses that have room for a reference. In 3:1 you will find "ᴿinto the temple at the hour of prayer, ᴿbeing the ninth *hour*." The ᴿ indicates that there is a reference to that word or phrase. At the end of this verse two references appear: "2:46" which goes with the ᴿ before "into" and "10:30; Ps 55:17" which goes with the ᴿ before "being."

Lord added to the church daily such as should be saved.   5:14

🔥 3 Now Peter and John went up together ᴿinto the temple at the hour of prayer, ᴿ*being* the ninth *hour*.   2:46 · 10:30; Ps 55:17

2   And a certain man lame from his mother's womb was carried, whom they laid daily at the gate of the temple which is called Beautiful, ᴿto ask alms of them that entered into the temple; v. 10

3   Who seeing Peter and John about to go into the temple asked an alms.

4   And Peter, fastening his eyes upon him with John, said, Look on us.

5   And he gave heed unto them,

11   And as the lame man which was healed held Peter and John, all the people ran together unto them in the porch that is called Solomon's, greatly wondering.

12   And when Peter saw *it*, he answered unto the people, Ye men of Israel, why marvel ye at this? or why look ye so ᵀearnestly on us, as though by our own power or ᵀholiness we had made this man to walk?   *intently · godliness*

13   ᴿThe God of Abraham, and of Isaac, and of Jacob, the God of our fathers, ᴿhath glorified his Son Jesus; whom ye delivered up, and denied him in the presence of

(🕊 2:42–47   🔥 3:1–4)   **E.**

2:42–47 Being in the Church—Converts were apparently immediately incorporated into the body of believers that became the church. Being involved in the Jerusalem church clearly must have changed the lives of these new believers dramatically. This

F.   The end-of-verse reference system includes some references enclosed in brackets that have conceptual connections with the original verse rather than another use of the word or phrase. In 3:21, "ᴿrestitution of all things" references "Ma 17:11; [Ro 8:21]" at the end of the verse. The Matthew reference is about the prophecy given Malachi that there will be restoration of all things. There is a direct connection and a related use of the same terminology. In the bracketed Roman's reference believers play a part in the redemption of creation from the bondage of sin. It is a related concept with different terminology. Also at the end of verses are translation notes. In 4:2 "ᵀgrieved" has a note at the end of the verse "*greatly disturbed.*" This note indicates that there is another way of translating the word that may be helpful to the reader.

18 But those things, which God before had shewed by the mouth of all his prophets, that Christ should suffer, he hath so fulfilled. **19** ᴿRepent ye therefore, and be converted, that your sins may be blotted out, when the times of refreshing shall come from the presence of the Lord;   [2:38; 26:20]

20 And he shall send Jesus Christ, which before was preached unto you:

F.   21 Whom the heaven must receive until the times of ᴿrestitution of all things, ᴿwhich God hath spoken by the mouth of all his holy prophets since the world began.   Ma 17:11; [Ro 8:21] · Lk 1:70

22 For Moses truly said unto the fathers, ᴿA prophet shall the Lord your God raise up unto you of your brethren, like unto me; him shall ye hear in all things whatsoever he shall say unto you.   7:37

every one of you from his iniquities.   Is 42:1; Ma 1:21

4 And as they spake unto the people, the priests, and the captain of the temple, and the Sad'-du-cees, came upon them,

2 Being ᵀgrieved that they taught the people, and preached through Jesus the resurrection from the dead.   *greatly disturbed*

3 And they laid hands on them, and put *them* in ᵀhold unto the next day: for it was now ᵀeventide.   *custody · evening*

4 Howbeit many of them which heard the word believed; and the number of the men was about five thousand.

5 And it came to pass on the morrow, that their rulers, and elders, and scribes,

3:20–21 **G.**

G.   World's Visual Reference System™ also includes prophecies about the second coming of our Lord. There is a 👑 in the text and a footnote at the bottom right of the text that indicates which verses are included in the prophecy.

Index to Major Notes and Charts

The

OLD TESTAMENT

The First Book of Moses Called
GENESIS

AUTHOR: Nowhere in the Book of Genesis is the author named. Although the events of the book end 300 years before Moses was born, the rest of the Bible and most of church historians attribute the authorship of Genesis to Moses. Both the Old and New Testaments have many references to Moses as its author (Ex 7:14; Le 1:1–2; Nu 33:2; De 1:1; Da 9:11–13; Mal 4:4; Ma 8:4; Mk 12:26; Lk 16:29; Jo 7:19; Ac 26:22; Ro 10:19). Both early Jewish and Christian writers name Moses as the author.

KEY VERSE: Ge 3:15

TIME: C. 4000–1804 B.C.

THEME: After the initial story of the world's creation, Genesis (beginnings) covers two basic subjects: God and man. God creates man. Man disobeys God and alienates himself from God. Genesis is the story then of the subsequent interactions between God and man that bring them back together into a right relationship. As such, the book points to the beginnings of the way of change, of restoration, and of a new way of life. Genesis sets the tone for the rest of the Bible with clear teaching on following God's call, believing in His promises, and being obedient to His commands. The main characters who dominate the story are the patriarchs: Abraham, Isaac, Jacob and Joseph.

IN the beginning God created the heaven and the earth.

2   And the earth was without form, and void; and darkness *was* upon the face of the deep. ᴿAnd the Spirit of God moved upon the face of the waters.   Is 40:13, 14

3   ᴿAnd God said, Let there be light: and there was light. Ps 33:6, 9

4   And God saw the light, that *it was* good: and God divided the light from the darkness.

5   And God called the light Day, and the ᴿdarkness he called Night.

And the evening and the morning were the first day.   Ps 19:2

6   And God said, ᴿLet there be a firmament in the midst of the waters, and let it divide the waters from the waters.   Job 37:18; 2 Pe 3:5

7   And God made the firmament, ᴿand divided the waters which *were* under the firmament from the waters which *were* ᴿabove the firmament: and it was so.   Job 38:8–11; Pr 8:27–29 · Ps 148:4

8   And God called the ᵀfirma-

1:1–3

1:1 Creation—Biblical revelation begins with a simple, strong, and sublime affirmation. Instead of arguing the existence of God, it declares that the very existence of the universe depends on the creative power of God. The world we live in was created by God and belongs to Him. His absolute ownership requires our faithful stewardship of all things. **1:1 *In the beginning.*** No information is given to us about what happened before the creation of the physical universe, though John 1:1 speaks of this time. It is possible that the rise, rebellion, and judgment of Satan transpired before the events of this chapter. **God.** This standard Hebrew term for deity *Elohim* is in the form called the plural of majesty or plural of intensity. In contrast to the ordinary plural (gods), this plural means "the fullness of deity" or "God—very God." Furthermore, the use of the plural allows for the later revelation of the Trinity (see 11:7; Ma 28:19; Jo 1:1–3).   **1:3 *Let there be light.*** These words express a principal theme of the Bible: God bringing light into darkness (see Is 9:1–2). Here, God produced physical light. The New Testament records God sending His Son to be the light of the world (Jo 8:12), bringing release from the spiritual darkness of bondage to sin. In the end, there will no longer be any darkness at all and we will be face to face with the source of light (Re 21:23).   **1:7 *divided the waters.*** The description of upper and lower waters is somewhat mysterious; it has been theorized that this is simply a reference to the division between the water of the seas and rivers on the surface of the earth and the water vapor which is part of the atmosphere.

ment Heaven. And the evening and the morning were the second day.   *expanse*

9 And God said, [R] Let the waters under the heaven be gathered together unto one place, and let the dry *land* appear: and it was so.   Ps 104:6–9; Je 5:22; 2 Pe 3:5

10 And God called the dry *land* Earth; and the gathering together of the waters called he Seas: and God saw that *it was* good.

11 And God said, Let the earth [R] bring forth grass, the herb yielding seed, *and* the [R] fruit tree yielding fruit after his kind, whose seed *is* in itself, upon the earth: and it was so.   He 6:7 · Lk 6:44

12 And the earth brought forth grass, *and* herb yielding seed after his kind, and the tree yielding fruit, whose seed *was* in itself, after his kind: and God saw that *it was* good.

13 And the evening and the morning were the third day.

14 And God said, Let there be [R] lights in the firmament of the heaven to divide the day from the night; and let them be for signs, and for [R] seasons, and for days, and years: De 4:19 · Ps 104:19

15 And let them be for lights in the firmament of the heaven to give light upon the earth: and it was so.

16 And God made two great lights; the [R] greater light to rule the day, and the [R] lesser light to rule the night: *he made* the stars also.   Ps 136:8 · De 17:3; Ps 8:3

17 And God set them in the firmament of the [R] heaven to give light upon the earth,   Je 33:20, 25

18 And to [R] rule over the day and over the night, and to divide the light from the darkness: and God saw that *it was* good.   Je 31:35

19 And the evening and the morning were the fourth day.

20 And God said, Let the waters bring forth abundantly the moving creature that hath life, and fowl *that* may fly above the earth in the open firmament of heaven.

21 And [R] God created great [T] whales, and every living creature that moveth, which the waters brought forth abundantly, after their kind, and every winged fowl after his kind: and God saw that *it was* good.   Ps 104:25–28 · *sea creatures*

22 And God blessed them, saying, [R] Be fruitful, and multiply, and fill the waters in the seas, and let fowl multiply in the earth.   8:17

23 And the evening and the morning were the fifth day.

24 And God said, Let the earth bring forth the living creature after his kind, cattle, and creeping thing, and beast of the earth after his kind: and it was so.

25 And God made the beast of the earth after his kind, and cattle after their kind, and every thing that creepeth upon the earth after his kind: and God saw that *it was* good.

1:11–12 seed . . . kind. God not only created plant life; He also set in motion the process that makes plant life reproduce. **1:14 *for signs, and for seasons.*** Some have mistakenly viewed these words as a biblical basis for astrology. The signs in this case relate to phases of the moon and the relative positions of stars that mark the passage of time from the vantage point of earth. The two words form a pair that may be translated *seasonal signs.* **1:16 *he made the stars also.*** This is a remarkable statement. In the ancient Middle East, other religions worshipped, deified, and mystified the stars. Israel's neighbors revered the stars and looked to them for guidance. In contrast, the biblical creation story gives the stars only the barest mention, as though the writer shrugged and said, *And, oh, yes, He also made the stars.* Such a statement showed great contempt for ancient Babylonian astrology (Ps 29; 93). **1:24 *living creature.*** This expression contains the word sometimes used for the soul, but the word can also mean "life," "being," "living thing," or "person," depending on the context. The same phrase is used for man in 2:7.

26 And God said, [R]Let us make man in our image, after our likeness: and let them have dominion over the fish of the sea, and over the fowl of the air, and over the cattle, and over all the earth, and over every creeping thing that creepeth upon the earth.   Jam 3:9

27 So God created man in his *own* image, in the image of God created he him; [R]male and female created he them.   Ma 19:4

28 And God blessed them, and God said unto them, Be fruitful, and multiply, and replenish the earth, and [R]subdue it: and have dominion over the fish of the sea, and over the fowl of the air, and over every living thing that moveth upon the earth.   1 Co 9:27

29 And God said, Behold, I have given you every herb bearing seed, which *is* upon the face of all the earth, and every tree, in the which *is* the fruit of a tree yielding seed; to you it shall be for meat.

30 And to [R]every beast of the earth, and to every fowl of the air, and to every thing that creepeth upon the earth, wherein *there is*

life, *I have given* every green herb for meat: and it was so.   Ps 145:15

31 And [R]God saw every thing that he had made, and, behold, *it was* very good. And the evening and the morning were the sixth day.   [Ps 104:24; 1 Ti 4:4]

2 Thus the heavens and the earth were finished, and [R]all the host of them.   Ps 33:6

2 [R]And on the seventh day God ended his work which he had made; and he rested on the seventh day from all his work which he had made.   Ex 20:9–11; He 4:4, 10

3 And God [R]blessed the seventh day, and sanctified it: because that in it he had rested from all his work which God created and made.   [Is 58:13]

4 [R]These *are* the generations of the heavens and of the earth when they were created, in the day that the LORD God made the earth and the heavens,   1:1; Ps 90:1, 2

5 And every plant of the field before it was in the earth, and every herb of the field before it grew: for the LORD God had not

1:27–28

1:26 *in our image.* Since God is spirit (Jo 4:24), there can be no "image" or "likeness" of Him in the normal sense of these words. The traditional view of this passage is that God's image in man is in specific moral, ethical, and intellectual abilities. A more recent view, based on a possible interpretation of Hebrew grammar and the knowledge of the Middle East, interprets the phrase as meaning "Let us make man *as* our image." In ancient times an emperor might command statues of himself to be placed in remote parts of his empire. These symbols would declare that these areas were under his power and reign. So God placed humankind as living symbols of Himself on earth to represent His reign. This interpretation fits well with the command that follows—to reign over all that God has made. **1:28** *replenish the earth, and subdue it.* The word translated *subdue* means "bring into bondage." This harsh term is used elsewhere of military conquest (Ze 9:15) and of God subduing our iniquities (Mi 7:19). Since this direction was given before the fall, it appears that the need to subdue the earth is not because of sin but because God left part of the arranging and ordering of the creation as work for mankind to do. Whatever the case, subdue does not mean "destroy" or "ruin." It does mean to "act as managers who have the authority to run everything as God planned." This command applies equally to male and female. **2:2** *he rested on the seventh day.* God did not rest because of fatigue, but because of His accomplishment. God is never weary (Is 40:28–29). The verb translated "rested" is related to the word for Sabbath, which means "rest." God's rest on the seventh day showed that He was satisfied with the work He had done. **2:4** *the LORD God.* This is a significant term. The word translated *God* is the same word as in 1:1. The word translated *LORD* is the proper name of God, Yahweh (or Jehovah; see Ex 3:14–15). The God of chapter 1 and the LORD God of chapter 2 are one and the same.

R caused it to rain upon the earth, and *there was* not a man R to till the ground. 7:4; Job 5:10 · 3:23

6 But there went up a mist from the earth, and watered the whole face of the ground.

7 And the LORD God formed man *of* the R dust of the ground, and breathed into his nostrils the breath of life; and R man became a living soul. Ps 103:14 · 1 Co 15:45

8 And the LORD God planted R a garden eastward in R Eden; and there he put the man whom he had formed. Is 51:3 · 4:16

9 And out of the ground made the LORD God to grow R every tree that is pleasant to the sight, and good for food; R the tree of life also in the midst of the garden, and the tree of knowledge of good and evil. Eze 31:8 · [Re 2:7; 22:2, 14]

10 And a river went out of Eden to water the garden; and from thence it was parted, and became into four T heads. *riverheads*

11 The name of the first *is* Pi'-son: that *is* it which compasseth R the whole land of Hav'-i-lah, where *there is* gold; 25:18

12 And the gold of that land *is* good: R there *is* bdellium and the onyx stone. Nu 11:7

13 And the name of the second river *is* Gi'-hon: the same *is* it that compasseth the whole land of T E-thi-o'-pi-a. *Cush*

14 And the name of the third river *is* R Hid'-de-kel: T that *is* it which goeth toward the east of Assyria. And the fourth river *is* Eu-phra'-tes. Da 10:4 · The *Tigris*

15 And the LORD God took the man, and put him into the garden of Eden to dress it and to keep it.

16 And the LORD God commanded the man, saying, Of every tree of the garden thou mayest freely eat:

17 But of the tree of the knowledge of good and evil, thou shalt not eat of it: for in the day that thou eatest thereof thou shalt surely R die. Ro 5:12; 1 Co 15:21, 22

18 And the LORD God said, *It is* not good that the man should be alone; R I will make him an help meet for him. 1 Co 11:8, 9

19 R And out of the ground the LORD God formed every beast of ⚡ 2:18

2:6 *mist.* The precise meaning of this word is uncertain. Obviously it refers to some manner of irrigation before the Lord brought the cycles of rain into being. 2:7 *the breath of life.* Although God created light with a mere word (1:3), He created man by fashioning a body out of mud and clay, transforming the clay into something new, and then breathing life into it. This "breath of life" is something which only God can bestow. Medical knowledge enables doctors to keep a human body "alive," keeping the heart pumping and the vital organs functioning, but it does not enable them to keep or to call back the breath of life. Some have speculated that the "breath of life" is the human soul, but later on, animals are also described as having the "breath of life" in their nostrils (7:22), which would seem to indicate that this is simply a reference to the miracle of living, breathing flesh. 2:15–17 **The First Covenant**—In biblical times the purpose of a covenant was to establish an agreement between two persons or groups. The elements of a covenant included a promise on the part of one person and the conditions that needed to be fulfilled, on the part of the other person, in order for the promises to be carried out by both parties to the covenant. The Edenic Covenant is the first covenant mentioned in the Bible. God gave Adam a place in His creation and charged him with the responsibility of caring for the garden. The only condition in the covenant was that Adam could not allow himself to eat of the fruit of the tree of the knowledge of good and evil or he would die. This covenant was terminated by Adam's disobedience which also resulted in man's spiritual and physical death. God then established a new covenant with Adam in Genesis 3:14–21. 2:17 *shalt surely die.* These emphatic words are made of two forms of the verb meaning "to die." The point is not that the guilty person would drop dead on the instant, but that death would surely happen—there is no escape (He 9:27). 2:18 *It is not good.* Until this point, everything in creation was very good.

the field, and every fowl of the air; and [R]brought *them* unto [T]Adam to see what he would call them: and whatsoever Adam called every living creature, that *was* the name thereof.   1:20, 24 · Ps 8:6 · *the man*

20 And Adam gave names to all cattle, and to the fowl of the air, and to every beast of the field; but for Adam there was not found an help meet for him.

21 And the LORD God caused a [R]deep sleep to fall upon Adam, and he slept: and he took one of his ribs, and closed up the flesh instead thereof;   1 Sa 26:12

22 And the rib, which the LORD God had taken from man, made he a woman, [R]and brought her unto the man.   3:20; 1 Ti 2:13

23 And Adam said, This *is* now [R]bone of my bones, and flesh of my flesh: she shall be called Woman, because she was taken out of Man.   29:14; Ep 5:28–30

24 [R]Therefore shall a man leave his father and his mother, and shall cleave unto his wife: and they shall be one flesh.   Ma 19:5

25 [R]And they were both naked, the man and his wife, and were not [R]ashamed.   3:7, 10 · Is 47:3

3 Now [R]the serpent was [R]more [T]subtil than any beast of the field which the LORD God had made. And he said unto the woman, Yea, hath God said, Ye shall not eat of every tree of the garden?   1 Ch 21:1 · 2 Co 11:3 · *cunning*

2   And the woman said unto the serpent, We may eat of the fruit of the trees of the garden:

3   But of the fruit of the tree which *is* in the midst of the garden, God hath said, Ye shall not eat of it, neither shall ye [R]touch it, lest ye die.   Ex 19:12, 13; Re 22:14

4   [R]And the serpent said unto

2:19 *to see what he would call them.* In giving each animal its name, Adam demonstrated his right as God's agent (1:26–28), the one set in place as lord of the created order.   **2:20 *help meet for him.*** Some have felt that calling the woman man's helper indicates that she is inferior in value, but this is far from true. In fact, the term "help" is used to describe God Himself, when He comes to our aid. The word "helper" indicates role, not value or position. The helper Adam needed was not merely a servant or a slave, nor another man exactly like himself. He needed a compliment, equal in value and with the same intelligence, personality, spirituality, and ethical and moral sense; but with different qualities and a different role, a helper who could join with him in his work of subduing the earth.   **2:21 *he took one of his ribs.*** God's use of Adam's rib was fitting. He might have started over with dust and clay. But by using a part of Adam himself, the identification of Adam with his partner would be ensured. As Martin Luther observed, God might have taken a bone from a toe, and thus signified that Adam was to rule over her; or He might have taken a bone from his head to indicate her rule over him. But by taking a bone from his side, God implied equality and mutual respect.   **2:24 *one flesh.*** This phrase suggests both a physical, sexual bonding and a lifelong relationship. They are still separate persons, but together they are as one (Ep 5:31). In the New Testament, Jesus refers to this text as the foundation of the biblical view of marriage (Ma 19:5). A married couple functions as "we," rather than "me and you." They are a new unit, separate from the family units they each came from. This does not mean that they will no longer relate to their extended families, but that their "one flesh" is a unit distinct from either family.   **3:1 *the serpent.*** With no introduction, Satan appears in the garden of Eden. This is the first clue in Scripture of creation outside the one Adam and Eve experienced. It is interesting to note that Eve expressed no surprise at the serpent speaking to her in intelligible language.   **3:3 *Ye shall not eat of it, neither shall ye touch it.*** Some interpreters suggest that the woman was already sinning by adding to the word of God, for these words were not part of God's instructions in 2:17. Scripture, however, always refers to the eating of the fruit as the sin, and never comments on Eve's addition. Her words reflected the original command well enough, and indeed they would have ensured that the command would be kept.

the woman, Ye shall not surely die: Jo 8:44; [2 Co 11:3; 1 Ti 2:14]
5   For God doth know that in the day ye eat thereof, then your eyes shall be opened, and ye shall be as ᵀgods, knowing good and evil.   *God*
6   And when the woman ᴿsaw that the tree *was* good for food, and that it *was* pleasant to the eyes, and a tree to be desired to make *one* wise, she took of the fruit thereof, and did eat, and gave also unto her husband with her; and he did eat.   1 Jo 2:16
7   And the eyes of them both were opened, ᴿand they knew that they *were* naked; and they sewed fig leaves together, and made themselves aprons.   2:25
8   And they heard ᴿthe voice of the LORD God walking in the garden in the cool of the day: and Adam and his wife ᴿhid themselves from the presence of the LORD God amongst the trees of the garden.   Job 38:1 · Je 23:24
9   And the LORD God called unto Adam, and said unto him, Where *art* thou?

10   And he said, I heard thy voice in the garden, ᴿand I was afraid, because I *was* naked; and I hid myself.   Ex 3:6; De 9:19; 1 Jo 3:20
11   And he said, Who told thee that thou *wast* naked? Hast thou eaten of the tree, whereof I commanded thee that thou shouldest not eat?
12   And the man said, ᴿThe woman whom thou gavest *to be* with me, she gave me of the tree, and I did eat.   [Pr 28:13]
13   And the LORD God said unto the woman, What *is* this *that* thou hast done? And the woman said, ᴿThe serpent ᵀbeguiled me, and I did eat.   2 Co 11:3; 1 Ti 2:14 · *deceived*
14   And the LORD God said unto the serpent, Because thou hast done this, thou *art* cursed above all cattle, and above every beast of the field; upon thy belly shalt thou go, and ᴿdust shalt thou eat all the days of thy life: Is 65:25; Mi 7:17
✝15   And I will put enmity between thee and the woman, and between thy seed and her seed; it

✝ 3:15—Ga 4:4

3:5 ye shall be as gods. God's fullness of knowledge was only one of the superiorities that set Him apart from the woman. But the serpent combined all of God's superiority over the woman into this one audacious appeal to her pride. **3:6–7 Sin's Consequences**—At first Adam's sin does not appear to be all that significant. All he did was take a bite of some fruit. But Scripture takes it very seriously. Adam's sin was one of disobedience and rebellion. God told Adam not to eat the fruit of the "tree of the knowledge of good and evil" under penalty of death (2:17). That action of eating the fruit changed Adam's whole nature as well as his relationship with God. Adam became a sinner and as such he died. His spiritual death was immediate, the physical death progressive. Adam, who began the human race, then became the source of sin for the world. We are all sinners by nature because Adam sinned (Ro 5:12–14). We inherit sin from Adam in our natures in the same way we inherit many of our physical characteristics from our parents. Sin is a universal part of our spiritual inheritance. **3:14–21 The Covenant with Adam**—The Adamic Covenant is the second covenant God made with man. It sets forth conditions that will be in effect until the curse of death is lifted (Is 11:6–10; Ro 8:18–23). In Christ's death and resurrection we have the beginning (firstfruits) of the lifting of the curse. The ultimate lifting of the curse will happen as Christ establishes his final reign on earth. **3:14 unto the serpent.** The Lord turned first to the serpent and brought judgment upon him. God did not excuse the woman because she was deceived, but He did bring the harsher judgment on the one who had deceived her. **3:15 Christ**—This passage is sometimes referred to as the "preaching of Messiah in the garden of Eden," because it introduces the One who will deliver mankind from the power of the Tempter. The seed of the serpent, those of the human race who choose evil and thus give themselves into the control of the Evil One, would hate and destroy the Seed of the woman, who was Jesus Christ. But in that very act, Evil condemned shall bruise thy head, and thou shalt bruise his heel.

16 Unto the woman he said, I will greatly multiply thy sorrow and thy conception; [R]in sorrow thou shalt bring forth children; [R]and thy desire *shall be* to thy husband, and he shall rule over thee.   Is 13:8; Jo 16:21 · 4:7

17 And unto Adam he said, Because thou hast hearkened unto the voice of thy wife, and hast eaten of the tree, of which I commanded thee, saying, Thou shalt not eat of it: [R]cursed *is* the ground for thy sake; in [T]sorrow shalt thou eat *of* it all the days of thy life;   Ro 8:20–22; He 6:8 · *toil*

18 Thorns also and thistles shall it bring forth to thee; and thou shalt eat the herb of the field;

19 In the sweat of thy face shalt thou eat bread, till thou return unto the ground; for out of it wast thou taken: for dust thou *art*, and unto dust shalt thou return.

20 And Adam called his wife's name Eve; because she was the mother of all living.

21 Unto Adam also and to his wife did the LORD God make coats of skins, and clothed them.

22 And the LORD God said, Behold, the man is become as one of us, to know good and evil: and now, lest he put forth his hand, and take also of the tree of life, and eat, and live for ever:

23 Therefore the LORD God sent him forth from the garden of Eden, [R]to till the ground from whence he was taken.   4:2; 9:20

24 So he drove out the man; and he placed at the east of the garden of Eden [R]Cher'-u-bims, and a flaming sword which turned every way, to keep the way of the tree of life.   Ps 104:4; Eze 10:1–20

4 And Adam knew Eve his wife; and she conceived, and bare Cain, and said, I have gotten a man from the LORD.

2 And she again bare his brother [T]Abel. And Abel was a keeper of sheep, but Cain was a tiller of the ground.   Lit. *Breath* or *Nothing*

3 And in process of time it came to pass, that Cain brought of the fruit [R]of the ground an offering unto the LORD.   Nu 18:12

4 And Abel, he also brought of

3:20   4:1–2

---

itself. Jesus rose triumphant from the grave, having paid the blood atonement for the sin of the world and conquered death forever. Thus the Seed of woman crushed the head of the serpent. **3:16 *thy sorrow and thy conception.*** The woman's joy in conceiving and bearing children would be saddened by the pain of it. ***desire . . . rule.*** The word *desire* can also mean "an attempt to usurp authority or control" as in 4:7. The last two lines of this verse could be paraphrased, "You will now have a tendency to try to dominate your husband and he will have the tendency to act as a tyrant." Each strives for control and neither lives in the best interest of the other (Ph 2:3–4). The antidote is in the restoration of mutual respect and dignity through Jesus Christ (Ep 5:21–23). **3:17–19 *cursed is the ground . . . In the sweat of thy face.*** Humans sometimes tend to look upon work itself as a curse, but it is important to remember that work in itself is part of the "very good" creation. The curse on the ground simply means that work is now painful and tiresome toil instead of the pure satisfaction that it was designed to be. ***unto dust shalt thou return.*** The word of God was sure: God had stated that they would certainly die (2:17). Now they were served notice concerning the process of aging and decay that was already at work (5:5; 6:3). **3:22 *tree of life.*** Adam and Eve apparently had free access to this tree before the fall, and by continuing to eat its fruit they would live forever. The penalty for sin was not instant death, but banishment from this tree and eventual death and decay. One day this tree will be planted anew and its fruit will be for the healing of the nations (Re 22:2). **4:3 *Cain brought . . . an offering.*** Genesis does not explain how the practice of sacrificial worship began, but it is clear that Adam and Eve's two sons understood the custom. Some people assume that Cain's offering was unsuitable because it was not a blood

Continued on the next page

Rthe firstlings of his flock and of the fat thereof. And the LORD had Rrespect unto Abel and to his offering: Nu 18:17 · He 11:4

5   But unto Cain and to his offering he had not respect. And Cain was very Twroth, and his countenance fell.   angry

6   And the LORD said unto Cain, Why art thou wroth? and why is thy countenance fallen?

7   If thou doest well, shalt thou not be accepted? and if thou doest not well, sin lieth at the door. And unto thee *shall be* his desire, and thou Tshalt rule over him.   should

8   And Cain talked with Abel his brother: and it came to pass, when they were in the field, that Cain rose up against Abel his brother, and Rslew him.   Ma 23:35

9   And the LORD said unto Cain, Where *is* Abel thy brother? And he said, I know not: *Am* I Rmy brother's keeper?   1 Co 8:11–13

10   And he said, What hast thou done? the voice of thy brother's blood Rcrieth unto me from the ground.   He 12:24; Re 6:9, 10

11   And now *art* thou cursed from the earth, which hath opened her mouth to receive thy brother's blood from thy hand;

12   When thou tillest the ground, it shall not henceforth yield unto thee her strength; a fugitive and a vagabond shalt thou be in the earth.

13   And Cain said unto the LORD, My Tpunishment *is* greater than I can bear.   iniquity

14   Behold, thou hast driven me out this day from the face of the earth; and from thy face shall I be hid; and I shall be a fugitive and a vagabond in the earth; and it shall come to pass, Rthat every one that findeth me shall slay me.   9:6

15   And the LORD said unto him, Therefore whosoever slayeth Cain, vengeance shall be taken on him Rsevenfold. And the LORD set a mark upon Cain, lest any finding him should kill him.   Ps 79:12

16   And Cain went out from the Rpresence of the LORD, and dwelt in the land of TNod, on the east of Eden.   Jon 1:3 · Lit. *Wandering*

17   And Cain knew his wife; and she conceived, and bare E'-noch: and he builded a city, Rand called the name of the city, after the name of his son, E'-noch.   Ps 49:11

18   And unto E'-noch was born I'-rad: and I'-rad begat Me-hu'-ja-el: and Me-hu'-ja-el begat Me-thu'-sa-el: and Me-thu'-sa-el begat La'-mech.

19   And La'-mech took unto him Rtwo wives: the name of the one *was* A'-dah, and the name of the other Zil'-lah.   2:24; 16:3; 1 Ti 3:2

offering, and blood is required for the forgiveness of sins (He 9:22). But nothing in this chapter indicates that Cain and Abel were coming to God for forgiveness. Their sacrifices were acts of worship, and as such a bloodless offering was not necessarily inappropriate (see Le 6:14–23). Apparently the deficiency was in Cain's heart, not in the actual offering. Abel's offering was "more excellent" than Cain's because of his faith in the Lord (He 11:4).   **4:8 *slew him.*** The murder was stunning in its lack of precedent, its suddenness, and its finality. Jesus spoke of this ghastly event as a historical fact (Ma 23:35). **4:17 *Cain knew his wife.*** The identity of Cain's wife has long been a source of puzzlement and argument to the readers and critics of the Book of Genesis. Some have postulated that God created other humans outside of the garden of Eden, but the Scriptures give no such indication, and in fact Adam refers to his wife as "the mother of all living" (3:20). It makes the most sense to assume that Cain married one of his sisters. While this idea seems repugnant to us today, it must be remembered that Adam and Eve's children had a near perfect gene pool, and there would not have been any genetic complications with close intermarrying. God's strict prohibition against siblings and other close relatives marrying did not come until much later (Le 18); even Abraham's wife Sarah was his half sister. ***Enoch.*** The fact that Cain named a city after his son indicates the rapid and dramatic increase in population.

20 And A'-dah bare Ja'-bal: he was the father of such as dwell in tents, and *of such as have* cattle.
21 And his brother's name *was* Ju'-bal: he was the father of all such as handle the harp and ᵀorgan.   *flute*
22 And Zil'-lah, she also bare Tu'-bal–cain, an ᵀinstructer of every artificer in brass and iron: and the sister of Tu'-bal–cain *was* Na'-a-mah.   Lit. *craftsman in bronze*
23 And La'-mech said unto his wives, A'-dah and Zil'-lah, Hear my voice; ye wives of La'-mech, hearken unto my speech: for I have slain a man to my wounding, and a young man to my hurt.
24 ᴿ If Cain shall be avenged sevenfold, truly La'-mech seventy and sevenfold.   v. 15
25 And Adam knew his wife again; and she bare a son, and called his name ᵀSeth: For God, *said she,* hath appointed me another seed instead of Abel, whom Cain slew.   Lit. *Appointed*
26 And to Seth, to him also there was born a son; and he called his name E'-nos: then began men to call upon the name of the LORD.

5 This *is* the book of the generations of Adam. In the day that God created man, in ᴿthe likeness of God made he him;   1:26; 9:6
2 Male and female created he them; and blessed them, and called their name Adam, in the day when they were created.
3 And Adam lived an hundred and thirty years, and begat *a son* in his own likeness, after his image; and called his name Seth:
4 And the days of Adam after he had begotten Seth were eight hundred years: ᴿand he begat sons and daughters: 1:28; 4:25
5 And all the days that Adam lived were nine hundred and thirty years: ᴿand he died.   [He 9:27]
6 And Seth lived an hundred and five years, and begat E'-nos:
7 And Seth lived after he begat E'-nos eight hundred and seven years, and begat sons and daughters:
8 And all the days of Seth were nine hundred and twelve years: and he died.
9 And E'-nos lived ninety years, and begat Ca-i'-nan:
10 And E'-nos lived after he begat Ca-i'-nan eight hundred and fifteen years, and begat sons and daughters:
11 And all the days of E'-nos were nine hundred and five years: and he died.
12 And Ca-i'-nan lived seventy years, and begat Ma-ha'-la-le-el:
13 And Ca-i'-nan lived after he begat Ma-ha'-la-le-el eight hundred

4:25

4:25 Seth. While it is certain that Adam and Eve had other daughters, and possibly other sons as well, the death of righteous Abel and the banishment of their firstborn, Cain, had left them with no one to carry on their line for good and for the promise of the Messiah. Seth is specifically mentioned among Adam and Eve's children because it would be through his descendants that the Messiah would come. His name is related to a Hebrew verb meaning "to place" or "to set" for he was appointed to take this special place in the plan of God. **4:26 *began men to call upon the name of the LORD.*** These words can hardly mean that only now did people begin to pray to God. Rather, the verb *call* means "to make proclamation." That is, this is the beginning of preaching, of witnessing, and testifying in the name of the Lord (12:8). **5:3 *an hundred and thirty years.*** The long lives of the people of the early chapters of Genesis have led to considerable speculation. One suggestion is that these ages were possible because of tremendously different climate and environmental conditions that were in effect before the flood. **5:5 *and he died.*** God created humans for eternity; if Adam and Eve had not disobeyed, they would have lived forever. There is a profound sadness in Adam's death, for it reminds us of Adam's mortality—and hence our own.

and forty years, and begat sons and daughters:

14 And all the days of Ca-i'-nan were nine hundred and ten years: and he died.

15 And Ma-ha'-la-le-el lived sixty and five years, and begat Ja'-red:

16 And Ma-ha'-la-le-el lived after he begat Ja'-red eight hundred and thirty years, and begat sons and daughters:

17 And all the days of Ma-ha'-la-le-el were eight hundred ninety and five years: and he died.

18 And Ja'-red lived an hundred sixty and two years, and he begat [R]E'-noch: Jude 14, 15

19 And Ja'-red lived after he begat E'-noch eight hundred years, and begat sons and daughters:

20 And all the days of Ja'-red were nine hundred sixty and two years: and he died.

21 And E'-noch lived sixty and five years, and begat Me-thu'-se-lah:

22 And E'-noch [R]walked with God after he begat Me-thu'-se-lah three hundred years, and begat sons and daughters: [Mi 6:8]

23 And all the days of E'-noch were three hundred sixty and five years:

24 And [R]E'-noch walked with God: and he *was* not; for God [R]took him.   Jude 14 · 2 Ki 2:10; Ps 49:15

25 And Me-thu'-se-lah lived an hundred eighty and seven years, and begat La'-mech:

26 And Me-thu'-se-lah lived after he begat La'-mech seven hundred eighty and two years, and begat sons and daughters:

27 And all the days of Me-thu'-se-lah were nine hundred sixty and nine years: and he died.

28 And La'-mech lived an hundred eighty and two years, and begat a son:

29 And he called his name [R]Noah, saying, This *same* shall comfort us concerning our work and toil of our hands, because of the ground which the LORD hath cursed.   Lk 3:36; He 11:7

30 And La'-mech lived after he begat Noah five hundred ninety and five years, and begat sons and daughters:

31 And all the days of La'-mech were seven hundred seventy and seven years: and he died.

32 And Noah was five hundred years old: and Noah begat [R]Shem, Ham, and Ja'-pheth.   6:10; 7:13

6 And it came to pass, [R]when men began to multiply on the face of the earth, and daughters were born unto them,   1:28

2 That the sons of God saw the daughters of men that they *were* fair; and they [R]took them wives of all which they chose.   De 7:3, 4

3 And the LORD said, [R]My spirit shall not always [R]strive with man, for that he also *is* flesh: yet his days

5:21–24   5:29

5:21–24 *for God took him.* Only Enoch and Elijah were taken by God without experiencing death (2 Ki 2:11). This was both a testimony of Enoch's deep faith in God (He 11:5–6) and a strong reminder at the beginning of biblical history that for God's people, there is life in God's presence after our physical bodies have died.   **6:2** *sons of God . . . daughters of men.* This passage is very difficult to interpret. Some believe that the "sons of God" were the men of the righteous line of Seth, while the "daughters of men" were Cain's offspring. This does not account for the fact that their offspring were giants, men of extraordinary size and talents; it is also problematic in that it assumes that Cain's descendants were universally more sinful than Seth's descendants. Since Noah was the only descendant of Seth who was considered righteous, this is obviously not accurate. A second view is that the "sons of God" were angelic beings. The phrase "sons of God" is used elsewhere in Scripture to refer to angelic beings (Job 1:6), but it seems impossible since angels in heaven do not marry (Ma 22:30). It may be, however, that these "sons of God" were some of the rebellious angels who had joined Satan (Jude 6; 2 Pe 2:4); they took on human form (as Satan was apparently able to take on the form

the seventeenth day of the month, the same day were all ᴿthe fountains of the great deep broken up, and the ᴿwindows of heaven were opened.　　　　　　　Is 51:10 · Ps 78:23
12　And the rain was upon the earth forty days and forty nights.
13　In the selfsame day entered Noah, and Shem, and Ham, and Ja'-pheth, the sons of Noah, and Noah's wife, and the three wives of his sons with them, into the ark;
14　ᴿThey, and every beast after his kind, and all the cattle after their kind, and every creeping thing that creepeth upon the earth after his kind, and every fowl after his kind, every bird of every ᴿsort.　6:19 · 1:21
15　And they went in unto Noah into the ark, two and two of all flesh, wherein is the breath of life.
16　And they that went in, went in male and female of all flesh, ᴿas God had commanded him: and the Lᴏʀᴅ shut him in.　　　　vv. 2, 3
17　ᴿAnd the flood was forty days upon the earth; and the waters increased, and ᵀbare up the ark, and it was lift up above the earth.　　vv. 4, 12; 8:6 · lifted
18　And the waters prevailed, and were increased greatly upon the earth; ᴿand the ark went upon the face of the waters.　　Ps 104:26
19　And the waters prevailed exceedingly upon the earth; and all the high hills, that were under the whole heaven, were covered.
20　Fifteen cubits upward did the waters prevail; and the mountains were covered.
21　ᴿAnd all flesh died that moved upon ᵀthe earth, both of fowl, and of cattle, and of beast, and of every creeping thing that creep-

eth upon the earth, and every man:　　v. 4; 6:7, 13, 17 · the land
22　All in ᴿwhose nostrils was the breath of life, of all that was in the dry land, died.　　　　2:7
23　And every living substance was destroyed which was upon the face of the ground, both man, and cattle, and the creeping things, and the fowl of the heaven; and they were destroyed from the earth: and ᴿNoah only remained alive, and they that were with him in the ark.　　Lk 17:26, 27; He 11:7
24　ᴿAnd the waters prevailed upon the earth an hundred and fifty days.　　　　8:3, 4

8 And God remembered Noah, and every living thing, and all the cattle that was with him in the ark: and God made a wind to pass over the earth, and the waters asswaged;
2　The fountains also of the deep and the windows of heaven were ᴿstopped, and the rain from heaven was restrained;　　De 11:17
3　And the waters returned from off the earth continually: and after the end ᴿof the hundred and fifty days the waters were abated.　7:24
4　And the ark rested in the seventh month, on the seventeenth day of the month, upon the mountains of Ar'-a-rat.
5　And the waters decreased continually until the tenth month: in the tenth month, on the first day of the month, were the tops of the mountains seen.
6　And it came to pass at the end of forty days, that Noah opened

7:23–24　　8:1

7:16 shut him in. The Lord who had drawn them now closed the door on them. That shut door was a symbol of closure, safety, and God's deliverance. **7:19 the high hills, that were under the whole heaven, were covered.** This explicit declaration, accompanied by the assertion in verse 21 that every living thing died, makes it clear that this was no localized event, but in actuality a worldwide catastrophic flood (see 8:5). Jesus affirmed the historicity of the "days of Noe" when he compared them to the end days (Ma 24:37–38; Lk 17:26–27). Peter similarly used the story of Noah and the flood as a pattern for the final judgment (1 Pe 3:20; 2 Pe 2:5; 3:5–6).

Rthe window of the ark which he had made: 6:16

7   And he sent forth a raven, which went forth to and fro, until the waters were dried up from off the earth.

8   Also he sent forth a dove from him, to see if the waters were abated from off the face of the ground;

9   But the dove found no rest for the sole of her foot, and she returned unto him into the ark, for the waters *were* on the face of the whole earth: then he put forth his hand, and took her, and pulled her in unto him into the ark.

10   And he stayed yet other seven days; and again he sent forth the dove out of the ark;

11   And the dove came in to him in the evening; and, lo, in her mouth *was* an olive leaf pluckt off: so Noah knew that the waters were abated from off the earth.

12   And he stayed yet other seven days; and sent forth the dove; which returned not again unto him any more.

13 And it came to pass in the six hundredth and first year, in the first *month*, the first *day* of the month, the waters were dried up from off the earth: and Noah removed the covering of the ark, and looked, and, behold, the face of the ground was dry.

14   And in the second month, on the seven and twentieth day of the month, was the earth dried.

15   And God spake unto Noah, saying,

16   Go forth of the ark, Rthou, and thy wife, and thy sons, and thy sons' wives with thee.   7:13

17   Bring forth with thee every living thing that *is* with thee, of all flesh, *both* of fowl, and of cattle, and of every creeping thing that creepeth upon the earth; that they may breed abundantly in the earth, and Rbe fruitful, and multiply upon the earth.   1:22, 28; 9:1, 7

18   And Noah went forth, and his sons, and his wife, and his sons' wives with him:

19   Every beast, every creeping thing, and every fowl, *and* whatsoever creepeth upon the earth, after their Tkinds, went forth out of the ark.   Lit. *families*

20   And Noah builded an Raltar unto the LORD; and took of every clean beast, and of every clean fowl, and offered burnt offerings on the altar.   12:7; Ex 29:18, 25

21   And the LORD smelled Ra sweet savour; and the LORD said in his heart, I will not again curse the ground any more for man's sake; for the Rimagination of man's heart *is* evil from his youth; neither will I again smite any more every thing living, as I have done.   Ep 5:2 · Ro 1:21; Ep 2:1–3

22   RWhile the earth remaineth, seedtime and harvest, and cold and heat, and summer and winter, and Rday and night shall not cease.   Is 54:9 · Ps 74:16; Je 33:20, 25

9 And God blessed Noah and his sons, and said unto them,

8:15–16   9:1

8:14 *was the earth dried.* After more than a full year, the waters had returned to their place (7:11). As in the beginning, God brought the waters of earth into their place (1:9–13). The flood began in Noah's 600th year, in the 2nd month, on day 17 (7:11) and ended in Noah's 601st year, in the 2nd month, on day 27 (8:14). **8:20 an altar.** This is the first mention of sacrificial worship since the days of Cain and Abel (4:3–5); yet we may assume that the principle of sacrificial worship was perpetuated through the line of faithful people (ch. 5). **8:22 *While the earth remaineth.*** The words of this verse are a poem of powerful effect. These words might easily have become a song of faith, the response of the people of God to the promise He made (v. 21). Later in Israel's history, the prophets recalled God's great promise to Noah (Is 54:9–10). **9:1–19 God's Promise to Noah**—Only when we think of God as Creator, as well as Redeemer, can we

[R] Be fruitful, and multiply, and replenish the earth.   1:28, 29

2   [R] And the fear of you and the dread of you shall be upon every beast of the earth, and upon every fowl of the air, upon all that moveth *upon* the earth, and upon all the fishes of the sea; into your hand are they delivered.   Ps 8:6

3   Every moving thing that liveth shall be meat for you; even as the [R] green herb have I given you all things.   Col 2:16; [1 Ti 4:3, 4]

4   [R] But flesh with the life thereof, *which is* the blood thereof, shall ye not eat.   Le 7:26; 17:10–16

5   And surely your blood of your lives will I require; at the hand of every beast will I require it, and [R] at the hand of man; at the hand of every man's brother will I require the life of man.   4:9, 10

6   [R] Whoso sheddeth man's blood, by man shall his blood be shed: for in the image of God made he man.   Ex 21:12–14; Le 24:17

7   And you, be ye fruitful, and multiply; bring forth abundantly in the earth, and multiply therein.

8   And God spake unto Noah, and to his sons with him, saying,

9   And I, behold, I establish [R] my covenant with you, and with your [T] seed after you;   Is 54:9 · *descendants*

10   [R] And with every living creature that *is* with you, of the fowl, of the cattle, and of every beast of the earth with you; from all that go out of the ark, to every beast of the earth.   Ps 145:9

11   And [R] I will establish my covenant with you; neither shall all flesh be cut off any more by the waters of a flood; neither shall there any more be a flood to destroy the earth.   8:21; Is 54:9

12   And God said, This *is* the token of the covenant which I make between me and you and every living creature that *is* with you, for perpetual generations:

13   I do set [R] my bow in the cloud, and it shall be for a [T] token of a covenant between me and the earth.   Eze 1:28; Re 4:3 · *sign*

14   And it shall come to pass, when I bring a cloud over the earth, that the [T] bow shall be seen in the cloud: *rainbow*

15   And [R] I will remember my covenant, which *is* between me and you and every living creature of all flesh; and the waters shall no more become a flood to destroy all flesh.   De 7:9; Eze 16:60

16   And the bow shall be in the cloud; and I will look upon it, that I may remember [R] the everlasting covenant between God and every living creature of all flesh that *is* upon the earth.   17:13, 19; He 13:20

17   And God said unto Noah, This *is* the [T] token of the covenant,

9:8–9   9:16–17

---

begin to understand His covenant of redemption as being related to the covenant of creation (Ge 1:26–30; 2:15–17). God doesn't abandon His creation. On the contrary, though evil has corrupted it, He graciously (for it is undeserved) establishes a covenantal relationship with Noah's descendants as well as with every beast of the earth. This note of universality is given further expression by Hosea (2:18) and Jonah (4:11). When Paul encourages Roman believers about struggles in this life, he reminds them that they are not alone, but assures them that the whole creation also groans and suffers, eagerly anticipating that final redemption from the curse of sin. The promise given here is to never destroy the earth again by flood (v.11). The rainbow is then a testimony of the existence of this promise.   **9:4 *blood.*** This restriction gets more attention in Leviticus (see Le 17:11–12). Blood represents the animal's life. It may be used in sacrifice, for all life belongs to the Lord.   **9:6 *image of God.*** Sin did not destroy man as the image of God. God values human life more highly than animal life because only humankind possesses God's image.   **9:9 *covenant.*** This is the second occurrence in Genesis of the important concept of covenant (6:18). God promised that He would establish His covenant with Noah and here He accomplished this great work.

which I have established between me and all flesh that *is* upon the earth.   *sign*

18 And the sons of Noah, that went forth of the ark, were Shem, and Ham, and Ja'-pheth: ᴿand Ham *is* the father of Canaan.   10:6

19 These *are* the three sons of Noah: and of them was the whole earth ᵀoverspread.   *populated*

20 And Noah began *to be* ᴿan ᵀhusbandman, and he planted a vineyard: Pr 12:11; Je 31:24 · *farmer*

21 And he drank of the wine, and was drunken; and he was uncovered within his tent.

22 And Ham, the father of Canaan, saw the nakedness of his father, and told his two brethren without.

23 And Shem and Ja'-pheth took a garment, and laid *it* upon both their shoulders, and went backward, and covered the nakedness of their father; and their faces *were* backward, and they saw not their father's nakedness.

24 And Noah awoke from his wine, and knew what his younger son had done unto him.

25 And he said, Cursed *be* Canaan; a ᴿservant of servants shall he be unto his brethren.   Jos 9:23

26 And he said, ᴿBlessed *be* the Lord God of Shem; and Canaan shall be his servant.   Ps 144:15

✝27 God shall enlarge Ja'-pheth, ᴿand he shall dwell in the tents of Shem; and Canaan shall be his servant.   Ep 2:13, 14; 3:6

28 And Noah lived after the flood three hundred and fifty years.

29 And all the days of Noah were nine hundred and fifty years: and he died.

10 Now these *are* the generations of the sons of Noah, Shem, Ham, and Ja'-pheth: ᴿand unto them were sons born after the flood.   9:1, 7, 19

2 ᴿThe sons of Ja'-pheth; Go'-mer, and Ma'-gog, and Ma'-dai, and Ja'-van, and Tu'-bal, and Me'-shech, and Ti'-ras.   1 Ch 1:5–7

3 And the sons of Go'-mer; Ash'-ke-naz, and Ri'-phath, and To-gar'-mah.

4 And the sons of Ja'-van; E-li'-shah, and Tar'-shish, Kit'-tim, and Dod'-a-nim.

5 By these were ᴿthe isles of the Gentiles divided in their lands; every one after his tongue, after their families, in their nations.   11:8; Ps 72:10; Je 2:10; 25:22

6 ᴿAnd the sons of Ham; Cush, and Miz'-ra-im, and ᵀPhut, and Canaan.   1 Ch 1:8–16 · Or *Put*

7 And the sons of Cush; Se'-ba, and Hav'-i-lah, and Sab'-tah, and Ra'-a-mah, and Sab'-te-chah: and the sons of Ra'-a-mah; She'-ba, and De'-dan.

8 And Cush begat ᴿNimrod: he began to be a mighty one in the earth.   Mi 5:6

9 He was a mighty ᴿhunter before the Lord: wherefore it is said,

✝9:27—Lk 3:36

9:26–27 Shem. Shem was given precedence over his brothers. Eber and Abram were descended from Shem (11:10–30), so Shem's blessing is ultimately a blessing on Israel. **9:29 and he died.** Noah's death was the end of an era. Only he and his family spanned two worlds, that of the earth before and after the flood. His long life (950 years) gave him opportunity to transmit to his many descendants the dramatic story that he had lived out with his family. Peoples in places and cultures the world over have memories and stories of a great flood in antiquity. The details differ, but the stories remain. **10:2 the sons of Japheth.** The listing of Japheth's descendants is briefer than the others. Among the persons and peoples mentioned is Javan, an ancient name for the Greek people. It is thought that many of Japheth's descendants migrated to Europe.   **10:6 the sons of Ham.** Cush is the ancient name for Ethiopia; Mizraim is a name for Egypt. **10:7–11 Nimrod.** Like Lamech the descendant of Cain, Nimrod's infamy was proverbial. His territory was in the lands of the east, the fabled ancient cities of Mesopotamia. The

Even as Nimrod the mighty hunter before the LORD.   Je 16:16

10 [R]And the beginning of his kingdom was [R]Babel, and E'-rech, and Ac'-cad, and Cal'-neh, in the land of Shi'-nar.   Mi 5:6 · 11:9

11 Out of that land [T]went [R]forth Assh'-ur, and builded Nin'-e-veh, and the city Re-ho'-both, and Ca'-lah,   he went to Assyria · 25:18

12 And Re'-sen between Nin'-e-veh and Ca'-lah: the same is [T]a great city.   the principal city

13 And Miz'-ra-im begat Lu'-dim, and An'-a-mim, and Le'-ha-bim, and Naph'-tu-him,

14 And Path-ru'-sim, and Cas'-lu-him, (out of whom came Phi-lis'-tim,) and Caph'-to-rim.

15 And Canaan begat Si'-don his firstborn, and [R]Heth,   23:3

16 And the Jeb'-u-site, and the Am'-or-ite, and the Gir'-ga-site,

17 And the Hi'-vite, and the Ark'-ite, and the Si'-nite,

18 And the Ar'-vad-ite, and the Zem'-a-rite, and the Ha'-math-ite: and afterward were the families of the Ca'-naan-ites spread abroad.

19 And the border of the Ca'-naan-ites was from Si'-don, as thou comest to Ge'-rar, unto Ga'-za; as thou goest, unto Sodom, and Go-mor'-rah, and Ad'-mah, and Ze-bo'-im, even unto La'-sha.

20 These are the sons of Ham, after their families, after their tongues, in their countries, and in their nations.

21 Unto Shem also, the father of all the children of E'-ber, the brother of Ja'-pheth the elder, even to him were children born.

22 The children of Shem; E'-lam, and Assh'-ur, and Ar-phax'-ad, and Lud, and A'-ram.

23 And the children of A'-ram; Uz, and Hul, and Ge'-ther, and [T]Mash.   Meshech, 1 Ch 1:17

24 And Ar-phax'-ad begat [R]Sa'-lah; and Sa'-lah begat E'-ber.   11:12

25 And unto E'-ber were born two sons: the name of one was [T]Pe'-leg; for in his days was the earth divided; and his brother's name was Jok'-tan.   Lit. Division

26 And Jok'-tan begat Al-mo'-dad, and She'-leph, and Ha'-zar–ma'-veth, and Je'-rah,

27 And Ha-do'-ram, and U'-zal, and Dik'-lah,

28 And [T]O'-bal, and A-bim'-a-el, and She'-ba,   Ebal, 1 Ch 1:22

29 And O'-phir, and Hav'-i-lah, and Jo'-bab: all these were the sons of Jok'-tan.

30 And their dwelling was from Me'-sha, as thou goest unto Se'-phar a mount of the east.

31 These are the sons of Shem, after their families, [T]after their tongues, in their lands, after their nations.   according to their languages

32 These are the families of the sons of Noah, after their generations, in their nations: [R]and by these were the nations divided in the earth after the flood.   9:19; 11:8

11 And the whole earth was of one [T]language, and of one speech.   Lit. lip

2 And it came to pass, as they journeyed from the east, that they found a plain in the land [R]of Shi'-nar; and they dwelt there.   Da 1:2

3 And they said one to another, [T]Go to, let us make brick, and burn them throughly. And they had brick

prophet Micah would later use the name Nimrod to describe the region of Assyria, which would come under God's judgment (Mi 5:5–6). **10:21–24 Eber.** This is the name that gives rise to the term *Hebrew,* which is first used of Abram in 14:13. Eber descended from Shem, the one of Noah's sons who was appointed to carry on the messianic line. Abram was a direct descendant of Eber. **10:32 the families of the sons of Noah.** Although not every ancient people group is listed in this "Table of the Nations," its clear teaching is that all the varied peoples of the earth, no matter of what land or language, are descended from Noah. **11:2 the land of Shinar.** This is the region of ancient Babylon in Mesopotamia (10:10), part of modern Iraq.

for stone, and ^Tslime had they for morter.　　　　*Come · asphalt*

4　And they said, Go to, let us build us a city and a tower, whose top *may reach* unto heaven; and let us make us a name, lest we ^Rbe scattered abroad upon the face of the whole earth.　　　　De 4:27

5　^RAnd the Lord came down to see the city and the tower, which the children of men builded.　18:21

6　And the Lord said, Behold, ^Rthe people *is* one, and they have all one language; and this they begin to do: and now nothing will be restrained from them, which they have imagined to do.　9:19

7　Go to, let us go down, and there ^Rconfound their language, that they may not understand one another's speech.　Is 33:19; Je 5:15

8　So ^Rthe Lord scattered them abroad from thence upon the face of all the earth: and they left off to build the city.　De 32:8; Ps 92:9

9　Therefore is the name of it called Babel; because the Lord did there confound the language of all the earth: and from thence did the Lord scatter them abroad upon the face of all the earth.

10　^RThese *are* the generations of Shem: Shem *was* an hundred years old, and begat Ar-phax'-ad two years after the flood:　1 Ch 1:17

11　And Shem lived after he begat Ar-phax'-ad five hundred years, and begat sons and daughters.

12　And Ar-phax'-ad lived five and thirty years, ^Rand begat Sa'-lah:　Lk 3:35

13　And Ar-phax'-ad lived after he begat Sa'-lah four hundred and three years, and begat sons and daughters.

14　And Sa'-lah lived thirty years, and begat E'-ber:

15　And Sa'-lah lived after he begat E'-ber four hundred and three years, and begat sons and daughters.

16　And E'-ber lived four and thirty years, and begat Pe'-leg:

17　And E'-ber lived after he begat Pe'-leg four hundred and thirty years, and begat sons and daughters.

18　And Pe'-leg lived thirty years, and begat Re'-u:

19　And Pe'-leg lived after he begat Re'-u two hundred and nine years, and begat sons and daughters.

20　And Re'-u lived two and thirty years, and begat Se'-rug:

21　And Re'-u lived after he begat Se'-rug two hundred and seven years, and begat sons and daughters.

22　And Se'-rug lived thirty years, and begat Na'-hor:

23　And Se'-rug lived after he begat Na'-hor two hundred years, and begat sons and daughters.

🔥 11:6–9

11:4 Pride—God divided the human race into different language groups because they had refused to obey His command to fill the earth, and had become united for an evil purpose. This does not mean that God wants the world to remain divided. Christ came to reconcile the world to God (2 Co 5:19), and when we are in Christ we are not only reconciled to God, but to one another (Ep 2:11–19). The unity God destroyed by judgment at Babel was restored by grace on the day of Pentecost. On that day people from different nations came together to hear the gospel in their own languages. **11:7 *let us go down.*** The plural "Us" in this passage is similar to the language of 1:26–28. The plural pronoun emphasizes the majesty of the speaker. **11:9 *Babel.*** There is a pun in this name that no Hebrew reader would miss. The verb for *confuse* sounds similar to the name of the city. **confound . . . scatter.** Because of their pride and arrogance, God scattered the peoples of the earth and confused their language, but one day peoples of all languages and cultures will unite to celebrate the grace of God's risen Son, lifting their voices together in praise of the Lamb (Re 5:8–14). **11:10–25 *the generations.*** This genealogy shows that Abram was a descendant of Noah through Shem, just as Noah was a descendant of Adam through Seth. It is interesting

24 And Na'-hor lived nine and twenty years, and begat Te'-rah:
25 And Na'-hor lived after he begat Te'-rah an hundred and nineteen years, and begat sons and daughters.
26 And Te'-rah lived seventy years, and [R]begat Abram, Na'-hor, and Ha'-ran. Jos 24:2; 1 Ch 1:26
27 Now these *are* the generations of Te'-rah: Te'-rah begat [R]Abram, Na'-hor, and Ha'-ran; and Ha'-ran begat Lot. v. 31; 17:5
28 And Ha'-ran died before his father Te'-rah in the land of his nativity, in Ur of the Chal'-dees.
29 And Abram and Na'-hor took them wives: the name of Abram's wife *was* Sa'-rai; and the name of Na'-hor's wife, Mil'-cah, the daughter of Ha'-ran, the father of Mil'-cah, and the father of Is'-cah.
30 But [R]Sa'-rai was barren; she *had* no child. 16:1, 2; Lk 1:36
31 And Te'-rah took Abram his son, and Lot the son of Ha'-ran his son's son, and Sa'-rai his daughter in law, his son Abram's wife; and they went forth with them from [R]Ur of the Chal'-dees, to go into [R]the land of Canaan; and

they came unto Ha'-ran, and dwelt there. 15:7; Ne 9:7; Ac 7:4 · 10:19
32 And the days of Te'-rah were two hundred and five years: and Te'-rah died in Ha'-ran.

12 Now the LORD had said unto Abram, Get thee out of thy country, and from thy kindred, and from thy father's house, unto a land that I will shew thee:
2 And I will make of thee a great nation, and I will bless thee, and make thy name great; [R]and thou shalt be a blessing: Ga 3:14
3 And I will bless them that bless thee, and curse him that curseth thee: and in thee shall all families of the earth be blessed.
4 So Abram departed, as the LORD had spoken unto him; and Lot went with him: and Abram *was* seventy and five years old when he departed out of Ha'-ran.
5 And Abram took Sa'-rai his wife, and Lot his brother's son, and all their substance that they had gathered, and [R]the souls that they had gotten [R]in Ha'-ran; and they went forth to go into the land

12:1-2 † 12:3—Ga 3:8

to note that while the people mentioned in this genealogy lived to be very old, they did not reach the great ages of the peoples before the flood. Instead, their lives appear to be growing progressively shorter. **11:28 Ur of the Chaldees.** For generations, scholars have believed this to be the famous Ur located near the ancient delta in the Persian Gulf where the Tigris and Euphrates Rivers flow together. More recently, some scholars have noted the tablets at Ebla that speak of an Ur in the region of north Syria and suggest that this is the city of Haran's death. **11:29 Sarai.** The name Sarai means "princess," implying a person of noble birth. Later we learn that Sarai was Abram's half sister (20:12). **12:1 LORD.** Even though the name Yahweh (translated LORD) is not explained until Exodus 3:14–15, it is used here to make it clear to the readers that this was the same God who later formed the nation of Israel, and who was the creator (2:4). **12:1–3 God's Covenant with Abram**—The covenant with Abram is the first covenant that pertains to the rule of God. It is unconditional, and depends only on God who obligates Himself in grace, indicated by the unconditional declaration, "I will." The Abrahamic covenant is also the basis of other covenants and it promises blessings in three areas: (1) national—"I will make of thee a great nation," (2) personal—"I will bless thee and make thy name great; and (3) universal—"in thee shall all families of the earth be blessed." The Abrahamic Covenant is an important link in all that God began to do, has done throughout history, and will continue to do until the consummation of history. God blesses Abram and all his descendants through the Messiah, who is Abram's progeny and provides salvation for the entire world. **12:2–3 I will bless thee.** There are seven elements in God's promise to Abram. The number seven is often used in Scripture to suggest fullness and completeness.

of Canaan; and into the land of Canaan they came.   14:14 · 11:31

6 And Abram ^Rpassed through the land unto the place of ^TSi'-chem, unto the plain of Mo'-reh. And the Ca'-naan-ite *was* then in the land.   He 11:9 · Or *Shechem*

7 And the LORD appeared unto Abram, and said, ^RUnto thy seed will I give this land: and there builded he an altar unto the LORD, who appeared unto him.   Ga 3:16

8 And he removed from thence unto a mountain on the east of Beth'–el, and pitched his tent, *having* Beth'–el on the west, and Ha'-i on the east: and there he builded an altar unto the LORD, and ^Rcalled upon the name of the LORD.   4:26; 13:4; 21:33

9 And Abram journeyed, ^Rgoing on still toward the south.   13:1

10 And there was ^Ra famine in the land: and Abram ^Rwent down into Egypt to sojourn there; for the famine *was* ^Rgrievous in the land.   26:1 · Ps 105:13 · 43:1

11 And it came to pass, when he was come near to enter into Egypt, that he said unto Sa'-rai his wife, Behold now, I know that thou *art* ^Ra ^Tfair woman to look upon: v. 14; 26:7; 29:17 · *beautiful*

12 Therefore it shall come to pass, when the Egyptians shall see thee, that they shall say, This *is* his wife: and they ^Rwill kill me, but they will save thee alive.   20:11

13 ^RSay, I pray thee, thou *art* my sister: that it may be well with me for thy sake; and my soul shall live because of thee.   20:1–18; 26:6–11

14 And it came to pass, that, when Abram was come into Egypt, the Egyptians beheld the woman that she *was* very fair.

15 The princes also of Pharaoh saw her, and commended her before Pharaoh: and the woman was taken into Pharaoh's house.

16 And he entreated Abram well for her sake: and he ^Rhad sheep, and oxen, and he asses, and menservants, and maidservants, and she asses, and camels.   13:2

17 And the LORD ^Rplagued Pharaoh and his house with great plagues because of Sa'-rai Abram's wife.   20:18; 1 Ch 16:21

18 And Pharaoh called Abram, and said, ^RWhat *is* this *that* thou hast done unto me? why didst thou not tell me that she *was* thy wife?   20:9, 10; 26:10

19 Why saidst thou, She *is* my sister? so I might have taken her to me to wife: now therefore behold thy wife, take *her*, and go thy way.

20 ^RAnd Pharaoh commanded *his* men concerning him: and they sent him away, and his wife, and all that he had.   [Pr 21:1]

13 And Abram went up out of Egypt, he, and his wife, and all that he had, and ^RLot with him, ^Rinto the south.   12:4; 14:12, 16 · 12:9

2 ^RAnd Abram *was* very rich in cattle, in silver, and in gold.   24:35

3 And he went on his journeys ^Rfrom the south even to Beth'–el, unto the place where his tent had been at the beginning, between Beth'–el and Ha'-i;   12:8, 9

4 Unto the place of the altar, which he had made there at the first: and there Abram ^Rcalled on the name of the LORD.   Ps 116:17

5 And Lot also, which went with

12:7 *Unto thy seed.* The land of Canaan was a gift to the descendants of Abram. God owned the land (Ps 24:1); it was His to do with as He pleased. The people of Canaan had lost their right to occupy the land due to their awful depravity (see 15:16). Thus God declared that this land would become the land of Israel (15:18–21; 17:6–8). **12:8** *called upon the name of the Lord.* This was not a private prayer but a public proclamation. Abram was telling others about the Lord. **12:11** *fair woman.* Sarai's physical beauty was remarkable considering her age. She was ten years younger than Abram, or about 65 (12:4; 17:17). **12:13** *my sister.* Sarai *was* Abram's half sister, the daughter of his father but not of his mother (20:12). **12:17** *the LORD plagued Pharaoh.* This is the first example of the cursing and blessing element of God's promise (see 12:2–3).

Abram, had flocks, and herds, and tents.

6   And ^Rthe land was not able to ^Tbear them, that they might dwell together: for their substance was great, so that they could not dwell together.   36:7 · support

7   And there was ^Ra strife between the herdmen of Abram's cattle and the herdmen of Lot's cattle: ^Rand the Ca'-naan-ite and the Per'-iz-zite dwelled then in the land.   26:20 · 12:6; 15:20, 21

8   And Abram said unto Lot, ^RLet there be no strife, I pray thee, between me and thee, and between my herdmen and thy herdmen; for we be brethren.   1 Co 6:7

9   ^RIs not the whole land before thee? separate thyself, I pray thee, from me: if thou wilt take the left hand, then I will go to the right; or if thou depart to the right hand, then I will go to the left. 20:15; 34:10

10   And Lot lifted up his eyes, and beheld all the plain of Jordan, that it was well watered every where, before the LORD ^Rdestroyed Sodom and Go-mor'-rah, even as the garden of the LORD, like the land of Egypt, as thou comest unto Zo'-ar.   19:24

11   Then Lot chose ^Thim all the plain of Jordan; and Lot journeyed east: and they separated themselves the one from the other. for himself

12   Abram dwelled in the land of Canaan, and Lot dwelled in the cities of the plain, and pitched his tent ^Ttoward Sodom.   as far as

13   But the men of Sodom ^Rwere wicked and sinners before the LORD exceedingly.   2 Pe 2:7, 8

14   And the LORD said unto Abram, after that Lot ^Rwas separated from him, Lift up now thine eyes, and look from the place where thou art ^Rnorthward, and southward, and eastward, and westward: v. 11 · 28:14

15   For all the land which thou seest, ^Rto thee will I give it, and to thy seed for ever.   De 34:4; Ac 7:5

16   And ^RI will make thy seed as the dust of the earth: so that if a man can number the dust of the earth, then shall thy seed also be numbered.   22:17; Ex 32:13; Nu 23:10

17   Arise, walk through the land in the length of it and in the breadth of it; for I will give it unto thee.

18   ^RThen Abram removed his tent, and came and ^Rdwelt in the plain of Mam'-re, ^Rwhich is in He'-bron, and built there an altar unto the LORD.   26:17 · 14:13 · 23:2; 35:27

14 And it came to pass in the days of Am'-ra-phel king of Shi'-nar, A'-ri-och king of El'-la-sar, Ched-or-la'-o-mer king of E'-lam, and Ti'-dal king of nations;

2   That these made war with Be'-ra king of Sodom, and with Bir'-sha king of Go-mor'-rah, Shi'-nab king of Ad'-mah, and Shem-e'-ber king of Ze-boi'-im, and the king of Be'-la, which is Zo'-ar.

3   All these were joined together in the vale of Sid'-dim, ^Rwhich is the salt sea.   Nu 34:12; De 3:17

4   Twelve years ^Rthey served Ched-or-la'-o-mer, and in the thirteenth year they rebelled.   9:26

5   And in the fourteenth year came Ched-or-la'-o-mer, and the kings that were with him, and smote ^Rthe Reph'-a-ims in Ash'-te-roth Kar-na'-im, and ^Rthe Zu'-zims in Ham, and the E'-mims in Sha'-veh Kir-i-a-tha'-im,   15:20 · De 2:20

6   ^RAnd the Ho'-rites in their mount Se'-ir, unto El–pa'-ran, which is by the wilderness.   36:20

13:7 **the Canaanite and the Perizzite.** As in 12:6, the point of this phrase is that the land was already populated; Abram and Lot did not come into an empty region but had to compete for land for their rapidly growing herds and flocks.   **13:14–17** This section forms part of the set of texts that set the stage for the Abrahamic covenant (see the list at 15:1–21). This section builds on 12:1–3,7 the passage in which God first gave His great promise to Abram.   **14:3** **the vale of Siddim.** This valley is most likely submerged under the waters of the Dead Sea today.

7   And they returned, and came to En–mish'-pat, which *is* Ka'-desh, and smote all the country of the Am'-a-lek-ites, and also the Am'-or-ites, that dwelt [R]in Haz'-e-zon–ta'-mar.   2 Ch 20:2

8   And there went out the king of Sodom, and the king of Go-mor'-rah, and the king of Ad'-mah, and the king of Ze-boi'-im, and the king of Be'-la (the same *is* Zo'-ar;) and they joined battle with them in the vale of Sid'-dim;

9   With Ched-or-la'-o-mer the king of E'-lam, and with Ti'-dal king of [T]nations, and Am'-ra-phel king of Shi'-nar, and A'-ri-och king of El'-la-sar; four kings [T]with five.   He *Goyim · against*

10   And the vale of Sid'-dim *was full of* [R]slimepits; and the kings of Sodom and Go-mor'-rah fled, and fell there; and they that remained fled [R]to the mountain. 11:3 · 19:17, 30

11   And they took [R]all the goods of Sodom and Go-mor'-rah, and all their [T]victuals, and went their way.   vv. 16, 21 · *provisions*

12   And they took Lot, Abram's [R]brother's son, [R]who dwelt in Sodom, and his goods, and departed.   11:27; 12:5 · 13:12

13   And there came one that had escaped, and told Abram the [R]He-brew; for he dwelt in the plain of Mam'-re the Am'-or-ite, brother of Esh'-col, and brother of A'-ner:

[R]and these *were* confederate with Abram.   39:14; 40:15 · v. 24; 21:27, 32

14   And [R]when Abram heard that [R]his brother was taken captive, he armed his trained *servants,* born in his own house, three hundred and eighteen, and pursued *them* unto Dan.   19:29 · v. 12; 13:8

15   And he divided himself against them, he and his servants, by night, and [R]smote them, and pursued them unto Ho'-bah, which *is* [T]on the left hand of Damas-cus.   Is 41:2, 3 · north

16   And he brought back all the goods, and also brought again his brother Lot, and his goods, and the women also, and the people.

17   And the king of Sodom [R]went out to meet him after his return from the [T]slaughter of Ched-or-la'-o-mer, and of the kings that *were* with him, at the valley of Sha'-veh, which *is* the king's [T]dale.   1 Sa 18:6 · *defeat · valley*

18   And [R]Mel-chiz'-e-dek king of Sa'-lem brought forth bread and wine: and he *was* the priest of the most high God.   Ps 110:4; He 7:1–10

19   And he blessed him, and said, [R]Blessed *be* Abram of the most high God, [R]possessor of heaven and earth: Ru 3:10 · v. 22

20   And [R]blessed be the most high God, which hath delivered thine enemies into thy hand. And he gave him tithes of all.   24:27

14:14 *three hundred and eighteen.* The fact that Abram could find this many fighting men from among his own servants is an indication of the great wealth and honor that the Lord had given him (12:2–3). **14:18 *Melchizedek.*** This name means "My King is Righteous." Melchizedek was a contemporary of Abram who worshipped the living God. He is described as the "king of Salem," an older shorter name for Jerusalem. The word is based on the root from which the word *shalom* (peace) comes. Melchizedek is a mysterious figure, apparently appearing from nowhere, and with no explanation of his family or background. He is a priest of God Most High, even though there is no indication that he is of Abram's family or even a descendant of Shem. The writer of Hebrews compares Melchizedek with another priest, the Lord Jesus Christ (see He 5:9; Ps 110:4). **14:20 *blessed be the most high God.*** When we bless God, we acknowledge Him as the source of all our blessings (Ps 103:1–2). ***tithes.*** This is the first mention of tithing in the Bible. Even though there is no record of tithing as a command until much later (De 14:22), the concept of a tenth belonging to God was apparently known. Abram's gift indicates that he considered Melchizedek a true priest of the living God; in giving this gift Abram was giving to the Lord.

21 And the king of Sodom said unto Abram, Give me the persons, and take the goods to thyself.

22 And Abram said to the king of Sodom, I [R]have lift up mine hand unto the LORD, the most high God, [R]the possessor of heaven and earth,   Da 12:7 · v. 19

23 That [R]I will not *take* from a thread even to a shoelatchet, and that I will not take any thing that *is* thine, lest thou shouldest say, I have made Abram rich: 2 Ki 5:16

24 Save only that which the young men have eaten, and the portion of the men which went with me, A'-ner, Esh'-col, and Mam'-re; let them take their portion.

15 After these things the word of the LORD came unto Abram in a vision, saying, [R]Fear not, Abram: I *am* thy shield, *and* thy exceeding great reward.   21:17

2 [R]And Abram said, Lord GOD, what wilt thou give me, [R]seeing I go childless, and the [T]steward of my house *is* this E-li-e'-zer of Damascus?   17:18 · Ac 7:5 · *heir*

3 And Abram said, Behold, to me thou hast given no seed: and, lo, [T]one born in my house is mine heir.   Lit. *a son of my house,* a servant

4 And, behold, the word of the LORD *came* unto him, saying, This

shall not be thine heir; but he that [R]shall come forth out of thine own bowels shall be thine heir. Ga 4:28

5 And he brought him forth abroad, and said, Look now toward heaven, and tell the stars, if thou be able to number them: and he said unto him, [R]So shall thy seed be.   Ro 4:18; He 11:12

6 And he [R]believed in the LORD; and he counted it to him for righteousness.   21:1; Ro 4:3, 9, 22; Ga 3:6

7 And he said unto him, I *am* the LORD that brought thee out of [R]Ur of the Chal'-dees, to give thee this land to inherit it.   11:28, 31

8 And he said, Lord GOD, [R]whereby shall I know that I shall inherit it?   1 Sa 14:9, 10; Lk 1:18

9 And he said unto him, Take me an heifer of three years old, and a she goat of three years old, and a ram of three years old, and a turtledove, and a young pigeon.

10 And he took unto him all these, and [R]divided them in the midst, and laid each piece one against another: but [R]the birds divided he not.   Je 34:18 · Le 1:17

11 And when the [T]fowls came down upon the carcases, Abram drove them away.   *vultures*

15:1–6

14:22 *the LORD, the most high God.* Abraham identified Yahweh, translated here as "the LORD," with the most high God for whom Melchizedek was priest. This is a clear statement that he and Melchizedek worshipped the same God. **15:1–21** This section is one of the texts that present the Abrahamic covenant (see 17:1–22; 18:1–15; 22:15–18; 26:23–24; 35:9–15; compare also 12:1–3, 7; 13:14–17). **15:2 *Eliezer of Damascus.*** This man had the honor of being Abram's heir because Abram and Sarai had no child of their own. Some have wondered if Eliezer is also the unnamed servant of Abraham who went on the quest for a wife for Isaac (24:2–5). **15:6 *he believed.*** Almost ten years had passed since the original promises were given. As Abram grew older and still had no children, it was natural for him to wonder how the promises could be fulfilled. In answer to Abram's questions, God, who had revealed Himself in word, and who had faithfully protected him and sustained him, again pledged His word of promise. Abram believed and his faith was accounted to him as righteousness. Some have thought that in Old Testament times people were saved by their good deeds rather than by faith, but this idea is mistaken. Abram was not saved because of righteous living or obedience, but by believing in God and so being declared righteous by Him. The only valid work is the work of faith (Jo 6:28–29; Jam 2:2). **15:9 *Take me.*** Abram prepared the sacrifice, but God enacted the sign (v. 17). This emphasizes the unilateral, unconditional nature of the covenant.

12 And when the sun was going down, [R]a deep sleep fell upon Abram; and, lo, an horror of great darkness fell upon him. 2:21; 28:11
13 And he said unto Abram, Know of a surety [R]that thy seed shall be a stranger in a land *that is* not theirs, and shall serve them; and they shall afflict them four hundred years;   Ex 1:11; Ac 7:6
14 And also that nation, whom they shall serve, will I judge: and afterward [R]shall they come out with great substance.   Ex 12:36
15 And thou shalt go [R]to thy fathers in peace; thou shalt be buried in a good old age.   25:8; 47:30
16 But in the fourth generation they shall come hither again: for the iniquity of the Am'-or-ites [R]*is* not yet full.   1 Ki 11:12; Ma 23:32
17 And it came to pass, that, when the sun went down, and it was dark, behold a smoking [T]furnace, and a burning [T]lamp that [R]passed between those pieces. *oven · torch* · Je 34:18, 19
18 In the same day the LORD made a covenant with Abram, saying, [R]Unto thy seed have I given this land, from the river of Egypt unto the great river, the river Eu-phra'-tes: Nu 34:3; Ac 7:5
19 The Ken'-ites, and the Ken'-iz-zites, and the Kad'-mon-ites,
20 And the Hit'-tites, and the Per'-iz-zites, and the Reph'-a-ims,
21 And the Am'-or-ites, and the Ca'-naan-ites, and the Gir'-ga-shites, and the Jeb'-u-sites.

16 Now Sa'-rai Abram's wife [R]bare him no children: and she had an handmaid, [R]an Egyptian, whose name *was* [R]Ha'-gar.   11:30; 15:2, 3 · 12:16; 21:9 · Ga 4:24
2 [R]And Sa'-rai said unto Abram, Behold now, the LORD [R]hath restrained me from bearing: I pray thee, go in unto my maid; it may be that I may obtain children by her. And Abram hearkened to the voice of Sa'-rai.   30:3 · 20:18
3 And Sa'-rai Abram's wife took Ha'-gar her maid the Egyptian, after Abram [R]had dwelt ten years in the land of Canaan, and gave her to her husband Abram to be his wife.   12:4, 5
4 And he went in unto Ha'-gar, and she conceived: and when she saw that she had conceived, her

15:12 *horror . . . darkness.* These two words give great emphasis to the meaning "an overwhelmingly dark terror." This kind of reaction to the indescribable holiness of the Lord (Is 6:3; 40:25) is natural—Abram was about to experience the presence of the Almighty. This was a moment of profound dread and holy awe. **15:13 *four hundred years.*** Moses wrote down the story of Abram's life from the vantage point of the generation who fulfilled this prophecy (Ex 12:40–42). **15:17 *between those pieces.*** This last element has profound implications. In solemn agreements between equals (parity treaties), both parties would pass between the bloody pieces of slain animals and birds. The symbol would be evident to all: "May I become like this if I do not keep my part of the agreement." But Abram was not to walk this grisly pathway. Only God made the journey in the symbols of smoke and fire. The fulfillment of the promise of God to Abram, the Abrahamic covenant, is as sure as the ongoing life of the Lord. **15:18 *this land.*** God's promise to Abram included his descendants and the Promised One, the Seed of Genesis 3:15. But the promise also included the land of Canaan. God removed the people of Israel from the land of Canaan several times, but He never revoked His everlasting promise 17:8). The promise will be fulfilled in its fullness when Jesus Christ returns (Is 9:1–7). ***the river of Egypt.*** The "river of Egypt" may refer to the Nile, or it may be what is called today the Wadi el Arish, a smaller watercourse at the natural boundary of Egypt and the land of Israel. ***the river Euphrates.*** This is the northern arm of the Euphrates in Syria. **15:20 *Rephaims.*** A people of unusually tall stature; they are called giants in 2 Samuel 21:15–22 (see Nu 13:33; De 2:11; 3:11). **16:2 *go in unto my maid.*** This seems to have been an accepted practice in the ancient middle east. If a woman was unable to bear children, she might use her servant as a surrogate mother, and adopt the child as her own.

mistress was [R]despised in her eyes. 1 Sa 1:6, 7; [Pr 30:21, 23]

5 And Sa'-rai said unto Abram, My wrong *be* upon thee: I have given my maid into thy bosom; and when she saw that she had conceived, I was despised in her eyes: [R]the LORD judge between me and thee. 31:53; Ex 5:21

6 But Abram said unto Sa'-rai, Behold, thy maid *is* in thy hand; do to her as it pleaseth thee. And when Sa'-rai dealt hardly with her, [R]she fled from her face. v. 9

7 And the angel of the LORD found her by a fountain of water in the wilderness, by the fountain in the way to Shur.

8 And he said, Ha'-gar, Sa'-rai's maid, whence camest thou? and whither wilt thou go? And she said, I flee from the face of my mistress Sa'-rai.

9 And the angel of the LORD said unto her, Return to thy mistress, and [R]submit thyself under her hands. [Tit 2:9]

10 And the angel of the LORD said unto her, [R]I will multiply thy seed exceedingly, that it shall not be numbered for multitude. 17:20

11 And the angel of the LORD said unto her, Behold, thou *art* with child, and shalt bear a son, and shalt call his name [T]Ish'-ma-el; because the LORD hath heard thy affliction. Lit. *God Hears*

12 And he will be a wild man; his hand *will be* against every man, and every man's hand against him;

and he shall dwell in the presence of all his brethren.

13 And she called the name of the LORD that spake unto her, Thou God seest me: for she said, Have I also here looked after him [R]that seeth me? 31:42

14 Wherefore the well was called [R]Be'-er-la-hai'–roi; behold, *it is* [R]between Ka'-desh and Be'-red. 24:62 · 14:7; Nu 13:26

15 And [R]Ha'-gar bare Abram a son: and Abram called his son's name, which Ha'-gar bare, Ish'-ma-el. Ga 4:22

16 And Abram *was* fourscore and six years old, when Ha'-gar bare Ish'-ma-el to Abram.

17 And when Abram was ninety years old and nine, the LORD appeared to Abram, and said unto him, I *am* the Almighty God; [R]walk before me, and be thou perfect. 2 Ki 20:3

2 And I will make my covenant between me and thee, and will multiply thee exceedingly.

3 And Abram fell on his face: and God talked with him, saying,

4 As for me, behold, my covenant *is* with thee, and thou shalt be [R]a father of many nations. [Ro 4:11, 12, 16]

5 Neither shall thy name any more be called Abram, but thy name shall be [T]Abraham; for a father of many nations have I made thee. Lit. *Father of a Multitude*

6 And I will make thee exceed-

16:7–11   17:1–5

16:11 **Ishmael.** The name Ishmael uses the divine name El, and means "God hears."
17:4 **covenant.** While the peoples who descended directly from Abram (the nation of Israel, the Midianites, Ishmaelites, and Edomites) were certainly numerous, Abram was "father of many" in a much broader sense yet. The message of the New Testament reveals that God's promise to Abram is to be fulfilled in the community of faith in every nation. So certain was the promise, that his name was changed to Abraham, as an everlasting reminder of God's gracious covenant. Furthermore, the emphatic "as for me" underscores the identity of the all sufficient God who takes the initiative for establishing the covenantal relationship. This relationship is both spiritual and personal, anticipating the divine pledge, "and I will be their God." The wonder of it all is that we who believe in Jesus Christ are part of that "multitude of nations" who share in the faith of Abraham "who is the father of us all." **17:5 Abram . . . Abraham.** This name change is significant. Abram means "exalted Father." Abraham means "Father of Many"—a direct reflection of his new role.

ing fruitful, and I will make ᴿ nations of thee, and kings shall come out of thee.   v. 16; 35:11

7 And I will establish my covenant between me and thee and thy seed after thee in their generations for an everlasting covenant, to be a God unto thee, and to ᴿ thy seed after thee.   Ro 9:8

8 And ᴿ I will give unto thee, and to thy seed after thee, the land wherein thou art a stranger, all the land of Canaan, for an everlasting possession; and ᴿ I will be their God.   Ac 7:5 · Ex 6:7; 29:45

9 And God said unto Abraham, ᴿ Thou shalt keep my covenant therefore, thou, and thy seed after thee in their generations.   Ex 19:5

10 This is my covenant, which ye shall keep, between me and you and thy seed after thee; ᴿ Every man child among you shall be circumcised.   Ac 7:8

11 And ye shall circumcise the flesh of your foreskin; and it shall be ᴿ a token of the covenant betwixt me and you.   [Ro 4:11]

12 And he that is eight days old shall be circumcised among you, every man child in your generations, he that is born in the house, or bought with money of any stranger, which is not of thy seed.

13 He that is born in thy house, and he that is bought with thy money, must needs be circumcised: and my covenant shall be in your flesh for an everlasting covenant.

14 And the uncircumcised man child whose flesh of his foreskin is not circumcised, that soul ᴿ shall be cut off from his people; he hath broken my covenant.   Ex 4:24–26

15 And God said unto Abraham, As for Sa′-rai thy wife, thou shalt not call her name Sa′-rai, but ᵀ Sa-rah shall her name be.   Lit. Princess

16 And I will bless her, and give thee a son also of her: yea, I will bless her, and she shall be a mother ᴿ of nations; kings of people shall be of her.   35:11; 1 Pe 3:6

17 Then Abraham fell upon his face, ᴿ and laughed, and said in his heart, Shall a child be born unto him that is an hundred years old? and shall Sarah, that is ninety years old, bear?   v. 3; 18:12; 21:6

18 And Abraham ᴿ said unto God, O that Ish′-ma-el might live before thee!   18:23

19 And God said, Sarah thy wife shall bear thee a son indeed; and thou shalt call his name Isaac: and I will establish my ᴿ covenant with him for an everlasting covenant, and with his seed after him.   22:16; Ma 1:2

20 And as for Ish′-ma-el, I have heard thee: Behold, I have blessed him, and will make him fruitful, and ᴿ will multiply him exceedingly; ᴿ twelve princes shall he beget, ᴿ and I will make him a great nation.   16:10 · 25:12–16 · 21:13, 18

21 But my ᴿ covenant will I establish with Isaac, ᴿ which Sarah shall

17:15–17   17:19—Ma 1:2

17:8 the land . . . an everlasting possession. The promise clearly included the Israelite people *and* the land of Canaan. The two are linked in the language of the covenant in chapter 15. Even though God removed Israel more than once from the land, He promised them ultimate possession of Canaan. **17:13 circumcised.** Circumcision in and of itself did not make people acceptable to God. It was meant as a tangible symbol of God's covenant in their lives, as an outward sign standing for the inward reality of a thorough commitment to God. In the New Testament, the apostle Paul speaks of having a "circumcised heart," pointing to the fact that a circumcised body means nothing if the heart is not in accord (Ro 2:25–29). **17:15 Sarai . . . Sarah.** Both names come from the same root, meaning "Princess." No explanation is given for the change in Sarah's name, but like the name change from Abram to Abraham (vv. 4–5) the new name accompanied a new relationship with God. **17:19 Isaac.** The name Isaac means "laughter" (see 21:1–6).

bear unto thee at this set time in the next year.   26:2–5 · 21:2

22 And he left off talking with him, and God went up from Abraham.

23 And Abraham took Ish'-ma-el his son, and all that were born in his house, and all that were bought with his money, every male among the men of Abraham's house; and circumcised the flesh of their foreskin in the selfsame day, as God had said unto him.

24 And Abraham *was* ninety years old and nine, when he was circumcised in the flesh of his foreskin.

25 And Ish'-ma-el his son *was* thirteen years old, when he was circumcised in the flesh of his foreskin.

26 In the selfsame day was Abraham circumcised, and Ish'-ma-el his son.

27 And ᴿall the men of his house, born in the house, and bought with money of the stranger, were circumcised with him.   18:19

18 And the Lᴏʀᴅ appeared unto him in the ᴿplains of Mam'-re: and he sat in the tent door in the heat of the day;   13:18

2 And he lift up his eyes and looked, and, lo, three men stood by him: ᴿand when he saw *them,* he ran to meet them from the tent door, and bowed himself toward the ground,   19:1; 1 Pe 4:9

3 And said, My Lord, if now I have found favour in thy sight, pass not ᵀaway, I pray thee, from thy servant: on by

4 Let ᴿa little water, I pray you, be ᵀfetched, and wash your feet, and rest yourselves under the tree: 19:2; 24:32; 43:24 · *brought*

5 And I will fetch a morsel of bread, and ᴿcomfort ye your hearts; after that ye shall pass on: for therefore are ye come to your servant. And they said, So do, as thou hast said.   Ju 19:5; Ps 104:15

6 And Abraham hastened into the tent unto Sarah, and said, Make ready quickly three measures of fine meal, knead *it,* and make cakes upon the hearth.

7 And Abraham ran unto the herd, and fetcht a calf tender and good, and gave *it* unto a young man; and he hasted to dress it.

8 And ᴿhe took butter, and milk, and the calf which he had ᵀdressed, and set *it* before them; and he stood by them under the tree, and they did eat.   19:3 · *prepared*

9 And they said unto him, Where *is* Sarah thy wife? And he said, Behold, in the tent.

10 And he said, I will certainly return unto thee ᴿaccording to the time of life; and, lo, ᴿSarah thy wife shall have a son. And Sarah heard *it* in the tent door, which *was* behind him.   2 Ki 4:16 · Ro 9:9

11 Now Abraham and Sarah *were* old *and* well stricken in age; *and* it ceased to be with Sarah ᴿafter the manner of women.   31:35

12 Therefore Sarah laughed within herself, saying, After I am waxed old shall I have pleasure, my ᴿlord being old also?   1 Pe 3:6

13 And the Lᴏʀᴅ said unto Abraham, Wherefore did Sarah laugh, saying, Shall I of a surety bear a child, which am old?

14 ᴿIs any thing too hard for the Lᴏʀᴅ? ᴿAt the time appointed I will return unto thee, according to the

18:9–14

18:1 *the Lᴏʀᴅ appeared.* This was the fifth time the Lord appeared to Abraham since he came into the land of Canaan (12:7; 13:14–17; 15:1–21; 17:1–22). **18:2–3 *three men.*** Verse 1 states that the Lord appeared to Abraham, then the next verse refers to "three men." It seems clear from verses 1, 13 and 17 that one of the three was the Lord Himself, and from 19:1 on the other two are referred to as angels. Apparently all three were in human form, and were able to eat the meal that Abraham had prepared. Many have speculated that this was an appearance of the pre-incarnate Christ.

time of life, and Sarah shall have a son. Ma 19:26 · 2 Ki 4:16

15 Then Sarah denied, saying, I laughed not; for she was afraid. And he said, Nay; but thou didst laugh.

16 And the men rose up from thence, and looked toward Sodom: and Abraham went with them to bring them on the way.

17 And the LORD said, ᴿShall I hide from Abraham that thing which I do; Ps 25:14; Am 3:7

18 Seeing that Abraham shall surely become a great and mighty nation, and all the nations of the earth shall be blessed in him?

19 For I know him, that he will command his children and his household after him, and they shall keep the way of the LORD, to do justice and judgment; that the LORD may bring upon Abraham that which he hath spoken of him.

20 And the LORD said, Because ᴿthe cry of Sodom and Go-mor'-rah is great, and because their sin is very grievous; 19:13; Eze 16:49, 50

21 ᴿI will go down now, and see whether they have done altogether according to the cry of it, which is come unto me; and if not, I will know. 11:5; Ex 3:8; Ps 14:2

22 And the men turned their faces from thence, ᴿand went toward Sodom: but Abraham stood yet before the LORD. 19:1

23 And Abraham drew near, and said, ᴿWilt thou also destroy the righteous with the wicked? Ex 23:7

24 ᵀPeradventure there be fifty righteous within the city: wilt thou also destroy and not spare the place for the fifty righteous that are therein? Suppose

25 That be far from thee to do after this manner, to slay the righteous with the wicked: and ᴿthat the righteous should be as the wicked, that be far from thee: ᴿShall not the Judge of all the earth do right? Is 3:10, 11 · Ps 58:11

26 And the LORD said, ᴿIf I find in Sodom fifty righteous within the city, then I will spare all the place for their sakes. Eze 22:30

27 And Abraham answered and said, Behold now, I have taken upon me to speak unto the Lord, which am but dust and ashes:

28 Peradventure there shall lack five of the fifty righteous: wilt thou destroy all the city for lack of five? And he said, If I find there forty and five, I will not destroy it.

29 And he spake unto him yet again, and said, Peradventure there shall be forty found there. And he said, I will not do it for forty's sake.

30 And he said unto him, Oh let not the Lord be angry, and I will speak: Peradventure there shall thirty be found there. And he said, I will not do it, if I find thirty there.

31 And he said, Behold now, I have taken upon me to speak unto the Lord: Peradventure there shall be twenty found there. And he said, I will not destroy it for twenty's sake.

32 And he said, ᴿOh let not the Lord be angry, and I will speak yet but this once: Peradventure ten shall be found there. ᴿAnd he said, I will not destroy it for ten's sake. Ju 6:39 · Jam 5:16

33 And the LORD went his way, as soon as he had left communing with Abraham: and Abraham returned unto his place.

19 And there came two angels to Sodom at even; and Lot sat in the gate of Sodom: and Lot seeing them rose up to meet them; and he bowed himself with his face toward the ground;

✝18:18—Ac 3:25   ❦19:1–11

18:19 For I know him. Some translations say, "I have chosen him." The language speaks of the intimate relationship which motivates the Lord to accomplish His purpose in Abraham (22:12). **do justice and judgment.** One idea in two words—"genuine righteousness."

2   And he said, Behold now, my lords, turn in, I pray you, into your servant's house, and tarry all night, and wash your feet, and ye shall rise up early, and go on your ways. And they said, Nay; but we will abide in the street all night.

3   And he ᵀpressed upon them greatly; and they turned in unto him, and entered into his house; ᴿand he made them a feast, and did bake unleavened bread, and they did eat.   *urged them* · Ex 23:15

4   But before they lay down, the men of the city, *even* the men of Sodom, compassed the house round, both old and young, all the people from every quarter:

5   And they called unto Lot, and said unto him, Where *are* the men which came in to thee this night? bring them out unto us, that we ᴿmay know them.   Ro 1:24, 27

6   And ᴿLot went out at the door unto them, and shut the door after him,   Ju 19:23

7   And said, I pray you, brethren, do not so wickedly.

8   ᴿBehold now, I have two daughters which have not known man; let me, I pray you, bring them out unto you, and do ye to them as *is* good in your eyes: only unto these men do nothing; ᴿfor therefore came they under the shadow of my roof.   Ju 19:24 · 18:5

9   And they said, Stand back. And they said *again,* This one *fellow* ᴿcame in to sojourn, and he will needs be a judge: now will we deal worse with thee, than with them. And they pressed sore upon the man, *even* Lot, and came near to break the door.   2 Pe 2:7, 8

10   But the men put forth their hand, and pulled Lot into the house to them, and shut to the door.

11   And they ᴿsmote the men that *were* at the door of the house with blindness, both small and great: so that they wearied themselves to find the door.   20:17

12   And the men said unto Lot, Hast thou here any besides? son in law, and thy sons, and thy daughters, and whatsoever thou hast in the city, ᴿbring *them* out of this place: 7:1; 2 Pe 2:7, 9

13   For we will destroy this place, because the cry of them ᵀis waxen great before the face of the LORD; and ᴿthe LORD hath sent us to destroy it.   *has grown* · Le 26:30-3

14   And Lot went out, and spake unto his sons in law, which married his daughters, and said, Up, get you out of this place; for the LORD will destroy this city. ᴿBut he seemed as one that ᵀmocked unto his sons in law. Ex 9:21 · *joked*

✍15   And when the morning arose, then the angels hastened Lot, saying, Arise, take thy wife, and thy two daughters, which are here; lest thou be consumed in the iniquity of the city.

16   And while he lingered, the men laid hold upon his hand, and upon the hand of his wife, and upon the hand of his two daughters; the ᴿLORD being merciful unto him: and they brought him

✍ 19:15

19:2 *my lords.* This is a greeting of respect for special visitors. **19:5 *know them.*** This term usually refers to sexual relations between a man and a woman (4:1), here it is referring to homosexual activity, which God has declared is an abomination (Le 18:22). **19:16 *the LORD being merciful unto him.*** This is the whole point of the story. God could have destroyed the city of Sodom with no word to Lot or Abraham (18:17). But because of His mercy, God's angels grabbed Lot and his family and brought them forcibly to safety. In this passage, Lot appears weak, indecisive, and unsure of whether he really wants to be rescued. However, the New Testament speaks a good word for Lot's character, calling him a "righteous man" and telling us that he was grieved by the sin he saw in Sodom and Gomorrah (2 Pe 2:6-8).

forth, and set him [T]without the city.   Ex 34:7; Lk 18:13 · *outside*
17 And it came to pass, when they had brought them forth [T]abroad, that he said, Escape for thy life; [R]look not behind thee, neither stay thou in all the plain; escape to the mountain, lest thou be consumed.   *outside* · Ma 24:16–18
18 And Lot said unto them, Oh, [R]not so, my Lord: Ac 10:14
19 Behold now, thy servant hath found grace in thy sight, and thou hast magnified thy mercy, which thou hast shewed unto me in saving my life; and I cannot escape to the mountain, lest some evil take me, and I die:
20 Behold now, this city *is* near to flee unto, and it *is* a little one: Oh, let me escape thither, (*is* it not a little one?) and my soul shall live.
21 And he said unto him, See, [R]I have accepted thee concerning this thing also, that I will not overthrow this city, for the which thou hast spoken.   Job 42:8, 9; Ps 145:19
🕯22 Haste thee, escape thither; for [R]I cannot do any thing till thou be come thither. Therefore the name of the city was called Zo'-ar.   Ex 32:10; De 9:14
23 The sun was risen upon the earth when Lot entered into Zo'-ar.
24 Then the LORD rained upon Sodom and upon Go-mor'-rah brimstone and [R]fire from the LORD out of heaven;   Le 10:2
25 And he overthrew those cities, and all the plain, and all the inhabitants of the cities, and that which grew upon the ground.
🕯26 But his wife looked back from behind him, and she became [R]a pillar of salt.   v. 17

27 And Abraham gat up early in the morning to the place where [R]he stood before the LORD: 18:22
28 And he looked toward Sodom and Go-mor'-rah, and toward all the land of the plain, and beheld, and, lo, [R]the smoke of the country went up as the smoke of a furnace.   Re 9:2; 18:9
29 And it came to pass, when God destroyed the cities of the plain, that God [R]remembered Abraham, and sent Lot out of the midst of the overthrow, when he overthrew the cities in the which Lot dwelt.   8:1; 18:23; De 7:8; 9:5, 27
30 And Lot went up out of Zo'-ar, and [R]dwelt in the mountain, and his two daughters with him; for he feared to dwell in Zo'-ar: and he dwelt in a cave, he and his two daughters.   vv. 17, 19
31 And the firstborn said unto the younger, Our father *is* old, and *there is* not a man in the earth [R]to come in unto us after the manner of all the earth: 38:8, 9; De 25:5
32 Come, let us make our father drink wine, and we will lie with him, that we [R]may preserve [T]seed of our father. [Mk 12:19] · *the lineage*
33 And they made their father drink wine that night: and the firstborn went in, and lay with her father; and he perceived not when she lay down, nor when she arose.
34 And it came to pass on the morrow, that the firstborn said unto the younger, Behold, I lay yesternight with my father: let us make him drink wine this night also; and go thou in, *and* lie with him, that we may preserve seed of our father.

🕯 19:22–25 🕯 19:26

19:22 *Zoar.* This name means "Insignificant in Size." **19:23–26 *brimstone and fire.*** This may be simply a supernatural judgment on the cities, but some have also theorized that the fire and brimstone which "rained" down on them may have been from a volcanic eruption. In any case, it is clear that the destruction was a judgment from God, and that it was under His control. **19:26 *pillar of salt.*** Near the Dead Sea, which is believed to now cover the site of Sodom and Gomorrah, there are numerous rock salt formations, including pillars about the size of a human. Jesus referred to the fate of Lot's wife as a historical fact (Lk 17:32).

35 And they made their father drink wine that night also: and the younger arose, and lay with him; and he perceived not when she lay down, nor when she arose.

36 Thus were both the daughters of Lot with child by their father.

37 And the firstborn bare a son, and called his name Moab: [R]the same *is* the father of the Mo'-ab-ites unto this day.   Nu 25:1; De 2:9

38 And the younger, she also bare a son, and called his name Ben-am'-mi: [R]the same *is* the father of the children of Ammon unto this day.   Nu 21:24; De 2:19

20 And Abraham journeyed from thence toward the south country, and dwelled between [R]Ka'-desh and Shur, and sojourned in Ge'-rar.   12:9; 16:7, 14

2 And Abraham said of Sarah his wife, [R]She *is* my sister: and A-bim'-e-lech king of Ge'-rar sent, and [R]took Sarah.   12:11–13; 26:7 · 12:15

3 But [R]God came to A-bim'-e-lech [R]in a dream by night, and said to him, [R]Behold, thou *art but* a dead man, for the woman which thou hast taken; for she *is* a man's wife.   Ps 105:14 · Job 33:15 · v. 7

4 But A-bim'-e-lech had not come near her: and he said, Lord, [R]wilt thou slay also a righteous nation?   18:23–25; Nu 16:22

5 Said he not unto me, She *is* my sister? and she, even she herself said, He *is* my brother: in the integrity of my heart and innocency of my hands have I done this.

6 And God said unto him in a dream, Yea, I know that thou didst this in the integrity of thy heart; for [R]I also withheld thee from sinning against me: therefore suffered I thee not to touch her.   31:7

7 Now therefore restore the man *his* wife; [R]for he *is* a prophet, and he shall pray for thee, and thou shalt live: and if thou restore *her* not, know thou that thou shalt surely die, thou, and all that *are* thine.   1 Sa 7:5; 2 Ki 5:11; Job 42:8

8 Therefore A-bim'-e-lech rose early in the morning, and called all his servants, and told all these things in their ears: and the men were [T]sore afraid.   *very*

9 Then A-bim'-e-lech called Abraham, and said unto him, What hast thou done unto us? and what have I offended thee, [R]that thou hast brought on me and on my kingdom a great sin? thou hast done deeds unto me that ought not to be done.   26:10; 39:9

10 And A-bim'-e-lech said unto Abraham, What sawest thou, that thou hast done this thing?

11 And Abraham said, Because I thought, Surely [R]the fear of God *is* not in this place; and they will slay me for my wife's sake.   42:1

12 And yet indeed *she is* my sister; she *is* the daughter of my father, but not the daughter of my mother; and she became my wife.

13 And it came to pass, when [R]God caused me to wander from my father's house, that I said unto her, This *is* thy kindness which thou shalt shew unto me; at every place whither we shall come, say of me, He *is* my brother.   12:1–9, 11

19:36–38 *Moab . . . Ben-ammi.* The shameful act of incest led to the births of two sons whose descendants (the Moabites and the Ammonites) would greatly trouble Israel. **20:2 *She is my sister.*** The complete truth told in such a way as to deceive or mislead is still a falsehood. Abraham's words were true: "She is my sister," but the message he intended to convey was false: "She is not married to me." His intent was deceit and the consequences he reaped were the same as if he had directly lied. A man speaks the real truth when he speaks the truth in his heart (Ps 15:2). **20:3 *God came . . . in a dream.*** Presumably, Abimelech was a pagan king. Yet God warned him of the wrong he was about to commit. This is another instance of the protective care that the Lord gives His people (31:24; Nu 22:12–20). **20:12 *indeed she is my sister.*** Later the law would prohibit the marriage of people so closely related, but in the early years of the earth it was apparently acceptable for half siblings to marry (see note on 4:17).

14 And A-bim'-e-lech ᴿtook sheep, and oxen, and menservants, and womenservants, and gave *them* unto Abraham, and restored him Sarah his wife.   12:16
15 And A-bim'-e-lech said, Behold, ᴿmy land *is* before thee: dwell where it pleaseth thee.   47:6
16 And unto Sarah he said, Behold, I have given thy brother a thousand *pieces* of silver: ᴿbehold, he *is* to thee ᴿa covering of the eyes, unto all that *are* with thee, and with all *other:* thus she was ᵀreproved.   26:11 · 24:65 · *justified*
17 So Abraham prayed unto God: and God healed A-bim'-e-lech, and his wife, and his maidservants; and they bare *children*.
18 For the LORD ᴿhad fast closed up all the wombs of the house of A-bim'-e-lech, because of Sarah Abraham's wife.   12:17

21 And the LORD ᴿvisited Sa-rah as he had said, and the LORD did unto Sarah ᴿas he had spoken. 1 Sa 2:21 · 17:16, 19, 21
2 For Sarah ᴿconceived, and bare Abraham a son in his old age, ᴿat the set time of which God had spoken to him.   Ac 7:8 · 18:10
3 And Abraham called the name of his son that was born unto him, whom Sarah bare to him, ᴿIsaac.ᵀ   17:19, 21 · Lit. *Laughter*
4 And Abraham circumcised his son Isaac being eight days old, as God had commanded him.
5 And ᴿAbraham was an hundred years old, when his son Isaac was born unto him.   17:1, 17
6 And Sarah said, ᴿGod hath

made me to laugh, *so that* all that hear will laugh with me.   Is 54:1
7 And she said, Who would have said unto Abraham, that Sarah should have given children suck? ᴿfor I have born *him* a son in his old age.   18:11, 12
8 And the child grew, and was weaned: and Abraham made a great feast the *same* day that Isaac was weaned.
9 And Sarah saw the son of Ha'-gar the Egyptian, which she had born unto Abraham, ᴿmocking.ᵀ   [Ga 4:29] · *scoffing*, lit. *laughing*
10 Wherefore she said unto Abraham, ᴿCast out this bondwoman and her son: for the son of this bondwoman shall not be heir with my son, *even* with Isaac.   25:6
11 And the thing was very grievous in Abraham's sight ᴿbecause of his son.   17:18
12 And God said unto Abraham, Let it not be grievous in thy sight because of the lad, and because of thy bondwoman; in all that Sarah hath said unto thee, hearken unto her voice; for ᴿin Isaac shall thy seed be called. [Ro 9:7, 8]; He 11:18
13 And also of the son of the bondwoman will I make ᴿa nation, because he *is* thy seed. 17:20
14 And Abraham rose up early in the morning, and took bread, and a ᵀbottle of water, and gave *it* unto Ha'-gar, putting *it* on her shoulder, and the ᵀchild, and ᴿsent her away: and she departed, and

20:17   21:1–8   21:12—Ro 9:7

21:1 *and the LORD visited Sarah as he had said.* The Bible stresses that the Lord causes conceptions; that children are a gift of the Lord (Ps 127:3). The verb *visit* is an extraordinary choice here, indicating that the Lord entered directly into the affairs of His people.   **21:3 *Isaac.*** Isaac means "He (God) Is Laughing (Now)." At one time Abraham and Sarah had both laughed at the improbability of having a son in their old age (17:17; 18:12); now with the birth of the promised child their laughter took on a happier meaning. **21:12 *hearken unto her voice.*** As painful as the situation was, God confirmed that Sarah was right that Ishmael would have to leave. Only Isaac was the child of promise, the one through whom the covenant would be fulfilled. This complicated situation was part of the price Abraham had to pay for trying to bring about God's promises in his own time. Nevertheless, God is merciful and He did not abandon Hagar and Ishmael.

wandered in the wilderness of Be'-er–she'-ba.   *skin · youth ·* Jo 8:35

15 And the water was spent in the bottle, and she [T] cast the child under one of the shrubs.   *placed*

16 And she went, and sat her down [T] over against *him* a good way off, as it were a bowshot: for she said, Let me not see the death of the child. And she sat over against *him*, and lift up her voice, and wept.   *opposite*

17 And [R] God heard the voice of the lad; and the angel of God called to Ha'-gar out of heaven, and said unto her, What aileth thee, Ha'-gar? fear not; for God hath heard the voice of the lad where he *is*.   Ex 3:7; De 26:7; Ps 6:8

18 Arise, lift up the lad, and hold him [T] in thine hand; for I will make him a great nation.   *with*

19 And [R] God opened her eyes, and she saw a well of water; and she went, and filled the bottle with water, and gave the lad drink.   3:7; Nu 22:31; 2 Ki 6:17

20 And God [R] was with the lad; and he grew, and dwelt in the wilderness, [R] and became an archer.   28:15; 39:2, 3, 21 · 16:12

21 And he dwelt in the wilderness of Pa'-ran: and his mother [R] took him a wife out of the land of Egypt.   24:4

22 And it came to pass at that time, that [R] A-bim'-e-lech and Phi'-chol the chief captain of his host spake unto Abraham, saying, [R] God *is* with thee in all that thou doest: 20:2, 14; 26:26 · 26:28; Is 8:10

23 Now therefore [R] swear unto me here by God that thou wilt not deal falsely with me, nor with my son, nor with my son's son: *but* according to the kindness that I have done unto thee, thou shalt do unto me, and to the land wherein thou hast sojourned.   Jos 2:12

24 And Abraham said, I will swear.

25 And Abraham reproved A-bim'-e-lech because of a well of water, which A-bim'-e-lech's servants had violently taken away.

26 And A-bim'-e-lech said, I [T] wot not who hath done this thing: neither didst thou tell me, neither yet heard I *of it*, but to day.   *know*

27 And Abraham took sheep and oxen, and gave them unto A-bim'-e-lech; and both of them [R] made a covenant.   26:31; 31:44

28 And Abraham set seven ewe lambs of the flock by themselves.

29 And A-bim'-e-lech said unto Abraham, [R] What *mean* these seven ewe lambs which thou hast set by themselves?   33:8

30 And he said, For *these* seven ewe lambs shalt thou take of my hand, that [R] they may be a witness unto me, that I have digged this well.   31:48, 52

31 Wherefore he called that place Be'-er–she'-ba; because there they sware both of them.

32 Thus they made a covenant at Be'-er–she'-ba: then A-bim'-e-lech rose up, and Phi'-chol the chief captain of his host, and they returned into the land of the Phi-lis'-tines.

33 And *Abraham* planted a grove in Be'-er–she'-ba, and called there

21:16–21

21:17 God heard. What wonderful words these are! There is no pain of His people that He does not see or hear about (Is 40:27–28; He 2:10,18; 4:15). Even though Ishmael was not the son of promise, God still had His hand on his life. **21:23 kindness.** This exceedingly important term, sometimes translated *loyal love* or *loving-kindness* is often used in the Psalms to describe God's character (Ps 100:5). Here we see its proper context in a binding relationship. The term basically describes covenant loyalty (24:12). **21:27 covenant.** This is a binding agreement between two equals, similar to today's business contracts. **21:28–31 seven ewe lambs . . . Beer-sheba.** The Hebrew number seven is similar in sound to the verb meaning "to swear" (v. 24). Thus Beer-sheba would be the well where they swore and the well of the seven ewe lambs.

on the name of the LORD, ^Rthe everlasting God.   35:11; Ex 15:18
34   And Abraham sojourned in the
Phi-lis'-tines' land many days.

22 And it came to pass after
these things, that ^RGod did
^Ttempt Abraham, and said unto
him, Abraham: and he said, Be-
hold, *here* I *am.*   1 Co 10:13 · test
2   And he said, Take now thy son,
^Rthine only *son* Isaac, whom thou
lovest, and get thee into the land
of Mo-ri'-ah; and offer him there
for a burnt offering upon one of
the mountains which I will tell thee
of.   Jo 3:16; 1 Jo 4:9
3   And Abraham rose up early
in the morning, and saddled his
^Tass, and took two of his young
men with him, and Isaac his son,
and ^Tclave the wood for the burnt
offering, and rose up, and went
unto the place of which God had
told him.   donkey · split
4   Then on the third day Abraham lifted up his eyes, and saw
the place afar off.
5   And Abraham said unto his
young men, Abide ye here with
the ass; and I and the ^Tlad will
go yonder and worship, and come
again to you.   Lit. *young man*
6   And Abraham took the wood
of the burnt offering, and ^Rlaid *it*
upon Isaac his son; and he took
the fire in his hand, and a knife;
and they went both of them together.   Jo 19:17
7   And Isaac spake unto Abra-
ham his father, and said, My father:
and he said, Here *am* I, my son.
And he said, Behold the fire and
the wood: but where *is* the ^Tlamb
for a burnt offering?   goat
8   And Abraham said, My son,
God will provide himself a ^Rlamb
for a burnt offering: so they went
both of them together.   Jo 1:29, 36
9   And they came to the place
which God had told him of; and
Abraham built an altar there, and
laid the wood in order, and bound
Isaac his son, and ^Rlaid him on the
altar upon the wood.   [He 11:17–19]
10   And Abraham stretched forth
his hand, and took the knife to
slay his son.
11   And the ^Rangel of the LORD
called unto him out of heaven, and
said, Abraham, Abraham: and he
said, Here *am* I.   16:7–11
12   And he said, Lay not thine
hand upon the lad, neither do thou
any thing unto him: for now I know
that thou fearest God, seeing thou
hast not withheld thy son, thine
only *son* from me.
13   And Abraham lifted up his
eyes, and looked, and behold behind *him* a ram caught in a thicket
by his horns: and Abraham went
and took the ram, and offered him

21:34 *the Philistines' land.* The name Palestine comes from the word for Philistine.
22:5 *worship, and come again to you.* Abraham's comment to his servants is a
significant avowal of his faith in God. Even though he was going to sacrifice his son, he
was confident that they both would return.   **22:8 *God will provide.*** Abraham's faith in
God's promise is shown in his response to a very real and terrible test. Many times this
is seen as a test of the quality of Abraham's love for God—who would he choose, God
or his son? However, there is no sign that Abraham made this mistake. He knew beyond
a shadow of doubt that Isaac was given to him directly by God, the son of promise.
Therefore it was right that he should love his son of promise as a gift from God. God's
covenant said that a great nation would descend from Isaac, therefore it would be so.
Abraham's test was not "whom do you love most?" but "do you really believe Me?"
The answer was a resounding, "Yes!" Abraham carried his faith to the knife edge on
his son's flesh. God had promised, and it would be so, even if Isaac had to be raised
from the dead to make His words come to pass (He 11:17–19).   **22:9 *bound Isaac
his son.*** Surely Isaac could have struggled or run away at this point, but there is no
evidence that he did so. Apparently Isaac's faith and trust both in God and in his father
was sufficient to stand the test.

up for a burnt offering in the stead of his son.

14 And Abraham called the name of that place [T]Je-ho'-vah–ji'-reh: as it is said *to* this day, In the mount of the LORD it shall be seen. Lit. *The* LORD *Will Provide or See*

15 And the angel of the LORD called unto Abraham out of heaven the second time,

16 And said, [R]By myself have I sworn, saith the LORD, for because thou hast done this thing, and hast not withheld thy son, thine only *son:* Ps 105:9; [He 6:13, 14]

17 That in blessing I will bless thee, and in multiplying I will multiply thy seed [R]as the stars of the heaven, [R]and as the sand which *is* upon the sea shore; and thy seed shall possess the gate of his enemies; De 1:10 · 1 Ki 4:20

18 [R]And in thy seed shall all the nations of the earth be blessed; because thou hast obeyed my voice. [Ac 3:25, 26]; Ga 3:8, 9, 16, 18

19 So Abraham returned unto his young men, and they rose up and went together to [R]Be'-er–she'-ba; and Abraham dwelt at Be'-er–she'-ba. 21:31

20 And it came to pass after these things, that it was told Abraham, saying, Behold, [R]Mil'-cah, she hath also born children unto thy brother Na'-hor; 24:15

21 [R]Huz his firstborn, and Buz his brother, and Kem'-u-el the father [R]of Ar'-am, Job 1:1 · Job 32:2

22 And Che'-sed, and Ha'-zo, and Pil'-dash, and Jid'-laph, and Be-thu'-el.

23 And [R]Be-thu'-el begat [T]Rebekah: these eight Mil'-cah did

bear to Na'-hor, Abraham's brother. 24:15 · *Rebecca,* Ro 9:10

24 And his concubine, whose name *was* Reu'-mah, she bare also Te'-bah, and Ga'-ham, and Tha'-hash, and Ma'-a-chah.

23 And Sarah was an hundred and seven and twenty years old: *these were* the years of the life of Sarah.

2 And Sarah died in [R]Kir'-jath-ar'-ba; the same *is* [R]He'-bron in the land of Canaan: and Abraham came to mourn for Sarah, and to weep for her. 35:27 · v. 19

3 And Abraham stood up from before his dead, and spake unto the sons of [R]Heth, saying, 2 Ki 7:6

4 [R]I *am* a stranger and a sojourner with you: [R]give me a possession of a buryingplace with you, that I may bury my dead out of my sight. Ps 39:12 · Ac 7:5, 16

5 And the children of Heth answered Abraham, saying unto him,

6 Hear us, my lord: thou *art* [R]a mighty prince among us: in the choice of our sepulchres bury thy dead; none of us shall withhold from thee his sepulchre, but that thou mayest bury thy dead. 24:35

7 And Abraham stood up, and bowed himself to the people of the land, *even* to the children of Heth.

8 And he communed with them, saying, If it be your mind that I should bury my dead out of my sight; hear me, and intreat for me to E'-phron the son of Zo'-har,

9 That he may give me the cave of [R]Mach-pe'-lah, which he hath, which *is* in the end of his field; for as much money as it is worth he shall give it me for a possession of a buryingplace amongst you. 25:9

22:14 Jehovah-jireh. As God provided a ram to take the place of Abraham's son, so one day He would provide His own Son to take our place. Some believe that Mt. Moriah later became part of the city of Jerusalem, and was the site of Solomon's temple. **22:17 I will bless thee.** In the Hebrew, this is stated by doubling the verbs (blessing I will bless you, multiplying I will multiply you), a Hebrew idiom that powerfully emphasizes the certainty of the action. **22:18 seed.** Here this is a grand play on words. The seed was Isaac, and by extension the Jewish nation. Specifically the Seed was one descendant of Abraham, Jesus the Messiah.

10   And E'-phron dwelt among the children of Heth: and E'-phron the Hit'-tite answered Abraham in the audience of the children of Heth, *even* of all that went in at the gate of his city, saying,

11   Nay, my lord, hear me: the field give I thee, and the cave that *is* therein, I give it thee; in the presence of the sons of my people give I it thee: bury thy dead.

12   And Abraham bowed down himself before the people of the land.

13   And he spake unto E'-phron in the audience of the people of the land, saying, But if thou *wilt give it*, I pray thee, hear me: I will give thee money for the field; take *it* of me, and I will bury my dead there.

14   And E'-phron answered Abraham, saying unto him,

15   My lord, hearken unto me: the land *is worth* four hundred ᴿshek'-els of silver; what *is* that betwixt me and thee? bury therefore thy dead.   Ex 30:13; Eze 45:12

16   And Abraham hearkened unto E'-phron; and Abraham weighed to E'-phron the silver, which he had named in the audience of the sons of Heth, four hundred shek'-els of silver, current *money* with the merchant.

17   And ᴿthe field of E'-phron, which *was* in Mach-pe'-lah, which *was* before Mam'-re, the field, and the cave which *was* therein, and all the trees that *were* in the field,

that *were* in all the borders round about, were made sure   49:29–32

18   Unto Abraham for a possession in the presence of the children of Heth, before all that went in at the gate of his city.

19   And after this, Abraham buried Sarah his wife in the cave of the field of Mach-pe'-lah before Mam'-re: the same *is* He'-bron in the land of Canaan.

20   And the field, and the cave that *is* therein, ᴿwere ᵀmade sure unto Abraham for a possession of a buryingplace by the sons of Heth.   Je 32:10, 11 · *deeded to*

24

And Abraham was old, *and* well stricken in age: and the LORD ᴿhad blessed Abraham in all things.   Ps 112:3; [Ga 3:9]

2   And Abraham said unto his eldest servant of his house, that ᴿruled over all that he had, ᴿPut, I pray thee, thy hand under my thigh: v. 10; 39:4–6 · 47:29; 1 Ch 29:24

3   And I will make thee ᴿswear by the LORD, the God of heaven, and the God of the earth, that ᴿthou shalt not take a wife unto my son of the daughters of the Ca'-naan-ites, among whom I dwell: 14:19, 22 · De 7:3; 2 Co 6:14–17

4   But thou shalt go unto my country, and to my kindred, and take a wife unto my son Isaac.

5   And the servant said unto him, Peradventure the woman will not be willing to follow me unto this land: must I needs bring thy son again unto the land from whence thou camest?

23:13 *I will give thee money for the field.* Abraham would not have been offering "money" as we think of it today; minted coins were not invented until at least 650 B.C. Instead, trading was done by barter, or with precious metals by weight.   **23:15** *what is that betwixt me and thee?* The dialogue in this chapter gives a wonderfully detailed example of the bargaining process of the day. Abraham clearly understood Ephron's generous statement as a politely phrased way of setting his price.   **23:20** *field . . . cave . . . were made sure unto Abraham.* It is interesting to note that the only piece of the promised land that Abraham ever personally possessed was this field and cave to bury his wife.   **24:2** *his eldest servant.* Some have thought that this might be Eliezer of Damascus, the one who had been named as Abraham's heir before the births of Ishmael and Isaac.   **24:3** *the daughters of the Canaanites.* This was not an issue of racism, as is sometimes thought—it was theological. The Canaanite peoples worshiped the false gods Baal and Asherah (De 7:3).

6   And Abraham said unto him, Beware thou that thou [T]bring not my son thither again.   *take*
7   The LORD God of heaven, which took me from my father's house, and from the land of my kindred, and which spake unto me, and that sware unto me, saying, Unto thy seed will I give this land; he shall send his angel before thee, and thou shalt take a wife unto my son from thence.
8   And if the woman will not be willing to follow thee, then [R]thou shalt be clear from this my oath: only [T]bring not my son thither again.   Jos 2:17–20 · *take*
9   And the servant put his hand under the thigh of Abraham his master, and sware to him concerning that matter.
10   And the servant took ten camels of the camels of his master, and departed; for all [T]the goods of his master *were* in his hand: and he arose, and went to Mes-o-po-ta'-mi-a, unto [R]the city of Na'-hor.   Lit. *good things* · 11:31, 32
11   And he made his camels to kneel down without the city by a well of water at the time of the evening, *even* the time that women go out to draw *water.*
12   And he said, O LORD God of my master Abraham, I pray thee, [T]send me good speed this day, and shew kindness unto my master Abraham.   *give me success*
13   Behold, [R]I stand *here* by the well of water; and [R]the daughters of the men of the city come out to draw water: v. 43 · Ex 2:16
14   And let it come to pass, that the damsel to whom I shall say, Let down thy pitcher, I pray thee, that I may drink; and she shall say, Drink, and I will give thy camels drink also: *let the same be* she *that* thou hast appointed for thy servant Isaac; and thereby shall I know that thou hast shewed kindness unto my master.
15   And it came to pass, before he had done speaking, that, behold, Rebekah came out, who was born to Be-thu'-el, son of [R]Mil'-cah, the wife of Na'-hor, Abraham's brother, with her pitcher upon her shoulder.   22:20, 23
16   And the damsel [R]*was* very fair to look upon, a virgin, neither had any man known her: and she went down to the well, and filled her pitcher, and came up.   26:7; 29:17
17   And the servant ran to meet her, and said, Let me, I pray thee, drink a little water of thy pitcher.
18   [R]And she said, Drink, my lord: and she hasted, and let down her pitcher upon her hand, and gave him drink.   vv. 14, 46; [1 Pe 3:8, 9]
19   And when she had done giving him drink, she said, I will draw *water* for thy camels also, until they have done drinking.
20   And she hasted, and emptied her pitcher into the trough, and ran again unto the well to draw *water,* and drew for all his camels.
21   And the man wondering at her held his peace, to wit whether [R]the LORD had made his journey prosperous or not.   vv. 12–14, 27, 52
22   And it came to pass, as the camels had done drinking, that the man took a golden [T]earring of half

24:12 *O LORD God of my master Abraham.* This language does not mean that the servant himself did not believe in God. The servant was making his appeal on the basis of God's covenant loyalty to Abraham.   **24:15 Providence**—Abraham sent his servant to choose Isaac's bride, confident that his servant would be led by the Lord and that in God's providence he would make the right choice. The servant prayed for very specific guidance, and God sent him Rebekah. He was impressed not only with her physical beauty, but also with her kind, generous, and hospitable character. His decision was confirmed when her parents gave their consent and she agreed to return with him. Today we must remember to seek the Lord's guidance and trust in His providence just as Abraham's servant, Rebekah, and her family did.

a shek'-el weight, and two bracelets for her hands of ten *shek'-els*
weight of gold; *nose ring*
23 And said, Whose daughter *art*
thou? tell me, I pray thee: is there
room *in* thy father's house for us
to lodge in?
24 And she said unto him, ᴿI *am*
the daughter of Be-thu'-el the son
of Mil'-cah, which she bare unto
Na'-hor. v. 15; 22:23
25 She said moreover unto him,
We have both straw and ᵀprov-
ender enough, and room to lodge
in. *food*
26 And the man ᴿbowed down
his head, and worshipped the
LORD. vv. 48, 52; Ex 4:31
27 And he said, Blessed *be* the
LORD God of my master Abraham,
who hath not left destitute my master of ᴿhis mercy and his truth: I
being in the way, the LORD ᴿled me
to the house of my master's brethren. 32:10; Ps 98:3 · vv. 21, 48
28 And the damsel ran, and told
them of her mother's house these
things.
29 And Rebekah had a brother,
and his name *was* ᴿLaban: and
Laban ran out unto the man, unto
the well. 29:5, 13
30 And it came to pass, when he
saw the ᵀearring and bracelets
upon his sister's hands, and when
he heard the words of Rebekah his
sister, saying, Thus spake the man
unto me; that he came unto the
man; and, behold, he stood by the
camels at the well. *nose ring*
31 And he said, Come in, ᴿthou
blessed of the LORD; wherefore
standest thou ᵀwithout? for I have
prepared the house, and room for
the camels. Ru 3:10 · *outside*
32 And the man came into the
house: and he ungirded his camels, and gave straw and provender for the camels, and water to
ᴿwash his feet, and the men's feet
that *were* with him. Jo 13:5, 13–15
33 And there was set *meat* before him to eat: but he said, I will

not eat, until I have told mine er-
rand. And he said, Speak on.
34 And he said, I *am* Abraham's
servant.
35 And the LORD ᴿhath blessed
my master greatly; and he is become great: and he hath given
him flocks, and herds, and silver,
and gold, and menservants, and
maidservants, and camels, and
ᵀasses. v. 1; 13:2 · *donkeys*
36 And Sarah my master's wife
bare a son to my master when she
was old: and ᴿunto him hath he
given all that he hath. 21:10; 25:5
37 And my master ᴿmade me
swear, saying, Thou shalt not take
a wife to my son of the daughters
of the Ca'-naan-ites, in whose land
I dwell: vv. 2–4
38 ᴿBut thou shalt go unto my father's house, and to my kindred,
and take a wife unto my son. v. 4
39 ᴿAnd I said unto my master,
ᵀPeradventure the woman will not
follow me. v. 5 · *Perhaps*
40 And he said unto me, The
LORD, before whom I walk, will
send his angel with thee, and prosper thy way; and thou shalt take
a wife for my son of my kindred,
and of my father's house:
41 ᴿThen shalt thou be clear from
this my oath, when thou comest
to my kindred; and if they give not
thee *one*, thou shalt be clear from
my oath. v. 8
42 And I came this day unto the
well, and said, ᴿO LORD God of my
master Abraham, if now thou do
prosper my way which I go: v. 12
43 ᴿBehold, I stand by the well
of water; and it shall come to pass,
that when the virgin cometh forth
to draw *water*, and I say to her,
Give me, I pray thee, a little water
of thy pitcher to drink; v. 13
44 And she say to me, Both drink
thou, and I will also draw for thy
camels: *let* the same *be* the woman
whom the LORD hath appointed out
for my master's son.
45 ᴿAnd before I had done speaking in mine heart, behold, Re-

bekah came forth with her pitcher on her shoulder; and she went down unto the well, and drew *water:* and I said unto her, Let me drink, I pray thee.   v. 15

46 And she made haste, and let down her pitcher from her *shoulder,* and said, Drink, and I will give thy camels drink also: so I drank, and she made the camels drink also.

47 And I asked her, and said, Whose daughter *art* thou? And she said, The daughter of Be-thu′-el, Na′-hor's son, whom Mil′-cah bare unto him: and I put the [T]earring upon her face, and the bracelets upon her hands.   *nose ring*

48 And I bowed down my head, and worshipped the LORD, and blessed the LORD God of my master Abraham, which had led me in the right way to take my master's brother's daughter unto his son.

49 And now if ye will [R]deal kindly and truly with my master, tell me: and if not, tell me; that I may turn to the right hand, or to the left.   47:29; Jos 2:14

50 Then Laban and Be-thu′-el answered and said, [R]The thing proceedeth from the LORD: we cannot speak unto thee bad or good.   Ps 118:23; Ma 21:42; Mk 12:11

51 Behold, Rebekah [R]*is* before thee, take *her,* and go, and let her be thy master's son's wife, as the LORD hath spoken.   20:15

52 And it came to pass, that, when Abraham's servant heard their words, he worshipped the LORD, *bowing himself* to the earth.

53 And the servant brought forth jewels of silver, and jewels of gold, and raiment, and gave *them* to Rebekah: he gave also to her

brother and to her mother [R]precious things.   2 Ch 21:3; Ez 1:6

54 And they did eat and drink, he and the men that *were* with him, and tarried all night; and they rose up in the morning, and he said, [R]Send me away unto my master.   vv. 56, 59; 30:25

55 And her brother and her mother said, Let the damsel abide with us *a few* days, at the least ten; after that she shall go.

56 And he said unto them, Hinder me not, seeing the LORD hath prospered my way; send me away that I may go to my master.

57 And they said, We will call the damsel, and [T]enquire at her mouth.   *ask her personally*

58 And they called Rebekah, and said unto her, Wilt thou go with this man? And she said, I will go.

59 And they sent away Rebekah their sister, and her nurse, and Abraham's servant, and his men.

60 And they blessed Rebekah, and said unto her, Thou *art* our sister, be thou [R]*the mother* of thousands of millions, and [R]let thy seed possess the gate of those which hate them.   17:16 · 22:17; 28:14

61 And Rebekah arose, and her damsels, and they rode upon the camels, and followed the man: and the servant took Rebekah, and went his way.

62 And Isaac came from the way of the [R]well La-hai′-roi; for he dwelt in the south country.   16:14

63 And Isaac went out [R]to meditate in the field at the eventide: and he lifted up his eyes, and saw, and, behold, the camels *were* coming.   Jos 1:8; Ps 1:2; 77:12; 119:15

64 And Rebekah lifted up her

✒ 24:58–60

24:50 *The thing proceedeth from the LORD.* It appears that the family of Bethuel and Laban also worshipped the living God, or at least acknowledged Him along with other gods (see 31:19; Jos 24:2).   **24:60** *they blessed Rebekah.* These words are not mere sentiment, nor are they a magical charm, but a prayer for God's blessing on her life. *gate.* The possession of the gates of one's enemies meant power over them (22:17).

eyes, and when she saw Isaac, she lighted off the camel.

65 For she *had* said unto the servant, What man *is* this that walketh in the field to meet us? And the servant *had* said, It *is* my master: therefore she took a vail, and covered herself.

66 And the servant told Isaac all things that he had done.

67 And Isaac brought her into his mother Sarah's tent, and ᴿtook Rebekah, and she became his wife; and he loved her: and Isaac was comforted after his mother's *death*.   25:20

25 Then again Abraham took a wife, and her name *was* Ketu'-rah.

2 And ᴿshe bare him Zim'-ran, and Jok'-shan, and Me'-dan, and Mid'-i-an, and Ish'-bak, and Shu'-ah.   1 Ch 1:32, 33

3 And Jok'-shan begat She'-ba, and De'-dan. And the sons of De'-dan were As-shu'-rim, and Le-tu'-shim, and Le-um'-mim.

4 And the sons of Mid'-i-an; E'-phah, and E'-pher, and Ha'-noch, and A-bi'-dah, and El-da'-ah. All these *were* the children of Ke-tu'-rah.

5 And ᴿAbraham gave all that he had unto Isaac.   24:35, 36

6 But unto the sons of the concubines, which Abraham had, Abraham gave gifts, and ᴿsent them away from Isaac his son, while he yet lived, eastward, unto ᴿthe east country.   21:14 · Ju 6:3

7 And these *are* the days of the years of Abraham's life which he lived, an hundred threescore and fifteen years.

8 Then Abraham gave up the ghost, and died in a good old age, an old man, and full *of years*; and ᴿwas gathered to his people.   35:29

9 And his sons Isaac and Ish'-ma-el buried him in the cave of Mach-pe'-lah, in the field of E'-phron the son of Zo'-har the Hit'-tite, which *is* before Mam'-re;

10 ᴿThe field which Abraham purchased of the sons of Heth: ᴿthere was Abraham buried, and Sarah his wife.   23:3–16 · 49:31

11 And it came to pass after the death of Abraham, that God blessed his son Isaac; and Isaac dwelt by the well La-hai'–roi.

12 Now these *are* the ᴿgenerations of Ish'-ma-el, Abraham's son, whom Ha'-gar the Egyptian, Sarah's ᵀhandmaid, bare unto Abraham: 11:10, 27; 16:15 · *maidservant*

13 And ᴿthese *are* the names of the sons of Ish'-ma-el, by their names, according to their generations: the firstborn of Ish'-ma-el,

24:67

24:67 he loved her. The love of Isaac for Rebekah is a wonderful fulfillment and illustration of God's original purpose for marriage. Realizing it was not good for man to be alone (Ge 2:18), the Creator graciously created Eve, a helper for Adam. God Himself then performed history's first wedding. Isaac and Rebekah serve not only as a lovely example of godly marriage, but also as a beautiful picture of the love between Christ and the church in the New Testament. Rebekah, like the church, loved her bridegroom without first seeing him (compare Ge 24:58 with 1 Pe 1:8). Like the church, Rebekah was prayed for by her bridegroom (Ge 24:63; Ro 8:34). Isaac, having previously been presented for offering on Mt. Moriah (Ge 22:1–14), was content to await the arrival of his bride. He was an early portrayal of the Son of God who now awaits the arrival of His bride in heaven (He 10:12–14). **25:1 took a wife.** In 1 Chronicles 1:32, Keturah is described as Abraham's concubine. It is not really known exactly what position she had in Abraham's household, or when the relationship began. Her sons had a status similar to that of Ishmael, Abraham's son by Hagar (ch. 16), but without Ishmael's particular blessing (16:10–16). **25:2 Midian.** This son was the father of the Midianites, some of whom later bought Joseph from his brothers (37:28,36). **25:11 God blessed.** God blessed Isaac because He had already established "an everlasting covenant" with him (17:19; He 11:17). Later God renewed the covenant with Isaac personally (26:2–5).

Ne-ba'-joth; and Ke'-dar, and Ad'-be-el, and Mib'-sam,   1 Ch 1:29-31

14 And Mish'-ma, and Du'-mah, and Mas'-sa,

15 Ha'-dar, and Te'-ma, Je'-tur, Na'-phish, and Ked'-e-mah:

16 These *are* the sons of Ish'-ma-el, and these *are* their names, by their towns, and by their ᵀcastles; twelve princes according to their nations.   *settlements* or *camps*

17 And these *are* the years of the life of Ish'-ma-el, an hundred and thirty and seven years: and he gave up the ghost and died; and was gathered unto his people.

18 ᴿAnd they dwelt from Hav'-i-lah unto Shur, that *is* before Egypt, as thou goest toward Assyria: *and* he ᵀdied in the presence of all his brethren.   20:1 · Lit. *fell*

19 And these *are* the generations of Isaac, Abraham's son: ᴿAbraham begat Isaac: Ma 1:2

20 And Isaac was forty years old when he took Rebekah to wife, ᴿthe daughter of Be-thu'-el the Syrian of Pa'-dan-a'-ram, ᴿthe sister to Laban the Syrian.   22:23 · 24:29

21 And Isaac intreated the LORD for his wife, because she *was* barren: ᴿand the LORD was intreated of him, and ᴿRebekah his wife conceived.   1 Sa 1:17 · Ro 9:10-13

22 And the children struggled together within her; and she said, If *it be* so, why *am* I thus? And she went to enquire of the LORD.

23 And the LORD said unto her, ᴿTwo nations *are* in thy womb, and two manner of people shall be separated from thy bowels; and ᴿ*the one* people shall be stronger than *the other* people; and ᴿthe elder shall serve the younger.   24:60 · 2 Sa 8:14 · Ro 9:12

24 And when her days to be delivered were fulfilled, behold, *there were* twins in her womb.

25 And the first came out red, all over like an hairy garment; and they called his name Esau.

26 And after that came his brother out, and ᴿhis hand took hold on Esau's heel; and ᴿhis name was called Jacob: and Isaac *was* threescore years old when she bare them.   Ho 12:3 · 27:36

27 And the boys grew: and Esau was ᴿa cunning hunter, a man of the field; and Jacob *was* a plain man, dwelling in tents.   27:3, 5

28 And Isaac loved Esau, because he did eat of *his* venison: ᴿbut Rebekah loved Jacob.   27:6-10

29 And Jacob ᵀsod pottage: and Esau came from the field, and he *was* faint: *cooked a stew*

30 And Esau said to Jacob, Feed me, I pray thee, with that same red *pottage*; for I *am* faint: therefore was his name called E'-dom.

31 And Jacob said, Sell me this day thy birthright.

32 And Esau said, Behold, I *am* at the point to die: and what profit shall this birthright do to me?

33 And Jacob said, Swear to me this day; and he sware unto him: and ᴿhe sold his birthright unto Jacob.   He 12:16

34 Then Jacob gave Esau bread and pottage of lentiles; and ᴿhe did eat and drink, and rose up, and went his way: thus Esau despised *his* birthright.   Is 22:13

25:21 *intreated.* The Hebrew verb here indicates that Isaac prayed passionately for his wife. For examples of passionate prayer, see Ex 8:30; 2 Sa 21:14; 24:25. **25:25** *Esau.* This name sounds like the Hebrew word that means "hairy." **25:26** *Jacob.* The Hebrew word that means "heel" sounds similar to the name Jacob. The name may mean either "He Who Grasps at the Heel (of Another)" or "He (the Lord) Is at His Heels (Is His Protector)." **25:30** *Edom.* This name means "red." The nickname is here connected to the red stew for which he traded his birthright; many have speculated that Esau may have had ruddy skin, or even red hair since the name stuck and even became the name of his land and the nation of his descendants (36:8).

26 And there was a famine in the land, beside [R] the first famine that was in the days of Abraham. And Isaac went unto [R] A-bim'-e-lech king of the Phi-lis'-tines unto Ge'-rar.   12:10 · 20:1, 2

2 And the LORD appeared unto him, and said, [R] Go not down into Egypt; dwell in [R] the land which I shall tell thee of: 17:1; 18:1; 35:9 · 12:1

3 [R] Sojourn in this land, and [R] I will be with thee, and will bless thee; for unto thee, and unto thy seed, I will give all these countries, and I will perform the oath which I sware unto Abraham thy father;   Ps 39:12; He 11:9 · 28:13, 15

4 And [R] I will make thy seed to multiply as the stars of heaven, and will give unto thy seed all these countries; [R] and in thy seed shall all the nations of the earth be blessed;   Ex 32:13 · Ga 3:8

5 [R] Because that Abraham obeyed my voice, and kept my charge, my commandments, my statutes, and my laws.   22:16, 18

6 And Isaac dwelt in Ge'-rar:

7 And the men of the place asked *him* of his wife; and [R] he said, She *is* my sister: for he feared to say, *She is* my wife; lest, *said he,* the men of the place should kill me for Rebekah; because she [R] *was* fair to look upon. 12:13; 20:2, 12, 13 · 12:11; 24:16

8 And it came to pass, when he had been there a long time, that A-bim'-e-lech king of the Phi-lis'-tines looked out at a window, and saw, and, behold, Isaac *was* sporting with Rebekah his wife.

9 And A-bim'-e-lech called Isaac, and said, Behold, [T] of a surety she *is* thy wife: and how saidst thou, She *is* my sister? And Isaac said unto him, Because I said, Lest I die for her.   *obviously*

10 And A-bim'-e-lech said, What *is* this thou hast done unto us? one of the people might [T] lightly have lien with thy wife, and [R] thou shouldest have brought guiltiness upon us.   *soon* · 20:9

11 And A-bim'-e-lech charged all *his* people, saying, He that toucheth this man or his wife shall surely be put to death.

12 Then Isaac sowed in that land, and [T] received in the same year [R] an hundredfold: and the LORD blessed him.   *reaped* · Mk 4:8

13 And the man [R] waxed great, and went forward, and grew until he became very great: [Pr 10:22]

14 For he had possession of flocks, and possession of herds, and great store of servants: and the Phi-lis'-tines [R] envied him.   37:11

15 For all the wells which his father's servants had digged in the days of Abraham his father, the Phi-lis'-tines had stopped them, and filled them with earth.

16 And A-bim'-e-lech said unto Isaac, Go from us; for [R] thou art much mightier than we.   Ex 1:9

17 And Isaac departed thence, and [T] pitched his tent in the valley of Ge'-rar, and dwelt there. *camped*

18 And Isaac digged again the wells of water, which they had digged in the days of Abraham his father; for the Phi-lis'-tines had stopped them after the death of Abraham: [R] and he called their names after the names by which his father had called them. 21:31

19 And Isaac's servants digged in

26:1 Philistines. The Philistines are thought to have come to the coastland of Canaan following their defeat by the Egyptians around 1200 B.C. The Egyptians called them the "Sea Peoples"; they were apparently Greek peoples who migrated eastward (see 1 Sa 4:1; 2 Sa 5:17). **26:3 bless thee.** The Lord fulfilled His promise to Abraham concerning Isaac (17:19). He established His everlasting covenant with Isaac, just as He had with Abraham. **26:7 sister.** Rebekah was Isaac's close relative, but she was not his sister (she was his first cousin once removed). Isaac was even more deceitful than his father Abraham (20:2,12). **26:12–13 blessed.** God's special work for Abraham was extended to the son.

the valley, and found there a well of ᵀspringing water.   *running*
20 And the herdmen of Ge'-rar did strive with Isaac's herdmen, saying, The water *is* ours: and he called the name of the well E'-sek; because they strove with him.
21 And they digged another well, and strove for that also: and he called the name of it Sit'-nah.
22 And he removed from thence, and digged another well; and for that they strove not: and he called the name of it Re-ho'-both; and he said, For now the LORD hath made room for us, and we shall be fruitful in the land.
23 And he went up from thence to Be'-er–she'-ba.
24 And the LORD appeared unto him the same night, and said, ᴿI *am* the God of Abraham thy father: fear not, for I *am* with thee, and will bless thee, and multiply thy seed for my servant Abraham's sake.   Ex 3:6; Ac 7:32
25 And he ᴿbuilded an altar there, and ᴿcalled upon the name of the LORD, and pitched his tent there: and there Isaac's servants digged a well.   22:9; 33:20 · Ps 116:17
26 Then A-bim'-e-lech went to him from Ge'-rar, and A-huz'-zath one of his friends, ᴿand Phi'-chol the chief captain of his army.   21:22
27 And Isaac said unto them, Wherefore come ye to me, ᴿseeing ye hate me, and have ᴿsent me away from you?   Ju 11:7 · v. 16
28 And they said, We saw certainly that the LORD ᴿwas with thee: and we said, Let there be now an oath betwixt us, *even* betwixt us and thee, and let us make a covenant with thee;   21:22
29 That thou wilt do us no hurt, as we have not touched thee, and

as we have done unto thee nothing but good, and have sent thee away in peace: ᴿthou *art* now the blessed of the LORD. 24:31; Ps 115:15
30 ᴿAnd he made them a feast, and they did eat and drink.   19:3
31 And they rose up ᵀbetimes in the morning, and ᴿsware one to another: and Isaac sent them away, and they departed from him in peace.   *early* · 21:31
32 And it came to pass the same day, that Isaac's servants came, and told him concerning the well which they had digged, and said unto him, We have found water.
33 And he called it She'-bah: ᴿtherefore the name of the city *is* Be'-er–she'-ba unto this day. 21:31
34 ᴿAnd Esau was forty years old when he took to wife Judith the daughter of Be-e'-ri the Hit'-tite, and Bash'-e-math the daughter of E'-lon the Hit'-tite: 28:8; 36:2
35 Which ᴿwere a grief of mind unto Isaac and to Rebekah. 27:46

27 And it came to pass, that when Isaac was old, and ᴿhis eyes were dim, so that he could not see, he called Esau his eldest son, and said unto him, My son: and he said unto him, Behold, *here am* I.   48:10; 1 Sa 3:2
2 And he said, Behold now, I am old, I ᴿknow not the day of my death: [Pr 27:1; Jam 4:14]
3 ᴿNow therefore take, I pray thee, thy weapons, thy quiver and thy bow, and go out to the field, and take me *some* venison;   25:28
4 And make me savoury meat, such as I love, and bring *it* to me, that I may eat; that my soul ᴿmay bless thee before I die.   49:28
5 And Rebekah heard when

26:24

26:25 *called upon the name of the Lord.* Isaac followed the practice of his father (12:8). At this altar Isaac not only prayed to the Lord, he also affirmed the reality of the living God in this special land (12:8; 21:33). **26:34** *Hittite.* Because the Hittite's believed in many different gods, Esau's marriages were unacceptable for one belonging to God's covenant family. **27:4** *my soul.* This phrase is simply a substitute for the personal pronoun, "I."

Isaac spake to Esau his son. And Esau went to the field to hunt *for* venison, *and* to bring *it*.

6 And Rebekah spake unto Jacob her son, saying, Behold, I heard thy father speak unto Esau thy brother, saying,

7 Bring me [T]venison, and make me [T]savoury meat, that I may eat, and bless thee before the LORD before my death.   *game · tasty food*

8 Now therefore, my son, [R]obey my voice according to that which I command thee.   vv. 13, 43

9 Go now to the flock, and fetch me from thence two good kids of the goats; and I will make them [R]savoury meat for thy father, such as he loveth: v. 4

10 And thou shalt bring *it* to thy father, that he may eat, and that he [R]may bless thee before his death.   v. 4; 48:16

11 And Jacob said to Rebekah his mother, Behold, [R]Esau my brother *is* a hairy man, and I *am* a smooth man: 25:25

12 My father peradventure will [R]feel me, and I shall seem to him as a deceiver; and I shall bring [R]a curse upon me, and not a blessing.   vv. 21, 22 · 9:25; De 27:18

13 And his mother said unto him, [R]Upon me *be* thy curse, my son: only obey my voice, and go fetch me *them*.   1 Sa 25:24

14 And he went, and fetched, and brought *them* to his mother: and his mother made savoury meat, such as his father loved.

15 And Rebekah took [R]goodly[T] raiment of her eldest son Esau, which *were* with her in the house,

and put them upon Jacob her younger son: v. 27 · *choice clothes*

16 And she put the skins of the kids of the goats upon his hands, and upon the smooth of his neck:

17 And she gave the savoury meat and the bread, which she had prepared, into the hand of her son Jacob.

18 And he came unto his father, and said, My father: and he said, Here *am* I; who *art* thou, my son?

19 And Jacob said unto his father, I *am* Esau thy firstborn; I have done according as thou [T]badest me: arise, I pray thee, sit and eat of my [T]venison, [R]that thy soul may bless me.   *told · game ·* v. 4

20 And Isaac said unto his son, How *is it* that thou hast found *it* so quickly, my son? And he said, Because the LORD thy God brought *it* to me.

21 And Isaac said unto Jacob, Come near, I pray thee, that I may feel thee, my son, whether thou *be* my very son Esau or not.

22 And Jacob went near unto Isaac his father; and he felt him, and said, The voice *is* Jacob's voice, but the hands *are* the hands of Esau.

23 And he [T]discerned him not, because [R]his hands were hairy, as his brother Esau's hands: so he blessed him.   *recognized ·* v. 16

24 And he said, *Art* thou my very son Esau? And he said, I *am*.

25 And he said, Bring *it* near to me, and I will eat of my son's venison, that my soul may bless thee. And he brought *it* near to him, and he did eat: and he brought him wine, and he drank.

27:8 *obey my voice . . . which I command thee.* Rebekah certainly appears calculating and devious in this passage, but God had told her before they were even born that the younger son would have precedence over the older (25:23). He had not, however, told her to make sure that it happened, and the results of her deception were family strife and the loss of her younger son. **27:18–29 Falsehood**—Jacob may have felt justified in deceiving his father, since Esau had already sold him the birthright. Esau had clearly demonstrated his contempt of the position (including the spiritual responsibility) which was his by right, while Jacob valued and desired it. However, lofty purposes and aspirations cannot justify deceit and trickery. We must be content to leave the fulfillment of God's promises in His hand and wait for His time.

26 And his father Isaac said unto him, Come near now, and kiss me, my son.

27 And he came near, and ᴿ kissed him: and he smelled the smell of his raiment, and blessed him, and said, See, the smell of my son *is* as the smell of a field which the LORD hath blessed: 29:13

28 Therefore ᴿ God give thee of the dew of heaven, and the fatness of the earth, and plenty of ᵀ corn and wine: He 11:20 · *grain*

29 ᴿ Let people serve thee, and nations bow down to thee: be lord over thy brethren, and ᴿ let thy mother's sons bow down to thee: ᴿ cursed *be* every one that curseth thee, and blessed *be* he that blesseth thee.   Is 45:14 · 37:7, 10; 49:8 · 12:2, 3

30 And it came to pass, as soon as Isaac had made an end of blessing Jacob, and Jacob ᵀ was yet scarce gone out from the presence of Isaac his father, that Esau his brother came in from his hunting.   *had scarcely*

31 And he also had made ᵀ savoury meat, and brought it unto his father, and said unto his father, Let my father arise, and ᴿ eat of his son's venison, that thy soul may bless me.   *tasty food* · v. 4

32 And Isaac his father said unto him, Who *art* thou? And he said, I *am* thy son, thy firstborn Esau.

33 And Isaac trembled very exceedingly, and said, Who? where *is* he that hath taken venison, and brought *it* me, and I have eaten of all before thou camest, and have blessed him? yea, ᴿ *and* he shall be blessed.   25:23; Ro 11:29

34 And when Esau heard the words of his father, he cried with a great and exceeding bitter cry, and said unto his father, Bless me, *even* me also, O my father.

35 And he said, Thy brother came with ᵀ subtilty, and hath taken away thy blessing.   *deceit*

36 And he said, ᴿ Is not he rightly named ᵀ Jacob? for he hath supplanted me these two times: he took away my birthright; and, behold, now he hath taken away my blessing. And he said, Hast thou not reserved a blessing for me?   25:26, 32–34 · Lit. *Supplanter*

37 And Isaac answered and said unto Esau, Behold, I have made him thy ᵀ lord, and all his brethren have I given to him for servants; and with corn and wine have I sustained him: and what shall I do now unto thee, my son?   *master*

38 And Esau said unto his father, Hast thou but one blessing, my father? bless me, *even* me also, O my father. And Esau lifted up his voice, ᴿ and wept.   He 12:17

39 And Isaac his father answered and said unto him, Behold, thy dwelling shall be the fatness of the earth, and of the dew of heaven from above;

40 And by thy sword shalt thou live, and ᴿ shalt serve thy brother; and ᴿ it shall come to pass when thou shalt have the dominion, that thou shalt break his yoke from off thy neck.   [Ob 18–20] · 2 Ki 8:20–22

41 And Esau ᴿ hated Jacob because of the blessing wherewith his father blessed him: and Esau said in his heart, ᴿ The days of mourning for my father are at hand; ᴿ then will I slay my brother Jacob.   37:4, 5, 8 · 50:2–4, 10 · Ob 10

42 And these words of Esau her elder son were told to Rebekah: and she sent and called Jacob her younger son, and said unto him, Behold, thy brother Esau, as touching thee, doth ᴿ comfort himself, *purposing* to kill thee.   Ps 64:5

43 Now therefore, my son, obey

27:26

27:29 people serve thee. Isaac predicted that Jacob's descendants would obtain supremacy over other peoples. Jesus, as the King of kings, and a descendant of Jacob, ultimately fulfilled this prediction (1 Ti 6:14–16).

my voice; and arise, flee thou to Laban my brother to Ha'-ran;

44 And ᵀtarry with him a ᴿfew days, until thy brother's fury turn away; *stay · 31:41*

45 Until thy brother's anger turn away from thee, and he forget *that* which thou hast done to him: then I will send, and fetch thee from thence: why should I be ᵀdeprived also of you both in one day? *bereaved*

46 And Rebekah said to Isaac, ᴿI am weary of my life because of the daughters of Heth: ᴿif Jacob take a wife of the daughters of Heth, such as these *which are* of the daughters of the land, what good shall my life do me? *28:8 · 24:3*

28 And Isaac called Jacob, and ᴿblessed him, and charged him, and said unto him, ᴿThou shalt not take a wife of the daughters of Canaan. *27:33 · 24:3*

2 Arise, go to Pa'-dan–a'-ram, to the house of Be-thu'-el thy mother's father; and take thee a wife from thence of the daughters of ᴿLaban thy mother's brother. *24:29*

3 And God Almighty bless thee, and make thee fruitful, and multiply thee, that thou mayest be ᵀa multitude of people; *an assembly*

4 And give thee ᴿthe blessing of Abraham, to thee, and to thy seed with thee; that thou mayest inherit the land ᴿwherein thou art

a stranger, which God gave unto Abraham. *12:2, 3; 22:17; Ga 3:8 · 17:8*

5 And Isaac sent away Jacob: and he went to Pa'-dan–a'-ram unto Laban, son of Be-thu'-el the Syrian, the brother of Rebekah, Jacob's and Esau's mother.

6 When Esau saw that Isaac had blessed Jacob, and sent him away to Pa'-dan–a'-ram, to take him a wife from thence; and that as he blessed him he gave him a charge, saying, Thou shalt not take a wife of the daughters of Canaan;

7 And that Jacob obeyed his father and his mother, and was gone to Pa'-dan–a'-ram;

8 And Esau seeing ᴿthat the daughters of Canaan pleased not Isaac his father; *24:3; 26:34, 35; 27:46*

9 Then went Esau unto Ish'-ma-el, and ᴿtook unto the wives which he had ᴿMa'-ha-lath the daughter of Ish'-ma-el Abraham's son, ᴿthe sister of Ne-ba'-joth, to be his wife. *26:34, 35 · 36:2, 3 · 25:13*

10 And Jacob went out from Be'-er–she'-ba, and went toward ᴿHa'-ran. *12:4, 5; 27:43; 2 Ki 19:12; Ac 7:2*

11 And he ᵀlighted upon a certain place, and tarried there all night, because the sun was set; and he took of the stones of that place, and ᵀput *them for* his pillows, and lay down in that place to sleep. *came to · Lit. put it at his head*

12 And he dreamed, and behold a ladder set up on the earth, and

---

27:46 daughters of Heth. Intermarrying with the pagan women of Canaan was dangerous because they would bring their pagan gods and pagan worship into their new homes. **28:2 Padan-aram.** This is a region of Haran in northern Aram (Syria) near the Euphrates River. **28:3 God Almighty.** This Hebrew name, *El Shaddai* is used by or in the hearing of Abraham, Isaac, and Jacob (35:11). God later identified Himself to Moses with this same name (Ex 6:3). **28:9 Mahalath.** This daughter of Ishmael is probably the same woman as Bashemath (36:3). Her name means "dance." **28:10–15 Jacob's Dream**—The ladder of Jacob's dream reminds us of Jesus' words about the angels "ascending and descending upon the Son of man" (Jo 1:51), vividly depicting Himself as the Way into the heavenlies. Certainly Jacob did not deserve such grace after cheating his brother out of the blessings of Isaac. Indeed, he was already suffering by being banished from the fellowship of his family. Nevertheless, God mercifully confirmed the covenant promises made to Abraham and Isaac concerning the land and the descendants. His words, "I am with thee, and will keep thee" speak of God's personal presence for protection and guidance, anticipating Jacob's return to the land, so that all the promises might be fulfilled. Surely the grace of God goes far beyond our small expectations.

the top of it reached to heaven: and behold the angels of God ascending and descending on it.

13 And, behold, the LORD stood above it, and said, [R]I *am* the LORD God of Abraham thy father, and the God of Isaac: [R]the land whereon thou liest, to thee will I give it, and to thy seed;   26:24 · 13:15, 17; 26:3

✝14 And thy seed shall be as the dust of the earth, and thou shalt spread abroad to the west, and to the east, and to the north, and to the south: and in thee and in thy seed shall all the families of the earth be blessed.

✗15 And, behold, I *am* with thee, and will keep thee in all *places* whither thou goest, and will bring thee again into this land; for [R]I will not leave thee, until I have done *that* which I have spoken to thee of.   De 7:9

16 And Jacob awaked out of his sleep, and he said, Surely the LORD is in [R]this place; and I knew *it* not.   Ex 3:5; Jos 5:15; Ps 139:7–12

17 And he was afraid, and said, How dreadful *is* this place! this *is* none other but the house of God, and this *is* the gate of heaven.

18 And Jacob rose up early in the morning, and took the stone that he had put *for* his pillows, and [R]set it up *for* a pillar, and poured oil upon the top of it.   31:13

19 And he called the name of [R]that place [T]Beth'-el: but the name of that city *was called* Luz at the first.   Ju 1:23 · Lit. *House of God*

20 And Jacob vowed a vow, saying, If God will be with me, and will keep me in this way that I go, and will give me [R]bread to eat, and raiment to put on,   1 Ti 6:8

21 So that [R]I come again to my father's house in peace; then shall the LORD be my God: Ju 11:31

22 And this stone, which I have set *for* a pillar, [R]shall be God's house: [R]and of all that thou shalt give me I will surely give the tenth unto thee.   35:7, 14 · 14:20; [Le 27:30]

29 Then Jacob went on his journey, [R]and came into the land of the people of the east.   25:6

2 And he looked, and behold a well in the field, and, lo, there *were* three flocks of sheep lying by it; for out of that well they watered the flocks: and a great stone *was* upon the well's mouth.

3 And thither were all the flocks gathered: and they rolled the stone from the well's mouth, and watered the sheep, and put the stone again upon the well's mouth in his place.

4 And Jacob said unto them, My brethren, whence *be* ye? And they said, Of Ha'-ran *are* we.

5 And he said unto them, Know ye [R]Laban the son of Na'-hor? And they said, We know *him.*   24:24

6 And he said unto them, [R]*Is* he well? And they said, *He is* well: and, behold, Ra'-chel his daughter [R]cometh with the sheep.   43:27 · 24:11

7 And he said, Lo, *it is* yet high day, neither *is it* time that the cattle should be gathered together: water ye the sheep, and go *and* feed *them.*

8 And they said, We cannot, until all the flocks be gathered together, and *till* they roll the stone from the well's mouth; then we water the sheep.

9 And while he yet spake with them, Ra'-chel came with her father's sheep: for she kept them.

10 And it came to pass, when Jacob saw Ra'-chel the daughter of Laban his mother's brother, and the

✝ 28:14—Ma 1:2   ✗ 28:15

28:22 the tenth. Jacob promised to give a tenth of his possessions to God. Abraham had given the same proportion to Melchizedek, the priest of the most high God. Later the Mosaic law required giving a tenth to God (De 14:22). **29:5 son.** This term is being used in a loose sense. Nahor was actually the grandfather of Laban (22:20–23; 24:15,50). **29:6 Rachel.** This name is a term of endearment meaning "Ewe Lamb."

sheep of Laban his mother's brother, that Jacob went near, and [R]rolled the stone from the well's mouth, and watered the flock of Laban his mother's brother.   Ex 2:17

11 And Jacob kissed Ra'-chel, and lifted up his voice, and wept.

12 And Jacob told Ra'-chel that he *was* her father's [T]brother, and that he *was* Rebekah's son: and she ran and told her father.   *relative*

13 And it came to pass, when Laban heard the tidings of Jacob his sister's son, that [R]he ran to meet him, and embraced him, and kissed him, and brought him to his house. And he told Laban all these things.   24:29–31; Lk 15:20

14 And Laban said to him, [R]Surely thou *art* my bone and my flesh. And he abode with him the space of a month.   37:27; Ju 9:2

15 And Laban said unto Jacob, Because thou *art* my brother, shouldest thou therefore serve me for [T]nought? tell me, [R]what *shall* thy wages *be*?   *nothing* · 30:28; 31:41

16 And Laban had two daughters: the name of the elder *was* Leah, and the name of the younger *was* Ra'-chel.

17 Leah *was* [T]tender eyed; but Ra'-chel was [R]beautiful and well favoured.   *delicate* or *soft* · 12:11, 14; 26:7

✎18 And Jacob loved Ra'-chel; and said, [R]I will serve thee seven years for Ra'-chel thy younger daughter.   31:41; 2 Sa 3:14

19 And Laban said, *It is* better that I give her to thee, than that I should give her to another man: abide with me.

✎20 And Jacob [R]served seven years for Ra'-chel; and they seemed unto him *but* a few days, for the love he had to her.   30:26

21 And Jacob said unto Laban, Give *me* my wife, for my days are fulfilled, that I may [R]go in unto her.   Ju 15:1

22 And Laban gathered together all the men of the place, and [R]made a feast.   Ju 14:10; Jo 2:1, 2

23 And it came to pass in the evening, that he took Leah his daughter, and brought her to him; and he went in unto her.

24 And Laban gave unto his daughter Leah [R]Zil'-pah his maid *for* an handmaid.   30:9, 10

25 And it came to pass, that in the morning, behold, it *was* Leah: and he said to Laban, What *is* this thou hast done unto me? did not I serve with thee for Ra'-chel? wherefore then hast thou [R]beguiled me?   27:35; 31:7; 1 Sa 28:12

26 And Laban said, It must not be so done in our country, to give the younger before the firstborn.

27 [R]Fulfil her week, and we will give thee this also for the service which thou shalt serve with me yet seven other years.   31:41

28 And Jacob did so, and fulfilled her week: and he gave him Ra'-chel his daughter to wife also.

29 And Laban gave to Ra'-chel his daughter [R]Bil'-hah his handmaid to be her maid.   30:3–5

30 And he went in also unto Ra'-chel, and he loved also Ra'-chel more than Leah, and served with him [R]yet seven other years.   30:26

✎31 And when the LORD saw that Leah *was* hated, he opened

✎ 29:18   ✎ 29:20   ✎ 29:31–30:2

29:21–25 Deception—Many times we see God's prohibitions as mere taboos. We somehow imagine that God says no just because He can, instead of acknowledging both His goodwill towards us, and His wisdom. God does not merely prohibit lying because He can, it is because it is destructive. Jacob learned through experience that trickery and deceit bring complicated and painful consequences. False dealing destroys trust in a relationship, and once trust has been broken it is difficult, if not impossible, to entirely restore it. **29:31 *hated*.** God was kind to Leah in her predicament. Even though she was the unloved wife, it was through her son Judah that the messianic line was carried out.

her womb: but Ra'-chel *was* barren.

32   And Leah conceived, and bare a son, and she called his name Reuben: for she said, Surely the LORD hath [R]looked upon my affliction; now therefore my husband will love me.   Ex 3:7; 4:31

33   And she conceived again, and bare a son; and said, Because the LORD hath heard that I *was* [T]hated, he hath therefore given me this *son* also: and she called his name Simeon.   *unloved*

34   And she conceived again, and bare a son; and said, Now this time will my husband be [T]joined unto me, because I have born him three sons: therefore was his name called Levi.   *attached to*

35   And she conceived again, and bare a son: and she said, Now will I praise the LORD: therefore she called his name [R]Judah; and [T]left bearing.   49:8; Ma 1:2 · *stopped*

30 And when Ra'-chel saw that she bare Jacob no children, Ra'-chel [R]envied her sister; and said unto Jacob, Give me children, or else I die.   37:11

2   And Jacob's anger was kindled against Ra'-chel: and he said, [R]*Am* I in God's stead, who hath withheld from thee the fruit of the womb?   16:2; 1 Sa 1:5

3   And she said, Behold my maid Bil'-hah, go in unto her; and she shall bear [T]upon my knees, that I may also [T]have children by her.   to be *upon* · Lit. *be built up*

4   And she gave him Bil'-hah her handmaid [R]to[T] wife: and Jacob went in unto her.   16:3, 4 · *as*

5   And Bil'-hah conceived, and bare Jacob a son.

6   And Ra'-chel said, God hath [R]judged me, and hath also heard my voice, and hath given me a son: therefore called she his name Dan.   Ps 35:24; 43:1

7   And Bil'-hah Ra'-chel's maid conceived again, and bare Jacob a second son.

8   And Ra'-chel said, With [T]great wrestlings have I wrestled with my sister, and I have prevailed: and she called his name Naph'-ta-li.   Lit. *wrestlings of God*

9   When Leah saw that she had left bearing, she took Zil'-pah her maid, and [R]gave her Jacob [T]to wife.   v. 4 · *as*

10   And Zil'-pah Leah's maid bare Jacob a son.

11   And Leah said, A [T]troop cometh: and she called his name Gad.   *fortune*

12   And Zil'-pah Leah's maid bare Jacob a second son.

13   And Leah said, Happy am I, for the daughters [R]will call me blessed: and she called his name Asher.   Pr 31:28; Lk 1:48

14   And Reuben went in the days of wheat harvest, and found mandrakes in the field, and brought them unto his mother Leah. Then Ra'-chel said to Leah, Give me, I pray thee, of thy son's mandrakes.

15   And she said unto her, [R]*Is it* a small matter that thou hast taken my husband? and wouldest thou take away my son's mandrakes also? And Ra'-chel said, Therefore he shall lie with thee to night for thy son's mandrakes.   [Nu 16:9, 13]

16   And Jacob came out of the field in the evening, and Leah went out to meet him, and said, Thou must come in unto me; for surely I have hired thee with my son's mandrakes. And he lay with her that night.

17   And God hearkened unto Leah, and she conceived, and bare Jacob the fifth son.

18   And Leah said, God hath given me my hire, because I have given my maiden to my husband: and she called his name Is'-sa-char.

30:6   30:13

30:14 mandrakes. This is a plant which was regarded as an aid to conception. Its aroma was associated with lovemaking (Song 7:13).

19 And Leah conceived again, and bare Jacob the sixth son.
20 And Leah said, God hath endued me *with* a good [T]dowry; now will my husband dwell with me, because I have born him six sons: and she called his name Zeb'-u-lun.   endowment
21 And afterwards she bare a [R]daughter, and called her name Dinah.   34:1
22 And God [R]remembered Ra'-chel, and God hearkened to her, and [R]opened her womb. 19:29 · 29:31
23 And she conceived, and bare a son; and said, God hath taken away [R]my reproach: 1 Sa 1:6; Is 4:1
24 And she called his name Joseph; and said, [R]The LORD shall add to me another son.   35:16–18
25 And it came to pass, when Ra'-chel had born Joseph, that Jacob said unto Laban, Send me away, that I may go unto mine own place, and to my country.
26 Give *me* my wives and my children, [R]for whom I have served thee, and let me go: for thou knowest my service which I have done thee.   29:18–20, 27, 30; Ho 12:12
27 And Laban said unto him, I pray thee, if I have found favour in thine eyes, [T]*tarry: for* [R]I have learned by experience that the LORD hath blessed me for thy sake.   stay · 26:24; 39:3; Is 61:9
28 And he said, [R]Appoint me thy wages, and I will give *it*.   29:15
29 And he said unto him, Thou knowest how I have served thee, and how thy cattle was with me.
30 For *it was* little which thou hadst before I *came*, and it is *now* increased unto a multitude; and the LORD hath blessed thee [T]since my coming: and now when shall I [R]provide for mine own house also?   Lit. *at my foot* · [1 Ti 5:8]
31 And he said, What shall I give thee? And Jacob said, Thou shalt not give me any thing: if thou wilt do this thing for me, I will again feed *and* keep thy flock.
32 I will pass through all thy flock to day, removing from thence all the speckled and spotted [T]cattle, and all the brown cattle among the sheep, and the spotted and speckled among the goats: and [R]*of such* shall be my hire.   sheep · 31:8
33 So shall my [R]righteousness answer for me in time to come, when it shall come [T]for my hire before thy face: every one that *is* not speckled and spotted among the goats, and brown among the sheep, that shall be counted stolen with me.   Ps 37:6 · *about my wages*
34 And Laban said, Behold, I would it might be according to thy word.
35 And he removed that day the he goats that were ringstraked[T] and spotted, and all the she goats that were speckled and spotted, *and* every one that had *some* white in it, and all the brown among the sheep, and gave *them* into the hand of his sons.   streaked
36 And he set three days' journey [T]betwixt himself and Jacob: and Jacob fed the rest of Laban's flocks.   between
37 And [R]Jacob took him rods of green poplar, and of the hazel and chesnut tree; and [T]pilled white

30:19–24

30:22 *remembered . . . hearkened to her . . . opened.* These three verbs emphasize conception as a gift from God. **30:25 *own place.*** Even though Jacob had lived for twenty years with Laban's family, he had not adopted that place as his own. He never forgot that promise and covenant of God were for the land of Canaan, and he knew that he must return. **30:27 *blessed.*** God had promised to bless others through Abraham's descendants (12:2–3). Now God blessed Laban through Jacob. **30:37 *rods of green poplar.*** Just what significance these sticks hold is unknown. Some have theorized that they were simply symbols of Jacob's faith in God. Whatever the case, God blessed Jacob by causing Laban's stock to give birth to speckled and spotted young.

^Tstrakes in them, and made the white appear which *was* in the rods.   31:9–12 · *peeled · strips*

38 And he set the rods which he had ^Tpilled before the flocks in the gutters in the watering troughs when the flocks came to drink, that they should conceive when they came to drink.   *peeled*

39 And the flocks conceived before the rods, and brought forth cattle ^Tringstraked, speckled, and spotted.   *streaked*

40 And Jacob did separate the lambs, and set the faces of the flocks toward the ^Tringstraked, and all the brown in the flock of Laban; and he put his own flocks by themselves, and put them not ^Tunto Laban's cattle.   *streaked · with*

41 And it came to pass, whensoever the stronger ^Tcattle did conceive, that Jacob laid the rods before the eyes of the cattle in the gutters, that they might conceive among the rods.   *livestock*

42 But when the cattle were feeble, he put *them* not in: so the feebler were Laban's, and the stronger Jacob's.

43 And the man increased exceedingly, and had much cattle, and maidservants, and menservants, and camels, and asses.

31 And he heard the words of Laban's sons, saying, Jacob hath taken away all that *was* our father's; and of *that* which *was* our father's hath he gotten all this ^Rglory.^T   Ps 49:16 · *wealth*

2 And Jacob beheld the countenance of Laban, and, behold, it *was* not toward him as before.

3 And the LORD said unto Jacob, ^RReturn unto the land of thy fathers, and to thy kindred; and I will ^Rbe with thee.   28:15 · 46:4

4 And Jacob sent and called Ra'-chel and Leah to the field unto his flock,

5 And said unto them, I see your father's countenance, that it *is* not toward me as before; but the God of my father ^Rhath been with me.   21:22; Is 41:10; He 13:5

6 And ^Rye know that with all my ^Tpower I have served your father.   vv. 38–41; 30:29 · *might*

7 And your father hath deceived me, and changed my wages ten times; but God ^Rsuffered him not to hurt me.   Ps 37:2

8 If he said thus, ^RThe speckled shall be thy wages; then all the ^Tcattle bare speckled: and if he said thus, The ^Tringstraked shall be thy hire; then bare all the cattle ringstraked.   30:32 · *flocks · streaked*

9 Thus God hath ^Rtaken away the cattle of your father, and given *them* to me.   vv. 1, 16

10 And it came to pass at the time that the ^Tcattle conceived, that I lifted up mine eyes, and saw in a dream, and, behold, the rams which leaped upon the cattle *were* ^Tringstraked, speckled, and ^Tgrisled.   *flocks · streaked · gray-spotted*

11 And ^Rthe angel of God spake unto me in a dream, *saying,* Jacob: And I said, Here *am* I.   22:11

12 And he said, Lift up now thine eyes, and see, all the rams which leap upon the cattle *are* ringstraked, speckled, and grisled: for ^RI have seen all that Laban doeth unto thee.   Ps 139:3

13 I *am* the God of Beth'–el, ^Rwhere thou anointedst the pillar, *and* where thou vowedst a vow unto me: now arise, get thee out

---

31:7 *deceived me.* Jacob had surely lived up to his name, deceiving his old father and tricking his brother out of the birthright. But in Laban he met his match, and tasted some of his own medicine. The consequences of dishonesty reach both ways. Because of his own trickery, Jacob had to flee from his home. He apparently never saw his mother again, and his relationship with his father and his only brother was broken. Lying not only harms the liar, but it also affects those he lies to. Because of Laban's trickery, Jacob was saddled with an unloved wife, quarreling sons, and consistent domestic strife.

from this land, and return unto the land of thy kindred.   28:16–22

14 And Ra'-chel and Leah answered and said unto him, *Is there* yet any portion or inheritance for us in our father's house?

15 Are we not counted of him strangers? for [R]he hath sold us, and hath quite devoured also our money.   29:15, 20, 23, 27; Ne 5:8

16 For all the riches which God hath taken from our father, that *is* ours, and our children's: now then, whatsoever God hath said unto thee, do.

17 Then Jacob rose up, and set his sons and his wives upon camels;

18 And he carried away all his cattle, and all his goods which he had gotten, the cattle of his getting, which he had gotten in Pa'-dan– a'-ram, for to go to Isaac his father in the land of [R]Canaan.   17:8

19 And Laban went to shear his sheep: and Ra'-chel had stolen the images that *were* her father's.

20 And Jacob stole away unawares to Laban the Syrian, in that he told him not that he fled.

21 So he fled with all that he had; and he rose up, and passed over the river, and [R]set his face *toward* the mount Gil'-e-ad.   46:28

22 And it was told Laban on the third day that Jacob was fled.

23 And he took [R]his brethren with him, and pursued after him seven days' journey; and they overtook him in the [T]mount Gil'-e-ad.   13:8 · *mountains of*

24 And God [R]came to Laban the Syrian in a dream by night, and said unto him, Take heed that thou [R]speak not to Jacob either good or bad.   20:3 · 24:50

25 Then Laban overtook Jacob. Now Jacob had pitched his tent in the mount: and Laban with his brethren pitched in the mount of Gil'-e-ad.

26 And Laban said to Jacob, What hast thou done, that thou hast stolen away unawares to me, and carried away my daughters, as captives *taken* with the sword?

27 Wherefore didst thou flee away secretly, and steal away from me; and didst not tell me, that I might have sent thee away with [T]mirth, and with songs, with [T]tabret, and with harp?   *joy · timbrel*

28 And hast not suffered me [R]to kiss my sons and my daughters? thou hast now done foolishly in *so* doing.   Ru 1:9, 14; 1 Ki 19:20

29 It is in the power of my hand to do you hurt: but the [R]God of your father spake unto me [R]yesternight, saying, Take thou heed that thou speak not to Jacob either good or bad.   28:13 · v. 24

30 And now, *though* thou wouldest needs be gone, because thou sore longedst after thy father's house, *yet* wherefore hast thou [R]stolen my gods?   Jos 24:2

31 And Jacob answered and said to Laban, Because I was [R]afraid: for I said, Peradventure thou wouldest take by force thy daughters from me.   26:7; 32:7, 11

32 With whomsoever thou findest thy gods, [R]let him not live: before our brethren discern thou what *is* thine with me, and take *it* to thee. For Jacob knew not that Ra'-chel had stolen them.   44:9

33 And Laban went into Jacob's tent, and into Leah's tent, and into the two maidservants' tents; but he found *them* not. Then went he out of Leah's tent, and entered into Ra'-chel's tent.

34 Now Ra'-chel had taken the im-

31:19 *images.* Laban's family may have been polytheistic (believing in many gods), as Abraham's father Terah evidently was (Jos 24:1–3). Considering the evidence of verses 25– 50 it seems likely that they worshipped Yahweh along with other "lesser gods." In this culture, the possession of the images was the right of the principal heir. Rachel probably did not steal the idols in order to worship them, but because they represented ownership of her father's property.

ages, and put them in the camel's ^Tfurniture, and sat upon them. And Laban searched all the tent, but found *them* not.   *saddle*

35 And she said to her father, Let it not displease my lord that I cannot ^Rrise up before thee; for the custom of women *is* upon me. And he searched, but found not the images.   Ex 20:12; Le 19:32

36 And Jacob was ^Twroth, and ^Tchode with Laban: and Jacob answered and said to Laban, What *is* my trespass? what *is* my sin, that thou hast so hotly pursued after me?   *angry · rebuked*

37 Whereas thou hast searched all my stuff, what hast thou found of all thy household stuff? set *it* here before my brethren and thy brethren, that they may judge betwixt us both.

38 This twenty years *have* I *been* with thee; thy ewes and thy she goats have not cast their young, and the rams of thy flock have I not eaten.

39 That which was torn *of beasts* I brought not unto thee; I bare the loss of it; of my hand didst thou require it, *whether* stolen by day, or stolen by night.

40 *Thus* I was; in the day the drought consumed me, and the frost by night; and my sleep departed from mine eyes.

41 Thus have I been twenty years in thy house; I ^Rserved thee fourteen years for thy two daughters, and six years for thy ^Tcattle: and ^Rthou hast changed my wages ten times.   29:20, 27–30 · *flock* · v. 7

42 Except the God of my father, the God of Abraham, and ^Rthe fear of Isaac, had been with me, surely thou hadst sent me away now empty. ^RGod hath seen mine affliction and the labour of my hands, and ^Rrebuked *thee* yesternight.   Is 8:13 · Ex 3:7 · 1 Ch 12:17

43 And Laban answered and said unto Jacob, *These* daughters *are* my daughters, and *these* children *are* my children, and *these* ^Tcattle *are* my cattle, and all that thou seest *is* mine: and what can I do this day unto these my daughters, or unto their children which they have born?   *flock*

44 Now therefore come thou, let us make a ^Tcovenant, I and thou; and let it be for a witness between me and thee.   *treaty*

45 And Jacob ^Rtook a stone, and set it up *for* a pillar.   Jos 24:26, 27

46 And Jacob said unto his brethren, Gather stones; and they took stones, and made an heap: and they did eat there upon the heap.

47 And Laban called it Je'-gar–sa-ha-du'-tha: but Jacob called it Gal'-e-ed.

48 And Laban said, ^RThis heap *is* a witness between me and thee this day. Therefore was the name of it called Gal'-e-ed;   Jos 24:27

49 And ^TMiz'-pah; for he said, The LORD watch between me and thee, when we are absent one from another.   Lit. *Watch*

50 If thou shalt afflict my daughters, or if thou shalt take *other* wives beside my daughters, no man *is* with us; see, God *is* witness betwixt me and thee.

51 And Laban said to Jacob, Behold this heap, and behold *this* pillar, which I have cast betwixt me and thee;

52 This heap *be* witness, and *this* pillar *be* witness, that I will not pass ^Tover this heap to thee, and that thou shalt not pass ^Tover this heap and this pillar unto me, for harm.   *beyond*

53 The God of Abraham, and the

31:44 *covenant.* This instance of a covenant was an agreement between two equals. **31:49** *Mizpah.* This name means "Outlook Point" and is related to the Hebrew word meaning "to watch." God above had His eyes on both men to make them keep their covenant. **31:53** *The God of Abraham.* The wording in Laban's oath suggests that

Continued on the next page

God of Na'-hor, the God of their father, ᴿjudge betwixt us. And Jacob ᴿsware by ᴿthe fear of his father Isaac.   16:5 · 21:23 · v. 42

54 Then Jacob offered sacrifice upon the mount, and called his brethren to eat bread: and they did eat bread, and tarried all night in the mount.

55 And early in the morning Laban rose up, and kissed his sons and his daughters, and ᴿblessed them: and Laban departed, and returned unto his place.   28:1

32 And Jacob went on his way, and ᴿthe angels of God met him.   Nu 22:31; 2 Ki 6:16, 17

2 And when Jacob saw them, he said, This *is* God's host: and he called the name of that place ᵀMaha-na'-im.   Lit. *Double Camp*

3 And Jacob sent messengers before him to Esau his brother ᴿunto the land of Se'-ir, ᴿthe country of E'-dom.   14:6 · De 2:5; Jos 24:4

4 And he commanded them, saying, ᴿThus shall ye speak unto my lord Esau; Thy servant Jacob saith thus, I have sojourned with Laban, and stayed there until now: Pr 15:1

5 And ᴿI have oxen, and asses, flocks, and menservants, and womenservants: and I have sent to tell my lord, that ᴿI may find grace in thy sight.   30:43 · 33:8, 15

6 And the messengers returned to Jacob, saying, We came to thy brother Esau, and also ᴿhe cometh to meet thee, and four hundred men with him.   33:1

7 Then Jacob was greatly afraid and distressed: and he divided the people that *was* with him, and the flocks, and herds, and the camels, into two bands;

8 And said, If Esau come to the one company, and ᵀsmite it, then the other company which is left shall escape.   *attack*

9 ᴿAnd Jacob said, O God of my father Abraham, and God of my father Isaac, the LORD which saidst unto me, Return unto thy country, and to thy kindred, and I will deal well with thee: [Ps 50:15]

10 I am not worthy of the least of all the mercies, and of all the truth, which thou hast shewed unto thy servant; for with my staff I passed over this Jordan; and now I am become two bands.

11 Deliver me, I pray thee, from the hand of my brother, from the hand of Esau: for I fear him, lest he will come and smite me, *and* the mother with the children.

12 And ᴿthou saidst, I will surely do thee good, and make thy seed as the ᴿsand of the sea, which cannot be numbered for multitude.   28:13–15 · 22:17

13 And he lodged there that same night; and took of that which came to his hand ᴿa present for Esau his brother;   43:11

14 Two hundred she goats, and twenty he goats, two hundred ewes, and twenty rams,

15 Thirty ᵀmilch camels with their colts, forty ᵀkine, and ten bulls, twenty ᵀshe asses, and ten foals.   *milk · cows · female donkeys*

16 And he delivered *them* into the hand of his servants, every drove by themselves; and said unto his servants, Pass over before me, and put a space betwixt drove and drove.

17 And he commanded the foremost, saying, When Esau my brother meeteth thee, and asketh thee, saying, Whose *art* thou? and

---

Abraham, Nahor, and their father Terah all worshipped the same One True God. Joshua records the fact that Terah at least worshipped other gods as well (Jos 24:1–3). It is possible that they were henotheistic—worshipping God not as the only God but as the most important and powerful among many. **32:11 *Deliver me, I pray thee.*** Jacob did not pray in generalities. He named his concerns openly, and concluded with another appeal to God's promises. Christians today can likewise base their prayers on God's proven character and His promises in the Bible.

whither goest thou? and whose *are* these before thee?

18 Then thou shalt say, *They be* thy servant Jacob's; it *is* a present sent unto my lord Esau: and, behold, also he *is* behind us.

19 And so commanded he the second, and the third, and all that followed the droves, saying, On this manner shall ye speak unto Esau, when ye find him.

20 And say ye moreover, Behold, thy servant Jacob *is* behind us. For he said, I will appease him with the present that goeth before me, and afterward I will see his face; peradventure he will accept ^Tof me.   Lit. *my face*

21 So went the present over before him: and himself lodged that night in the ^Tcompany.   *camp*

22 And he rose up that night, and took his two wives, and his two womenservants, and his eleven sons, ^Rand passed over the ford Jab'-bok.   Nu 21:24; De 3:16

23 And he took them, and sent them over the brook, and sent over that he had.

24 And Jacob was left alone; and there wrestled a man with him until the breaking of the day.

25 And when he saw that he prevailed not against him, he ^Ttouched the ^Thollow of his ^Tthigh; and the hollow of Jacob's thigh was out of joint, as he wrestled with him.   *struck · socket · hip*

26 And ^Rhe said, Let me go, for the day breaketh. And he said, ^RI will not let thee go, except thou bless me.   Lk 24:28 · Ho 12:4

27 And he said unto him, What *is* thy name? And he said, Jacob.

28 And he said, Thy name shall be called no more Jacob, but ^TIsrael: for as a prince hast thou power with God and with men, and hast prevailed.   *Prince with God*

29 And Jacob asked *him,* and said, Tell *me,* I pray thee, thy name. And he said, Wherefore *is* it *that* thou dost ask after my name? And he blessed him there.

30 And Jacob called the name of the place ^TPe-ni'-el: for ^RI have seen God face to face, and my life is preserved.   Lit. *Face of God* · Is 6:5

31 And as he passed over Pe-nu'-el the sun rose upon him, and he ^Thalted upon his thigh.   *limped*

32 Therefore the children of Israel eat not *of* the ^Tsinew which shrank, which *is* upon the ^Thollow of the ^Tthigh, unto this day: because he ^Ttouched the hollow of Jacob's thigh in the sinew that shrank.   *muscle · socket · hip · struck*

33 And Jacob lifted up his eyes, and looked, and, behold, ^REsau came, and with him four hundred men. And he divided the children unto Leah, and unto Ra'-chel, and unto the two ^Thandmaids.   32:6 · *maidservants*

2 And he put the handmaids and their children foremost, and Leah and her children after, and Ra'-chel and Joseph hindermost.

3 And he passed over before them, and ^Rbowed himself to the

32:24–30

32:24 *wrestled a man with him.* Some believe that the man who wrestled with Jacob was the pre-incarnate Jesus Christ. Others believe the Man was the Angel of God (21:17; 31:11). In any case, Jacob wrestled with a manifestation of God (vv. 28–30), and because of God's mercy he survived. **32:28 *Israel.*** Before Jacob wrestled with the angel, his name, "One who Supplants," described a man who was deceitful in character. Afterwards he was given the new status of a champion, "One who Strives (or Prevails) with God." **32:30 *God face to face.*** The dramatic name ("Face of God") given to the location shows the awesome nature of the encounter. Here God's messenger in human form was the same as God Himself, a fact which Jacob recognized to his amazement. In Hebrew thought, the penalty for seeing God face to face was death (Ex 33:20), yet Jacob had passed through such an experience and had survived.

ground seven times, until he came near to his brother.   18:2; 42:6

4 ᴿAnd Esau ran to meet him, and embraced him, ᴿand fell on his neck, and kissed him: and they wept.   32:28 · 45:14, 15

5 And he lifted up his eyes, and saw the women and the children; and said, Who *are* those with thee? And he said, The children ᴿwhich God hath graciously given thy servant.   48:9; [Ps 127:3]; Is 8:18

6 Then the handmaidens came near, they and their children, and they bowed themselves.

7 And Leah also with her children came near, and bowed themselves: and after came Joseph near and Ra′-chel, and they bowed themselves.

8 And he said, What *meanest* thou by all this drove which I met? And he said, *These are* to find grace in the sight of my lord.

9 And Esau said, I have enough, my brother; keep that thou hast unto thyself.

10 And Jacob said, Nay, I pray thee, if now I have found grace in thy sight, then receive my present at my hand: for therefore I ᴿhave seen thy face, as though I had seen the face of God, and thou wast pleased with me.   2 Sa 3:13

11 Take, I pray thee, my blessing that is brought to thee; because God hath dealt graciously with me, and because I have enough. And he urged him, and he took *it.*

12 And he said, Let us take our journey, and let us go, and I will go before thee.

13 And he said unto him, My lord knoweth that the children *are* ᵀtender, and the flocks and herds with young *are* with me: and if men should overdrive them one day, all the flock will die.   *weak*

14 Let my lord, I pray thee, pass over before his servant: and I will lead on ᵀsoftly, according as the ᵀcattle that goeth before me and the children be able to endure, until I come unto my lord ᴿunto Se′-ir.   *slowly* · *livestock* · 32:3; 36:8

15 And Esau said, Let me now leave with thee *some* of the folk that *are* with me. And he said, What needeth it? ᴿlet me find grace in the sight of my lord.   34:11

16 So Esau returned that day on his way unto Se′-ir.

17 And Jacob journeyed to Suc′-coth, and built him an house, and made ᵀbooths for his cattle: therefore the name of the place is called Suc′-coth.   *shelters*

18 And Jacob came to Sha′-lem, a city of She′-chem, which *is* in the land of Canaan, when he came from Pa′-dan-a′-ram; and pitched his tent before the city.

19 And he bought a parcel of a field, where he had spread his tent, at the hand of the children of Ha′-mor, She′-chem's father, for an hundred pieces of money.

20 And he erected there an altar, and ᴿcalled it ᵀEl-e-lo′-he-Is′-ra-el.   35:7 · *Lit. God, the God of Israel*

34 And ᴿDinah the daughter of Leah, which she bare unto Jacob, went out to see the daughters of the land.   30:21

2 And when She′-chem the son of Ha′-mor the Hi′-vite, prince of the country, saw her, he took her, and lay with her, and defiled her.

3 And his soul clave unto Dinah the daughter of Jacob, and he loved the damsel, and spake kindly unto the damsel.

4 And She′-chem ᴿspake unto

33:11 *Take, I pray thee, my blessing.* Before, Jacob had done all he could to take Esau's blessing (25:29–34; 27:1–45). Now a wiser man, Jacob wanted to bless his brother with what God had given him. **33:20** *he erected there an altar.* The name Jacob gave this altar reflected his mature faith in "God, the God of Israel." The God of Jacob's fathers was now Jacob's personal God, for He had fulfilled His promises and protected him (28:13–15).

his father Ha'-mor, saying, Get me this damsel to wife. Ju 14:2

5　And Jacob heard that he had defiled Dinah his daughter: now his sons were with his cattle in the field: and Jacob [R]held his peace until they were come. 2 Sa 13:22

6　And Ha'-mor the father of She'-chem went out unto Jacob to [T]commune with him. *speak*

7　And the sons of Jacob came out of the field when they heard *it:* and the men were grieved, and they were very wroth, because he had wrought folly in Israel in lying with Jacob's daughter; which thing ought not to be done.

8　And Ha'-mor communed with them, saying, The soul of my son She'-chem longeth for your daughter: I pray you give her him to wife.

9　And make ye marriages with us, *and* give your daughters unto us, and take our daughters unto you.

10　And ye shall dwell with us: and the land shall be before you; dwell and trade ye therein, and get you possessions therein.

11　And She'-chem said unto her father and unto her brethren, Let me find [T]grace in your eyes, and what ye shall say unto me I will give. *favour*

12　Ask me never so much dowry and gift, and I will give according as ye shall say unto me: but give me the damsel to wife.

13　And the sons of Jacob answered She'-chem and Ha'-mor his father [R]deceitfully, and said, because he had defiled Dinah their sister: 31:7; Ex 8:29

14　And they said unto them, We cannot do this thing, to give our sister to one that is [R]uncircumcised; for [R]that *were* a reproach unto us: Ex 12:48 · Jos 5:2–9

15　But in this will we consent unto you: If ye will be as we *be,* that every male of you be circumcised;

16　Then will we give our daughters unto you, and we will take your daughters to us, and we will dwell with you, and we will become one people.

17　But if ye will not hearken unto us, to be circumcised; then will we take our daughter, and we will be gone.

18　And their words pleased Ha'-mor, and She'-chem Ha'-mor's son.

19　And the young man deferred not to do the thing, because he had delight in Jacob's daughter: and he *was* more honourable than all the house of his father.

20　And Ha'-mor and She'-chem his son came unto the [R]gate of their city, and communed with the men of their city, saying, Ru 4:1

21　These men *are* peaceable with us; therefore let them dwell in the land, and trade therein; for the land, behold, *it is* large enough for them; let us take their daughters to us for wives, and let us give them our daughters.

22　Only [T]herein will the men consent unto us for to dwell with us, to be one people, if every male among us be circumcised, as they *are* circumcised. *on this condition*

23　*Shall* not their cattle and their [T]substance and every [T]beast of theirs *be* ours? only let us consent unto them, and they will dwell with us. *property · animal*

24　And unto Ha'-mor and unto She'-chem his son hearkened all that [R]went out of the gate of his city; and every male was circumcised, all that went out of the gate of his city. 23:10, 18

25　And it came to pass on the third day, when they were sore, that two of the sons of Jacob, Simeon and Levi, Dinah's brethren, took

---

34:25 *slew all the males.* Jacob's sons were correct that God did not want them to intermarry with the pagan Canaanite families. According to later Levitical law, they were even correct that rape was punishable by death. However, their treacherous pretended

Continued on the next page

each man his sword, and came upon the city boldly, and slew all the males.

26 And they ᴿslew Ha'-mor and She'-chem his son with the edge of the sword, and took Dinah out of She'-chem's house, and went out.   49:5, 6

27 The sons of Jacob came upon the slain, and ᵀspoiled the city, because they had defiled their sister.   *plundered*

28 They took their sheep, and their oxen, and their asses, and that which *was* in the city, and that which *was* in the field,

29 And all their wealth, and all their little ones, and their wives took they captive, and spoiled even all that *was* in the house.

30 And Jacob said to Simeon and Levi, Ye have troubled me ᴿto make me ᵀto stink among the inhabitants of the land, among the Ca'-naan-ites and the Per'-iz-zites: and I *being* few in number, they shall gather themselves together against me, and slay me; and I shall be destroyed, I and my house. Ex 5:21; 2 Sa 10:6 · *obnoxious*

31 And they said, Should he deal with our sister as with an harlot?

35 And God said unto Jacob, Arise, go up to Beth'-el, and dwell there: and make there an altar unto God, that appeared unto thee when thou fleddest from the face of Esau thy brother.

2 Then Jacob said unto his household, and to all that *were* with him, Put away the strange gods that *are* among you, and be clean, and change your garments:

3 And let us arise, and go up to Beth'-el; and I will make there an altar unto God, ᴿwho answered me in the day of my distress, ᴿand was with me in the way which I went. 32:7, 24; Ps 107:6 · 28:15, 20; 31:3, 42

4 And they gave unto Jacob all the ᵀstrange gods which *were* in their hand, and *all their* earrings which *were* in their ears; and Jacob hid them under the oak which *was* by She'-chem.   *foreign*

5 And they journeyed: and ᴿthe terror of God was upon the cities that *were* round about them, and they did not pursue after the sons of Jacob.   Ex 15:16; 23:27; [De 2:25]

6 So Jacob came to ᴿLuz, which *is* in the land of Canaan, that *is*, Beth'-el, he and all the people that *were* with him.   48:3

7 And he built there an altar, and called the place ᵀEl–beth'–el: because there God appeared unto him, when he fled from the face of his brother.   *God of the House of God*

8 But ᴿDeb'-o-rah Rebekah's nurse died, and she was buried ᵀbeneath Beth'–el under an oak: and the name of it was called Al'-lon–bach'-uth.   24:59 · *below*

9 And God appeared unto Jacob again, when he came out of Pa'-dan–a'-ram, and blessed him.

10 And God said unto him, Thy name *is* Jacob: thy name shall not be called any more Jacob,

35:1–3   35:10–11

friendship and the massacre of all the men of Shechem, along with their greedy looting of all the Shechemites goods, was clearly not a justifiable execution of justice, and God condemned their violence and anger (49:5–7). **35:2 strange gods.** Jacob's command included the idols that Rachel had stolen (31:22–35) as well as any idols among his servants. These were not gods Jacob himself had been worshipping, but he had apparently been allowing others in his household to do so. **35:10–12 Israel shall be thy name.** The renewal of God's covenant with Jacob was introduced by confirming Jacob's change of name to Israel, the one who "wrestled with God and prevailed." The promises made to Abraham and Isaac were once again repeated, underscoring the continuity of the covenant. Furthermore, a rather significant phrase is added, "be fruitful and multiply," which incorporated the creation ordinance, thus exhibiting the continuity with the covenant of creation. The covenant Lord is the God of creation and of redemption.

R but Israel shall be thy name: and he called his name Israel.　32:28

11　And God said unto him, I *am* God Almighty: be fruitful and multiply; a nation and a company of nations shall be of thee, and kings shall come out of thy loins;

12　And the R land which I gave Abraham and Isaac, to thee I will give it, and to thy seed after thee will I give the land. 12:7; 13:15; 26:3, 4

13　And God R went T up from him in the place where he talked with him.　17:22; 18:33 · *departed*

14　And Jacob R set up a pillar in the place where he talked with him, *even* a pillar of stone: and he poured a drink offering thereon, and he poured oil thereon.　28:18, 19

15　And Jacob called the name of the place where God spake with him, R Beth'–el.　28:19

16　And they journeyed from Beth'–el; and there was but a little way to come to Eph'-rath: and Ra'-chel travailed, and she had hard labour.

17　And it came to pass, when she was in hard labour, that the midwife said unto her, Fear not; thou shalt have this son also.

18　And it came to pass, as her soul was in departing, (for she died) that she called his name T Ben–o'–ni: but his father called him Benjamin.　Lit. *Son of My Sorrow*

19　And Ra'-chel died, and was buried in the way to R Eph'-rath, which *is* Beth'–le-hem.　Ma 2:6

20　And Jacob set a pillar upon her grave: that *is* the pillar of Ra'-chel's grave unto this day.

21　And Israel journeyed, and spread his tent beyond R the tower of T E'-dar.　Mi 4:8 · Or *Eder*

22　And it came to pass, when Israel dwelt in that land, that Reuben went and R lay with Bil'-hah

his father's concubine: and Israel heard *it*. Now the sons of Jacob were twelve:　49:4; 1 Ch 5:1

23　The sons of Leah; Reuben, Jacob's firstborn, and Simeon, and Levi, and Judah, and Is'-sa-char, and Zeb'-u-lun:

24　The sons of Ra'-chel; Joseph, and Benjamin:

25　And the sons of Bil'-hah, Ra'-chel's handmaid; Dan, and Naph'-ta-li:

26　And the sons of Zil'-pah, Leah's handmaid; Gad, and Asher: these *are* the sons of Jacob, which were born to him in Pa'-dan–a'-ram.

27　And Jacob came unto Isaac his father unto R Mam'-re, unto the R city of Ar'-bah, which *is* He'-bron, where Abraham and Isaac sojourned. 13:18; 18:1; 23:19 · Jos 14:15

28　And the days of Isaac were an hundred and fourscore years.

29　And Isaac gave up the ghost, and died, and R was gathered unto his people, *being* old and full of days: and his sons Esau and Jacob buried him.　15:15; 25:8; 49:33

36 Now these *are* the generations of Esau, R who *is* E'-dom.　25:30

2　Esau took his wives of the daughters of Canaan; A'-dah the daughter of E'-lon the R Hit'-tite, and R A-hol-i-ba'-mah the daughter of A'-nah the daughter of Zib'-e-on the Hi'-vite;　2 Ki 7:6 · v. 25

3　And Bash'-e-math Ish'-ma-el's daughter, sister of Ne-ba'-joth.

4　And R A'-dah bare to Esau El'-i-phaz; and Bash'-e-math bare Reu'-el;　1 Ch 1:35

5　And A-hol-i-ba'-mah bare Je'-ush, and Ja-a'-lam, and Ko'-rah: these *are* the sons of Esau, which were born unto him in the land of Canaan.

6　And Esau took his wives, and

35:16 Ephrath. This is an alternative name for the region around Bethlehem (v. 19; 48:7; Ru 1:2; Mi 5:2). The King of Glory would one day be born near the birthplace of Benjamin (Ma 2:1). **35:27 Jacob came unto Isaac his father.** After more than 20 years of exile Jacob finally visited his father. Sadly, his mother Rebekah was probably dead since she is not mentioned.

his sons, and his daughters, and all the persons of his house, and his cattle, and all his beasts, and all his ᵀsubstance, which he had got in the land of Canaan; and went into the country from the face of his brother Jacob.   *goods*

7   For their riches were more than that they might dwell together; and ᴿthe land wherein they were strangers could not bear them because of their cattle.   17:8

8   Thus dwelt Esau in ᴿmount Se'-ir: Esau *is* E'-dom.   De 2:5

9   And these *are* the generations of Esau the father of the E'-domites in mount Se'-ir:

10   These *are* the names of Esau's sons; ᴿEl'-i-phaz the son of A'-dah the wife of Esau, Reu'-el the son of ᵀBash'-e-math the wife of Esau.   1 Ch 1:35 · He *Basemath*

11   And the sons of El'-i-phaz were Te'-man, Omar, Ze'-pho, and Ga'-tam, and Ke'-naz.

12   And Tim'-na was concubine to El'-i-phaz Esau's son; and she bare to El'-i-phaz ᴿAm'-a-lek: these *were* the sons of A'-dah Esau's wife.   Ex 17:8–16; Nu 24:20

13   And these *are* the sons of Reu'-el; Na'-hath, and Ze'-rah, Sham'-mah, and Miz'-zah: these were the sons of ᵀBash'-e-math Esau's wife.   He *Basemath*

14   And these were the sons of ᵀA-hol-i-ba'-mah, the daughter of A'-nah the daughter of Zib'-e-on, Esau's wife: and she bare to Esau Je'-ush, and Ja-a'-lam, and Ko'-rah.   Or *Oholibamah*

15   These *were* ᵀdukes of the sons of Esau: the sons of El'-i-phaz the firstborn *son* of Esau; duke Te'-man, duke Omar, duke Ze'-pho, duke Ke'-naz,   *chiefs*

16   Duke Ko'-rah, duke Ga'-tam, *and* duke Am'-a-lek: these *are* the dukes *that came* of El'-i-phaz in the land of E'-dom; these *were* the sons of A'-dah.

17   And these *are* the sons of Reu'-el Esau's son; duke Na'-hath, duke Ze'-rah, duke Sham'-mah, duke Miz'-zah: these *are* the dukes *that came* of Reu'-el in the land of E'-dom; these *are* the sons of Bash'-e-math Esau's wife.

18   And these *are* the sons of A-hol-i-ba'-mah Esau's wife; duke Je'-ush, duke Ja-a'-lam, duke Ko'-rah: these *were* the dukes *that came* of A-hol-i-ba'-mah the daughter of A'-nah, Esau's wife.

19   These *are* the sons of Esau, who *is* E'-dom, and these *are* their dukes.

20   ᴿThese *are* the sons of Se'-ir the Ho'-rite, who inhabited the land; Lo'-tan, and Sho'-bal, and Zib'-e-on, and A'-nah,   1 Ch 1:38–42

21   And Di'-shon, and E'-zer, and Di'-shan: these *are* the dukes of the Ho'-rites, the children of Se'-ir in the land of E'-dom.

22   And the children of Lo'-tan were Ho'-ri and He'-mam; and Lo'-tan's sister *was* Tim'-na.

23   And the children of Sho'-bal *were* these; Al'-van, and Ma-na'-hath, and E'-bal, She'-pho, and O'-nam.

24   And these *are* the children of Zib'-e-on; both A'-jah, and A'-nah: this *was that* A'-nah that found ᴿthe mules in the wilderness, as he fed the asses of Zib'-e-on his father.   Le 19:19

25   And the children of A'-nah *were* these; Di'-shon, and A-hol-i-ba'-mah the daughter of A'-nah.

26   And these *are* the children of Di'-shon; Hem'-dan, and Esh'-ban, and Ith'-ran, and Che'-ran.

27   The children of E'-zer *are* these; Bil'-han, and Za'-a-van, and ᵀA'-kan.   *Jakan,* 1 Ch 1:42

28   The children of Di'-shan *are* these; ᴿUz, and A'-ran.   Job 1:1

29   These *are* the ᵀdukes *that came* of the Ho'-rites; duke Lo'-tan, duke Sho'-bal, duke Zib'-e-on, duke A'-nah,   *chiefs*

36:12 *Amalek.* Esau's grandson Amalek founded a people that later would trouble the Israelites (Nu 14:39–45).

30 Duke Di′-shon, duke E′-zer, duke Di′-shan: these *are* the dukes *that came* of Ho′-ri, among their dukes in the land of Se′-ir.

31 And ᴿthese *are* the kings that reigned in the land of E′-dom, before there reigned any king over the children of Israel.   17:6, 16

32 And Be′-la the son of Be′-or reigned in E′-dom: and the name of his city *was* Din′-ha-bah.

33 And Be′-la died, and Jo′-bab the son of Ze′-rah of Boz′-rah reigned in his stead.

34 And Jo′-bab died, and Hu′-sham of the land of Tem′-a-ni reigned in his stead.

35 And Hu′-sham died, and Ha′-dad the son of Be′-dad, who smote Mid′-i-an in the field of Moab, reigned in his stead: and the name of his city *was* A′-vith.

36 And Ha′-dad died, and Sam′-lah of Mas-re′-kah reigned in his stead.

37 And Sam′-lah died, and Saul of ᴿRe-ho′-both *by* the river reigned in his stead.   10:11

38 And Saul died, and Ba′-al–ha′-nan the son of Ach′-bor reigned in his stead.

39 And Ba′-al–ha′-nan the son of Ach′-bor died, and Ha′-dar reigned in his stead: and the name of his city *was* Pa′-u; and his wife's name *was* Me-het′-a-bel, the daughter of Ma′-tred, the daughter of Mez′-a-hab.

40 And these *are* the names of the dukes *that came* of Esau, according to their families, after their places, by their names; duke Tim′-nah, duke ᵀAl′-vah, duke Je′-theth,   *Aliah,* 1 Ch 1:51

41 Duke ᵀA-hol-i-ba′-mah, duke E′-lah, duke Pi′-non, Or *Oholibamah*

42 Duke Ke′-naz, duke Te′-man, duke Mib′-zar,

43 Duke Mag′-di-el, duke I′-ram: these *be* the dukes of E′-dom, according to their habitations in the land of their possession: he *is* Esau the father of the E′-dom-ites.

37 And Jacob dwelt in the land wherein his father was a stranger, in the land of Canaan.

2 These *are* the generations of Jacob. Joseph, *being* seventeen years old, was feeding the flock with his brethren; and the lad *was* with the sons of Bil′-hah, and with the sons of Zil′-pah, his father's wives: and Joseph brought unto his father ᴿtheir evil report. 35:25

3 Now Israel loved Joseph more than all his children, because he *was* the son of his old age: and he ᴿmade him a coat of *many* colours.   Ju 5:30; 1 Sa 2:19

4 And when his brethren saw that their father loved him more than all his brethren, they ᴿhated him, and could not speak peaceably unto him.   1 Sa 17:28

5 And Joseph dreamed a dream,

36:40–43 *Esau the father of the Edomites.* Although Esau was not the heir of God's everlasting covenant with the family of Abraham, God still blessed his family and made them into a nation. **37:1** *a stranger.* The Lord had promised that this land would become a permanent possession of Abraham's family (12:7). To the third generation, that promise was still not realized. Jacob and his family were still aliens in the land. **37:2** *their evil.* Since Joseph in general demonstrated his integrity (see ch. 39), he was probably not slandering his brothers, but accurately reporting some negligence on their part. **37:3** *a coat of many colours.* This is the traditional translation. The Hebrew phrase may simply mean a garment with long sleeves. The robe was certainly distinctive in some way, and probably costly. **37:4** *hated him.* Because fallen and unregenerate man hates God, he displays hatred in his relations with others. The hatred of Joseph's brothers is attributed primarily to the love which Jacob had for his youngest son. As a result of their hatred the brothers were not able to speak kindly to Joseph, and the hatred led to a plot to kill him. Jesus remarked that the world's hatred of His people is a reflection of hatred against Himself (Jo 15:18). Love is the leading characteristic of the godly as hatred is the mark of the worldly person.

and he told *it* his brethren: and they hated him yet the more.

6 And he said unto them, Hear, I pray you, this dream which I have dreamed:

7 For, ^Rbehold, we *were* binding sheaves in the field, and, lo, my sheaf arose, and also stood upright; and, behold, your sheaves stood round about, and made obeisance to my sheaf. 42:6

8 And his brethren said to him, Shalt thou indeed reign over us? or shalt thou indeed have dominion over us? And they hated him yet the more for his dreams, and for his words.

9 And he dreamed yet another dream, and told it his brethren, and said, Behold, I have dreamed a dream more; and, behold, ^Rthe sun and the moon and the eleven stars made obeisance to me. 46:29

10 And he told *it* to his father, and to his brethren: and his father rebuked him, and said unto him, What *is* this dream that thou hast dreamed? Shall I and thy mother and ^Rthy brethren indeed come to bow down ourselves to thee to the earth? 27:29

11 And his brethren envied him; but his father ^Tobserved the saying. *kept the matter* in mind

12 And his brethren went to feed their father's flock in ^RShe'-chem. 33:18–20

13 And Israel said unto Joseph, Do not thy brethren feed *the flock* in She'-chem? come, and I will send thee unto them. And he said to him, Here *am* I.

14 And he said to him, Go, I pray thee, see whether it be well with thy brethren, and well with the flocks; and bring me word again. So he sent him out of the vale of

^RHe'-bron, and he came to She'-chem. 23:2, 19; 35:27; Jos 14:14, 15

15 And a certain man found him, and, behold, *he was* wandering in the field: and the man asked him, saying, What seekest thou?

16 And he said, I seek my brethren: tell me, I pray thee, where they feed *their flocks.*

17 And the man said, They are departed hence; for I heard them say, Let us go to Do'-than. And Joseph went after his brethren, and found them in Do'-than.

18 And when they saw him afar off, even before he came near unto them, ^Rthey conspired against him to slay him. Ma 21:38

19 And they said one to another, Behold, this dreamer cometh.

20 ^RCome now therefore, and let us slay him, and cast him into some pit, and we will say, Some evil beast hath devoured him: and we shall see what will become of his dreams. 37:22; Pr 1:11

21 And ^RReuben heard *it,* and he delivered him out of their hands; and said, Let us not kill him. 42:22

22 And Reuben said unto them, Shed no blood, *but* cast him into this pit that *is* in the wilderness, and lay no hand upon him; that he might rid him out of their hands, to deliver him to his father again.

23 And it came to pass, when Joseph was come unto his brethren, that they ^Rstript Joseph out of his coat, *his* coat of *many* colours that *was* on him; Ma 27:28

24 And they took him, and cast him into a pit: and the pit *was* empty, *there was* no water in it.

25 And they sat down to eat bread: and they lifted up their eyes and looked, and, behold, a company of ^RIsh'-me-el-ites came

---

37:17 Dothan. This is about ten miles north of Shechem, near Mount Gilboa. **37:21 *Let us not kill him.*** Reuben, as the firstborn son and principal heir, had the most to lose if Joseph's dreams came true. Yet Reuben intervened to spare Joseph's life. This was something of a contrast with his earlier wicked actions (35:22). **37:25 *Ishmeelites.*** The Ishmeelites of this passage were wandering traders. The name (referring to descendants of Ishmael, the son of Abraham and Hagar) is loosely equivalent with the name from Gil'-e-ad with their camels bearing spicery and ᴿbalm and myrrh, going to carry *it* down to Egypt. vv. 28, 36; 16:11, 12; 39:1 · Je 8:22

26 And Judah said unto his brethren, What profit *is it* if we slay our brother, and ᴿconceal his blood?   v. 20

27 Come, and let us sell him to the Ish'-me-el-ites, and let not our hand be upon him; for he *is* ᴿour brother *and* ᴿour flesh. And his brethren were content.   42:21 · 29:14

28 Then there passed by ᴿMid'-i-an-ites merchantmen; and they drew and lifted up Joseph out of the pit, and sold Joseph to the Ish'-me-el-ites for ᴿtwenty *pieces* of silver: and they brought Joseph into Egypt.   v. 25; Ju 6:1–3 · Ma 27:9

29 And Reuben returned unto the pit; and, behold, Joseph *was* not in the pit; and he ᴿrentᵀ his clothes.   v. 34; 44:13; Job 1:20 · *tore*

30 And he returned unto his brethren, and said, The ᵀchild *is* not; and I, whither shall I go?   lad

31 And they took ᴿJoseph's coat, and killed a kid of the goats, and dipped the coat in the blood;   v. 3

32 And they sent the coat of *many* colours, and they brought *it* to their father; and said, This have we found: ᵀknow now whether it *be* thy son's coat or no.   do you know

33 And he knew it, and said, *It is* my son's coat; an ᴿevilᵀ beast hath devoured him; Joseph is without doubt rent in pieces.   v. 20 · *wild*

34 And Jacob ᴿrentᵀ his clothes, and put sackcloth upon his loins,

and ᴿmourned for his son many days.   v. 29; 2 Sa 3:31 · *tore* · 50:10

35 And all his sons and all his daughters ᴿrose up to comfort him; but he refused to be comforted; and he said, For ᴿI will go down into the grave unto my son mourning. Thus his father wept for him.   2 Sa 12:17 · 42:38; 44:29, 31

36 And ᴿthe Mid'-i-an-ites sold him into Egypt unto Pot'-i-phar, an officer of Pharaoh's, *and* captain of the guard.   39:1

38 And it came to pass at that time, that Judah went down from his brethren, and ᴿturned in to a certain A-dul'-lam-ite, whose name *was* Hi'-rah.   2 Ki 4:8

2 And Judah ᴿsaw there a daughter of a certain Ca'-naan-ite, whose name *was* ᵀShu'-ah; and he ᵀtook her, and went in unto her.   34:2 · He *Shua*; 1 Ch 2:3 · *married*

3 And she conceived, and bare a son; and he called his name Er.

4 And she conceived again, and bare a son; and she called his name ᴿO'-nan.   46:12; Nu 26:19

5 And she yet again conceived, and bare a son; and called his name She'-lah: and he was at Che'-zib, when she bare him.

6 And Judah ᴿtook a wife for Er his firstborn, whose name *was* ᴿTa'-mar.   21:21 · Ru 4:12

7 And Er, Judah's firstborn, was wicked in the sight of the LORD; and the LORD slew him.

8 And Judah said unto O'-nan,

✂ 37:32–35

Midianite (Midian was another son of Abraham, by Keturah). Probably the families of the two half brothers had a strong alliance and were so closely associated that the names became interchangeable (v. 28).   **37:28 *twenty pieces of silver.*** The standard price for a slave in later Israelite law was 30 pieces of silver.   **37:29 *rent his clothes.*** Tearing one's clothes was a common expression of grief and dismay. Reuben's grief was genuine feeling for his younger brother mixed with fear that he, the oldest brother, would be blamed.   **38:1–30** At first glance it appears that the story of Judah and Tamar is an intrusion into the story of Joseph, but it is here for a reason. It provides a stunning contrast between the morals of Judah and Joseph. It illustrates the further disintegration of Jacob's family. If this process continued, Jacob's family, the family of promise, would become like the people of Canaan.   **38:8 *unto thy brother's wife.*** In order to maintain the family line and the name of the deceased, it was the custom in ancient times for the

Continued on the next page

Go in unto ^Rthy brother's wife, and marry her, and raise up seed to thy brother.   De 25:5, 6; Ma 22:24

9 And O'-nan knew that the seed should not be his; and it came to pass, when he went in unto his brother's wife, that he spilled *it* on the ground, lest that he should give seed to his brother.

10 And the thing which he did displeased the LORD: wherefore he slew ^Rhim also.   46:12; Nu 26:19

11 Then said Judah to Ta'-mar his daughter in law, Remain a widow at thy father's house, till She'-lah my son be grown: for he said, Lest peradventure he die also, as his brethren *did*. And Ta'-mar went and dwelt ^Rin her father's house.   Le 22:13

12 And in process of time the daughter of Shu'-ah Judah's wife died; and Judah was comforted, and went up unto his sheepshearers to Tim'-nath, he and his friend Hi'-rah the A-dul'-lam-ite.

13 And it was told Ta'-mar, saying, Behold thy father in law goeth up ^Rto Tim'-nath to shear his sheep.   Jos 15:10, 57; Ju 14:1

14 And she put her widow's garments off from her, and covered her with a vail, and wrapped herself, and ^Rsat in an open place, which *is* by the way to Tim'-nath; for she saw ^Rthat She'-lah was grown, and she was not given unto him to wife.   Pr 7:12 · vv. 11, 26

15 When Judah saw her, he thought her *to be* an harlot; because she had covered her face.

16 And he turned unto her by the way, and said, Go to, I pray thee, let me come in unto thee; (for he knew not that she *was* his daughter in law.) And she said, What wilt thou give me, that thou mayest come in unto me?

17 And he said, ^RI will send *thee* a kid from the flock. And she said, Wilt thou give *me* a pledge, till thou send *it*?   Ju 15:1; Eze 16:33

18 And he said, What pledge shall I give thee? And she said, ^RThy signet, and thy ^Tbracelets, and thy staff that *is* in thine hand. And he gave *it* her, and came in unto her, and she conceived by him.   v. 25; 41:42 · cord

19 And she arose, and went away, and ^Rlaid by her vail from her, and put on the garments of her widowhood.   v. 14

20 And Judah sent the kid by the hand of his friend the A-dul'-lam-ite, to receive *his* pledge from the woman's hand: but he found her not.

21 Then he asked the men of that place, saying, Where *is* the harlot, that *was* openly by the way side? And they said, There was no harlot in this *place*.

22 And he returned to Judah, and said, I cannot find her; and also the men of the place said, *that* there was no harlot in this *place*.

23 And Judah said, Let her take *it* to her, lest we be shamed: be-

---

dead man's brother to marry the widow and father a child that would carry on the man's family. This is called *levirate* marriage, from the Latin word meaning "husband's brother." The custom became part of the Mosaic law (De 25:5–10; Ru 4:1–12). **38:15–18 Fornication**—God designed sexual relations to be enjoyed exclusively within the framework of marriage: one man, for one woman, mutually committed for life. Outside of this framework, all sexual relations are sin. This is not because God wants to deprive His people of pleasure, but because He wants to protect them from the painful and destructive consequences of sin. Sexual union is not only a union of the body, but of the whole person (1 Co 6:15–20). Illicit sexual relations defile the temple of God, breed both physical and social disease, and serve as a source for many other sins. **38:18 *signet*.** This was an ancient means of identification. The signet was distinctively etched in stone, metal, or ivory. To confirm a business transaction, or make an order official, the signet was pressed into soft clay, leaving its distinctive impression. Basically, Judah gave Tamar the equivalent of a modern credit card.

hold, I sent this kid, and thou hast not found her.

24 And it came to pass about three months after, that it was told Judah, saying, Ta'-mar thy daughter in law hath played the harlot; and also, behold, she *is* with child by whoredom. And Judah said, Bring her forth, ^Rand let her be burnt.   Le 20:14; 21:9; De 22:21

25 When she *was* brought forth, she sent to her father in law, saying, By the man, whose these *are*, *am* I with child: and she said, ^RDiscern, I pray thee, whose *are* these, the signet, and ^Tbracelets, and staff.   v. 18; 37:32 · *cord*

26 And Judah ^Racknowledged *them*, and said, ^RShe hath been more righteous than I; because that I gave her not to She'-lah my son. And he knew her again ^Rno more.   37:33 · 1 Sa 24:17 · Job 34:31, 32

27 And it came to pass in the time of her travail, that, behold, twins *were* in her womb.

28 And it came to pass, when she travailed, that *the one* put out *his* hand: and the midwife took and bound upon his hand a scarlet thread, saying, This came out first.

29 And it came to pass, as he drew back his hand, that, behold, his brother came out: and she said, How hast thou broken forth? *this* breach *be* upon thee: therefore his name was called ^RPha'-rez.   46:12; Ru 4:12; 1 Ch 2:4; Ma 1:3

30 And afterward came out his brother, that had the scarlet thread upon his hand: and his name was called Zar'-ah.

39 And Joseph was brought down to Egypt; and ^RPot'-i-phar, an officer of Pharaoh, captain of the guard, an Egyptian, bought him of the hands of the Ish'-me-el-ites, which had brought him down thither.   37:36; Ps 105:17

2 And ^Rthe LORD was with Joseph, and he was a prosperous man; and he was in the house of his master the Egyptian.   Ac 7:9

3 And his master saw that the LORD *was* with him, and that the LORD ^Rmade all that he did to prosper in his hand.   Ps 1:3

4 And Joseph ^Rfound grace in his sight, and he served him: and he made him ^Roverseer over his house, and all *that* he had he put into his hand.   18:3; 19:19 · 24:2; 41:40

5 And it came to pass from the time *that* he had made him overseer in his house, and over all that he had, that ^Rthe LORD blessed the Egyptian's house for Joseph's sake; and the blessing of the LORD was upon all that he had in the house, and in the field.   2 Sa 6:11

6 And he left all that he had in Joseph's hand; and he knew not ought he had, save the bread which he did eat. And Joseph ^Rwas *a* ^Tgoodly *person*, and well favoured.   29:17; 1 Sa 16:12 · *handsome*

7 And it came to pass after these things, that his master's wife cast her eyes upon Joseph; and she said, Lie with me.

8 But he refused, and said unto his master's wife, Behold, my master ^Twotteth not what *is* with me in the house, and he hath committed all that he hath to my hand; *knows*

38:26 *She hath been more righteous.* Judah, one of the heirs of the everlasting covenant with the living God, was put to shame by a Canaanite woman. To his credit, Judah confessed his sins.   **38:29 *Pharez.*** Pharez was in the lineage of David, and eventually Jesus the Messiah (Ru 4:18; Ma 1:3).   **39:2 *the LORD was with Joseph.*** This key phrase of this section is repeated (vv. 21, 23). This phrase indicates that God cared for, protected, and blessed Joseph.   **39:4 *found grace.*** Joseph's life illustrates the principle that one who is faithful in little will be given charge over much (Ma 25:21; 1 Co 4:2).   **39:5 *the LORD blessed the Egyptian's house.*** God blessed Potiphar's house because of Joseph, just as He had blessed Laban because of Jacob.

9   *There is* none greater in this house than I; neither hath he kept back any thing from me but thee, because thou *art* his wife: how then can I do this great wickedness, and [R]sin against God?   Ps 51:4

10   And it came to pass, as she spake to Joseph day by day, that he hearkened [R]not unto her, to lie by her, *or* to be with her.   Pr 1:10

11   And it came to pass about this time, that *Joseph* went into the house to do his [T]business; and *there was* none of the men of the house there within.   *work*

12   And she [R]caught him by his garment, saying, Lie with me: and he left his garment in her hand, and fled, and got him out.   Pr 7:13

13   And it came to pass, when she saw that he had left his garment in her hand, and was fled [T]forth,   *outside*

14   That she called unto the men of her house, and spake unto them, saying, See, he hath brought in an [R]Hebrew unto us to [T]mock us; he came in unto me to lie with me, and I cried with a loud voice: 14:13; 41:12 · *laugh at*

15   And it came to pass, when he heard that I lifted up my voice and cried, that he left his garment with me, and fled, and got him out.

16   And she laid up his garment by her, until his lord came home.

17   And she [R]spake unto him according to these words, saying, The Hebrew servant, which thou hast brought unto us, came in unto me to mock me: Ex 23:1

18   And it came to pass, as I lifted up my voice and cried, that he left his garment with me, and fled out.

19   And it came to pass, when his master heard the words of his wife, which she spake unto him, saying, After this manner did thy servant to me; that his [R]wrath was kindled.   Pr 6:34, 35

20   And Joseph's master took him, and [R]put him into the prison, a place where the king's prisoners *were* bound: and he was there in the prison.   Ps 105:18; [1 Pe 2:19]

21   But the LORD was with Joseph, and shewed him mercy, and [R]gave him favour in the sight of the keeper of the prison.   Ac 7:9, 10

22   And the keeper of the prison [R]committed to Joseph's hand all the prisoners that *were* in the prison; and whatsoever they did there, he was the doer *of it.*   v. 4

23   The keeper of the prison [T]looked not to any thing *that was* under his hand; because [R]the LORD was with him, and *that* which he did, the LORD made *it* to prosper.   *did not look into* · vv. 2, 3

40 And it came to pass after these things, *that* the [R]butler of the king of Egypt and *his* baker had offended their lord the king of Egypt.   vv. 11, 13; Ne 1:11

2   And Pharaoh was wroth against two *of* his officers, against the chief of the butlers, and against the chief of the bakers.

3   [R]And he put them in ward in the house of the captain of the guard, into the prison, the place where Joseph *was* bound.   41:10

4   And the captain of the guard

39:9 sin against God. Joseph rejected the solicitation to sin, regarding it both as a wicked act of treachery against his master, and as a defiling and rebellious act before a holy God. Because Joseph's conscience was bound by God and His truth, he was able to resist this evil suggestion more than once. Pleasing God was more important to Joseph than engaging in the pleasures of sin for a season. His fear and reverence of God was the directing power of his life. **39:20 into the prison.** Surprisingly, Potiphar did not simply kill Joseph outright. It is possible that knowledge of Joseph's character (or his own wife's character) caused him to suspect that the story was not wholly true. **39:21 mercy.** This word can be translated *loyal love* (Ps 13:5). God faithfully kept His promises by staying with His people (12:1–3; 50:24). **39:23 the LORD made it to prosper.** Because of God's blessing, everything Joseph did prospered (Ps 1:1–3).

charged Joseph with them, and he served them: and they continued ^Ta season in ward. *in custody awhile*

5 And they ^Rdreamed a dream both of them, each man his dream in one night, each man according to the interpretation of his dream, the butler and the baker of the king of Egypt, which *were* bound in the prison.   37:5; 41:1

6 And Joseph came in unto them in the morning, and looked upon them, and, behold, they *were* ^Tsad.   *dejected*

7 And he asked Pharaoh's officers that *were* with him in the ward of his lord's house, saying, ^RWherefore look ye *so* sadly to day? Ne 2:2

8 And they said unto him, We have dreamed a dream, and *there is* no interpreter of it. And Joseph said unto them, ^RDo not interpretations *belong* to God? tell me *them,* I pray you.   [41:16; Da 2:11–47]

9 And the chief butler told his dream to Joseph, and said to him, In my dream, behold, a vine *was* before me;

10 And in the vine *were* three branches: and it *was* as though it budded, *and* her blossoms shot forth; and the clusters thereof brought forth ripe grapes:

11 And Pharaoh's cup *was* in my hand: and I took the grapes, and pressed them into Pharaoh's cup, and I gave the cup into Pharaoh's hand.

12 And Joseph said unto him, ^RThis *is* the interpretation of it: The three branches ^R*are* three days: Ju 7:14; Da 2:36; 4:18, 19 · 42:17

13 Yet within three days shall Pharaoh ^Rlift up thine head, and restore thee unto thy place: and thou shalt deliver Pharaoh's cup into his hand, after the former manner when thou wast his butler.   2 Ki 25:27; Ps 3:3; Je 52:31

14 But ^Rthink on me when it shall be well with thee, and ^Rshew kindness, I pray thee, unto me, and make mention of me unto Pharaoh, and bring me out of this house: Lk 23:42 · Jos 2:12; 1 Ki 2:7

15 For indeed I was ^Rstolen away out of the land of the Hebrews: ^Rand here also have I done nothing that they should put me into the dungeon.   37:26–28 · 39:20

16 When the chief baker saw that the interpretation was good, he said unto Joseph, I also *was* in my dream, and, behold, *I had* three white baskets on my head:

17 And in the uppermost basket *there was* of all manner of ^Tbakemeats for Pharaoh; and the birds did eat them out of the basket upon my head.   *baked goods*

18 And Joseph answered and said, ^RThis *is* the interpretation thereof: The three baskets *are* three days: v. 12

19 Yet within three days shall Pharaoh lift up thy head from off thee, and shall ^Rhang thee on a tree; and the birds shall eat thy flesh from off thee.   De 21:22

20 And it came to pass the third day, *which was* Pharaoh's birthday, that he made a feast unto all his servants: and he lifted up the head of the chief butler and of the chief baker among his servants.

21 And he ^Rrestored the chief butler unto his butlership again; and ^Rhe gave the cup into Pharaoh's hand: v. 13 · Ne 2:1

22 But he ^Rhanged the chief baker: as Joseph had interpreted to them.   v. 19; De 21:23; Es 7:10

23 Yet did not the chief butler remember Joseph, but ^Rforgat him.   Ps 31:12; Is 49:15; Am 6:6

40:8 *interpretations belong to God?* Joseph not only announced his faith, he then quickly acted upon it. Joseph had received dreams and visions as a younger man, and he had understood their meaning (37:5–11). **40:22** *he hanged the chief baker.* Pharaoh was clearly a ruthless ruler who rewarded those who served him well, but destroyed those he perceived as threats.

41 And it came to pass at the end of two full years, that [R]Pharaoh dreamed: and, behold, he stood by the river.   40:5; Ju 7:13

2 And, behold, there came up out of the river seven well favoured [T]kine and fatfleshed; and they fed in a meadow.   *cows*

3 And, behold, seven other kine came up after them out of the river, ill favoured and leanfleshed; and stood by the *other* kine upon the [T]brink of the river.   *bank*

4 And the [T]ill favoured and leanfleshed kine did eat up the seven well favoured and fat kine. So Pharaoh awoke.   *ugly and gaunt*

5 And he slept and dreamed the second time: and, behold, seven ears of corn came up upon one stalk, [T]rank and good.   *plump*

6 And, behold, seven thin [T]ears and blasted with the east wind sprung up after them.   *heads of grain*

7 And the seven thin ears devoured the seven rank and full ears. And Pharaoh awoke, and, behold, *it was* a dream.

8 And it came to pass in the morning that his spirit was troubled; and he sent and called for all [R]the magicians of Egypt, and all the wise men thereof: and Pharaoh told them his dream; but *there was* none that could interpret them unto Pharaoh.   Ex 7:11

9 Then spake the chief butler unto Pharaoh, saying, I do remember my faults this day:

10 Pharaoh was wroth with his servants, and put me in ward in the captain of the guard's house, *both* me and the chief baker:

11 And [R]we dreamed a dream in one night, I and he; we dreamed each man according to the interpretation of his dream.   Ju 7:15

12 And *there was* there with us a young man, [R]an Hebrew, [R]servant to the captain of the guard; and we told him, and he [R]interpreted to us our dreams; to each man according to his dream he did interpret.   39:14; 43:32 · 37:36 · 40:12

13 And it came to pass, [R]as he interpreted to us, so it was; me he restored unto mine office, and him he hanged.   40:21, 22

14 Then Pharaoh sent and called Joseph, and they brought him hastily [R]out of the dungeon: and he shaved *himself,* and changed his raiment, and came in unto Pharaoh.   [1 Sa 2:8]

15 And Pharaoh said unto Joseph, I have dreamed a dream, and *there is* none that can interpret it: [R]and I have heard say of thee, *that* thou canst understand a dream to interpret it.   Da 5:16

16 And Joseph answered Pharaoh, saying, [R]*It is* not in me: God shall give Pharaoh an answer of peace.   Da 2:30; Ac 3:12; [2 Co 3:5]

17 And Pharaoh said unto Joseph, In my dream, behold, I stood upon the bank of the river:

18 And, behold, there came up out of the river seven [T]kine, fatfleshed and well favoured; and they fed in a meadow: *cows*

19 And, behold, seven other kine came up after them, poor and very ill favoured and leanfleshed, such as I never saw in all the land of Egypt for [T]badness: *ugliness*

41:8 *magicians.* The Hebrew term is related to the word for *stylus,* a writing instrument. Thus the magicians were associated in some manner with writing and knowledge, no doubt of the occult. ***wise men.*** These were a class of scholars associated with the courts of the ancient Middle East. They were either functionaries of pagan religions, or merely observers and interpreters of life.   **41:14 *shaved.*** Egyptian men not only shaved their faces, but their entire bodies and heads. Egyptian officials scorned the "hairy" Canaanites, including the Hebrews (43:32). While he lived in Egypt Joseph apparently adopted the dress and manner of the Egyptians.   **41:16 *God.*** Joseph praised the power of the living God in the pagan court of Pharaoh. He would not take any credit to himself, nor did he try to use the situation to plead for his own release.

20 And the lean and the ill favoured kine did eat up the first seven fat kine:

21 And when they had eaten them up, it could not be known that they had eaten them; but they *were* still ᵀill favoured, as at the beginning. So I awoke. *ugly*

22 And I saw in my dream, and, behold, seven ears came up in one stalk, full and good:

23 And, behold, seven ᵀears, withered, thin, *and* ᵀblasted with the east wind, sprung up after them: *heads · blighted*

24 And the thin ears devoured the seven good ears: and ᴿI told *this* unto the magicians; but *there was* none that could declare *it* to me. *v. 8; Ex 7:11; Is 8:19; Da 4:7*

25 And Joseph said unto Pharaoh, The dream of Pharaoh *is* one: ᴿGod hath shewed Pharaoh what he *is* about to do. *Da 2:28, 29*

26 The seven good kine *are* seven years; and the seven good ears *are* seven years: the dream *is* one.

27 And the seven thin and ill favoured kine that came up after them *are* seven years; and the seven empty ears blasted with the east wind shall be ᴿseven years of famine. *2 Ki 8:1*

28 ᴿThis *is* the thing which I have spoken unto Pharaoh: What God *is* about to do he sheweth unto Pharaoh. *[vv. 25, 32; Da 2:28]*

29 Behold, there come ᴿseven years of great plenty throughout all the land of Egypt: *v. 47*

30 And there shall arise after them seven years of famine; and all the plenty shall be forgotten in the land of Egypt; and the famine ᴿshall consume the land; *Ps 105:16*

31 And the plenty shall not be known in the land by reason of that famine following; for it *shall be* very grievous.

32 And for that the dream was ᵀdoubled unto Pharaoh twice; *it is* because the ᴿthing *is* established by God, and God will shortly bring it to pass. *repeated · Nu 23:19*

33 Now therefore let Pharaoh look out a man ᵀdiscreet and wise, and set him over the land of Egypt. *discerning*

34 Let Pharaoh do *this*, and let him appoint officers over the land, and ᴿtake up the fifth part of the land of Egypt in the seven plenteous years. *[Pr 6:6–8]*

35 And let them gather all the food of those good years that come, and lay up corn under the ᵀhand of Pharaoh, and let them keep food in the cities. *authority*

36 And that food shall be for ᵀstore to the land against the seven years of famine, which shall be in the land of Egypt; that the land ᴿperish not through the famine. *a reserve for · 47:15, 19*

37 And ᴿthe thing was good in the eyes of Pharaoh, and in the eyes of all his servants. *Ps 105:19*

38 And Pharaoh said unto his servants, Can we find *such a one* as this *is*, a man ᴿin whom the Spirit of God *is*? *Nu 27:18; Da 6:3*

39 And Pharaoh said unto Joseph, Forasmuch as God hath shewed

---

41:32 *God, and God.* Joseph made it clear that he was speaking about the one God, not the numerous false gods that filled the Egyptian court, or Pharaoh himself who was believed to be a god (22:1; 42:18). **41:38** *in whom the Spirit of God is.* Even if he did not follow God himself, Pharaoh was at least acknowledging that Joseph was extraordinarily wise, and that the power of his God was obvious in his life. **41:39** *discreet and wise.* Joseph is an illustration of the instructions Paul gave Colosse: "Walk in wisdom toward them that are without" (Col 4:5). Pharaoh recognized that Joseph's wisdom was not the ordinary powers of a clever man, but something unique and outside of himself. Joseph was wise because he listened to God, not just because of his extraordinary intelligence and perspicacity. God's wisdom is moral. It discerns between good and evil. It is seen through prudence in secular affairs and comes through personal experience with the Lord.

thee all this, *there is* none so discreet and wise as thou *art:*

40 ᴿThou shalt be over my house, and according unto thy word shall all my people be ruled: only in the throne will I be greater than thou.   Ps 105:21; Ac 7:10

41 And Pharaoh said unto Joseph, See, I have ᴿset thee over all the land of Egypt.   Da 6:3

42 And Pharaoh took off his ring from his hand, and put it upon Joseph's hand, and ᴿarrayed him in ᵀvestures of fine linen, ᴿand put a gold chain about his neck;   Es 8:2, 15 · *garments* · Da 5:7

43 And he made him to ride in the second chariot which he had; ᴿand they cried before him, Bow the knee: and he made him *ruler* over all the land of Egypt.   Es 6:9

44 And Pharaoh said unto Joseph, I *am* Pharaoh, and without thee shall no man lift up his hand or foot in all the land of Egypt.

45 And Pharaoh called Joseph's name Zaph'-nath–pa-a-ne'-ah; and he gave him to wife As'-e-nath the daughter of Pot-i–phe'-rah priest of On. And Joseph went out over *all* the land of Egypt.

46 And Joseph *was* thirty years old when he ᴿstood before Pharaoh king of Egypt. And Joseph went out from the presence of Pharaoh, and went throughout all the land of Egypt.   1 Sa 16:21

47 And in the seven plenteous years the earth brought forth ᵀby handfuls.   *abundantly*

48 And he gathered up all the food of the seven years, which were in the land of Egypt, and laid up the food in the cities: the food of the field, which *was* round about every city, laid he up in the same.

49 And Joseph gathered corn as the sand of the sea, very much, un-

til he ᵀleft numbering; for *it was* without number.   *stopped*

50 And unto Joseph were born two sons before the years of famine came, which As'-e-nath the daughter of Pot-i–phe'-rah priest of On bare unto him.   48:5

51 And Joseph called the name of the firstborn Ma-nas'-seh: For God, *said he,* hath made me forget all my toil, and all my ᴿfather's house.   Ps 45:10

52 And the name of the second called he E'-phra-im: For God hath caused me to be ᴿfruitful in the land of my affliction.   49:22

53 And the seven years of plenteousness, that was in the land of Egypt, were ended.

54 And the seven years of dearth began to come, according as Joseph had said: and the dearth was in all lands; but in all the land of Egypt there was bread.

55 And when all the land of Egypt was famished, the people cried to Pharaoh for bread: and Pharaoh said unto all the Egyptians, Go unto Joseph; ᴿwhat he saith to you, do.   Jo 2:5

56 And the famine was over all the face of the earth: And Joseph opened all the storehouses, and ᴿsold unto the Egyptians; and the famine ᵀwaxed sore in the land of Egypt.   42:6 · *became severe*

57 ᴿAnd all countries came into Egypt to Joseph for to ᴿbuy *corn;* because that the famine was *so* sore in all lands.   Eze 29:12 · 27:28, 37

42 Now when Jacob saw that there was corn in Egypt, Jacob said unto his sons, Why do ye look one upon another?

2 And he said, Behold, I have heard that there is corn in Egypt:

🕊 41:50–42:2

41:45 Zaphnath-paaneah. This Egyptian name probably means something like "The God Speaks and Lives." **Asenath.** This name means "Belonging to (the Goddess) Neith." **Potipherah.** This name means "He Whom Ra (the sun god) Gave." Even though his father-in-law was the priest of a pagan god, Joseph and Asenath's sons were worshippers of the Lord, not Ra.

get you down thither, and buy for us from thence; that we may [R]live, and not die.   Ps 33:18, 19; Is 38:1

3   And Joseph's ten brethren went down to buy corn in Egypt.

4   But Benjamin, Joseph's brother, Jacob sent not with his brethren; for he said, [R]Lest peradventure mischief befall him.   v. 38

5   And the sons of Israel came to buy *corn* among those that came: for the famine was [R]in the land of Canaan.   26:1; Ac 7:11

6   And Joseph *was* the governor [R]over the land, *and* he *it was* that sold to all the people of the land: and Joseph's brethren came, and [R]bowed down themselves before him *with* their faces to the earth.   41:41, 55 · 37:7–10; 41:43; Is 60:14

7   And Joseph saw his brethren, and he knew them, but made himself [T]strange unto them, and spake roughly unto them; and he said unto them, Whence come ye? And they said, From the land of Canaan to buy food.   *a stranger*

8   And Joseph knew his brethren, but they knew not him.

9   And Joseph remembered the dreams which he dreamed of them, and said unto them, Ye *are* spies; to see the [T]nakedness of the land ye are come.   *exposed parts*

10   And they said unto him, Nay, my lord, but to buy food are thy servants come.

11   We *are* all one man's sons; we *are* [T]true *men*, thy servants are no spies.   *honest*

12   And he said unto them, Nay, but to see the nakedness of the land ye are come.

13   And they said, Thy servants *are* twelve brethren, the sons of one man in the land of Canaan; and, behold, the youngest *is* this day with our father, and one [R]*is* [T]not.   v. 32; 44:20; La 5:7 · *no more*

14   And Joseph said unto them, That *is it* that I spake unto you, saying, Ye *are* spies:

15   Hereby ye shall be proved: By the life of Pharaoh ye shall not go forth hence, except your youngest brother come hither.

16   Send one of you, and let him fetch your brother, and ye shall be kept in prison, that your words may be proved, whether *there be any* truth in you: or else by the life of Pharaoh surely ye *are* spies.

17   And he put them all together into [T]ward [R]three days.   *prison* · 40:4

18   And Joseph said unto them the third day, This do, and live; [R]*for* I fear God: Ex 1:17; Ne 5:15

19   If ye *be* true *men*, let one of your brethren be bound in the house of your prison: go ye, carry corn for the famine of your houses:

20   But [R]bring your youngest brother unto me; so shall your words be verified, and ye shall not die. And they did so.   43:5; 44:23

21   And they said one to another, We *are* verily guilty concerning our brother, in that we saw the anguish of his soul, when he besought us, and we would not hear; [R]therefore is this distress come upon us.   Pr 21:13; Ma 7:2

22   And Reuben answered them, saying, Spake I not unto you, saying, Do not sin against the child; and ye would not hear? there-

---

42:4 *Benjamin.* Jacob still played favorites, but this time there is no mention of jealousy among the other brothers as there had been before (37:8).   **42:6 *bowed down themselves before him.*** God fulfilled the dreams He gave to Joseph at the age of 17 (37:5–11).   **42:9 *Ye are spies.*** Joseph set out to learn whether his brothers had changed for the better. Would they betray each other when under pressure?   **42:18 *I fear God.*** Joseph gave his brothers a clue about who he was.   **42:22 *Spake I not unto you.*** Joseph's brothers were fearful because they knew they were guilty before God and that they deserved any punishment that God might choose to send. They must have been troubled by feelings of guilt for years, and even though they did not realize who Joseph really was, they immediately attributed their troubles to their guilt.

fore, behold, also his blood is [R] required.   Ps 9:12; Lk 11:50, 51

23   And they knew not that Joseph understood *them;* for he spake unto them by an interpreter.

24   And he turned himself [T]about from them, and wept; and returned to them again, and [T]communed with them, and took from them [R]Simeon, and bound him before their eyes.   *away · talked · 34:25*

25   Then Joseph [R]commanded to fill their sacks with corn, and to restore every man's money into his sack, and to give them provision for the way: and [R]thus did he unto them.   44:1 · [Ro 12:17, 20, 21]

26   And they laded their asses with the corn, and departed thence.

27   And as [R]one of them opened his sack to give his ass [T]provender in the inn, he [T]espied his money; for, behold, it *was* in his sack's mouth.   *43:21, 22 · feed · saw*

28   And he said unto his brethren, My money is restored; and, lo, *it is* even in my sack: and [T]their heart failed *them,* and they were afraid, saying one to another, What *is* this *that* God hath done unto us?   *their hearts sank*

29   And they came unto Jacob their father unto the land of Canaan, and told him all that befell unto them; saying,

30   The man, *who is* the lord of the land, [R]spake [T]roughly to us, and took us for spies of the country.   *v. 7 · harshly*

31   And we said unto him, We *are* [T]true *men;* we are no spies: *honest*

32   We *be* twelve brethren, sons of our father; one *is* not, and the youngest *is* this day with our father in the land of Canaan.

33   And the man, the lord of the country, said unto us, [R]Hereby shall I know that ye *are* [T]true *men;* leave one of your brethren *here* with me, and take *food for*

the famine of your households, and be gone: *vv. 15, 19, 20 · honest*

34   And bring your youngest brother unto me: then shall I know that ye *are* no spies, but *that* ye *are* true *men: so* will I deliver you your brother, and ye shall [T]traffick in the land.   *trade*

35   And it came to pass as they emptied their sacks, that, behold, every man's bundle of money *was* in his sack: and when *both* they and their father saw the bundles of money, they were afraid.

36   And Jacob their father said unto them, Me have ye [R]bereaved *of my children:* Joseph *is* not, and Simeon *is* not, and ye will take [R]Benjamin *away:* all these things are against me.   *43:14 · 35:18*

37   And Reuben spake unto his father, saying, Slay my two sons, if I bring him not to thee: deliver him into my hand, and I will bring him to thee again.

38   And he said, My son shall not go down with you; for his brother is dead, and he is left alone: if [T]mischief befall him by the way in the which ye go, then shall ye [R]bring down my gray hairs with sorrow to the grave. *calamity · 44:31*

43 And the famine *was* [R]sore[T] in the land.   45:6, 11 · *severe*

2   And it came to pass, when they had eaten up the corn which they had brought out of Egypt, their father said unto them, Go [R]again, buy us a little food.   44:25

3   And Judah spake unto him, saying, The man did solemnly [T]protest unto us, saying, Ye shall not see my face, except your brother *be* with you.   Lit. *warn*

4   If thou wilt send our brother with us, we will go down and buy thee food:

5   But if thou wilt not send *him,* we will not go down: for the man said unto us, Ye shall not see my

---

42:25 *money.* This refers to a certain weight of silver. Coins had not been invented at this time.

face, except your brother *be* with you."

6 And Israel said, Wherefore dealt ye *so* ᵀill with me, *as* to tell the man whether ye had yet a brother?   *wickedly*

7 And they said, The man asked us ᵀstraitly of our state, and of our kindred, saying, *Is* your father yet alive? have ye *another* brother? and we told him according to the tenor of these words: could we certainly know that he would say, Bring your brother down?   *pointedly about ourselves*

8 And Judah said unto Israel his father, Send the lad with me, and we will arise and go; that we may live, and not die, both we, and thou, *and* also our little ones.

9 I will be surety for him; of my hand shalt thou require him: ᴿif I bring him not unto thee, and set him before thee, then let me bear the blame for ever: Phile 18, 19

10 For except we had lingered, surely now we had returned this second time.

11 And their father Israel said unto them, If *it must be* so now, do this; take of the best fruits in the land in your vessels, and carry down the man a present, a little balm, and a little honey, spices, and myrrh, nuts, and almonds:

12 And take double money in your hand; and the money ᴿthat was brought again in the mouth of your sacks, carry *it* again in your hand; peradventure it *was* an oversight: vv. 21, 22; 42:25, 35

13 Take also your brother, and arise, go again unto the man:

14 And God Almighty ᴿgive you mercy before the man, that he may send away your other brother, and Benjamin. ᴿIf I be bereaved *of my children,* I am bereaved.   Ps 106:46 · 42:36; Es 4:16

15 And the men took that present, and they took double money in their hand, and Benjamin; and rose up, and went ᴿdown to Egypt, and stood before Joseph.   46:3, 6

16 And when Joseph saw Benjamin with them, he said to the ruler of his house, Bring *these* men home, and ᵀslay, and make ready; for *these* men shall dine with me at noon.   *slaughter an animal*

17 And the man did as Joseph ᵀbade; and the man brought the men into Joseph's house.   *ordered*

18 And the men were afraid, because they were brought into Joseph's house; and they said, Because of the money that was returned in our sacks at the first time are we brought in; that he may seek occasion against us, and fall upon us, and take us ᵀfor bondmen, and our asses.   *as slaves*

19 And they came near to the steward of Joseph's house, and they communed with him at the door of the house,

20 And said, O sir, ᴿwe came indeed down at the first time to buy food: 42:3, 10

21 And it came to pass, when we came to the ᵀinn, that we opened our sacks, and, behold, *every* man's money *was* in the mouth of his sack, our money in full weight: and we have brought it again in our hand.   *encampment*

22 And other money have we brought down in our hands to buy food: we cannot tell who put our money in our sacks.

23 And he said, Peace *be* to you, fear not: your God, and the God of your father, hath given you treasure in your sacks: I had your

---

43:8 *Send the lad with me.* Judah promised that he would keep Benjamin safe. Judah had changed tremendously (38:1). Instead of leaving the family, he protected his brother and was concerned about his father's welfare.   **43:23 *your God, and the God of your father.*** Surprisingly, the steward expressed his own faith in the God of Joseph and Jacob.

money. And he brought ᴿSimeon out unto them.   42:24
24   And the man brought the men into Joseph's house, and ᴿgave *them* water, and they washed their feet; and he gave their asses provender.   19:2; 24:32
25   And they made ready the present against Joseph ᵀcame at noon: for they heard that they should eat bread there.   *coming*
26   And when Joseph came home, they brought him the present which *was* in their hand into the house, and ᴿbowed themselves to him to the earth.   44:14
27   And he asked them of *their* welfare, and said, *Is* your father well, the old man ᴿof whom ye spake? *Is* he yet alive?   42:11, 13
28   And they answered, Thy servant our father *is* in good health, he *is* yet alive. And they bowed down their heads, and ᵀmade obeisance.   *prostrated themselves*
29   And he lifted up his eyes, and saw his brother Benjamin, ᴿhis mother's son, and said, *Is* this your younger brother, ᴿof whom ye spake unto me? And he said, God be gracious unto thee, my son.   35:17, 18 · 42:13
30   And Joseph made haste; for his ᵀbowels did yearn upon his brother: and he sought *where* to weep; and he entered into *his* chamber, and wept there.   *heart*
31   And he washed his face, and went out, and refrained himself, and said, ᵀSet on bread.   *Serve*
32   And they ᵀset on for him by himself, and for them by themselves, and for the Egyptians, which did eat with him, by themselves: because the Egyptians might not eat bread with the Hebrews; for that *is* an abomination unto the Egyptians.   *set a place*

33   And they sat before him, the firstborn according to his ᴿbirthright, and the youngest according to his youth: and the men marvelled one at another.   De 21:16, 17
34   And he took *and sent* ᵀmesses unto them from before him: but Benjamin's mess was ᴿfive times so much as any of theirs. And they drank, and were merry with him.   *servings* · 35:24; 45:22

44 And he commanded the ᴿsteward of his house, saying, ᴿFill the men's sacks *with* food, as much as they can carry, and put every man's money in his sack's mouth.   43:16 · 42:25
2   And put my cup, the silver cup, in the sack's mouth of the youngest, and his ᵀcorn money. And he did according to the word that Joseph had spoken.   *grain*
3   As soon as the morning was light, the men were sent away, they and their ᵀasses.   *donkeys*
4   *And* when they were gone out of the city, *and* not *yet* far off, Joseph said unto his steward, Up, follow after the men; and when thou dost overtake them, say unto them, Wherefore have ye ᴿrewarded evil for good?   1 Sa 25:21
5   *Is* not this *it* in which my lord drinketh, and whereby indeed he ᵀdivineth? ye have done evil in so doing.   *practises divination*
6   And he overtook them, and he spake unto them these same words.
7   And they said unto him, Wherefore saith my lord these words? ᵀGod forbid that thy servants should do according to this thing: *Far be it from us that*
8   Behold, ᴿthe money, which we found in our sacks' mouths, we brought again unto thee out of the land of Canaan: how then

---

43:26 *bowed.* For the second time (42:6) the brothers of Joseph bowed down to him, just as his dreams had predicted (37:5–11).   **43:32 *an abomination.*** This word can indicate the strongest revulsion, something that might cause physical illness (46:34). The Egyptians (who carefully shaved their entire bodies) may have been repulsed by the "hairy" Hebrews.

should we steal out of thy lord's house silver or gold? 43:21

9 With whomsoever of thy servants it be found, [R]both let him die, and we also will be my lord's [T]bondmen. 31:32 · slaves

10 And he said, Now also *let* it *be* according unto your words: he with whom it is found shall be my [T]servant; and ye shall be blameless. slave

11 Then they speedily took down every man his sack to the ground, and opened every man his sack.

12 And he searched, *and* began at the eldest, and [T]left at the youngest: and the cup was found in Benjamin's sack. finished with

13 Then they [R]rent their clothes, and laded every man his ass, and returned to the city. 37:29, 34

14 And Judah and his brethren came to Joseph's house; for he *was* yet there: and they [R]fell before him on the ground. 37:7, 10

15 And Joseph said unto them, What deed *is* this that ye have done? [T]wot ye not that such a man as I can certainly divine? know

16 And Judah said, What shall we say unto my lord? what shall we speak? or how shall we clear ourselves? God hath [R]found out the iniquity of thy servants: behold, [R]we *are* my lord's servants, both we, and *he* also with whom the cup is found. [Nu 32:23] · v. 9

17 And he said, [R]God forbid that I should do so: *but* the man in whose hand the cup is found, he shall be my servant; and as for you, get you up in peace unto your father. Pr 17:15

18 Then Judah came near unto him, and said, Oh my lord, let thy servant, I pray thee, speak a word in my lord's ears, and [R]let not thine anger burn against thy servant: for thou *art* even as Pharaoh. 18:30, 32; Ex 32:22

19 My lord asked his servants, saying, Have ye a father, or a brother?

20 And we said unto my lord, We have a father, an old man, and a child of his old age, [T]a little one; and his brother is dead, and he alone is left of his mother, and his father loveth him. who *is young*

21 And thou saidst unto thy servants, [R]Bring him down unto me, that I may set mine eyes upon him. 42:15, 20

22 And we said unto my lord, The lad cannot leave his father: for *if* he should leave his father, *his father* would die.

23 And thou saidst unto thy servants, [R]Except your youngest brother come down with you, ye shall see my face no more. 43:3, 5

24 And it came to pass when we came up unto thy servant my father, we told him the words of my lord.

25 And [R]our father said, Go again, *and* buy us a little food. 43:2

26 And we said, We cannot go down: if our youngest brother be with us, then will we go down: for we may not see the man's face, except our youngest brother *be* with us.

27 And thy servant my father said unto us, Ye know that [R]my wife bare me two *sons:* 46:19

28 And the one went out from me, and I said, Surely he is torn in pieces; and I saw him not since:

29 And if ye take this also from

44:15 *can certainly divine.* This curious verse is not very clear in meaning. Clearly a God-fearing man like Joseph who knew that only God can interpret dreams and visions (40:8) would not have been one to dabble with the occult. He may just have been trying to frighten his brothers by appearing to know things supernaturally (this would certainly have been backed up by his uncanny knowledge of their birth order in 43:33).
44:17 *get you up in peace unto your father.* Joseph was testing his brothers again, to see if they had changed in their attitude to the son of their father's favorite wife. Would they leave Benjamin a slave in Egypt as they had Joseph?

me, and [T]mischief befall him, ye shall bring down my gray hairs with sorrow to the grave. *calamity*

30 Now therefore when I come to thy servant my father, and the lad *be* not with us; seeing that his life is bound up in the lad's life;

31 It shall come to pass, when he seeth that the lad *is* not *with us,* that he will die: and thy servants shall bring down the gray hairs of thy servant our father with sorrow to the grave.

32 For thy servant became surety for the lad unto my father, saying, [R]If I bring him not unto thee, then I shall bear the blame to my father for ever. 43:9

33 Now therefore, I pray thee, [R]let thy servant [T]abide instead of the lad [T]a bondman to my lord; and let the lad go up with his brethren. Ex 32:32 · *remain · as a slave*

34 For how shall I go up to my father, and the lad *be* not with me? lest peradventure I see the evil that shall come on my father.

45 Then Joseph could not refrain himself before all them that stood by him; and he cried, Cause every man to go out from me. And there stood no man with him, while Joseph made himself known unto his brethren.

2 And he [R]wept aloud: and the Egyptians and the house of Pharaoh heard. 43:30; 46:29

3 And Joseph said unto his brethren, I *am* Joseph; doth my father yet live? And his brethren could not answer him; for they were troubled at his presence.

4 And Joseph said unto his brethren, Come near to me, I pray you. And they came near. And he said, I *am* Joseph your brother, [R]whom ye sold into Egypt. 39:1

5 Now therefore be not grieved, nor angry with yourselves, that ye sold me hither: [R]for God did send me before you to preserve life. Ps 105:16, 17

6 For these two years *hath* the [R]famine *been* in the land: and yet *there are* five years, in the which *there shall* neither *be* [T]earing nor harvest. 43:1; 47:4, 13 · *plowing*

7 And God [R]sent me before you to preserve you a [T]posterity in the earth, and to save your lives by a great deliverance. 50:20 · *a remnant*

8 So now *it was* not you *that* sent me hither, but [R]God: and he hath made me a father to Pharaoh, and lord of all his house, and a [R]ruler throughout all the land of Egypt. [Ro 8:28] · 41:43; 42:6

9 Haste ye, and go up to my father, and say unto him, Thus saith thy son Joseph, God hath made me lord of all Egypt: come down unto me, [T]tarry not: *delay*

10 And [R]thou shalt dwell in the land of Go'-shen, and thou shalt be near unto me, thou, and thy children, and thy children's children,

45:1–10

45:1–4 Real love—A profound comparison can be made between the life of Joseph and the life of Christ. Both Joseph and Jesus were persecuted unjustly (Ge 37:11–28; Ma 26:59). Both were lost to their brothers for a while (Ge 45:1–15; Ro 10:1–4). Both later forgave and restored their repentant brothers (Ge 45;1–15; Ze 8:1–8). **45:3 I am Joseph.** Joseph must have said this in Hebrew, finally dropping the ruse of the interpreter (42:23). **45:5 God did send me.** God often permits the wicked to carry out their evil plans in order to fulfill some larger purpose He has for the objects of their violence and cruelty. Since it is not possible for us to see the whole picture from God's perspective, we must exercise faith and believe that the God of all the earth will do right and that all things do work together for good to those who love God, who are called according to His purpose. Joseph was able to freely forgive his brothers partly because he recognized that their sin had been turned by God into something good. **45:10 thou shalt dwell in the land of Goshen.** This was God's plan, He had told Abraham that his descendants would live in a foreign land (15:13–16).

and thy flocks, and thy herds, and all that thou hast: 47:1
11　And there will I ᴿnourishᵀ thee; for yet *there are* five years of famine; lest thou, and thy household, and all that thou hast, come to poverty. 47:12 · *provide for*
12　And, behold, your eyes see, and the eyes of my brother Benjamin, that *it is* ᴿmy mouth that speaketh unto you. 42:23
13　And ye shall tell my father of all my glory in Egypt, and of all that ye have seen; and ye shall haste and ᴿbring down my father hither. 46:6–28; Ac 7:14
14　And he fell upon his brother Benjamin's neck, and wept; and Benjamin wept upon his neck.
15　Moreover he ᴿkissed all his brethren, and wept upon them: and after that his brethren talked with him. 48:10
16　And the ᵀfame thereof was heard in Pharaoh's house, saying, Joseph's brethren are come: and it pleased Pharaoh well, and his servants. *report*
17　And Pharaoh said unto Joseph, Say unto thy brethren, This do ye; lade your beasts, and go, get you unto the land of Canaan;
18　And take your father and your households, and come unto me: and I will give you the good of the land of Egypt, and ye shall eat ᴿthe ᵀfat of the land. 27:28; 47:6 · *best*
19　Now thou art commanded, this do ye; take you wagons out of the land of Egypt for your little ones, and for your wives, and bring your father, and come.
20　Also ᵀregard not your stuff; for the good of all the land of Egypt *is* yours. *be concerned about*
21　And the children of Israel did so: and Joseph gave them ᴿwagons,ᵀ according to the command-

ment of Pharaoh, and gave them provision for the way. 46:5 · *carts*
22　To all of them he gave each man ᴿchanges of ᵀraiment; but to Benjamin he gave three hundred *pieces* of silver, and ᴿfive changes of raiment. 2 Ki 5:5 · *clothing* · 43:34
23　And to his father he sent after this *manner*; ten asses laden with the good things of Egypt, and ten she asses laden with ᵀcorn and bread and ᵀmeat for his father ᵀby the way. *grain · food · for*
24　So he sent his brethren away, and they departed: and he said unto them, See that ye ᵀfall not out by the way. *be not troubled*
25　And they went up out of Egypt, and came into the land of Canaan unto Jacob their father,
26　And told him, saying, Joseph *is* yet alive, and he *is* governor over all the land of Egypt. ᴿAnd Jacob's heart fainted, for he believed them not. Ps 126:1
⤳27　And they told him all the words of Joseph, which he had said unto them: and when he saw the wagons which Joseph had sent to carry him, the spirit of Jacob their father revived:
28　And Israel said, *It is* enough; Joseph my son *is* yet alive: I will go and see him before I die.

46 And Israel took his journey with all that he had, and came to ᴿBe′-er–she′-ba, and offered sacrifices ᴿunto the God of his father Isaac. 28:10 · 26:24, 25
2　And God spake unto Israel ᴿin the visions of the night, and said, Jacob, Jacob. And he said, Here *am* I. 15:1; 22:11; 31:11
3　And he said, I *am* God, the God of thy father: fear not to go

⤳ 45:27–28

46:1　*Israel took his journey.* Jacob's journey to Egypt began a four-hundred-year sojourn away from the promised land of Canaan. Jacob entered Egypt with his twelve sons and their families; Jacob's descendants would leave Egypt as a small nation. **46:2　*Israel . . . Jacob.*** The fact that these names are used interchangeably indicates that the earlier negative connotations of the name Jacob had faded (31:11; 32:28; 35:10).

down into Egypt; for I will there
[R]make of thee a great nation: 12:2
4   I will go down with thee into
Egypt; and I will also surely bring
thee up *again:* and Joseph shall put
his hand upon thine eyes.
5   And Jacob rose up from Be'-er–
she'-ba: and the sons of Israel carried Jacob their father, and their
little ones, and their wives, in the
wagons [R]which Pharaoh had sent
to carry him.   45:19–21
6   And they took their cattle,
and their goods, which they had
gotten in the land of Canaan, and
came into Egypt, [R]Jacob, and all
his seed with him: Is 52:4; Ac 7:15
7   His sons, and his sons' sons
with him, his daughters, and his
sons' daughters, and all his seed
brought he with him into Egypt.
8   And these *are* the names of
the children of Israel, which came
into Egypt, Jacob and his sons:
Reuben, Jacob's firstborn.
9   And the sons of Reuben; Ha'-
noch, and [T]Phal'-lu, and Hez'-ron,
and Car'-mi.   *Pallu,* Nu 26:5
10   And the sons of Simeon; Jem'-
u-el, and Ja'-min, and O'-had, and
Ja'-chin, and Zo'-har, and Sha'-ul
the son of a Ca'-naan-i-tish woman.
11   And the sons of Levi; Ger'-
shon, Ko'-hath, and Me-ra'-ri.
12   And the sons of Judah; Er, and
O'-nan, and She'-lah, and Pha'-rez,
and Za'-rah: but Er and O'-nan
died in the land of Canaan. And
the sons of Pha'-rez were Hez'-ron
and Ha'-mul.
13   [R]And the sons of Is'-sa-char;
To'-la, and Phu'-vah, and Job, and
Shim'-ron.   1 Ch 7:1
14   And the sons of Zeb'-u-lun;
Se'-red, and E'-lon, and Jah'-le-el.
15   These *be* the [R]sons of Leah,
which she bare unto Jacob in Pa'-
dan–a'-ram, with his daughter
Dinah: all the [T]souls of his sons

and his daughters *were* thirty and
three.   35:23; 49:31 · *persons*
16   [R]And the sons of Gad; Ziph'-
i-on, and Hag'-gi, Shu'-ni, and
Ez'-bon, E'-ri, and Ar'-o-di, and
A-re'-li.   Nu 26:15
17   [R]And the sons of Asher; Jim'-
nah, and Ish'-u-ah, and Is'-u-i, and
Be-ri'-ah, and Se'-rah their sister:
and the sons of Be-ri'-ah; He'-ber,
and Mal'-chi-el.   Nu 26:44–47
18   These *are* the sons of Zil'-pah,
whom Laban gave to Leah his
daughter, and these she bare unto
Jacob, *even* sixteen souls.
19   The sons of Ra'-chel Jacob's
wife; Joseph, and Benjamin.
20   [R]And unto Joseph in the land
of Egypt were born Ma-nas'-seh
and E'-phra-im, which As'-e-nath
the daughter of Pot-i–phe'-rah priest
of On bare unto him.   48:1
21   [R]And the sons of Benjamin
were Be'-lah, and Be'-cher, and
Ash'-bel, Ge'-ra, and Na'-a-man,
E'-hi, and Rosh, Mup'-pim, and
Hup'-pim, and Ard.   1 Ch 7:6; 8:1
22   These *are* the sons of Ra'-chel,
which were born to Jacob: all the
souls *were* fourteen.
23   And the sons of Dan; [T]Hu'-
shim.   *Shuham,* Nu 26:42
24   [R]And the sons of Naph'-ta-li;
Jah'-ze-el, and Gu'-ni, and Je'-zer,
and Shil'-lem.   Nu 26:48
25   [R]These *are* the sons of Bil'-
hah, [R]which Laban gave unto Ra'-
chel his daughter, and she bare
these unto Jacob: all the souls *were*
seven.   30:5, 7 · 29:29
26   [R]All the souls that came with
Jacob into Egypt, which came out
of his loins, [R]besides Jacob's sons'
wives, all the souls *were* threescore
and six;   Ex 1:5 · 35:11
27   And the sons of Joseph,
which were born him in Egypt,
were two souls: [R]all the souls of
the house of Jacob, which came

46:11 *Gershon, Kohath, and Merari.* These sons of Levi became the founders of the Levitical families (Ex 6:16–19). Aaron and Moses descended from Kohath (Ex 6:20–25).
46:26–27 *threescore and six . . . threescore and ten.* When Joseph, his two sons, and Jacob himself are added, the number of males in Jacob's family equals seventy.

into Egypt, *were* threescore and ten. Ex 1:5; De 10:22; Ac 7:14

28 And he sent Judah before him unto Joseph, to direct his face unto Go'-shen; and they came [R]into the land of Go'-shen. 47:1
29 And Joseph made ready his [R]chariot, and went up to meet Is-rael his father, to Go'-shen, and presented himself unto him; and he [R]fell on his neck, and wept on his neck a good while. 41:43 · 45:14
30 And Israel said unto Joseph, [R]Now let me die, since I have seen thy face, because thou *art* yet alive. Lk 2:29, 30
31 And Joseph said unto his brethren, and unto his father's house, [R]I will go up, and [T]shew Pharaoh, and say unto him, My brethren, and my father's house, which *were* in the land of Canaan, are come unto me; 47:1 · *tell*
32 And the men *are* [R]shepherds, for their [T]trade hath been to feed cattle; and they have brought their flocks, and their herds, and all that they have. 47:3 · *occupation*
33 And it shall come to pass, when Pharaoh shall call you, and shall say, [R]What *is* your occupa-tion? 47:2, 3
34 That ye shall say, Thy ser-vants' trade hath been about cat-tle [R]from our youth even until now, both we, *and* also our fathers: that ye may dwell in the land of Go'-shen; for every shepherd *is*

[R]an abomination unto the Egyp-tians. 34:5; 37:17 · 43:32; Ex 8:26

47 Then Joseph came and told Pharaoh, and said, My fa-ther and my brethren, and their flocks, and their herds, and all that they have, are come out of the land of Canaan; and, behold, they *are* in [R]the land of Go'-shen. 50:8
2 And he took some of his breth-ren, *even* five men, and presented them unto Pharaoh.
3 And Pharaoh said unto his brethren, What *is* your occupa-tion? And they said unto Pharaoh, [R]Thy servants *are* shepherds, both we, *and* also our fathers. 46:32, 34
4 They said moreover unto Pha-raoh, For to sojourn in the land are we come; for thy servants have no pasture for their flocks; for the famine *is* sore in the land of Ca-naan: now therefore, we pray thee, let thy servants dwell in the land of Go'-shen.
5 And Pharaoh spake unto Jo-seph, saying, Thy father and thy brethren are come unto thee:
6 The land of Egypt *is* before thee; in the best of the land make thy father and brethren to dwell; in the land of Go'-shen let them dwell: and if thou knowest *any* men of activity among them, then make them rulers over my cattle.
7 And Joseph brought in Jacob his father, and set him before Pharaoh: and Jacob [R]blessed Pha-raoh. 2 Sa 14:22; 1 Ki 8:66; He 7:7

46:34 *every shepherd is an abomination unto the Egyptians.* God used the racial and ethnic prejudice of the Egyptians as a way of preserving the ethnic and spiritual identity of His own people. Jacob's family was already intermarrying with the Canaanites (ch. 38) and was in danger of losing its identity as the people of God. **47:5–6 *Pharoah.*** There is some uncertainty concerning the identity of this Pharaoh. Many believe he was Amenhotep I of the eleventh dynasty. Prior to his reign Egypt had suffered political and economic chaos for 200 years. Irrigation and building projects fell into ruin, and civil war raged. But Pharaoh Amenhotep was able to reunite Egypt, rebuilding the country and developing world trade. One of the reasons for his success no doubt stemmed from the fact that he was a generous man as we are told here. Not only was he generous to his own people, but he was kind to Israel. God had already promised to bless those who blessed the descendants of Abraham (Ge 12:3). The lesson is clear. If a pagan king can experience God's blessing for his liberality, how much more can born-again believers know the riches of heaven for their liberality? Solomon reminds us of this principle: "The liberal soul shall be made fat" (Pr 11:25).

8　And Pharaoh said unto Jacob, How old *art* thou?

9　And Jacob said unto Pharaoh, The days of the years of my pilgrimage *are* an [R]hundred and thirty years: few and evil have the days of the years of my life been, and [R]have not attained unto the days of the years of the life of my fathers in the days of their pilgrimage.　v. 28 · 11:10, 11; 25:7, 8; 35:28

10　And Jacob [R]blessed Pharaoh, and went out from before Pharaoh.　v. 7

11　And Joseph placed his father and his brethren, and gave them a possession in the land of Egypt, in the best of the land, in the land of [R]Ram′-e-ses, [R]as Pharaoh had commanded.　Ex 1:11; 12:37 · vv. 6, 27

12　And Joseph nourished his father, and his brethren, and all his father's household, with bread, according to *their* families.

13　And *there was* no bread in all the land; for the famine *was* very sore, so that the land of Egypt and *all* the land of Canaan [T]fainted by reason of the famine.　*languished*

14　[R]And Joseph gathered up all the money that was found in the land of Egypt, and in the land of Canaan, for the corn which they bought: and Joseph brought the money into Pharaoh's house.　42:6

15　And when money failed in the land of Egypt, and in the land of Canaan, all the Egyptians came unto Joseph, and said, Give us bread: for [R]why should we die in thy presence? for the money faileth.　v. 19

16　And Joseph said, Give your cattle; and I will give you for your cattle, if money fail.

17　And they brought their cattle unto Joseph: and Joseph gave them bread *in exchange* for horses, and for the flocks, and for the cattle of the herds, and for the asses: and he [T]fed them with bread for all their cattle for that year.　*supplied* or *refreshed*

18　When that year was ended, they came unto him the second year, and said unto him, We will not hide *it* from my lord, how that our money is spent; my lord also hath our herds of [T]cattle; there is [T]not ought left in the sight of my lord, but our bodies, and our lands:　*livestock · nothing*

19　Wherefore shall we die before thine eyes, both we and our land? buy us and our land for bread, and we and our land will be servants unto Pharaoh: and give *us* seed, that we may [R]live, and not die, that the land be not desolate.　43:8

20　And Joseph [R]bought all the land of Egypt for Pharaoh; for the Egyptians sold every man his field, because the famine prevailed over them: so the land became Pharaoh's.　Je 32:43

21　And as for the people, he [T]removed them to cities from *one* end of the borders of Egypt even to the *other* end thereof.　*moved*

22　Only the land of the priests bought he not; for the priests had a portion *assigned them* of Pharaoh, and did eat their portion which Pharaoh gave them: wherefore they sold not their lands.

23　Then Joseph said unto the people, Behold, I have bought you this day and your land for Pharaoh: lo, *here is* seed for you, and ye shall sow the land.

24　And it shall come to pass in the increase, that ye shall give the fifth *part* unto Pharaoh, and four parts shall be your own, for seed

47:12

47:8　How old art thou? Pharaoh's question suggests that the long ages of the patriarchal family were truly exceptional, even for this period. Jacob's final 147 years (47:28) were fewer than the 175 years of Abraham (25:7) and the 180 years of Isaac (35:28), but still a significant age.　**47:20　the land.** Pharaoh's ownership of all the land of Egypt would one day lead to gross abuses of power (see the Book of Exodus).

of the field, and for your food, and for them of your households, and for food for your little ones.

25 And they said, Thou hast saved our lives: let us find [T]grace in the sight of my lord, and we will be Pharaoh's servants.	favour

26 And Joseph made it a law over the land of Egypt unto this day, *that* Pharaoh should have the fifth *part;* [R]except the land of the priests only, *which* became not Pharaoh's.	v. 22

27 And Israel dwelt in the land of Egypt, in the country of Go'-shen; and they had possessions therein, and [R]grew, and multiplied exceedingly.	Ex 1:7; Ac 7:17

28 And Jacob lived in the land of Egypt seventeen years: so the whole age of Jacob was an hundred forty and seven years.

29 And the time drew nigh that Israel must die: and he called his son Joseph, and said unto him, If now I have found grace in thy sight, [R]put, I pray thee, thy hand under my thigh, and deal kindly and truly with me; [R]bury me not, I pray thee, in Egypt:	24:2–4 · 50:25

30 But I will lie with my fathers, and thou shalt carry me out of Egypt, and [R]bury me in their bury-ingplace. And he said, I will do as thou hast said.	50:5–13; He 11:21

31 And he said, Swear unto me. And he sware unto him. And [R]Is-rael bowed himself upon the bed's head.	1 Ki 1:47; He 11:21

48 And it came to pass after these things, that *one* told Jo-seph, Behold, thy father *is* sick: and he took with him his two sons, Ma-nas'-seh and E'-phra-im.

2 And *one* told Jacob, and said, Behold, thy son Joseph cometh unto thee: and Israel strengthened himself, and sat upon the bed.

3 And Jacob said unto Joseph, God [R]Almighty appeared unto me at [R]Luz in the land of Canaan, and blessed me,	43:14 · 28:13, 19; 35:6, 9

4 And said unto me, Behold, I will [R]make thee fruitful, and mul-tiply thee, and I will make of thee a multitude of people; and will [R]give this land to thy seed after thee [R]*for* an everlasting posses-sion.	46:3 · 35:12; Ex 6:8 · 17:8

5 And now thy two sons, E'-phra-im and Ma-nas'-seh, which were born unto thee in the land of Egypt before I came unto thee into Egypt, *are* mine; as Reuben and Simeon, they shall be mine.

6 And thy [T]issue, which thou be-gettest after them, shall be thine, *and* shall be called after the name of their brethren in their inheri-tance.	offspring

7 And as for me, when I came from Pa'-dan, [R]Ra'-chel died [T]by me in the land of Canaan in the way, when yet *there was* but a lit-tle way to come unto Eph'-rath: and I buried her there [T]in the way of Eph'-rath; the same *is* Beth'-le-hem.	35:9, 16, 19, 20 · beside · on

8 And Israel beheld Joseph's sons, and said, Who *are* these?

9 And Joseph said unto his fa-ther, They *are* my sons, whom God hath given me in this *place.* And he said, Bring them, I pray thee, unto me, and [R]I will bless them.	27:4; 47:15

10 Now [R]the eyes of Israel were dim [T]for age, *so that* he could not see. And he brought them near unto him; and he kissed them, and embraced them.	27:1; 1 Sa 3:2 · with

11 And Israel said unto Joseph, [R]I had not thought to see thy face:

48:8–10

47:29 *deal kindly and truly with me.* In other words, ''demonstrate to me the utmost covenant loyalty.'' Jacob showed his vigorous faith in God's promises by asking to be buried in the land promised to his descendants. **48:5–7 *Ephraim and Manasseh.*** As firstborn, Reuben should have received a double portion of the inheritance, but he had forfeited his birthright by his sins (35:22). By adopting Ephraim and Manasseh as his own sons, Jacob gave the double portion to Joseph.

and, lo, God hath shewed me also thy seed. 45:26

12 And Joseph brought them out from [T]between his knees, and he bowed himself with his face to the earth. *beside*

13 And Joseph took them both, E'-phra-im in his right hand toward Israel's left hand, and Ma-nas'-seh in his left hand toward Israel's right hand, and brought *them* near unto him.

14 And Israel stretched out his right hand, and [R]laid *it* upon E'-phra-im's head, who *was* the younger, and his left hand upon Ma-nas'-seh's head, guiding his hands wittingly; for Ma-nas'-seh *was* the firstborn. Ma 19:15

15 And he blessed Joseph, and said, God, [R]before whom my fathers Abraham and Isaac did walk, the God which fed me all my life long unto this day, 17:1

16 The Angel [R]which redeemed me from all evil, bless the lads; and let [R]my name be named on them, and the name of my fathers Abraham and Isaac; and let them grow into a multitude in the midst of the earth. 22:11, 15–18 · Ac 15:17

17 And when Joseph saw that his father [R]laid his right hand upon the head of E'-phra-im, it displeased him: and he held up his father's hand, to remove it from E'-phra-im's head unto Ma-nas'-seh's head. v. 14

18 And Joseph said unto his father, Not so, my father: for this *is* the firstborn; put thy right hand upon his head.

19 And his father refused, and said, [R]I know *it*, my son, I know *it*: he also shall become a people, and he also shall be great: but truly [R]his younger brother shall be greater than he, and his seed

shall become a multitude of nations. v. 14 · Nu 1:33, 35; De 33:17

20 And he blessed them that day, saying, [R]In thee shall Israel bless, saying, God make thee as E'-phra-im and as Ma-nas'-seh: and he set E'-phra-im before Ma-nas'-seh. Ru 4:11, 12

21 And Israel said unto Joseph, Behold, I die: but [R]God shall be with you, and bring you again unto the land of your fathers. 50:24

22 Moreover [R]I have given to thee one portion above thy brethren, which I took out of the hand [R]of the Am'-or-ite with my sword and with my bow. Jo 4:5 · 34:28

49 And Jacob called unto his sons, and said, Gather yourselves together, that I may tell you *that* which shall befall you [R]in the last days. Is 2:2; 39:6; Je 23:20; He 1:2

2 Gather yourselves together, and hear, ye sons of Jacob; and hearken unto Israel your father.

3 Reuben, thou *art* [R]my firstborn, my might, and the beginning of my strength, the excellency of dignity, and the excellency of power: 29:32

4 Unstable as water, thou shalt not excel; because thou [R]wentest up to thy father's bed; then defiledst thou *it:* he went up to my couch. 35:22; De 27:20; 1 Ch 5:1

5 Simeon and Levi *are* brethren; instruments of [T]cruelty *are in* their habitations. *violence*

6 O my soul, come not thou into their [T]secret; unto their assembly, mine honour, be not thou united: for in their [R]anger they slew a man, and in their selfwill they digged down a wall. *council* · 34:26

7 Cursed *be* their anger, for *it was* fierce; and their wrath, for it was cruel: I will divide them in Jacob, and scatter them in Israel.

48:22 *one portion above.* Jacob promised Joseph that he would one day return to the land of Canaan. The promise was fulfilled after Joseph's death (50:24–26). **49:5–7** *Simeon and Levi.* This prophecy was fulfilled when the Israelites settled in the promised land. Simeon's allotment was scattered within the larger portion of the tribe of Judah, and Levi's allotment was scattered cities throughout the land (Jos 21).

8   Judah, thou *art he* whom thy brethren shall praise: [R]thy hand *shall be* [T]in the neck of thine enemies; thy father's children shall bow down before thee.   Ps 18:40 · *on*
9   Judah *is* [R]a lion's whelp: from the prey, my son, thou art gone up: he stooped down, he couched as a lion, and as an old lion; who shall rouse him up?   Mi 5:8; [Re 5:5]
✝10   The sceptre shall not depart from Judah, nor a lawgiver from between his feet, until Shi'-loh come; and unto him *shall* the gathering of the people *be.*
11   Binding his foal unto the vine, and his ass's colt unto the choice vine; he washed his garments in wine, and his clothes in the blood of grapes:
12   His eyes *shall be* [T]red with wine, and his teeth [T]white with milk.   *darker than · whiter than*
13   Zeb'-u-lun shall dwell at the haven of the sea; and he *shall be* for an haven of ships; and his border *shall be* unto Zi'-don.
14   [R]Is'-sa-char *is* a strong ass couching down between two burdens: 1 Ch 12:32
15   And he saw that rest *was* good, and the land that *it was* pleasant; and bowed [R]his shoulder to bear, and became a servant unto tribute.   1 Sa 10:9
16   [R]Dan shall judge his people, as one of the tribes of Israel.   30:6
17   Dan shall be a serpent by the way, an adder in the path, that biteth the horse heels, so that his rider shall fall backward.
18   [R]I have waited for thy salvation, O LORD.   Ps 25:5; 40:1–3; Is 25:9

19   [R]Gad, a troop shall overcome him: but he shall overcome at the last.   30:11; De 33:20; 1 Ch 5:18
20   [R]Out of Asher his bread *shall be* [T]fat, and he shall yield royal dainties.   De 33:24; Jos 19:24–31 · *rich*
21   Naph'-ta-li *is* a hind let loose: he giveth goodly words.
22   Joseph *is* a fruitful bough, *even* a fruitful bough by a well; *whose* branches run over the wall:
23   The archers have [R]sorely[T] grieved him, and shot *at him,* and hated him: 37:4, 24; Ps 118:13 · *bitterly*
24   But his [R]bow abode in strength, and the arms of his hands were made strong by the hands of the mighty *God* of Jacob; (from thence *is* the shepherd, the stone of Israel:)   Ps 37:15
25   *Even* by the God of thy father, who shall help thee; [R]and by the Almighty, who shall bless thee with blessings of heaven above, blessings of the deep that lieth under, blessings of the breasts, and of the womb: 35:11
26   The blessings of thy father have prevailed above the blessings of my progenitors [R]unto the utmost bound of the everlasting hills: they shall be on the head of Joseph, and on the crown of the head of him that was separate from his brethren.   De 33:15
27   Benjamin shall ravin *as* a wolf: in the morning he shall devour the prey, [R]and at night he shall divide the spoil.   Ze 14:1
28   All these *are* the twelve tribes of Israel: and this *is it* that their fa-

✝ 49:10—Ac 13:23

49:10 *sceptre.* With these words, Jacob predicted that a royal line would rise from Judah's descendants. Shiloh is an obscure word, probably meaning "the one to whom it belongs." In other words, Judah's descendants would be the rulers of Israel until the coming of "Shiloh," the One to whom all royal authority belongs. In this context, Shiloh, like "the Seed," is a reference to the coming Messiah.   **49:11–12** *wine . . . blood.* The imagery in this verse describes the warfare that the Messiah will wage to establish His reign (Ps 2; 110; Re 19:11–21).   **49:24** *shepherd.* The image of God as a shepherd occurs many times in Scripture. This term would have had great significance for a family of shepherds. God shepherded and cared for their families just as they shepherded and cared for their own flocks. God is the one Good Shepherd (Ps 23; Jo 10).   **49:28** *the twelve tribes of*

Continued on the next page

ther spake unto them, and blessed them; every one according to his blessing he blessed them.

29 And he charged them, and said unto them, I ᴿam to be gathered unto my people: ᴿbury me with my fathers ᴿin the cave that *is* in the field of E′-phron the Hit′-tite,   35:29 · 2 Sa 19:37 · 23:16–20; 50:13

30 In the cave that *is* in the field of Mach-pe′-lah, which *is* before Mam′-re, in the land of Canaan, which Abraham bought with the field of E′-phron the Hit′-tite for a possession of a buryingplace.

31 There they buried Abraham and Sarah his wife; there they buried Isaac and Rebekah his wife; and there I buried Leah.

32 The purchase of the field and of the cave that *is* therein *was* from the children of Heth.

33 And when Jacob had made an end of commanding his sons, he gathered up his feet into the bed, and yielded up the ghost, and was gathered unto his people.

50 And Joseph fell upon his father's face, and wept upon him, and kissed him.

2 And Joseph commanded his servants the physicians to ᴿembalm his father: and the physicians embalmed Israel.   v. 26

3 And forty days were fulfilled for him; for so are fulfilled the days of those which are embalmed: and the Egyptians ᴿmourned for him threescore and ten days.   37:34; Nu 20:29; De 34:8

4 And when the days of his mourning were past, Joseph spake

unto ᴿthe house of Pharaoh, saying, If now I have found ᵀgrace in your eyes, speak, I pray you, in the ears of Pharaoh, saying,   Es 4:2 · *favour*

5 My father made me swear, saying, Lo, I die: in my grave which I have digged for me in the land of Canaan, there shalt thou bury me. Now therefore let me go up, I pray thee, and bury my father, and I will come again.

6 And Pharaoh said, Go up, and bury thy father, according as he made thee swear.

7 And Joseph went up to bury his father: and with him went up all the servants of Pharaoh, the elders of his house, and all the elders of the land of Egypt,

8 And all the house of Joseph, and his brethren, and his father's house: only their little ones, and their flocks, and their herds, they left in the land of Go′-shen.

9 And there went up with him both chariots and horsemen: and it was a very great company.

10 And they came to the threshingfloor of A′-tad, which *is* beyond Jordan, and there they ᴿmourned with a great and very sore lamentation: ᴿand he made a mourning for his father seven days.   Ac 8:2 · 1 Sa 31:13; Job 2:13

11 And when the inhabitants of the land, the Ca′-naan-ites, saw the mourning in the floor of A′-tad, they said, This *is* a grievous mourning to the Egyptians: wherefore

50:1

Israel. Jacob's blessings are prophecies about the destiny of each tribe. Some of the blessings are obscure, but the blessings on Judah and Joseph are clear prophecies from God about their destinies (compare Moses' blessing of the tribes of Israel, De 33).

50:5–6 *swear.* Bound by an oath, Joseph requested leave to bury his father in Canaan in a sepulchre ready for his remains. It seems today that we do not take vows as seriously as Joseph took his promise to his father, and every thing from casual promises to solemn marriage vows are broken with little remorse. Honoring vows, both in small matters and significant, honors God because He asks us to put "away lying, speak every man truth" (Ep 4:25). Broken vows result in broken hearts and ruined relationships, blasted memories, ineffective lives and testimonies. Even a foolish or wrong vow cannot be lightly set aside, but must be repented of before God. We must learn to promise wisely, and honor our promises faithfully.

the name of it was called [T]A'-bel–miz'-ra-im, which *is* beyond Jordan.   Lit. *Mourning of Egypt*

12 And his sons did unto him according as he commanded them:

13 For [R]his sons carried him into the land of Canaan, and buried him in the cave of the field of Mach-pe'-lah, which Abraham [R]bought with the field for a possession of a buryingplace of E'-phron the Hit'-tite, before Mam'-re.   49:29–31; Ac 7:16 · 23:16–20

14 And Joseph returned into Egypt, he, and his brethren, and all that went up with him to bury his father, after he had buried his father.

15 And when Joseph's brethren saw that their father was dead, [R]they said, Joseph will peradventure hate us, and will certainly requite us all the evil which we did unto him.   [Job 15:21]

16 And they sent a messenger unto Joseph, saying, Thy father did command before he died, saying,

17 So shall ye say unto Joseph, Forgive, I pray thee now, the trespass of thy brethren, and their sin; for they did unto thee evil: and now, we pray thee, forgive the trespass of the servants of the God of thy father. And Joseph wept when they spake unto him.

18 And his brethren also went and [R]fell down before his face; and they said, Behold, we *be* thy servants.   37:7–10; 41:43; 44:14

19 And Joseph said unto them, [R]Fear not: [R]for *am* I in the place of God?   45:5 · 30:2; 2 Ki 5:7

20 [R]But as for you, ye thought evil against me; *but* [R]God meant it unto good, to bring to pass, as *it is* this day, to save much people alive.   45:5, 7; Ps 56:5 · [Ac 3:13–15]

21 Now therefore fear ye not: [R]I will nourish you, and your little ones. And he comforted them, and spake kindly unto them.   [Ma 5:44]

22 And Joseph dwelt in Egypt, he, and his father's house: and Joseph lived an hundred and ten years.

23 And Joseph saw E'-phra-im's children of the third *generation:* the children also of Ma'-chir the son of Ma-nas'-seh [R]were brought up upon Joseph's knees.   30:3

24 And Joseph said unto his brethren, I die: and [R]God will surely visit you, and bring you out of this land unto the land [R]which he sware to Abraham, to Isaac, and to Jacob.   He 11:22 · 26:3; 35:12

25 And Joseph took an oath of the children of Israel, saying, God will surely visit you, and ye shall carry up my bones from hence.

26 So Joseph died, *being* an hundred and ten years old: and they embalmed him, and he was put in a coffin in Egypt.

50:19–21

50:20 *God meant it unto good.* God transformed the evil of a group of men into an exceedingly great work. Joseph not only saved the lives of numerous people in the ancient world, he also testified to the power and goodness of the living God.   **50:24 *to Abraham, to Isaac, and to Jacob.*** This phrase is the standard way of referring to God's covenant with Abraham's family (50:24; Ex 2:24; 3:16). The recital of the three names reaffirms the certainty of the promise and God's commitment to fulfill it.   **50:25 *carry up my bones.*** Hundreds of years later, Moses would keep the Israelites' oath by taking Joseph's bones with the people into the wilderness (Ex 13:19). Finally, Joshua would bury the bones of Joseph at Shechem (Jos 24:32).

The Second Book of Moses Called
EXODUS

AUTHOR: Exodus has been attributed to Moses since the time of Joshua (cf. 20:25; Jos 8:30–32), and there is a great deal of both internal and external evidence that supports Moses as the author. The claims in Joshua are backed by similar testimony from Malachi (4:4), the disciples (Jo 1:45), Paul (Ro 10:5), and Christ (Mk 7:10; 12:26; Lk 20:37; Jo 5:46–47; 7:19,22-23). Portions of the book itself claim the authorship of Moses (ch. 15; 17:8–14; 20:1–17; 24:4,7,12; 31:18; 34:1–27). The author of Exodus must have been a man familiar with the customs and climate of Egypt. Its consistency of style points to a single author and its ancient literary devices support its antiquity.

KEY VERSE: Ex 19:5–6

TIME: c. 1875–1445 B.C.

THEME: The main character of Exodus is clearly Moses. God gives him the job of leading the exodus from Egypt. Moses also takes on the job of establishing, at God's direction, the essential elements of the Jewish patterns of life and worship. He is simultaneously God's designated representative of the people to God and God's messenger and representative to the people. The critical events in Exodus are the Passover and the giving of the Ten Commandments. The remainder of the Old Testament continually refers back to God's deliverance of Israel from Egypt and the law as delivered at Sinai. In these events God's identity and purpose is revealed. There are many signs and wonders of His power. Aspects of His nature and His expectations of the people also become increasingly clear.

N OW these *are* the names of the children of Israel, which came into Egypt; every man and his household came with Jacob.

2   Reuben, Simeon, Levi, and Judah,

3   Is′-sa-char, Zeb′-u-lun, and Benjamin,

4   Dan, and Naph′-ta-li, Gad, and Asher.

5   And all the souls that came out of the loins of Jacob were ᴿseventy souls: for Joseph was in Egypt *already*.   Ge 46:26, 27

6   And Joseph died, and all his brethren, and all that generation.

7   ᴿAnd the children of Israel were fruitful, and increased abundantly, and multiplied, and waxed exceeding mighty; and the land was filled with them.   Ps 105:24

8   Now there arose up a new king over Egypt, ᴿwhich knew not Joseph.   Ac 7:18, 19

9   And he said unto his people, Behold, the people of the children of Israel *are* more and ᴿmightier than we: Ge 26:16

10   Come on, let us ᴿdeal wisely with them; lest they multiply, and it come to pass, that, when there falleth out any war, they join also unto our enemies, and fight against us, and *so* get them up out of the land.   Ps 105:25; [Pr 16:25]

11   Therefore they did set over

1:1 Israel. Originally, Israel was called Jacob. His twelve sons became the founders of the twelve tribes of the nation Israel.   **1:2–4** The sons are listed according to their mothers and their ages. Reuben, Simeon, Levi, Judah, Issachar and Zebulun were all sons of Leah. Benjamin was the son of Rachel. Dan and Naphtali were sons of Bilhah, the maid of Rachel. Gad and Asher were sons of Zilpah, the maid of Leah (for each son's birth, see Ge 29:31–35; 35:16–20,23–26).   **1:8 a new king.** This king did not remember Joseph, his privileged position in the older pharaoh's administration, his administrative skill that saved the Egyptians from starvation, and his enrichment of the pharaoh's treasury. This pharaoh was probably one of the Hyksos kings who descended from foreign invaders. Ethnically they were a minority in Egypt, and they may have perceived the growing numbers of Hebrews as a personal challenge.   **1:11 Pithom and Raamses.** These storage cities are mentioned according to the names by which

them taskmasters to afflict them with their burdens. And they built for Pharaoh ᴿtreasure cities, Pi'-thom and Ra-am'-ses.   1 Ki 9:19

12 But the more they afflicted them, the more they multiplied and grew. And they were grieved because of the children of Israel.

13 And the Egyptians made the children of Israel to ᴿserve with ᵀrigour: 5:7–19; Ge 15:13 · *harshness*

14 And they ᴿmade their lives bitter with hard bondage, in morter, and in brick, and in all manner of service in the field: all their service, wherein they made them serve, *was* with rigour.   Nu 20:15

✎ 15 And the king of Egypt spake to the ᴿHebrew midwives, of which the name of the one *was* Shiph'-rah, and the name of the other Pu'-ah: 2:6

16 And he said, When ye do the office of a midwife to the Hebrew women, and see *them* upon the stools; if it *be* a ᴿson, then ye shall kill him: but if it *be* a daughter, then she shall live.   Ma 2:16

17 But the midwives feared God, and did not ᴿas the king of Egypt commanded them, but saved the men children alive.   Da 3:16, 18

18 And the king of Egypt called for the midwives, and said unto them, Why have ye done this thing, and have saved the men children alive?

19 And the midwives said unto Pharaoh, Because the Hebrew women *are* not as the Egyptian women; for they ᵀ*are* lively, and are delivered ere the midwives come in unto them.   Bear quickly

20 ᴿTherefore God dealt well with the midwives: and the people multiplied, and waxed very mighty.   Ec 8:12; [Is 3:10]; He 6:10

21 And it came to pass, because the midwives feared God, ᴿthat he made them houses.   [Ps 127:1]

22 And Pharaoh ᵀcharged all his people, saying, ᴿEvery son that is born ye shall cast into the river, and every daughter ye shall save alive.   commanded · Ac 7:19

✎ **2** And there went ᴿa man of the house of Levi, and took *to wife* a daughter of Levi.   6:16–20

2 And the woman conceived, and bare a son: and when she saw him that he *was a* goodly *child*, she hid him three months.

3 And when she could not longer hide him, she took for him an ark of bulrushes, and daubed it with slime and with pitch, and put the child therein; and she laid *it* in the flags by the river's brink.

4 ᴿAnd his sister stood afar off, to ᵀwit what would be done to him.   15:20; Nu 26:59 · *know*

5 And the ᴿdaughter of Pharaoh came down to wash *herself* at the river; and her maidens walked along by the river's side; and when she saw the ark among

✎ 1:15–22   ✎ 2:1–10

they were known in later times. The Pharaoh Ramses (whose name presumably relates to the name of one of these cities) was not yet in power. **1:11–22 to afflict them.** Long before the sons of Israel came to Egypt, Abraham received a remarkable revelation from the Lord (Ge 15:13–16): his descendants would be strangers in a foreign land and would be enslaved and oppressed for four hundred years. "In all their affliction He was afflicted" (Is 63:9). At the point when Israel's afflictions became unbearable they cried for help, and God responded in faithfulness to His promise. **1:15 king of Egypt.** This king was probably not the Hyksos king alluded to in verses 8–14. This king, perhaps Thutmose I (c. 1539–1514 B.C.), ruled Egypt when Moses was born (2:1–10). **Hebrew midwives.** The names of these women (Shiphrah—"beautiful one," and Puah—"splendid one") are preserved in this account because they were godly women with a courageous faith. At the same time, the names of the pharaohs—the "important" people of the day—are omitted. **1:17 feared.** The Hebrew term for "fear" is the word regularly used for piety, obedience, and the true worship of God (20:20; Ge 22:12). **2:2 bare a son.** This was not their first child, both Miriam and Aaron were older than Moses (v. 4; 7:7).

the flags, she sent her maid to fetch it.   7:15; Ac 7:21

6   And when she had opened *it*, she saw the child: and, behold, the babe wept. And she had compassion on him, and said, This *is one* of the Hebrews' children.

7   Then said his sister to Pharaoh's daughter, Shall I go and call to thee a nurse of the Hebrew women, that she may nurse the child for thee?

8   And Pharaoh's daughter said to her, Go. And the maid went and called the child's mother.

9   And Pharaoh's daughter said unto her, Take this child away, and nurse it for me, and I will give *thee* thy wages. And the woman took the child, and nursed it.

10   And the child grew, and she brought him unto Pharaoh's daughter, and he became her son. And she called his name ᵀMoses: and she said, Because I drew him out of the water.   Lit. *Drawn Out*

11   And it came to pass in those days, when Moses was grown, that he went out unto his brethren, and looked on their burdens: and he spied an Egyptian smiting an Hebrew, one of his brethren.

12   And he looked this way and that way, and when he saw that there *was* no man, he slew the Egyptian, and hid him in the sand.

13   And ᴿwhen he went out the second day, behold, two men of the Hebrews ᴿstrove together: and he said to him that did the wrong, Wherefore smitest thou thy fellow?   Ac 7:26–28 · Pr 25:8

14   And he said, ᴿWho made thee a prince and a judge over us? intendest thou to kill me, as thou killedst the Egyptian? And Moses ᴿfeared, and said, Surely this thing is known.   Ge 19:9 · Ju 6:27

15   Now when Pharaoh heard this thing, he sought to slay Moses. But ᴿMoses fled from the face of Pharaoh, and dwelt in the land of ᴿMid'-i-an: and he sat down by a well.   Ac 7:29 · 3:1

16   Now the priest of Mid'-i-an had seven daughters: ᴿand they came and drew *water*, and filled the ᴿtroughs to water their father's flock.   Ge 24:11 · Ge 30:38

17   And the ᴿshepherds came and drove them away: but Moses stood up and helped them, and watered their flock.   1 Sa 25:7

18   And when they came to Reu'-el their father, he said, How *is it that* ye are come so soon to day?

19   And they said, An Egyptian delivered us out of the hand of the

2:6 *one of the Hebrews' children.* A Hebrew baby would have been circumcised on the eighth day. Although circumcision was practiced in Egypt, it was not done to infants. Upon unwrapping the infant's clothing, the women would have seen his special mark. **2:10** *Because I drew him out.* In Hebrew, the name Moses means "he who draws out." In this manner, Moses' name can refer the reader to the living God, who is the true Deliverer, and also to Moses, who was used by God to deliver the Israelites from the Red Sea (chs. 14–15). The one who was drawn out of water would be the means of drawing the Israelite nation out of water. **2:11** *when Moses was grown.* The years of Moses' experience in the pharaoh's court are not detailed. Yet Stephen, the New Testament martyr, reported the long-held and surely accurate tradition: "Moses was educated in all the learning of the Egyptians, and he was a man of power in words and deeds" (Ac 7:22). The training Moses received was the best education the world had to offer at the time. He would have learned three languages: Egyptian, Akkadian, and Hebrew. When Moses came into the presence of Pharaoh to demand freedom for his people, he was no "uneducated slave," but had received an education on par with the king's. **2:15** *the land of Midian.* This is the region of the Sinai Peninsula and Arabian deserts where the seminomadic Midianites lived (for the Abrahamic origin of this people group, see Ge 25:1). **2:16** *the priest of Midian.* This man appears to have been a foreigner who had come to worship the true and living God. **2:18** *Reuel.* Reuel is also called Jethro (4:18). **2:19** *An Egyptian.* Moses apparently still dressed and spoke as an Egyptian, rather than as a Hebrew.

shepherds, and also drew *water* enough for us, and watered the flock.

20 And he said unto his daughters, And where *is* he? why *is* it *that* ye have left the man? call him, that he may eat bread.

21 And Moses was content to dwell with the man: and he gave Moses Zip-po'-rah his daughter.

22 And she bare *him* a son, and he called his name Ger'-shom: for he said, I have been [R]a stranger in a strange land.   Ge 23:4; Le 25:23

23 And it came to pass in process of time, that the king of Egypt died: and the children of Israel sighed by reason of the bondage, and they cried, and [R]their cry came up unto God by reason of the bondage.   3:7, 9; Jam 5:4

24 And God heard their groaning, and God remembered his [R]covenant with Abraham, with Isaac, and with Jacob.   Ge 12:1-3

25 And God [R]looked upon the children of Israel, and God had respect unto *them*.   4:31; Lk 1:25

3 Now Moses kept the flock of Je'-thro his father in law, the priest of Mid'-i-an: and he led the flock to the backside of the desert, and came to the mountain of God, *even* to Ho'-reb.

2 And [R]the angel of the LORD appeared unto him in a flame of fire out of the midst of a bush: and he looked, and, behold, the bush burned with fire, and the bush *was* not consumed.   Lk 20:37

3 And Moses said, I will now turn aside, and see this great sight, why the bush is not burnt.

4 And when the LORD saw that he turned aside to see, God called [R]unto him out of the midst of the bush, and said, Moses, Moses. And he said, Here *am* I.   De 33:16

5 And he said, Draw not nigh hither: put off thy shoes from off thy feet, for the place whereon thou standest *is* holy ground.

6 Moreover he said, [R]I *am* the God of thy father, the God of Abraham, the God of Isaac, and the God of Jacob. And Moses hid his face; for [R]he was afraid to look upon God.   Ge 28:13 · 1 Ki 19:13

7 And the LORD said, [R]I have surely seen the affliction of my people which *are* in Egypt, and have heard their cry by reason of their taskmasters; [R]for I know their sorrows;   Ps 106:44 · Ge 18:21

8 And I am come down to deliver them out of the hand of the Egyptians, and to bring them up out of that land unto a good land and a large, unto a land [R]flowing with milk and honey; unto the place of the Ca'-naan-ites, and the Hit'-tites, and the Am'-or-ites, and the Per'-iz-zites, and the Hi'-vites, and the Jeb'-u-sites.   13:5; Je 11:5

9 Now therefore, behold, [R]the cry of the children of Israel is come

2:21-22   3:1-6

2:22 Gershom. Gershom means "a stranger there." Moses was doubly removed from his land. He and his people, the Israelites, were strangers in Egypt, and now he was estranged even from his people.   **2:23 the king of Egypt died.** The death of Pharaoh (likely Thutmose III, who died about 1447 B.C.) meant that Moses could return to Egypt (4:19).   **3:1 Horeb.** This alternate name for Mount Sinai means "desolate place." Yet because of God's appearance on the mountain, this desolate place would become holy. Usually the site of this mountain is identified as Jebel el-Musa, a mountain in the southern Sinai Peninsula.   **3:2 angel.** The word *angel* simply means "messenger" (Mal 1:1). In the Old Testament, the term "the Angel of the Lord" is used numerous times, and is identified with God as well as being distinguished from Him. In this passage, having mentioned that the Angel of the Lord appeared to Moses, it is immediately established that it was the Lord Himself (v. 4).   **3:6 the God of thy father.** God identified Himself as the God worshiped by Abraham, Isaac, and Jacob. In announcing these names, the Lord was assuring Moses that the covenant He had made with them was still intact.

unto me: and I have also seen the oppression wherewith the Egyptians oppress them.   2:23

10 ᴿCome now therefore, and I will send thee unto Pharaoh, that thou mayest bring forth my people the children of Israel out of Egypt.   Ge 15:13, 14; Ac 7:6, 7

11 And Moses said unto God, ᴿWho *am* I, that I should go unto Pharaoh, and that I should bring forth the children of Israel out of Egypt?   4:10; 6:12; 1 Sa 18:18

12 And he said, Certainly I will be with thee; and this *shall be* a ᴿtoken unto thee, that I have sent thee: When thou hast brought forth the people out of Egypt, ye shall serve God upon this mountain.   4:8; 19:3

13 And Moses said unto God, Behold, *when* I come unto the children of Israel, and shall say unto them, The God of your fathers hath sent me unto you; and they shall say to me, What *is* his name? what shall I say unto them?

14 And God said unto Moses, ɪ ᴀᴍ ᴛʜᴀᴛ ɪ ᴀᴍ: and he said, Thus shalt thou say unto the children of Israel, ᴿI ᴀᴍ hath sent me unto you.   [Jo 8:24; He 13:8; Re 1:8; 4:8]

15 And God said moreover unto Moses, Thus shalt thou say unto the children of Israel, The Lᴏʀᴅ God of your fathers, the God of Abraham, the God of Isaac, and the God of Jacob, hath sent me unto you: this *is* ᴿmy name for ever, and this *is* my memorial unto all generations.   Ps 30:4; 102:12; 135:13

16 Go, and gather the elders of Israel together, and say unto them, The Lᴏʀᴅ God of your fathers, the God of Abraham, of Isaac, and of Jacob, appeared unto me, saying, ᴿI have surely visited you, and *seen* that which is done to you in Egypt: Lk 1:68

17 And I have said, ᴿI will bring you up out of the affliction of Egypt unto the land of the Ca′-naan-ites, and the Hit′-tites, and the Am′-or-ites, and the Per′-iz-zites, and the Hi′-vites, and the Jeb′-u-sites, unto a land flowing with milk and honey.   Ge 15:13–21

18 And they shall hearken to thy voice: and thou shalt come, thou and the elders of Israel, unto the king of Egypt, and ye shall say unto him, The Lᴏʀᴅ God of the Hebrews hath ᴿmet with us: and now let us go, we beseech thee, three days' journey into the wilderness, that we may sacrifice to the Lᴏʀᴅ our God.   Nu 23:3, 4

19 And I am sure that the king of Egypt ᴿwill not let you go, no, not by a mighty hand.   5:2

20 And I will ᴿstretch out my hand, and smite Egypt with ᴿall my wonders which I will do in the midst thereof: and after that he will let you go.   6:6; 9:15 · Ac 7:36

21 And ᴿI will give this people favour in the sight of the Egyptians: and it shall come to pass, that, when ye go, ye shall not go empty: 1 Ki 8:50; Ps 105:37; 106:46

22 But every woman shall borrow of her neighbour, and of her that sojourneth in her house, jewels of silver, and jewels of gold, and raiment: and ye shall put *them* upon your sons, and upon your

3:13–14   3:22

3:14 *I AM THAT I AM.* The One who spoke to Moses declared Himself to be the Eternal One—uncaused and independent. Only the Creator of all things can call Himself the *I AM* in the absolute sense; all other creatures are in debt to Him for their existence. But in addition, God the Creator declares His relationship with the people of Israel. The future tense of the Hebrew verb related to God's name is used in verse 12: The I AM *will be* with His people. Thus God declares His covenantal relationship with Israel by His name. **3:15 *The Lᴏʀᴅ.*** Lᴏʀᴅ in capital letters is the form translators have chosen to represent the Hebrew name YHWH (also transliterated Yahweh, or Jehovah). The Hebrew word meaning "I Am" used in verse 14 is very similar.

daughters; and ye shall [T]spoil the Egyptians. *plunder*

4 And Moses answered and said, But, behold, they will not believe me, nor hearken unto my voice: for they will say, The LORD hath not appeared unto thee.

2 And the LORD said unto him, What *is* that in thine hand? And he said, A rod.

3 And he said, Cast it on the ground. And he cast it on the ground, and it became a serpent; and Moses fled from before it.

4 And the LORD said unto Moses, Put forth thine hand, and take it by the tail. And he put forth his hand, and caught it, and it became a rod in his hand:

5 That they may believe that the [R]LORD God of their fathers, the God of Abraham, the God of Isaac, and the God of Jacob, hath appeared unto thee. Ge 28:13; 48:15

6 And the LORD said furthermore unto him, Put now thine hand into thy bosom. And he put his hand into his bosom: and when he took it out, behold, his hand *was* leprous as snow.

7 And he said, Put thine hand into thy bosom again. And he put his hand into his bosom again; and plucked it out of his bosom, and, behold, [R]it was turned again as his *other* flesh. Nu 12:13–15

8 And it shall come to pass, if they will not believe thee, neither hearken to the voice of the [R]first sign, that they will believe the voice of the latter sign. 7:6–13

9 And it shall come to pass, if they will not believe also these two signs, neither hearken unto thy voice, that thou shalt take of the water of the [T]river, and pour *it* upon the dry *land:* and [R]the water which thou takest out of the river shall become blood upon the dry *land.* The Nile · 7:19, 20

10 And Moses said unto the LORD, O my Lord, I *am* not eloquent, neither heretofore, nor since thou hast spoken unto thy servant: but [R]I *am* slow of speech, and of a slow tongue. 6:12; Je 1:6

11 And the LORD said unto him, [R]Who hath made man's mouth? or who maketh the dumb, or deaf, or the seeing, or the blind? have not I the LORD? Ps 94:9; 146:8; Ma 11:5

12 Now therefore go, and I will be [R]with thy mouth, and teach thee what thou shalt say. Is 50:4

13 And he said, O my Lord, [R]send, I pray thee, by the hand *of him whom* thou wilt send. Jon 1:3

14 And the anger of the LORD was kindled against Moses, and he said, *Is* not Aaron the Levite thy [R]brother? I know that he can speak well. And also, behold, he cometh forth to meet thee: and when he seeth thee, he will be glad in his heart. Nu 26:59

15 And thou shalt speak unto him, and [R]put words in his mouth: and I will be with thy mouth, and with his mouth, and will teach you what ye shall do. Nu 23:5, 12

16 And he shall be thy spokesman unto the people: and he shall be, *even* he shall be to thee instead of a mouth, and [R]thou shalt be to him instead of God. 7:1, 2

17 And thou shalt take this rod in thine hand, wherewith thou shalt do signs.

18 And Moses went and returned to Je'-thro his father in law, and said unto him, Let me go, I pray thee, and return unto my brethren which *are* in Egypt, and see whether they be yet alive. And Je'-thro said to Moses, [R]Go in peace. Ge 43:23; Ju 18:6

19 And the LORD said unto Moses in Mid'-i-an, Go, return into Egypt:

4:1–5 4:6–8

4:6–7 *leprous.* The term *leprosy* included a wide variety of skin diseases. **4:19** *which sought thy life.* God promised Abraham that those who persecuted Israel would be

Continued on the next page

for ᴿall the men are dead which sought thy life.   Ma 2:20

20 And Moses took his wife and his sons, and set them upon an ass, and he returned to the land of Egypt: and Moses took ᴿthe rod of God in his hand.   v. 17; 17:9; Nu 20:8

21 And the LORD said unto Moses, When thou goest to return into Egypt, see that thou do all those wonders before Pharaoh, which I have put in thine hand: but ᴿI will harden his heart, that he shall not let the people go.   7:3

22 And thou shalt say unto Pharaoh, Thus saith the LORD, Israel *is* my son, *even* my firstborn:

23 And I say unto thee, Let my son go, that he may serve me: and if thou refuse to let him go, behold, ᴿI will slay thy son, *even* thy firstborn.   Ps 105:36; 135:8; 136:10

24 And it came to pass by the way in the inn, that the LORD ᴿmet him, and sought to kill him.   3:18

25 Then Zip-po'-rah took ᴿa sharp stone, and cut off the foreskin of her son, and cast *it* at his feet, and said, Surely a bloody husband *art* thou to me.   Ge 17:14

26 So he let him go: then she said, A bloody husband *thou art*, because of the circumcision.

27 And the LORD said to Aaron,

Go into the wilderness ᴿto meet Moses. And he went, and met him in ᴿthe mount of God, and kissed him.   v. 14 · 3:1; 18:5; 24:13

28 And Moses told Aaron all the words of the LORD who had sent him, and all the ᴿsigns which he had commanded him.   vv. 8, 9

29 And Moses and Aaron ᴿwent and gathered together all the elders of the children of Israel: 12:21

30 ᴿAnd Aaron spake all the words which the LORD had spoken unto Moses, and did the signs in the sight of the people.   vv. 15, 16

31 And the people believed: and when they heard that the LORD had visited the children of Israel, and that he ᴿhad looked upon their affliction, then they bowed their heads and worshipped.   2:25

5 And afterward Moses and Aaron went in, and told Pharaoh, Thus saith the LORD God of Israel, Let my people go, that they may hold ᴿa feast unto me in the wilderness.   3:18; 7:16; 10:9

2 And Pharaoh said, ᴿWho *is* the LORD, that I should obey his voice to let Israel go? I know not the LORD, neither will I let Israel go.   2 Ki 18:35; 2 Ch 32:14; Job 21:15

4:25

judged (Ge 12:3), and it is clear from history that God fulfilled His promise. In Exodus 14, the Egyptians attempted to destroy the Israelites by driving them into the Red Sea, but instead were drowned themselves. Those who threw Daniel to the lions were devoured by those same beasts (Da 6). Haman plotted to destroy all the Jews in Persia, and ended up signing his own death warrant (Es 7). "The LORD preserveth all them that love him" (Ps 145:20). **4:21 Pharaoh.** This Pharaoh was most likely Amenhotep II (c. 1447–1421). **I will harden his heart.** Some interpret these words to mean that God would confirm what Pharaoh had stubbornly determined to do. In the first five plagues, the hardening was attributed to Pharaoh (7:13,22; 8:15,19,32; 9:7). Then for the sixth plague, God hardened a heart that had already rejected Him (9:12). Others insist that God had determined Pharaoh's negative response to Moses long before Pharaoh could harden his heart. These interpreters point to this verse and to 9:16, in which God says that He raised up Pharaoh for the purpose of demonstrating His power. **4:24 sought to kill him.** The precise meaning of this passage is unclear. Apparently someone in Moses' family was not circumcised, despite God's command. It is possible that Moses had kept one of his sons uncircumcised in order to please his Midianite family. (The Midianites practiced adult male circumcision at the time of marriage, rather than infant circumcision as the Hebrews did). Moses' neglect of the sign of God's covenant was very serious, especially for the future leader of God's people. **5:2 Who is the LORD.** Later these words would haunt Pharaoh (12:31–32). Meanwhile, Pharaoh believed himself to be a

3   And they said, The God of the Hebrews hath [R]met with us: let us go, we pray thee, three days' journey into the desert, and sacrifice unto the LORD our God; lest he fall upon us with [R]pestilence, or with the sword.   4:24; Nu 23:3 · 9:15
4   And the king of Egypt said unto them, Wherefore do ye, Moses and Aaron, let the people from their works? get you unto your [R]burdens.   1:11; 2:11; 6:6
5   And Pharaoh said, Behold, the people of the land now *are* [R]many, and ye make them rest from their burdens.   1:7, 9
6   And Pharaoh commanded the same day the [R]taskmasters of the people, and their officers, saying,   vv. 10, 13, 14; 1:11; 3:7
7   Ye shall no more give the people straw to make [R]brick, as heretofore: let them go and gather straw for themselves.   1:14
8   And the [T]tale of the bricks, which they did make heretofore, ye shall lay upon them; ye shall not diminish *ought* thereof: for they *be* idle; therefore they cry, saying, Let us go *and* sacrifice to our God.   *quota*
9   Let there more work be laid upon the men, that they may labour therein; and let them not regard [T]vain words.   *false*
10   And the taskmasters of the people went out, and their officers, and they spake to the people, saying, Thus saith Pharaoh, I will not give you straw.
11   Go ye, get you straw where ye can find it: yet not ought of your work shall be diminished.

12   So the people were scattered abroad throughout all the land of Egypt to gather stubble instead of straw.
13   And the taskmasters [T]hasted *them*, saying, Fulfil your works, *your* daily tasks, as when there was straw.   *forced them to hurry*
14   And the [R]officers of the children of Israel, which Pharaoh's taskmasters had set over them, were [R]beaten, *and* demanded, Wherefore have ye not fulfilled your task in making brick both yesterday and to day, as heretofore?   v. 6 · Is 10:24
15   Then the officers of the children of Israel came and cried unto Pharaoh, saying, Wherefore dealest thou thus with thy servants?
16   There is no straw given unto thy servants, and they say to us, Make brick: and, behold, thy servants *are* beaten; but the fault *is* in thine own people.
17   But he said, Ye *are* idle, *ye are* idle: therefore ye say, Let us go *and* do sacrifice to the LORD.
18   Go therefore now, *and* work; for there shall no straw be given you, yet shall ye deliver the [T]tale of bricks.   *quota*
19   And the officers of the children of Israel did see *that* they *were* [T]in evil *case*, after it was said, Ye shall not [T]minish *ought* from your bricks of your daily task.   *in trouble · diminish any*
20   And they met Moses and Aaron, who stood in the way, as they came forth from Pharaoh:
21   [R]And they said unto them, The LORD look upon you, and judge;

god in his own right, and certainly felt no need to cave in to the demands of a god who claimed to be the champion of his slave labor force. **5:7–9 *let them go and gather straw for themselves.*** It is easy to rationalize our cruel treatment of others when it is in our selfish interest to do so. We often hear "Pharaoh's reasoning" about minority peoples or people on welfare today. Of course laziness and discontent is a genuine problem for some who are on welfare, or who feel oppressed (just as it is for some who were born into wealth and privilege), but too often we turn off the concern we should have for the poor and oppressed with the comfortable conviction that somehow they deserve their problems. If we continue in this attitude, we may be sure that God will judge our sin. God cares deeply for the weak, the poor, and the downtrodden; if we are genuine disciples we will share His concern.

because ye have made our savour to be abhorred in the eyes of Pharaoh, and in the eyes of his servants, to put a sword in their hand to slay us.   6:9; 14:11; 15:24; 16:2

22   And Moses returned unto the LORD, and said, Lord, wherefore hast thou ᵀso evil entreated this people? why *is* it *that* thou hast sent me?   *brought trouble on*

23   For since I came to Pharaoh to speak in thy name, he hath done evil to this people; neither hast thou delivered thy people at all.

6 Then the LORD said unto Moses, Now shalt thou see what I will do to Pharaoh: for ᴿwith a strong hand shall he let them go, and with a strong hand ᴿshall he drive them out of his land.   3:19 · 12:31, 33, 39

2   And God spake unto Moses, and said unto him, I *am* ᵀthe LORD: He *YHWH*

3   And I appeared unto Abraham, unto Isaac, and unto Jacob, by *the name of* God Almighty, but by my name ᵀJE-HO'-VAH was I not known to them.   He *YHWH*

4   ᴿAnd I have also established my covenant with them, to give them the land of Canaan, the land of their pilgrimage, ᴿwherein they were strangers.   Ge 12:7 · Ge 28:4

5   And ᴿI have also heard the groaning of the children of Israel, whom the Egyptians keep in bondage; and I have remembered my covenant.   [Job 34:28]; Ac 7:34

6   Wherefore say unto the children of Israel, I *am* the LORD, and ᴿI will bring you out from under the burdens of the Egyptians, and I will rid you out of their bondage, and I will ᴿredeem you with a stretched out arm, and with great judgments: Ps 136:11 · Ne 1:10

7   And I will take you to me for a people, and ᴿI will be to you a God: and ye shall know that I *am* the LORD your God, which bringeth you out from under the burdens of the Egyptians.   De 29:13

8   And I will bring you in unto the land, concerning the which I did ᴿswear to give it to Abraham, to Isaac, and to Jacob; and I will give it you for an heritage: I *am* the LORD.   Ge 15:18; 26:3; Nu 14:30

9   And Moses spake so unto the children of Israel: but they hearkened not unto Moses for anguish of spirit, and for cruel bondage.

10   And the LORD spake unto Moses, saying,

11   Go in, speak unto Pharaoh king of Egypt, that he let the children of Israel go out of his land.

12   And Moses spake before the LORD, saying, Behold, the children of Israel have not hearkened unto me; how then shall Pharaoh hear me, ᴿwho *am* of uncircumcised lips?   v. 30; 4:10; Je 1:6

13   And the LORD spake unto Moses and unto Aaron, and gave them a charge unto the children of Israel, and unto Pharaoh king of Egypt, to bring the children of Israel out of the land of Egypt.

14   These *be* the heads of their fathers' houses: ᴿThe sons of Reuben the firstborn of Israel; Ha'-noch, and Pal'-lu, Hez'-ron, and Car'-mi: these *be* the families of Reuben.   Nu 26:5–11; 1 Ch 5:3

15   ᴿAnd the sons of Simeon; Jem'-u-el, and Ja'-min, and O'-had, and Ja'-chin, and Zo'-har, and Sha'-ul the son of a Ca'-naan-i-tish woman: these *are* the families of Simeon.   Nu 26:12–14

16   And these *are* the names of the sons of Levi according to their generations; Ger'-shon, and Ko'-hath,

---

5:23 *speak in thy name.* It seems that Moses expected Pharaoh to cave in as soon as he heard the use of the Lord's name Yahweh (3:13–15; 5:1). Yet God had warned Moses that Pharaoh would do the opposite (3:19; 4:21).   **6:4** *my covenant.* This is a reference to the Abrahamic covenant celebrated in Genesis (Ge 12:1–3,7; 15:12–21; 17:1–16; 22:15–18).   **6:14–27** *their fathers'.* The family history of Moses, Aaron, and Miriam is important because all of Israel's future priests would come from this family.

and Me-ra'-ri: and the years of the life of Levi *were* an hundred thirty and seven years.

17 [R]The sons of Ger'-shon; Lib'-ni, and Shim'-i, according to their families.   1 Ch 6:17

18 And the sons of Ko'-hath; Am'-ram, and Iz'-har, and He'-bron, and Uz-zi'-el: and the years of the life of Ko'-hath *were* an hundred thirty and three years.

19 And [R]the sons of Me-ra'-ri; Ma'-ha-li and Mu'-shi: these *are* the families of Levi according to their generations.   1 Ch 6:19; 23:21

20 And [R]Am'-ram took him Joch'-e-bed his father's sister to wife; and she bare him Aaron and Moses: and the years of the life of Am'-ram *were* an hundred and thirty and seven years. 2:1, 2

21 And the sons of Iz'-har; Ko'-rah, and Ne'-pheg, and Zich'-ri.

22 And [R]the sons of Uz-zi'-el; Mish'-a-el, and El'-za-phan, and Zith'-ri.   Le 10:4

23 And Aaron took him E-lish'-e-ba, daughter of [R]Am-min'-a-dab, sister of Na-ash'-on, to wife; and she bare him [R]Na'-dab, and A-bi'-hu, [R]E-le-a'-zar, and Ith'-a-mar.   Ru 4:19, 20 · Le 10:1 · 28:1

24 And [R]the sons of Ko'-rah; As'-sir, and El'-ka-nah, and A-bi'-a-saph: these *are* the families of the Kor'-hites.   Nu 26:11

25 And E-le-a'-zar Aaron's son took him *one* of the daughters of Pu'-ti-el to wife; and she bare him Phin'-e-has: these *are* the heads of the fathers of the Levites according to their families.

26 These *are* that Aaron and Mo-ses, to whom the LORD said, Bring out the children of Israel from the land of Egypt according to their [R]armies.   12:17, 51; Nu 33:1

27 These *are* they which spake to Pharaoh king of Egypt, [R]to bring out the children of Israel from Egypt: these *are* that Moses and Aaron.   v. 13; 32:7; 33:1; Ps 77:20

28 And it came to pass on the day *when* the LORD spake unto Moses in the land of Egypt,

29 That the LORD spake unto Mo-ses, saying, I *am* the LORD: [R]speak thou unto Pharaoh king of Egypt all that I say unto thee.   7:2

30 And Moses said before the LORD, Behold, [R]I *am* of uncircum-cised lips, and how shall Pharaoh hearken unto me?   4:10; Je 1:6

7 And the LORD said unto Mo-ses, See, I have made thee a god to Pharaoh: and Aaron thy brother shall be [R]thy prophet. 4:15

2 Thou [R]shalt speak all that I command thee: and Aaron thy brother shall speak unto Pharaoh, that he send the children of Israel out of his land.   De 18:18

3 And I will harden Pharaoh's heart, and [R]multiply my [R]signs and my wonders in the land of Egypt.   11:9; Ac 7:36 · 4:7; De 4:34

4 But Pharaoh shall not hearken unto you, that I may lay my hand upon Egypt, and bring forth mine armies, *and* my people the children of Israel, out of the land of Egypt [R]by great judgments.   6:6

5 And the Egyptians [R]shall know that I *am* the LORD, when I stretch forth mine hand upon Egypt, and bring out the children of Israel from among them.   8:22

6 And Moses and Aaron [R]did as the LORD commanded them, so did they.   v. 2

7 And Moses *was* fourscore years old, and [R]Aaron fourscore

6:20   7:1–12:51

7:1 thy prophet. As Moses was the prophet of the Lord, so Aaron became Moses' prophet. Aaron would speak for Moses, for a prophet was the "mouth" of the one who sent him. **7:3 I will harden Pharaoh's heart.** It was a part of God's plan that Pharaoh would be inflexibly stubborn, thus setting the scene for God to deliver His people by powerful signs and wonders. **7:7 fourscore . . . fourscore and three.** These men

Continued on the next page

and three years old, when they spake unto Pharaoh.   Nu 33:39

8   And the LORD spake unto Moses and unto Aaron, saying,

9   When Pharaoh shall speak unto you, saying, [R]Shew a miracle for you: then thou shalt say unto Aaron, Take thy rod, and cast *it* before Pharaoh, *and* it shall become a serpent.   Is 7:11; Jo 2:18

10   And Moses and Aaron went in unto Pharaoh, and they did so [R]as the LORD had commanded: and Aaron cast down his rod before Pharaoh, and before his servants, and it [R]became a serpent.   v. 9 · 4:3

11   Then Pharaoh also called the wise men and [R]the sorcerers: now the magicians of Egypt, they also did in like manner with their enchantments.   Da 2:2; 2 Ti 3:8, 9

12   For they cast down every man his rod, and they became serpents: but Aaron's rod swallowed up their rods.

13   And he hardened Pharaoh's heart, that he hearkened not unto them; as the LORD had said.

14   And the LORD said unto Moses, [R]Pharaoh's heart *is* hardened, he refuseth to let the people go.   8:15; 10:1, 20, 27

15   Get thee unto Pharaoh in the morning; lo, he goeth out unto the water; and thou shalt stand by the river's brink [T]against he come; and [R]the rod which was turned to a serpent shalt thou take in thine hand.   *to meet him* · v. 10; 4:2, 3

16   And thou shalt say unto him, [R]The LORD God of the Hebrews hath sent me unto thee, saying, Let my people go, [R]that they may [T]serve me in the wilderness: and, behold, hitherto thou wouldest not hear.   4:22 · 3:12, 18; 4:23 · *worship*

17   Thus saith the LORD, In this thou shalt know that I *am* the LORD: behold, I will smite with the rod that *is* in mine hand upon the waters which *are* in the river, and they shall be turned to blood.

18   And the fish that *is* in the river shall die, and the river shall stink; and the Egyptians shall [R]lothe[T] to drink of the water of the river.   v. 24 · *be weary of*

19   And the LORD spake unto Moses, Say unto Aaron, Take thy rod, and stretch out thine hand upon the waters of Egypt, upon their streams, upon their rivers, and

🔥 7:9–13

had already lived as long as the average lifetime of our day before their principal life work had begun. Moses and Aaron each lived another forty years as leaders of the nation of Israel. **7:9–10 Miracles**—A miracle could be defined as the temporary suspension of some natural law (like turning a staff into a snake), or the manipulation of natural forces (such as weather) over which humans ordinarily have no jurisdiction. We tend to look for miracles only for their immediate results (healing, retribution, etc.), but in the Bible miracles are always for a "sign." The focus isn't on the actual miracle, but on the supernatural as a sign of God's working in the situation. This is clearly seen in the miracles of Jesus. If His purpose had just been physical healing, He would have set up a clinic and systematically healed everyone. Instead, His miracles were for a sign, to let people know who and what He was (Jo 20:30–31). **7:11 *wise men . . . sorcerers . . . magicians.*** The king's wise men were his counselors, men of learning and insight. In ancient times, the "wise men" of a court were often associated with occult practices. The power of these men may have been in trickery and slight-of-hand illusions, or demonic power. Later the royal courts of Israel had wise men (1 Ki 4:34; Pr 25:1), but the black arts of sorcery, divination, and astrology were forbidden (De 18:9–14). **7:12 *his rod . . . serpents.*** The text does not say whether this was a genuine transformation or a trick of Pharaoh's evil sorcerers. Whatever the case, their serpents were no match for the serpent of God's sign. **7:15 *unto the water . . . the river's brink.*** Pharaoh went to the waters of the Nile not to bathe but to be empowered. Pharaoh's bath in the Nile was a sacred Egyptian rite connected to his claim of divinity. The plague on the waters of the Nile was a direct attack on the Egyptian religion.

upon their ponds, and upon all their pools of water, that they may become blood; and *that* there may be blood throughout all the land of Egypt, both in *vessels of* wood, and in *vessels of* stone.

20 And Moses and Aaron did so, as the LORD commanded; and he lifted up the rod, and smote the waters that *were* in the river, in the sight of Pharaoh, and in the sight of his servants; and all the ᴿwaters that *were* in the river were turned to blood.   Ps 78:44

21 And the fish that *was* in the river died; and the river stank, and the Egyptians ᴿcould not drink of the water of the river; and there was blood throughout all the land of Egypt.   v. 18

22 And the magicians of Egypt did ᴿso with their enchantments: and Pharaoh's heart was hardened, neither did he hearken unto them; as the LORD had said.   8:7

23 And Pharaoh turned and went into his house, neither did he set his heart to this also.

24 And all the Egyptians digged round about the river for water to drink; for they could not drink of the water of the river.

25 And seven days were fulfilled, after that the LORD had smitten the river.

8 And the LORD spake unto Moses, Go unto Pharaoh, and say unto him, Thus saith the LORD, Let my people go, ᴿthat they may serve me.   3:12, 18; 4:23; 5:1, 3

2 And if thou ᴿrefuse to let *them* go, behold, I will smite all thy borders with frogs: 7:14; 9:2

3 And the river shall bring forth frogs abundantly, which shall go up and come into thine house, and into

thy bedchamber, and upon thy bed, and into the house of thy servants, and upon thy people, and into thine ovens, and into thy kneading-troughs:

4 And the frogs shall come up both on thee, and upon thy people, and upon all thy servants.

5 And the LORD spake unto Moses, Say unto Aaron, Stretch forth thine hand with thy rod over the streams, over the rivers, and over the ponds, and cause frogs to come up upon the land of Egypt.

6 And Aaron stretched out his hand over the waters of Egypt; and ᴿthe frogs came up, and covered the land of Egypt.   Ps 105:30

7 ᴿAnd the magicians did so with their ᵀenchantments, and brought up frogs upon the land of Egypt.   7:11, 22 · *secret arts*

8 Then Pharaoh called for Moses and Aaron, and said, ᴿIntreat the LORD, that he may take away the frogs from me, and from my people; and I will let the people go, that they may do sacrifice unto the LORD.   1 Ki 13:6

9 And Moses said unto Pharaoh, Glory over me: when shall I intreat for thee, and for thy servants, and for thy people, to destroy the frogs from thee and thy houses, *that* they may remain in the river only?

10 And he said, To morrow. And he said, *Be it* according to thy word: that thou mayest know that ᴿ*there is* none like unto the LORD our God.   1 Ch 17:20; Ps 86:8; Is 46:9

11 And the frogs shall depart from thee, and from thy houses, and from thy servants, and from thy people; they shall remain in the river only.

7:23 *turned and went into his house.* Pharaoh showed his utter disdain for the revelation of God's power and his complete lack of concern for the suffering of his own people. **8:7 *the magicians . . . with their enchantments.*** We do not know how or in what quantities the magicians produced frogs, but doing so hardly helped the situation. Clearly the power they had was not strong enough to counteract the plagues God sent. **8:8 *called for Moses and Aaron.*** Note that Pharaoh did not turn to his magicians to relieve the land of the frogs.

12 And Moses and Aaron went out from Pharaoh: and Moses [R]cried unto the LORD because of the frogs which he had brought against Pharaoh.   9:33; 10:18; 32:11

13 And the LORD did according to the word of Moses; and the frogs died out of the houses, out of the villages, and out of the fields.

14 And they gathered them together upon heaps: and the land stank.

15 But when Pharaoh saw that there was respite, [R]he hardened his heart, and hearkened not unto them; as the LORD had said.   9:34

16 And the LORD said unto Moses, Say unto Aaron, Stretch out thy rod, and smite the dust of the land, that it may become lice throughout all the land of Egypt.

17 And they did so; for Aaron stretched out his hand with his rod, and smote the dust of the earth, and [R]it became lice in man, and in beast; all the dust of the land became lice throughout all the land of Egypt.   Ps 105:31

18 And the magicians did so with their enchantments to bring forth lice, but they [R]could not: so there were lice upon man, and upon beast.   Da 5:8; 2 Ti 3:8, 9

19 Then the magicians said unto Pharaoh, This *is* the finger of God: and Pharaoh's heart was hardened, and he hearkened not unto them; as the LORD had said.

20 And the LORD said unto Moses, [R]Rise up early in the morning, and stand before Pharaoh; lo, he cometh forth to the water; and say unto him, Thus saith the LORD, Let my people go, that they may serve me.   7:15; 9:13

21 Else, if thou wilt not let my people go, behold, I will send swarms *of flies* upon thee, and upon thy servants, and upon thy people, and into thy houses: and the houses of the Egyptians shall be full of swarms *of flies*, and also the ground whereon they *are*.

22 And I will sever in that day the land of Go'-shen, in which my people dwell, that no swarms *of flies* shall be there; to the end thou mayest know that I *am* the LORD in the midst of the [R]earth.   9:29

23 And I will put a division between my people and thy people: to morrow shall this [R]sign be.   4:8

24 And the LORD did so; and [R]there came a grievous swarm *of flies* into the house of Pharaoh, and *into* his servants' houses, and into all the land of Egypt: the land was [T]corrupted by reason of the swarm *of flies*.   Ps 105:31 · *destroyed*

25 And Pharaoh called for Moses and for Aaron, and said, Go ye, sacrifice to your God in the land.

26 And Moses said, It is not meet so to do; for we shall sacrifice the abomination of the Egyptians to the LORD our God: lo, shall we sacrifice the abomination of the Egyptians before their eyes, and will they not stone us?

27 We will go [R]three days' journey into the wilderness, and sac-

---

8:15 Instability—The action of this Egyptian Pharaoh is a case study in instability. He gave permission for the people to go and then changed his mind more than once. He alternated between denying the power of God and actually admitting his sin. Pharaoh was a rebel against God, tossed about by his own lack of integrity. Believers can take warning from Pharaoh's behavior. The apostle James informs us that a double-minded man is unstable in all his ways (James 1:8). But stability isn't something we achieve by sheer willpower. Real integrity and stability comes from the security of our relationship with God. **8:18 *The magicians did . . . enchantments . . . but they could not.*** Perhaps the lack of announcement meant they had no time to prepare. The magicians could not duplicate God's work; further proof that this was no trick, but the hand of God. **8:26 *the abomination of the Egyptians.*** Moses employed the ethnic and cultural sensibilities of the Egyptians to free the Israelites (Ge 43:32; 46:34). The sacrificial animals of Israel would include sheep, something the Egyptians regarded as detestable.

rifice to the LORD our God, as [R]he shall command us.   3:18; 5:3 · 3:12
28 And Pharaoh said, I will let you go, that ye may sacrifice to the LORD your God in the wilderness; only ye shall not go very far away: [R]intreat for me.   1 Ki 13:6
29 And Moses said, Behold, I go out from thee, and I will intreat the LORD that the swarms *of flies* may depart from Pharaoh, from his servants, and from his people, to morrow: but let not Pharaoh [R]deal deceitfully any more in not letting the people go to sacrifice to the LORD.   vv. 8, 15
30 And Moses went out from Pharaoh, and intreated the LORD.
31 And the LORD did according to the word of Moses; and he removed the swarms *of flies* from Pharaoh, from his servants, and from his people; there remained not one.
32 And Pharaoh [R]hardened his heart at this time also, neither would he let the people go. Ps 52:2
9 Then the LORD said unto Moses, Go in unto Pharaoh, and tell him, Thus saith the LORD God of the Hebrews, Let my people go, that they may [R]serve me.   7:16
2 For if thou [R]refuse to let *them* go, and wilt hold them still,   8:2
3 Behold, the [R]hand of the LORD is upon thy cattle which *is* in the field, upon the horses, upon the asses, upon the camels, upon the oxen, and upon the sheep: *there shall be* a very [T]grievous murrain.   Ps 39:10 · *severe pestilence*
4 And the LORD shall [T]sever between the cattle of Israel and the cattle of Egypt: and there shall nothing die of all *that is* the children's of Israel.   *make a difference*
5 And the LORD appointed a set time, saying, To morrow the LORD shall do this thing in the land.
6 And the LORD did that thing on the morrow, and all the cattle

of Egypt died: but of the cattle of the children of Israel died not one.
7 And Pharaoh sent, and, behold, there was not one of the cattle of the Israelites dead. And the heart of Pharaoh was hardened, and he did not let the people go.
8 And the LORD said unto Moses and unto Aaron, Take to you handfuls of ashes of the furnace, and let Moses sprinkle it toward the heaven in the sight of Pharaoh.
9 And it shall become small dust in all the land of Egypt, and shall be [R]a boil breaking forth *with* [T]blains upon man, and upon beast, throughout all the land of Egypt.   De 28:27; Re 16:2 · *sores*
10 And they took ashes of the furnace, and stood before Pharaoh; and Moses sprinkled it up toward heaven; and it became a boil breaking forth *with* blains upon man, and upon beast.
11 And the magicians could not stand before Moses because of the [R]boils; for the boil was upon the magicians, and upon all the Egyptians.   Job 2:7; Re 16:1, 2
12 And the LORD hardened the heart of Pharaoh, and he [R]hearkened not unto them; [R]as the LORD had spoken unto Moses. 7:13 · 4:21
13 And the LORD said unto Moses, [R]Rise up early in the morning, and stand before Pharaoh, and say unto him, Thus saith the LORD God of the Hebrews, Let my people go, that they may [R]serve me.   8:20 · v. 1
14 For I will at this time send all my plagues upon thine heart, and upon thy servants, and upon thy people; [R]that thou mayest know that *there is* none like me in all the earth.   Ps 86:8; Is 45:5–8; Je 10:6, 7
15 For now I will [R]stretch out my hand, that I may smite thee and thy people with [R]pestilence; and thou shalt be cut off from the earth.   3:20; 7:5 · 5:3

9:11 *for the boil was upon the magicians.* The reference to the hapless magicians is almost humorous. Not only were they powerless, but they also suffered from the plague.

16 And in very deed for this *cause* have I raised thee up, for to ^Rshew *in* thee my power; and that my name may be declared throughout all the earth.   11:9; 14:17

17 As yet exaltest thou thyself against my people, that thou wilt not let them go?

18 Behold, to morrow about this time I will cause it to rain a very grievous hail, such as hath not been in Egypt since the foundation thereof even until now.

19 Send therefore now, *and* gather thy cattle, and all that thou hast in the field; *for upon* every man and beast which shall be found in the field, and shall not be brought home, the hail shall come down upon them, and they shall die.

20 He that feared the word of the LORD among the servants of Pharaoh made his servants and his cattle flee into the houses:

21 And he that regarded not the word of the LORD left his servants and his cattle in the field.

22 And the LORD said unto Moses, Stretch forth thine hand toward heaven, that there may be ^Rhail in all the land of Egypt, upon man, and upon beast, and upon every herb of the field, throughout the land of Egypt.   Re 16:21

23 And Moses stretched forth his rod toward heaven: and ^Rthe LORD sent thunder and hail, and the fire ran along upon the ground; and the LORD rained hail upon the land of Egypt.   Re 8:7

24 So there was hail, and fire mingled with the hail, very grievous, such as there was none like it in all the land of Egypt since it became a nation.

25 And the ^Rhail smote throughout all the land of Egypt all that *was* in the field, both man and beast; and the hail smote every herb of the field, and brake every tree of the field.   Ps 78:47; 105:32, 33

26 ^ROnly in the land of Go'-shen, where the children of Israel *were,* was there no hail.   12:13; Is 32:18, 19

27 And Pharaoh sent, and called for Moses and Aaron, and said unto them, I have sinned this time: ^Rthe LORD *is* righteous, and I and my people *are* wicked.   2 Ch 12:6

28 ^RIntreat the LORD (for *it is* enough) that there be no *more* mighty thunderings and hail; and I will let you go, and ye shall stay no longer.   8:8, 28; 10:17; Ac 8:24

29 And Moses said unto him, As soon as I am gone out of the city, I will ^Rspread abroad my hands unto the LORD; *and* the thunder shall cease, neither shall there be any more hail; that thou mayest know how that the ^Rearth *is* the LORD's.   Is 1:15 · Ps 24:1; 1 Co 10:26, 28

30 But as for thee and thy servants, ^RI know that ye will not yet fear the LORD God.   8:29; [Is 26:10]

31 And the flax and the barley was smitten: for the barley *was* in the ear, and the flax *was* bolled.

32 But the wheat and the ^Trie were not smitten: for they *were* ^Tnot grown up.   spelt · Lit. *darkened*

33 And Moses went out of the city from Pharaoh, and ^Rspread abroad his hands unto the LORD:

9:16 *for this cause have I raised thee up.* God used Pharaoh's stubbornness and disobedience to demonstrate His power. Pharaoh was not only an evil ruler in a powerful state; he was an evil man, ungodly, and unrighteous. Pharaoh set himself up as a god who maintained the stability of his kingdom. The Lord's judgment on him was an appropriate response to this fraud. **9:17 *exaltest thou thyself.*** Pharaoh was behaving like the king of Tyrus (Eze 28:1–10) and Satan, whom the king of Tyrus emulated (Eze 28:11–19). **9:19 *gather thy cattle.*** The fact that God was judging Pharaoh does not mean that He was unmerciful. The Lord could have destroyed Pharaoh and his people in a moment (v. 15), but instead He warned them of the calamities about to befall them. Apparently some of the Egyptians took the word of the Lord seriously. **9:27 *I have sinned.*** This was a stunning admission for such a proud man. Sadly, these words of contrition would not hold. Pharaoh repeated them later (10:16–17), only to take them back in the end.

and the thunders and hail ceased, and the rain was not poured upon the earth.   v. 29; 8:12
34 And when Pharaoh saw that the rain and the hail and the thunders were ceased, he sinned yet more, and hardened his heart, he and his servants.
35 And ᴿthe heart of Pharaoh was hardened, neither would he let the children of Israel go; as the LORD had spoken by Moses.   4:21

10 And the LORD said unto Moses, Go in unto Pharaoh: ᴿfor I have hardened his heart, and the heart of his servants, ᴿthat I might shew these my signs before him: Jo 12:40; Ro 9:18 · 7:4
2 And that ᴿthou mayest tell in the ears of thy son, and of thy son's son, what things I have wrought in Egypt, and my signs which I have done among them; that ye may ᴿknow how that I *am* the LORD.   Ps 44:1; 78:5; Joel 1:3 · 7:5, 17
3 And Moses and Aaron came in unto Pharaoh, and said unto him, Thus saith the LORD God of the Hebrews, How long wilt thou refuse to ᴿhumble thyself before me? let my people go, that they may serve me.   [Jam 4:10; 1 Pe 5:6]
4 Else, if thou refuse to let my people go, behold, to morrow will I bring the locusts into thy coast:
5 And they shall cover the face of the earth, that one cannot be able to see the earth: and ᴿthey shall eat the residue of that which is escaped, which remaineth unto you from the hail, and shall eat

every tree which groweth for you out of the field: 9:32; Joel 1:4; 2:25
6 And they shall ᴿfill thy houses, and the houses of all thy servants, and the houses of all the Egyptians; which neither thy fathers, nor thy fathers' fathers have seen, since the day that they were upon the earth unto this day. And he turned himself, and went out from Pharaoh.   8:3, 21
7 And Pharaoh's servants said unto him, How long shall this man be ᴿa snare unto us? let the men go, that they may serve the LORD their God: knowest thou not yet that Egypt is destroyed?   23:33
8 And Moses and Aaron were brought again unto Pharaoh: and he said unto them, Go, serve the LORD your God: *but* who *are* they that shall go?
9 And Moses said, We will go with our young and with our old, with our sons and with our daughters, with our flocks and with our herds will we go; for we *must hold* a feast unto the LORD.
10 And he said unto them, Let the LORD be so with you, as I will let you go, and your little ones: look *to it;* for evil *is* before you.
11 Not so: go now ye *that are* men, and serve the LORD; for that ye did desire. And they were driven out from Pharaoh's presence.
12 And the LORD said unto Moses, ᴿStretch out thine hand over the land of Egypt for the locusts, that they may come up upon the land of Egypt, and ᴿeat every herb

---

10:1 *I have hardened his heart.* Three verbs are used in Exodus to describe God's hardening of Pharaoh's heart. Usually the verb meaning "to make hard" is used (4:21). In 7:3 the verb "to make stiff" is used. Here the Hebrew verb that means "to make heavy" or "to make insensitive" is used. **10:3** *refuse to humble thyself.* Pharaoh's pride was his undoing. He believed himself to be a god and paraded himself like one. God resists the proud but gives grace to the humble (Ps 18:27; 1 Pe 5:5). **10:12–16 Repentance**—In Exodus 9 and 10 there are two vivid examples of "foxhole religion" recorded for us. This kind of "faith" freely acknowledges the person and power of God during a terrible crisis, and then promptly forgets all about Him when the danger passes. Just like little children, we want to avert punishment by saying, "I'm sorry, I'm sorry!" and then go about our business as usual. God is not interested in empty "I've sinned" confessions. Only true repentance from the heart is acceptable to God.

of the land, *even* all that the hail hath left. 7:19 · vv. 5, 15

13 And Moses stretched forth his rod over the land of Egypt, and the LORD brought an east wind upon the land all that day, and all *that* night; *and* when it was morning, the east wind brought the locusts.

14 And [R]the locusts went up over all the land of Egypt, and rested in all the coasts of Egypt: very grievous *were they;* [R]before them there were no such locusts as they, neither after them shall be such. Ps 78:46 · Joel 2:1–11; Re 9:3

15 For they [R]covered the face of the whole earth, so that the land was darkened; and they [R]did eat every herb of the land, and all the fruit of the trees which the hail had left: and there remained not any green thing in the trees, or in the herbs of the field, through all the land of Egypt. v. 5 · Ps 105:35

16 Then Pharaoh called for Moses and Aaron in haste; and he said, I have sinned against the LORD your God, and against you.

17 Now therefore forgive, I pray thee, my sin only this once, and [R]intreat[T] the LORD your God, that he may take away from me this death only. 9:28; 1 Ki 13:6 · *pray to*

18 And he [R]went out from Pharaoh, and intreated the LORD. 8:30

19 And the LORD turned a mighty strong west wind, which took away the locusts, and cast them [R]into the Red sea; there remained not one locust in all the [T]coasts of Egypt. Joel 2:20 · *territory*

20 But the LORD [R]hardened Pharaoh's heart, so that he would not let the children of Israel go. 4:21

21 And the LORD said unto Moses, Stretch out thine hand toward heaven, that there may be darkness over the land of Egypt, even darkness *which* may be felt.

22 And Moses stretched forth his hand toward heaven; and there was a thick darkness in all the land of Egypt three days:

23 They saw not one another, neither rose any from his place for three days: [R]but all the children of Israel had light in their dwellings. 8:22, 23

24 And Pharaoh called unto Moses, and said, Go ye, serve the LORD; only let your flocks and your herds be stayed: let your [R]little ones also go with you. v. 10

25 And Moses said, Thou must give us also sacrifices and burnt offerings, that we may sacrifice unto the LORD our God.

26 Our [R]cattle also shall go with us; there shall not an hoof be left behind; for thereof must we take to serve the LORD our God; and we know not with what we must serve the LORD, until we come thither. v. 9

27 But the LORD [R]hardened Pharaoh's heart, and he would not let them go. vv. 1, 20; 4:21; 14:4, 8

28 And Pharaoh said unto him, [R]Get thee from me, take heed to thyself, see my face no more; for in *that* day thou seest my face thou shalt die. v. 11

29 And Moses said, Thou hast spoken well, [R]I will see thy face again no more. 11:8; He 11:27

11 And the LORD said unto Moses, Yet will I bring one plague *more* upon Pharaoh, and upon Egypt; afterwards he will let you go hence: [R]when he shall let *you* go, he shall surely thrust you out hence altogether. 6:1; 12:39

2 Speak now in the ears of the

10:20 *But the LORD hardened Pharaoh's heart.* See 3:19; 4:21; 5:2; 7:3, 13–14.
10:22 thick darkness. This calamity was another direct attack on the Egyptian religious system. They worshipped many gods, but none so much as the sun. An enshrouding darkness that lasted three days was a clear statement that their gods, their Pharaoh with his supposed control of nature, and all Pharaoh's counselors were, in reality, helpless before the God of Israel. **10:27 *But the LORD hardened Pharaoh's heart.*** See 3:19; 4:21; 5:2; 7:3, 13–14.

people, and let every man ᵀborrow of his neighbour, and every woman of her neighbour, jewels of silver, and jewels of gold.   *ask*

3   ᴿAnd the LORD gave the people favour in the sight of the Egyptians. Moreover the man ᴿMoses *was* very great in the land of Egypt, in the sight of Pharaoh's servants, and in the sight of the people.   Ps 106:46 · 2 Sa 7:9; Es 9:4

4   And Moses said, Thus saith the LORD, About midnight will I go out into the midst of Egypt:

5   And ᴿall the firstborn in the land of Egypt shall die, from the firstborn of Pharaoh that sitteth upon his throne, even unto the firstborn of the maidservant that *is* behind the mill; and all the firstborn of beasts.   Ps 78:51; Am 4:10

6   ᴿAnd there shall be a great cry throughout all the land of Egypt, ᴿsuch as there was none like it, nor shall be like it any more.   12:30; Am 5:17 · 10:14

7   But against any of the children of Israel shall not a dog move his tongue, against man or beast: that ye may know how that the LORD doth put a difference between the Egyptians and Israel.

8   And ᴿall these thy servants shall come down unto me, and bow down themselves unto me, saying, Get thee out, and all the people that follow thee: and after that I will go out. ᴿAnd he went out from Pharaoh in a great anger.   12:31–33 · 10:29; He 11:27

9   And the LORD said unto Moses, ᴿPharaoh shall not hearken unto you; that ᴿmy wonders may be multiplied in the land of Egypt.   3:19; 7:4; 10:1 · 7:3; 9:16

10   And Moses and Aaron did all these wonders before Pharaoh: ᴿand the LORD hardened Pharaoh's heart, so that he would not let the children of Israel go out of his land.   Is 63:17; Jo 12:40; Ro 2:5

12 And the LORD spake unto Moses and Aaron in the land of Egypt, saying,

2   ᴿThis month *shall be* unto you the beginning of months: it *shall be* the first month of the year to you.   13:4; 23:15; 34:18; De 16:1

11:3 *favour.* After all that had happened, we might suppose that the Egyptians would have universally hated the Hebrews. Instead, most of the people felt positively towards them, even Pharaoh's own servants.   **11:7** *a difference between the Egyptians and Israel.* The institution of the Passover accentuated this great distinction. The Lord in His mercy protected His people even as He executed judgment on those who opposed Him.   **11:9–10** *wonders.* We tend to think that if God would only send a miracle, people would have to believe. Sadly, history shows that this is not true. Often those individuals who have seen God's mightiest miracles have responded by displaying a total lack of faith. Pharaoh had all the proof one could want of who God was, and did not believe. The Pharisees saw a man raised from the dead, and wanted to kill both the man and his healer (Jo 11:53; 12:9–11). God desires us to believe His word by faith, and not be dependent on supernatural and external signs and wonders. Miracles are signs, just as the creation itself is a sign of God's power and authority (Ro 1:19–20), but a person whose heart is hardened toward God will not be any more impressed with a miracle than with a sunset.   **12:1–14 The Passover**—There was only one Passover. The Passover feast has always been one of the primary elements of Jewish religious tradition and is their way of remembering the "pass over" by the Lord, sparing the people of a visit by "the destroyer" (v. 23). By celebrating it, Jews remember one of the key elements of their history. It points to their national identity and to their deliverance as a community of faith. One could say that it was a defining moment of their faith. For the Christian, the event clearly foreshadows the cross of Christ. He is our Passover Lamb who delivers us from death by taking it all on Himself. The parallels between Exodus 12 and the Christian Communion service are noteworthy (1 Co 11:23–26).   **12:2** *unto you the beginning of months.* This month, called Abib in 13:4 corresponds to April/May and is also called Nisan. The Hebrew people began to mark time in relation to the time of their departure from Egypt.

3   Speak ye unto all the congregation of Israel, saying, In the tenth *day* of this month they shall take to them every man a lamb, according to the house of *their* fathers, a lamb for an house:

4   And if the household be too little for the lamb, let him and his neighbour next unto his house take *it* according to the number of the ᵀsouls; every man according to his eating shall make your count for the lamb.   *persons*

5   Your lamb shall be ᴿwithout blemish, a male of the first year: ye shall take *it* out from the sheep, or from the goats: Mal 1:8

6   And ye shall keep it up until the ᴿfourteenth day of the same month: and the whole assembly of the congregation of Israel shall kill it in the evening.   Le 23:5

7   And they shall take of the blood, and strike *it* on the two side posts and on the upper door post of the houses, wherein they shall eat it.

8   And they shall eat the flesh in that night, ᴿroast with fire, and unleavened bread; *and* with bitter *herbs* they shall eat it.   De 16:7

9   Eat not of it raw, nor sodden at all with water, but roast *with* fire; his head with his legs, and with the purtenance thereof.

10   ᴿAnd ye shall let nothing of it remain until the morning; and that which remaineth of it until the morning ye shall burn with fire.   16:19; 23:18; 34:25

11   And thus shall ye eat it; *with* your loins girded, your shoes on your feet, and your staff in your hand; and ye shall eat it in haste: ᴿit *is* the Lᴏʀᴅ's passover.   vv. 13, 21

12   For I ᴿwill pass through the land of Egypt this night, and will smite all the firstborn in the land of Egypt, both man and beast; and ᴿagainst all the gods of Egypt I will execute judgment: ᴿI *am* the Lᴏʀᴅ.   11:4, 5 · Nu 33:4 · 6:2

13   And the blood shall be to you for a ᵀtoken upon the houses where ye *are:* and when I see the blood, I will pass over you, and the plague shall not be upon you to destroy *you*, when I smite the land of Egypt.   *sign*

14   And this day shall be unto you ᴿfor a memorial; and ye shall keep it a ᴿfeast to the Lᴏʀᴅ throughout your generations; ye shall keep it a feast by an ordinance for ever.   13:9 · Le 23:4, 5

15   ᴿSeven days shall ye eat unleavened bread; even the first day ye shall put away leaven out of your houses: for whosoever eateth leavened bread from the first day until the seventh day, ᴿthat soul shall be cut off from Israel.   Le 23:6 · Ge 17:14; Nu 9:13

16   And in the first day *there shall be* ᴿan holy convocation, and in the seventh day there shall be an holy convocation to you; no manner of work shall be done in them, save *that* which every man must eat, that only may be done of you.   Le 23:2, 7, 8; Nu 28:18, 25

17   And ye shall observe *the feast of* unleavened bread; for in this selfsame day have I brought your

✍ 12:13

12:5 *without blemish.* Sacrifice was not a way to get rid of unwanted animals. Only the very best lambs were suitable. The Passover lamb sacrificed for the Israelites was meant as a picture of the coming death of the perfect, sinless Savior, Jesus Christ. **12:8** *unleavened bread . . . bitter herbs.* The Passover meal is full of symbolism, the unleavened bread reminded them that the first Passover was eaten in haste, ready for flight. The bitter herbs were a reminder of the bitterness of the slavery from which they were rescued.   **12:12** *I will pass through . . . will smite.* The repetition of the pronoun *I* emphasizes that God did this, not an angel or some other agent.   **12:13** *token.* The term "token" can mean a reminder, memorial, or symbol, as it does here, or a miracle that points to the power of God.

armies ^Rout of the land of Egypt: therefore shall ye observe this day in your generations by an ordinance for ever. Nu 33:1

18 ^RIn the first *month*, on the fourteenth day of the month at even, ye shall eat unleavened bread, until the one and twentieth day of the month at even. v. 2

19 ^RSeven days shall there be no leaven found in your houses: for whosoever eateth that which is leavened, even that soul shall be cut off from the congregation of Israel, whether he be a stranger, or born in the land. 23:15; 34:18

20 Ye shall eat nothing leavened; in all your habitations shall ye eat unleavened bread.

21 Then Moses called for all the elders of Israel, and said unto them, ^RDraw out and take you a lamb according to your families, and kill the passover. Nu 9:4

22 ^RAnd ye shall take a bunch of hyssop, and dip *it* in the blood that *is* in the bason, and ^Rstrike the lintel and the two side posts with the blood that *is* in the bason; and none of you shall go out at the door of his house until the morning. He 11:28 · v. 7

23 For the LORD will pass through to smite the Egyptians; and when he seeth the blood upon the lintel, and on the two side posts, the LORD will pass over the door, and will not suffer ^Rthe destroyer to come in unto your houses to smite *you*. 1 Co 10:10

24 And ye shall ^Robserve this thing for an ordinance to thee and to thy sons for ever. 13:5, 10

25 And it shall come to pass, when ye be come to the land which the LORD will give you, according as he hath promised, that ye shall keep this service.

26 ^RAnd it shall come to pass, when your children shall say unto you, What mean ye by this service? De 32:7; Jos 4:6; Ps 78:6

27 That ye shall say, ^RIt *is* the sacrifice of the LORD's passover, who passed over the houses of the children of Israel in Egypt, when he smote the Egyptians, and delivered our houses. And the people ^Rbowed the head and worshipped. v. 11 · 4:31

28 And the children of Israel went away, and ^Rdid as the LORD had commanded Moses and Aaron, so did they. [He 11:28]

29 And it came to pass, that at midnight ^Rthe LORD smote all the firstborn in the land of Egypt, from the firstborn of Pharaoh that sat on his throne unto the firstborn of the captive that *was* in the dungeon; and all the firstborn of cattle. Nu 8:17; 33:4; Ps 135:8; 136:10

30 And Pharaoh rose up in the night, he, and all his servants, and all the Egyptians; and there was a great cry in Egypt; for *there was* not a house where *there was* not one dead.

31 And he ^Rcalled for Moses and Aaron by night, and said, Rise up, *and* get you forth from among my people, ^Rboth ye and the children of Israel; and go, serve the LORD, as ye have said. 10:28, 29 · 8:25; 11:1

32 ^RAlso take your flocks and

12:29 *and all the firstborn of cattle.* Though not nearly as awful as the death of firstborn children, the death of the livestock was a blow to the Egyptians economically. These deaths were also attacks on the power of their gods (v. 12). **12:29–33** *the LORD smote all the firstborn.* In the Passover we have a summary of God's eternal plan of salvation. Jesus, the final sacrifice, was killed at the time of the Passover feast; His blood provides salvation from eternal death. Note some similarities between the first and final Passover: (1) the blood of an innocent sacrifice must be shed, (2) the sacrifice must be blameless, and (3) the shed blood must be applied by faith. **12:32** *and bless me also.* At last Pharaoh capitulated (10:9,26). The death of his son—and the deaths of firstborn sons everywhere—must have shattered him to the core of his being.

your herds, as ye have said, and be gone; and bless me also. 10:9, 26
33 ᴿAnd the Egyptians were ᴿurgent upon the people, that they might send them out of the land in haste; for they said, We *be* all dead *men*.   10:7 · 11:8; Ps 105:38
34 And the people took their dough before it was leavened, their ᵀkneadingtroughs being bound up in their clothes upon their shoulders.   *dough*
35 And the children of Israel did according to the word of Moses; and they ᵀborrowed of the Egyptians jewels of silver, and jewels of gold, and raiment: *asked from*
36 And the LORD gave the people favour in the sight of the Egyptians, so that they ᵀlent unto them *such things as they required*. And they ᵀspoiled the Egyptians.   *granted · plundered*
37 And the children of Israel journeyed from ᴿRam'-e-ses to Suc'-coth, about six hundred thousand on foot *that were* men, beside children.   Ge 47:11; Nu 33:3
38 And a mixed multitude went up also with them; and flocks, and herds, *even* very much cattle.
39 And they baked unleavened cakes of the dough which they brought forth out of Egypt, for it was not leavened; because ᴿthey were thrust out of Egypt, and

could not tarry, neither had they prepared for themselves any victual.   vv. 31–33; 6:1; 11:1
40 Now the sojourning of the children of Israel, who dwelt in Egypt, *was* ᴿfour hundred and thirty years.   Ge 15:13, 16; Ac 7:6
41 And it came to pass at the end of the four hundred and thirty years, even the selfsame day it came to pass, that ᴿall the hosts of the LORD went out from the land of Egypt.   3:8, 10; 6:6; 7:4
42 It *is* ᴿa night to be much observed unto the LORD for bringing them out from the land of Egypt: this *is* that night of the LORD to be observed of all the children of Israel in their generations.   13:10
43 And the LORD said unto Moses and Aaron, This *is* ᴿthe ordinance of the passover: There shall no stranger eat thereof: Nu 9:14
44 But every man's servant that is bought for money, when thou hast ᴿcircumcised him, then shall he eat thereof.   Ge 17:12; Le 22:11
45 A foreigner and an hired servant shall not eat thereof.
✝46 In one house shall it be eaten; thou shalt not carry forth ought of the flesh abroad out of the house; ᴿneither shall ye break a bone thereof.   Ps 34:20

✝12:46—Jo 19:36

12:36 spoiled the Egyptians. Newly freed slaves do not usually make their escape with their masters pushing the family silver into their hands. Far from wanting to keep the Israelites in bondage, the rest of Egypt couldn't wait to get rid of them.   **12:37 Rameses.** The reference to Rameses most likely relates to the store city Raamses, mentioned in 1:11, perhaps Tel el-Maskhuta further to the east. **six hundred thousand . . . men.** This number of men would indicate a total population of perhaps three million men, women, and children (Nu 1:46).   **12:38 mixed multitude.** Apparently a number of Egyptians and perhaps other non-Hebrews joined the flight out of Egypt. Some of these people later caused trouble when things did not go as smoothly as expected (Nu 11:4).   **12:39 unleavened cakes.** The symbolism in this has to do with the haste of their departure, not (as some have supposed) that there is something evil in leaven itself. If leaven were intrinsically evil, the Israelites would have been forbidden to eat leaven at any time. In the New Testament, leaven is often used as a symbolic way of speaking about sin, but again, leaven in and of itself is not evil.   **12:40 four hundred and thirty years.** If the exodus took place around 1446 B.C., Jacob's arrival in Egypt would have been around 1876 B.C.   **12:46 neither . . . break a bone thereof.** Not breaking the bones of the lamb foreshadowed Jesus' death. None of the Savior's bones were broken, even though He suffered a horrible death (Ps 34:20; Jo 19:33–36).

47 ᴿAll the congregation of Israel shall keep it.   v. 6; Nu 9:13, 14

48 And when a stranger shall sojourn with thee, and will keep the passover to the Lᴏʀᴅ, let all his males be circumcised, and then let him come near and keep it; and he shall be as one that is born in the land: for no uncircumcised person shall eat thereof.

49 One law shall be to him that is homeborn, and unto the stranger that sojourneth among you.

50 Thus did all the children of Israel; as the Lᴏʀᴅ commanded Moses and Aaron, so did they.

51 And it came to pass the selfsame day, *that* the Lᴏʀᴅ did bring the children of Israel out of the land of Egypt by their armies.

13 And the Lᴏʀᴅ spake unto Moses, saying,

2 ᴿSanctifyᵀ unto me all the firstborn, whatsoever openeth the womb among the children of Israel, *both* of man and of beast: it *is* mine.   Le 27:26; Lk 2:23 · *Set apart*

3 And Moses said unto the people, ᴿRemember this day, in which ye came out from Egypt, out of the house of bondage; for ᴿby strength of hand the Lᴏʀᴅ brought you out from this *place:* ᴿthere shall no leavened bread be eaten.   12:42; De 16:3 · 3:20; 6:1 · 12:8, 19

4 ᴿThis day came ye out in the month A′-bib.   23:15; 34:18; De 16:1

5 And it shall be when the Lᴏʀᴅ shall bring thee into the land of the Ca′-naan-ites, and the Hit′-tites, and the Am′-or-ites, and the Hi′-

vites, and the Jeb′-u-sites, which he sware unto thy fathers to give thee, a land flowing with milk and honey, that thou shalt keep this service in this month.

6 ᴿSeven days thou shalt eat unleavened bread, and in the seventh day *shall be* a feast to the Lᴏʀᴅ.   12:15–20

7 Unleavened bread shall be eaten seven days; and there shall no leavened bread be seen with thee, neither shall there be leaven seen with thee in all thy quarters.

8 And thou shalt ᴿshew thy son in that day, saying, *This is done* because of that *which* the Lᴏʀᴅ did unto me when I came forth out of Egypt.   10:2; 12:26; Ps 44:1

9 And it shall be for ᴿa sign unto thee upon thine hand, and for a memorial between thine eyes, that the Lᴏʀᴅ's law may be in thy mouth: for with a strong hand hath the Lᴏʀᴅ brought thee out of Egypt.   De 6:8; 11:18; Ma 23:5

10 ᴿThou shalt therefore keep this ᵀordinance in his season from year to year.   12:14, 24 · *regulation*

11 And it shall be when the Lᴏʀᴅ shall ᴿbring thee into the land of the Ca′-naan-ites, as he sware unto thee and to thy fathers, and shall give it thee,   v. 5

12 That thou shalt ᵀset apart unto the Lᴏʀᴅ all that openeth the ᵀmatrix, and every firstling that cometh of a beast which thou hast; the males *shall be* the Lᴏʀᴅ's.   Lit. *cause to pass over · womb*

13 And ᴿevery firstling of an ass

13:1–22 *Sanctify unto me.* Before the dramatic story of the crossing of the Red Sea there is a record of foundational institutions that the Lord gave to Israel. These are: (1) the consecration of the firstborn (vv. 1–2); (2) the Feast of Unleavened Bread (vv. 3–10); and (3) the law concerning the firstborn (vv. 11–16). This is followed by the Lord's command to the Israelites to travel in an unexpected direction (vv. 17–22). **13:9 *sign.*** A similar commandment is found in Deuteronomy 6:8. Jews would fasten a small box containing passages of Scripture to their foreheads or arms during prayer, to serve as a memorial. The physical symbol was designed to be a reminder of the inner reality of making God's law the guiding rule of all we do. **13:13 *firstling of an ass.*** Donkeys were unclean animals, and could not be used as a sacrifice. Instead they were redeemed with a lamb. Similarly, a firstborn son was redeemed. God would never allow human sacrifice. Later the Lord claimed the Levites for Himself in exchange for the firstborn sons of the people (Nu 3:40–51).

thou shalt redeem with a lamb; and if thou wilt not redeem it, then thou shalt break his neck: and all the firstborn of man among thy children [R]shalt thou redeem.   Nu 18:15 · Nu 3:46, 47

14 [R]And it shall be when thy son asketh thee in time to come, saying, What *is* this? that thou shalt say unto him, [R]By strength of hand the LORD brought us out from Egypt, from the house of bondage: De 6:20; Jos 4:6 · vv. 3, 9

15 And it came to pass, when Pharaoh would hardly let us go, that the LORD slew all the firstborn in the land of Egypt, both the firstborn of man, and the firstborn of beast: therefore I sacrifice to the LORD all that openeth the matrix, being males; but all the firstborn of my children I redeem.

16 And it shall be for a token upon thine hand, and for frontlets between thine eyes: for by strength of hand the LORD brought us forth out of Egypt.

17 And it came to pass, when Pharaoh had let the people go, that God led them not *through* the way of the land of the Phi-lis'-tines, although that *was* near; for God said, Lest peradventure the people repent when they see war, and they return to Egypt:

18 But God [R]led the people about, *through* the way of the wilderness of the Red sea: and the children of Israel went up [T]harnessed out of the land of Egypt.   14:2; Nu 33:6 · *in orderly ranks*

19 And Moses took the bones of [R]Joseph with him: for he had straitly sworn the children of Israel, saying, God will surely visit

you; and ye shall carry up my bones away hence with you.   1:6

20 And [R]they took their journey from [R]Suc'-coth, and encamped in E'-tham, in the edge of the wilderness.   Nu 33:6–8 · 12:37

21 And the LORD went before them by day in a pillar of a cloud, to lead them the way; and by night in a pillar of fire, to give them light; to go by day and night:

22 He took not away the pillar of the cloud by day, nor the pillar of fire by night, *from* before the people.

14 And the LORD spake unto Moses, saying,

2 Speak unto the children of Israel, [R]that they turn and encamp before Pi–ha–hi'-roth, between Mig'-dol and the sea, over against Ba'-al–ze'-phon: before it shall ye encamp by the sea.   13:18

3 For Pharaoh will say of the children of Israel, [R]They *are* entangled in the land, the wilderness hath shut them in.   Ps 71:11

4 And I will harden Pharaoh's heart, that he shall follow after them; and I will be honoured upon Pharaoh, and upon all his host; [R]that the Egyptians may know that I *am* the LORD. And they did so.   v. 25; 7:5

5 And it was told the king of Egypt that the people fled: and the heart of Pharaoh and of his servants was turned against the people, and they said, Why have we done this, that we have let Israel go from serving us?

6 And he made ready his chariot, and took his people with him:

13:20–22

13:18 *the way of the wilderness.* The route the Israelites traveled from Egypt to Canaan has been disputed. The traditional route has the people moving in a southerly direction along the western shore of the Sinai Peninsula until they reached Mount Sinai in the far south central region of the peninsula. ***Red sea.*** This translation comes from the Septuagint (the Greek translation of the Old Testament); the Hebrew phrase means "Sea of Reeds." This phrase may refer to the ancient northern extension of the Red Sea. Many believe that it was one of the marshy lakes of the region. **13:19 *the bones of Joseph.*** The story of the last wish of Joseph and his death is found in Genesis 50:22–26.

7 And he took ᴿsix hundred chosen chariots, and all the chariots of Egypt, and captains over every one of them. 15:4

8 And the Lᴏʀᴅ hardened the heart of Pharaoh king of Egypt, and he pursued after the children of Israel: and the children of Israel went out with an high hand.

9 But the ᴿEgyptians pursued after them, all the horses *and* chariots of Pharaoh, and his horsemen, and his army, and overtook them encamping by the sea, beside Pi–ha–hi′-roth, before Ba′-al–ze′-phon. 15:9; Jos 24:6

10 And when Pharaoh drew nigh, the children of Israel lifted up their eyes, and, behold, the Egyptians marched after them; and they were sore afraid: and the children of Israel ᴿcried out unto the Lᴏʀᴅ. Jos 24:7; Ne 9:9; Ps 34:17

11 ᴿAnd they said unto Moses, Because *there were* no graves in Egypt, hast thou taken us away to die in the wilderness? wherefore hast thou dealt thus with us, to carry us forth out of Egypt? 5:21

12 ᴿ*Is* not this the word that we did tell thee in Egypt, saying, Let us alone, that we may serve the Egyptians? For *it had been* better for us to serve the Egyptians, than that we should die in the wilderness. 5:21; 6:9

13 And Moses said unto the people, Fear ye not, stand still, and see the ᵀsalvation of the Lᴏʀᴅ, which he will shew to you to day: for the Egyptians whom ye have seen to day, ye shall see them again no more for ever. *deliverance*

14 The Lᴏʀᴅ shall fight for you, and ye shall hold your peace.

15 And the Lᴏʀᴅ said unto Moses, Wherefore criest thou unto me? speak unto the children of Israel, that they go forward:

16 But ᴿlift thou up thy rod, and stretch out thine hand over the sea, and divide it: and the children of Israel shall go on dry *ground* through the midst of the sea. 4:17

17 And I, behold, I will harden the hearts of the Egyptians, and they shall follow them: and I will get me honour upon Pharaoh, and upon all his host, upon his chariots, and upon his horsemen.

18 And the Egyptians shall know that I *am* the Lᴏʀᴅ, when I have gotten me honour upon Pharaoh, upon his chariots, and upon his horsemen.

19 And the angel of God, ᴿwhich went before the camp of Israel, removed and went behind them; and the pillar of the cloud went from before their face, and stood behind them: 13:21, 22; [Is 63:9]

20 And it came between the camp of the Egyptians and the camp of Israel; and it was a cloud and darkness *to them*, but it gave light by night *to these:* so that the one came not near the other all the night.

21 And Moses stretched out his hand over the sea; and the Lᴏʀᴅ caused the sea to go *back* by a

🔥 14:21–30

14:11–12 *wherefore.* This marks the first of ten episodes of Israel's unbelief, beginning at the Red Sea, and concluding at Kadesh-barnea (Nu 14:22). Because of these ten events an entire generation was prevented from entering the promised land. The New Testament book of Hebrews recalls these events, using the promised land as a picture of heaven and warning that disobedience and unbelief will still keep people out of the final land of "rest" (He 4). **14:13 *the salvation of the Lᴏʀᴅ.*** The Hebrew word for salvation comes from a term that has to do with room or space. The people were under great pressure, squeezed between the waters before them and the armies of Pharaoh behind them. Salvation relieved the pressure in a most dramatic way. **14:19 *angel of God.*** The term "angel of God" is an alternative expression for the angel of the Lᴏʀᴅ. The pillar of cloud is later strongly associated with the Lord Himself (33:9–11).

strong east wind all that night, and made the sea dry *land,* and the waters were ᴿdivided.   Ps 74:13
22   And the children of Israel went into the midst of the sea upon the dry *ground:* and the waters *were* a wall unto them on their right hand, and on their left.
23   And the Egyptians pursued, and went in after them to the midst of the sea, *even* all Pharaoh's horses, his chariots, and his horsemen.
24   And it came to pass, that in the morning watch the Lᴏʀᴅ looked unto the host of the Egyptians through the pillar of fire and of the cloud, and troubled the host of the Egyptians,
25   And took off their chariot wheels, that they drave them heavily: so that the Egyptians said, Let us flee from the face of Israel; for the Lᴏʀᴅ ᴿfighteth for them against the Egyptians.   7:5
26   And the Lᴏʀᴅ said unto Moses, Stretch out thine hand over the sea, that the waters may come again upon the Egyptians, upon their chariots, and upon their horsemen.
27   And Moses stretched forth his hand over the sea, and the sea ᴿreturned to his strength when the morning appeared; and the Egyptians fled against it; and the Lᴏʀᴅ overthrew the Egyptians in the midst of the sea.   Jos 4:18
28   And the waters returned, and ᴿcovered the chariots, and the horsemen, *and* all the host of Pharaoh that came into the sea after them; there remained not so much as one of them.   Ps 78:53
29   But ᴿthe children of Israel walked upon dry *land* in the midst of the sea; and the waters *were* a wall unto them on their right hand, and on their left.   Is 11:15
30   Thus the Lᴏʀᴅ ᴿsaved Israel that day out of the hand of the Egyptians; and Israel saw the Egyptians dead upon the sea shore.   v. 13; Ps 106:8, 10; Is 63:8, 11
31   And Israel saw that great work which the Lᴏʀᴅ did upon the Egyptians: and the people feared the Lᴏʀᴅ, and ᴿbelieved the Lᴏʀᴅ, and his servant Moses.   4:31

15 Then sang Moses and the children of Israel this song unto the Lᴏʀᴅ, and spake, saying, I will ᴿsing unto the Lᴏʀᴅ, for he hath triumphed gloriously: the horse and his rider hath he thrown into the sea.   Is 12:1-6
2   The Lᴏʀᴅ *is* my strength and song, and he is become my salvation: he *is* my God, and I will prepare him an habitation; my father's God, and I will exalt him.
3   The Lᴏʀᴅ *is* a man of ᴿwar: the Lᴏʀᴅ *is* his name.   Re 19:11
4   ᴿPharaoh's chariots and his host hath he cast into the sea: ᴿhis chosen captains also are drowned in the Red sea.   14:28 · 14:7
5   The depths have covered them: ᴿthey sank into the bottom as a stone.   v. 10; Ne 9:11
6   ᴿThy right hand, O Lᴏʀᴅ, is become glorious in power: thy right hand, O Lᴏʀᴅ, hath dashed in pieces the enemy.   Ps 17:7; 118:15

14:25 the Lᴏʀᴅ fighteth for them. This was the confession the Lord demanded; word spread widely that the Lord fought for the Israelites. **14:31 the people . . . believed the Lᴏʀᴅ.** The same wording is used of Abraham's saving faith in Genesis 15:6 (see also Ro 4). The people were transformed spiritually even as they were delivered physically. **15:2 my father's God.** The Israelites had worshipped, believed, and obeyed. Today, Christians are part of Abraham's line because they also believe, obey, and worship the same God (Ga 3:6–7). Many faithful believers have preceded us. **15:3 the Lᴏʀᴅ is his name.** Other supposed gods had secret names that only guilds of priests knew. By knowing a god's secret name, a priest supposedly had special access to that god. But the living God had made His name known to all, and salvation is found in His name alone.

7   And in the greatness of thine excellency thou hast overthrown them that rose up against thee: thou sentest forth thy ᴿwrath, *which* consumed them ᴿas stubble.   Ps 78:49, 50 · De 4:24; He 12:29

8   And with the blast of thy nostrils the waters were gathered together, the floods stood upright as an heap, *and* the depths were congealed in the heart of the sea.

9   The enemy said, I will pursue, I will overtake, I will divide the spoil; my lust shall be satisfied upon them; I will draw my sword, my hand shall destroy them.

10   Thou didst blow with thy wind, the sea covered them: they sank as lead in the mighty waters.

11   ᴿWho *is* like unto thee, O Lᴏʀᴅ, among the ᵀgods? who *is* like thee, glorious in holiness, fearful *in* praises, ᴿdoing wonders?   De 3:24 · *mighty ones* · Ps 77:11

12   Thou stretchedst out thy right hand, the earth swallowed them.

13   Thou in thy mercy hast led forth the people *which* thou hast redeemed: thou hast guided *them* in thy strength unto ᴿthy holy habitation.   De 12:5; Ps 78:54

14   ᴿThe people shall hear, *and* be afraid: ᴿsorrow shall take hold on the inhabitants of ᵀPal-es-ti′-na.   Jos 2:9 · Ps 48:6 · Or *Philistia*

15   Then the dukes of E′-dom shall be amazed; the mighty men of Moab, trembling shall take hold upon them; all the inhabitants of Canaan shall melt away.

16   ᴿFear and dread shall fall upon them; by the greatness of thine arm they shall be *as* still as a stone; till thy people pass over, O Lᴏʀᴅ, till the people pass over, *which* thou hast purchased.   23:27

17   Thou shalt bring them in, and ᴿplant them in the ᴿmountain of thine inheritance, *in* the place, O Lᴏʀᴅ, *which* thou hast made for thee to dwell in, *in* the ᴿSanctuary, O Lᴏʀᴅ, *which* thy hands have established.   Ps 44:2 · Ps 2:6 · Ps 68:16

18   ᴿThe Lᴏʀᴅ shall reign for ever and ever.   2 Sa 7:16; Is 57:15

19   For the ᴿhorse of Pharaoh went in with his chariots and with his horsemen into the sea, and the Lᴏʀᴅ brought again the waters of the sea upon them; but the children of Israel went on dry *land* in the midst of the sea.   14:23

20   And Miriam the prophetess, the sister of Aaron, took a timbrel in her hand; and all the women went out after her ᴿwith timbrels and with dances.   Ps 30:11; 150:4

21   And Miriam ᴿanswered them, ᴿSing ye to the Lᴏʀᴅ, for he hath triumphed gloriously; the horse and his rider hath he thrown into the sea.   1 Sa 18:7 · v. 1

22   So Moses brought Israel from the Red sea, and they went

🌿 15:22–25

15:11 *Who is like unto thee?* Many times, the Bible uses the language of incomparability to describe the true God. In a world in which there are many supposed gods, the Lord is unique. He alone is God. He is not just better than other gods; there *are* no other gods. No person, god, or thing can be compared to the one true God (Ps 96:4; Is 40:25–26; Mi 7:18).   **15:18** *The Lᴏʀᴅ shall reign for ever and ever.* Ultimately, the salvation of Israel from Egypt points to the coming reign of the living God on earth over His redeemed people. This victory song ends with the assertion of the eternal rule of the Lord, promising the kingdom of God rather than the conquering of neighboring lands. Its emphasis is spiritual, not material. Now that deliverance from slavery in Egypt had been accomplished, the Hebrews would be formed by God into a nation which was designed to be a witness to the rest of the world of God's character and authority.   **15:20** *prophetess.* Although there is no record of women serving as priests in ancient Israel, women did serve as prophetesses (Deborah, Ju 4:4; the wife of Isaiah, Is 8:3; Huldah, 2 Ki 22:14). As a prophetess, Miriam spoke authoritatively from God. However, it is apparent that neither she nor Aaron had the level of intimacy with God that Moses had.

out into the wilderness of Shur; and they went three days in the wilderness, and found no water.

23 And when they came to [R]Ma'-rah, they could not drink of the waters of Ma'-rah, for they *were* bitter: therefore the name of it was called Ma'-rah.   Nu 33:8

24 And the people [R]murmured against Moses, saying, What shall we drink?   14:11; 16:2; Ps 106:13

25 And he cried unto the LORD; and the LORD shewed him a tree, *which* when he had cast into the waters, the waters were made sweet: there he made for them a statute and an ordinance, and there [R]he proved them,   Ps 66:10

26 And said, If thou wilt diligently hearken to the voice of the LORD thy God, and wilt do that which is right in his sight, and wilt give ear to his commandments, and keep all his statutes, I will put none of these diseases upon thee, which I have brought upon the Egyptians: for I *am* the LORD that healeth thee.

27 [R]And they came to E'-lim, where *were* twelve wells of water, and threescore and ten palm trees: and they encamped there by the waters.   Nu 33:9

16 And they took their journey from E'-lim, and all the congregation of the children of Israel came unto the wilderness of Sin, which *is* between E'-lim and [R]Si'-nai, on the fifteenth day of the second month after their departing out of the land of Egypt.   12:6

2 And the whole congregation of the children of Israel [R]mur-

mured against Moses and Aaron in the wilderness: 1 Co 10:10

3 And the children of Israel said unto them, Would to God we had died by the hand of the LORD in the land of Egypt, when we sat by the [T]flesh pots, *and* when we did eat bread to the full; for ye have brought us forth into this wilderness, to kill this whole assembly with hunger.   *pots of meat*

4 Then said the LORD unto Moses, Behold, I will rain [R]bread from heaven for you; and the people shall go out and gather a certain rate every day, that I may prove them, whether they will walk in my law, or no.   1 Co 10:3

5 And it shall come to pass, that on the sixth day they shall prepare *that* which they bring in; and [R]it shall be twice as much as they gather daily.   Le 25:21

6 And Moses and Aaron said unto all the children of Israel, [R]At even, then ye shall know that the LORD hath brought you out from the land of Egypt: 6:7

7 And in the morning, then ye shall see [R]the glory of the LORD; for that he heareth your murmurings against the LORD: and what *are* we, that ye murmur against us?   Is 35:2; 40:5; Jo 11:4, 40

8 And Moses said, *This shall be,* when the LORD shall give you in the evening flesh to eat, and in the morning bread to the full; for that the LORD heareth your murmurings which ye murmur against him: and what *are* we? your murmurings

15:26

15:24 *murmured.* The people's recent deliverance from the Egyptian armies makes this complaint seem fickle and a true test of God's mercy. We are like the Israelites far too often, turning from praise to complaint at a moment's notice. **15:27 *Elim.*** Elim means "place of trees." The wells and palms of this oasis would have been a welcome relief from the barren wasteland. **16:1 *wilderness of Sin.*** The location of this wasteland is uncertain; its position between Elim and Sinai depends on the location of Mount Sinai. (The name Sin has nothing to do with the English word "sin"). **16:4 *prove.*** In this sense, to prove does not mean "to provide evidence," but "to prove what one really is." **16:5 *twice as much.*** Gathering extra food on the sixth day would allow for the Sabbath rest (v. 25).

are not against us, but [R]against the LORD.   1 Sa 8:7

9 And Moses spake unto Aaron, Say unto all the congregation of the children of Israel, [R]Come near before the LORD: for he hath heard your murmurings.   Nu 16:16

10 And it came to pass, as Aaron spake unto the whole congregation of the children of Israel, that they looked toward the wilderness, and, behold, the glory of the LORD appeared in the cloud.

11 And the LORD spake unto Moses, saying,

12 [R]I have heard the murmurings of the children of Israel: speak unto them, saying, At even ye shall eat flesh, and in the morning ye shall be filled with bread; and ye shall know that I *am* the LORD your God.   v. 8; Nu 14:27

13 And it came to pass, that at even [R]the quails came up, and covered the camp: and in the morning the dew lay round about the host.   Ps 78:27–29; 105:40

14 And when the dew that lay was gone up, behold, upon the face of the wilderness *there lay* a small round thing, *as* small as the hoar frost on the ground.

15 And when the children of Israel saw *it,* they said one to another, [T]It *is* man'-na: for they wist not what it *was.* And Moses said unto them, [R]This *is* the bread which the LORD hath given you to eat.   *What is it?* · Ps 78:24; [Jo 6:31, 49]

16 This *is* the thing which the LORD hath commanded, Gather of it every man [R]according to his eating, an o'-mer for every man, *according to* the number of your persons; take ye every man for *them* which *are* in his tents.   12:4

17 And the children of Israel did so, and gathered, some more, some less.

18 And when they did [T]mete *it* with an o'-mer, [R]he that gathered much had nothing over, and he that gathered little had no lack; they gathered every man according to his eating.   *measure* · 2 Co 8:15

19 And Moses said, Let no man [R]leave of it till the morning.   12:10

20 Notwithstanding they hearkened not unto Moses; but some of them left of it until the morning, and it bred worms, and stank: and Moses was wroth with them.

21 And they gathered it every morning, every man according to his eating: and when the sun waxed hot, it melted.

22 And it came to pass, *that* on the sixth day they gathered twice as much bread, two o'-mers for one *man:* and all the rulers of the congregation came and told Moses.

23 And he said unto them, This *is that* which the LORD hath said,

🔥 16:12–25

16:10 *the glory of the LORD.* This is one of the grand appearances of God recorded in Exodus. We do not know exactly what the people saw in the cloud, but the sight certainly made them aware of God's majestic and somewhat ominous presence (Ps 97:2–5). **16:14 *a small round thing . . . as . . . frost on the ground.*** There have been many attempts to explain manna as a naturally occurring substance that still might be found in the desert, suggesting that it was some kind of plant or animal secretion. However, it is clear from the wording of these verses that this was not so. The description of the manna was necessary precisely because it was *not* a naturally occurring substance, or something they had ever seen before (Nu 11:1–15). **16:15–18 God's Provision**—It is easy to think we trust in God and believe He will supply all of our needs when we have food, shelter, and clothing. It is more difficult when the food is low, the clothing has disappeared, and there is no money to pay the rent. Sometimes God allows us to be in this kind of position so that we will have to learn to consciously rely on His providence. When we really place our lives in His hands, we will experience a depth of relationship which is worth far more than all the security in the world. **16:19 *Let no man leave of it.*** The Israelites' daily dependence on manna was an act of faith in God's provision.

To morrow *is* [R]the rest of the holy sabbath unto the LORD: bake *that* which ye will bake *to day,* and [T]seethe that ye will [T]seethe; and that which remaineth over lay up for you to be kept until the morning.   20:8–11; Ge 2:3; Ne 9:13, 14 · *boil*

24 And they laid it up till the morning, as Moses bade: and it did not [R]stink, neither was there any worm therein.   v. 20

25 And Moses said, Eat that to day; for to day *is* a sabbath unto the LORD: to day ye shall not find it in the field.

26 [R]Six days ye shall gather it; but on the seventh day, *which is* the sabbath, in it there shall be none.   20:9, 10

27 And it came to pass, *that* there went out *some* of the people on the seventh day for to gather, and they found none.

28 And the LORD said unto Moses, How long refuse ye to keep my commandments and my laws?

29 See, for that the LORD hath given you the sabbath, therefore he giveth you on the sixth day the bread of two days; abide ye every man in his place, let no man go out of his place on the seventh day.

30 So the people rested on the seventh day.

31 And the house of Israel called the name thereof [T]Man'-na: and it *was* like coriander seed, white; and the taste of it *was* like wafers *made* with honey.   Lit. *What?*

32 And Moses said, This *is* the thing which the LORD commandeth, Fill an o'-mer of it to be kept for your generations; that they may see the bread wherewith I have fed you in the wilderness, when I

brought you forth from the land of Egypt.

33 And Moses said unto Aaron, [R]Take a pot, and put an o'-mer full of man'-na therein, and lay it up before the LORD, to be kept for your generations.   He 9:4; Re 2:17

34 As the LORD commanded Moses, so Aaron laid it up [R]before the Testimony, to be kept. 25:16, 21

35 And the children of Israel did [R]eat man'-na [R]forty years, until they came to a land inhabited; they did eat man'-na, until they came unto the borders of the land of Canaan.   De 8:3, 16 · Nu 33:38

36 Now an o'-mer *is* the tenth *part* of an e'-phah.

17 And [R]all the congregation of the children of Israel journeyed from the wilderness of [R]Sin, after their journeys, according to the commandment of the LORD, and pitched in Reph'-i-dim: and *there was* no water for the people to drink.   16:1 · Nu 33:11–15

2   Wherefore the people did chide with Moses, and said, Give us water that we may drink. And Moses said unto them, Why chide ye with me? wherefore do ye [R]tempt the LORD?   [Ma 4:7]

🕎 3   And the people thirsted there for water; and the people [R]murmured against Moses, and said, Wherefore *is* this *that* thou hast brought us up out of Egypt, to kill us and our children and our cattle with thirst?   16:2, 3

4   And Moses [R]cried unto the LORD, saying, What shall I do unto this people? they be almost ready to [R]stone me.   14:15 · Jo 8:59; 10:31

5   And the LORD said unto Mo-

🕎 17:3–7

16:26 *Six days . . . the sabbath.* The characteristics of manna were a built-in reminder of the importance of the Sabbath day in the life of the people of Israel.   **16:31** *coriander seed . . . honey.* Apparently the manna was very tasty. It must also have been very nutritious since it was the staple of the Israelites for a full generation.   **16:32** *to be kept for your generations.* This pot of manna was not only a reminder of God's miraculous provision, but a miracle in itself since it did not spoil as did the extra manna Israelites gathered for themselves.

ses, [R]Go on before the people, and take with thee of the elders of Israel; and thy rod, wherewith thou smotest the river, take in thine hand, and go.   Eze 2:6

6   [R]Behold, I will stand before thee there upon the rock in Ho'-reb; and thou shalt smite the rock, and there shall come water out of it, that the people may drink. And Moses did so in the sight of the elders of Israel. Ps 78:15; [1 Co 10:4]

7   And he called the name of the place [R]Mas'-sah, and Mer'-i-bah, because of the chiding of the children of Israel, and because they tempted the LORD, saying, Is the LORD among us, or not?   Ps 81:7

8   Then came Am'-a-lek, and fought with Israel in Reph'-i-dim.

9   And Moses said unto Joshua, Choose us out men, and go out, fight with Am'-a-lek: to morrow I will stand on the top of the hill with [R]the rod of God in mine hand. 4:20

10   So Joshua did as Moses had said to him, and fought with Am'-a-lek: and Moses, Aaron, and Hur went up to the top of the hill.

11   And it came to pass, when Moses [R]held up his hand, that Israel prevailed: and when he let down his hand, Am'-a-lek prevailed.   [Jam 5:16]

12   But Moses' hands *were* heavy; and they took a stone, and put *it* under him, and he sat thereon; and Aaron and Hur stayed up his hands, the one on the one side, and the other on the other side; and his hands were steady until the going down of the sun.

13   And Joshua discomfited Am'-a-lek and his people with the edge of the sword.

14   And the LORD said unto Moses, [R]Write this *for* a memorial in a book, and rehearse *it* in the ears of Joshua: for I will utterly put out the remembrance of Am'-a-lek from under heaven.   24:4; Nu 33:2

15   And Moses built an altar, and called the name of it [T]Je-ho'-vah–nis'-si: Lit. *The* LORD *Is My Banner*

16   For he said, Because the LORD hath sworn *that* the LORD *will have* war with Am'-a-lek from generation to generation.

18 When [R]Je'-thro, the priest of Mid'-i-an, Moses' father in law, heard of all that God had done for Moses, and for Israel his people, *and* that the LORD had brought Israel out of Egypt;   2:16

2   Then Je'-thro, Moses' father in law, took Zip-po'-rah, Moses' wife, after he had sent her back,

3   And her [R]two sons; of which the name of the one *was* Ger'-shom; for he said, I have been an alien in a strange land: Ac 7:29

4   And the name of the other *was* E-li-e'-zer; for the God of my

18:2-3

17:7 Is the LORD among us. The people had seen God's power in the plagues, the exodus, the crossing of the Red Sea, and the provision of manna. Every day they saw the pillar of His presence. We can wonder at their lack of faith until we look at our own weakness. **17:8 Amalek.** The people of Amalek were descendants of Esau, and thus relatives of the Hebrews (Ge 36:12). Their attack on Israel was unprovoked. The Israelites—and the Lord—regarded this attack as particularly heinous (vv. 14–16). **17:14 Write this.** Some people allege that the first five books of the Old Testament were not actually written down until centuries after Moses' death. Others concede that Moses may have written certain small sections, such as the one to which this verse seems to refer (24:4). However, strong tradition supports the assertion that Moses really wrote all of the first five books; ancient Jews, including Jesus, referred to this portion of the Scripture as "the books of Moses." **17:16 the LORD hath sworn.** This Hebrew phrase is somewhat obscure, but appears to mean "Surely there is a hand on the throne of the LORD." In this phraseology, the Creator of the universe is pictured as seated on His throne while raising His hand in a solemn oath. It is a fearful thing for the wicked to fall into the hands of the just and righteous Judge of the universe.

father, *said he, was* mine ᴿhelp, and delivered me from the sword of Pharaoh: Ge 49:25

5   And Je′-thro, Moses' father in law, came with his sons and his wife unto Moses into the wilderness, where he encamped at ᴿthe mount of God: 3:1, 12; 4:27; 24:13

6   And he said unto Moses, I thy father in law Je′-thro am come unto thee, and thy wife, and her two sons with her.

7   And Moses went out to meet his father in law, and did obeisance, and ᴿkissed him; and they asked each other of *their* welfare; and they came into the tent.   4:27

8   And Moses told his father in law all that the Lᴏʀᴅ had done unto Pharaoh and to the Egyptians for Israel's sake, *and* all the ᵀtravail that had come upon them by the way, and *how* the Lᴏʀᴅ ᴿdelivered them.   hardship · Ps 81:7

9   And Je′-thro rejoiced for all the ᴿgoodness which the Lᴏʀᴅ had done to Israel, whom he had delivered out of the hand of the Egyptians.   [Is 63:7–14]

10   And Je′-thro said, ᴿBlessed *be* the Lᴏʀᴅ, who hath delivered you out of the hand of the Egyptians, and out of the hand of Pharaoh, who hath delivered the people from under the hand of the Egyptians.   2 Sa 18:28; 1 Ki 8:56

11   Now I know that the Lᴏʀᴅ *is* greater than all gods: for in the thing wherein they dealt ᴿproudly *he was* above them.   Lk 1:51

12   And Je′-thro, Moses' father in law, took a burnt ᴿoffering and sacrifices for God: and Aaron came, and all the elders of Israel, ᴿto eat

bread with Moses' father in law before God.   24:5 · De 12:7

13   And it came to pass on the morrow, that Moses ᴿsat to judge the people: and the people stood by Moses from the morning unto the evening.   De 33:4, 5; Ma 23:2

14   And when Moses' father in law saw all that he did to the people, he said, What *is* this thing that thou doest to the people? why sittest thou thyself alone, and all the people stand by thee from morning unto even?

15   And Moses said unto his father in law, Because the people come unto me to enquire of God:

16   When they have ᴿa matter, they come unto me; and I judge between one and another, and I do make *them* know the statutes of God, and his laws.   De 19:17

17   And Moses' father in law said unto him, The thing that thou doest *is* not good.

18   Thou wilt surely wear away, both thou, and this people that *is* with thee: for this thing *is* too heavy for thee; thou art not able to perform it thyself alone.

19   Hearken now unto my voice, I will give thee counsel, and God shall be with thee: Be thou for the people to ᴿGod-ward, that thou mayest ᴿbring the causes unto God: 4:16; 20:19 · Nu 9:8; 27:5

20   And thou shalt ᴿteach them ordinances and laws, and shalt shew them the way wherein they must walk, and ᴿthe work that they must do.   De 5:1 · De 1:18

21   Moreover thou shalt provide out of all the people able men, such as ᴿfear God, men of truth, hating

18:6 *her two sons.* Zipporah's two sons stayed with Moses and became part of the families of Israel. However, the subsequent history of the family of Gershom involved a return to idols and inappropriate priesthood (Ju 18:30).   **18:7 *did obeisance, and kissed him.*** The ancient Middle Eastern acts of bowing and kissing were not acts of worship, but signs of respect and reminders of obligations between two people.   **18:11 *Now I know that the Lᴏʀᴅ is greater.*** Jethro's words imply that he had once regarded the Lord as one among many gods, or perhaps as the principal deity over the lesser. Here he declares full faith in God as the supreme Deity.   **18:21 *covetousness.*** Jethro's five qualifications for judges are similar to the qualifications for elders in the New Testament

covetousness; and place *such* over them, *to be* rulers of thousands, *and* rulers of hundreds, rulers of fifties, and rulers of tens: Ge 42:18; 2 Sa 23:3

22 And let them judge the people at all seasons: and it shall be, *that* every great matter they shall bring unto thee, but every small matter they shall judge: so shall it be easier for thyself, and they shall bear *the burden* with thee.

23 If thou shalt do this thing, and God command thee *so,* then thou shalt be able to endure, and all this people shall also go to their ᴿplace in peace. 16:29

24 So Moses hearkened to the voice of his father in law, and did all that he had said.

25 And Moses chose able men out of all Israel, and made them heads over the people, rulers of thousands, rulers of hundreds, rulers of fifties, and rulers of tens.

26 And they judged the people at all seasons: the ᴿhard ᵀcauses they brought unto Moses, but every small matter they judged themselves. Job 29:16 · *cases*

27 And Moses let his father in law depart; and ᴿhe went his way into his own land. Nu 10:29, 30

19 In the third month, when the children of Israel were gone

forth out of the land of Egypt, the same day came they *into* the wilderness of Si'-nai.

2 For they were departed from ᴿReph'-i-dim, and were come *to* the desert of Si'-nai, and had pitched in the wilderness; and there Israel camped before ᴿthe mount. 17:1 · 3:1, 12; 18:5

3 And ᴿMoses went up unto God, and the Lᴏʀᴅ ᴿcalled unto him out of the mountain, saying, Thus shalt thou say to the house of Jacob, and tell the children of Israel; Ac 7:38 · 3:4

4 Ye have seen what I did unto the Egyptians, and *how* ᴿI bare you on eagles' wings, and brought you unto myself. Is 63:9; Re 12:14

✎5 Now therefore, if ye will obey my voice indeed, and keep my covenant, then ᴿye shall be a peculiar treasure unto me above all people: for all the earth *is* mine: Ps 135:4; Tit 2:14; 1 Pe 2:9

6 And ye shall be unto me a ᴿkingdom of priests, and an holy nation. These *are* the words which thou shalt speak unto the children of Israel. [1 Pe 2:5, 9; Re 1:6; 5:10]

7 And Moses came and called for the ᴿelders of the people, and

✎ 19:5

(1 Ti 3:1–13). In particular, the men recommended by Jethro were to be God-fearing and haters of dishonesty. As such they would not be susceptible to bribery, and justice would not be perverted. God takes no bribes (De 10:17), so neither must a judge. A bribe blinds the eyes. Human justice must reflect divine justice, which is impartial (Ro 2:11). **19:5–8 God Gives His Covenant**—The covenant with Moses is the second covenant that pertains to the rule of God. It is different than the Abrahamic covenant in that it is conditional. It is introduced by the conditional formula "if ye will obey my voice indeed . . . . ye shall be a peculiar treasure unto me." This covenant was given to the nation Israel so that those who believed God's promises given to Abraham in the Abrahamic Covenant (Ge 12:1–3) would know how they should live. The Mosaic Covenant in its entirety governs three areas of their lives: (1) the commandments governed their personal lives (Ex 20:1–26); (2) the law governed their social lives particularly as they related to one another (Ex 21:1–24:11); and (3) the ordinances governed their religious lives so that the people would know how to approach God (Ex 24:12–31:18). The Mosaic Covenant did not replace the Abrahamic Covenant. It was added alongside the Abrahamic Covenant so that the people of Israel would know how to live until "the seed," Christ, comes and makes the complete and perfect sacrifice. The Mosaic Covenant was never given so that by keeping it people could be saved, but so that they might realize that they cannot do what God wants, even when God writes it down on stone tablets. The law was given that man might realize that he is helpless and that his only hope is to receive the righteousness of God by faith in Jesus (Ga 3:17–24).

[T]laid before their faces all these words which the LORD commanded him.   4:29, 30 · *set*

8   And [R]all the people answered together, and said, All that the LORD hath spoken we will do. And Moses returned the words of the people unto the LORD.   4:31; 24:3, 7

9   And the LORD said unto Moses, Lo, I come unto thee [R]in a thick cloud, [R]that the people may hear when I speak with thee, and believe thee for ever. And Moses told the words of the people unto the LORD.   Ma 17:5 · Jo 12:29, 30

10   And the LORD said unto Moses, Go unto the people, and [R]sanctify[T] them to day and to morrow, and let them wash their clothes,   Le 11:44, 45 · *consecrate*

11   And be ready against the third day: for the third day the LORD will come down in the sight of all the people upon mount Si'-nai.

12   And thou shalt set bounds unto the people round about, saying, Take heed to yourselves, *that ye go not* up into the mount, or touch the border of it: [R]whosoever toucheth the mount shall be surely put to death: 34:3; He 12:20

13   There shall not an hand touch it, but he shall surely be stoned, or shot through; whether *it be* beast or man, it shall not live: when the trumpet soundeth long, they shall come up to the mount.

14   And Moses went down from the mount unto the people, and sanctified the people; and they washed their clothes.

15   And he said unto the people, Be ready against the third day: come not [T]at *your* wives.   *near to*

16   And it came to pass on the third day in the morning, that there were [R]thunders and lightnings, and a thick cloud upon the

mount, and the voice of the trumpet exceeding loud; so that all the people that *was* in the camp [R]trembled.   He 12:18, 19 · He 12:21

17   And Moses brought forth the people out of the camp to meet with God; and they stood at the nether part of the mount.

18   And mount Si'-nai was altogether on a smoke, because the LORD descended upon it in fire: and the smoke thereof ascended as the smoke of a furnace, and the whole mount quaked greatly.

19   And when the voice of the trumpet sounded long, and waxed louder and louder, [R]Moses spake, and [R]God answered him by a voice.   He 12:21 · Ne 9:13; Ps 81:7

20   And the LORD came down upon mount Si'-nai, on the top of the mount: and the LORD called Moses *up* to the top of the mount; and Moses went up.

21   And the LORD said unto Moses, Go down, [T]charge the people, lest they break through unto the LORD [R]to gaze, and many of them perish.   *warn* · 1 Sa 6:19

22   And let the priests also, which come near to the LORD, sanctify themselves, lest the LORD break forth upon them.

23   And Moses said unto the LORD, The people cannot come up to mount Si'-nai: for thou chargedst us, saying, Set bounds about the mount, and sanctify it.

24   And the LORD said unto him, Away, get thee down, and thou shalt come up, thou, and Aaron with thee: but let not the priests and the people break through to come up unto the LORD, lest he break forth upon them.

25   So Moses went down unto the people, and spake unto them.

19:16 ***the voice of the trumpet exceeding loud.*** Amazingly, one of the heavenly visitors played the trumpet rather than someone in the camp of Israel (compare Is 27:13; 1 Co 15:52; 1 Th 4:16). No wonder they trembled (20:18–19).   **19:18** ***the LORD descended.*** Even though we know God is everywhere, language such as this gives us a greater appreciation of His merciful grace.

20 And God spake ^Rall these words, saying,   De 5:22

2   ^RI *am* the LORD thy God, which have brought thee out of the land of Egypt, ^Rout of the house of bondage.   Ho 13:4 · 13:3

3   ^RThou shalt have no other gods before me.   De 6:14

4   ^RThou shalt not make unto thee any graven image, or any likeness *of any thing* that *is* in heaven above, or that *is* in the earth beneath, or that *is* in the water under the earth: Le 19:4; 26:1

5   ^RThou shalt not bow down thyself to them, nor serve them: for I the LORD thy God *am* a jealous God, visiting the iniquity of the fathers upon the children unto the third and fourth *generation* of them that hate me;   Is 44:15, 19

6   And shewing mercy unto thousands of them that love me, and keep my commandments.

7   ^RThou shalt not take the name of the LORD thy God in vain; for the LORD ^Rwill not hold him guiltless that taketh his name in vain.   Le 19:12; [Ma 5:33–37] · Mi 6:11

20:1 *And God spake.* The following words of God are known as the law of Moses, but this is only because they were delivered to the people from God through Moses, not because Moses invented them.   **20:1–17 The Ten Commandments**—The first four Commandments (20:1–11) lay out the basics of the relationship with God. God is not a mere abstraction or figment of imagination. He is the God who spoke dramatically to the patriarchs and continues to speak to us. Our responsibility is to have a relationship with Him whereby we explicitly recognize Him, listen to what He says and then obey. What He wants isn't all that complicated. He is the Creator and Master of the world, as we know it. Any view of God that makes Him less, falls short of what is required to make the relationship between God and man work. For example if God is not the creator and sustainer of the world, then the perspective of Genesis 1:28 and our responsibility as stewards of His creation don't make much sense. The last six Commandments (20:12–17) give us the basics for living—with our families, our neighbors and our communities. Disregarding and disobeying any of these commands leads to the breakdown and possible destruction of those relationships. The relationship between a parent and a child can only go downhill if the basic respect for the parent has not been created and maintained. Adultery clearly has enormous potential to destroy a marriage because it creates distrust where trust should be. Trust is one of the foundational blocks of the marriage relationship. While many would like to say that these Commandments are limiting, confining and outdated, in reality, they provide the basis for a society to function harmoniously. Only when a culture places limits on itself, is it able to prosper. Followed correctly, these Commandments provide safety and freedom, the same way a fish functions best within the confines of water. In the water it lives and prospers. On land it dies.   **20:3** *no other gods.* God is not to be viewed as one god among many, or even as the highest among many. He is the one and only.   **20:4** *not make . . . any likeness.* This command has often been misunderstood as a prohibition against all kinds of art. In fact, God used many "likenesses" of created things to beautify His tabernacle, including carved images and woven pictures. The prohibition was not against art, but against attempting to "picture" God. Any statue, icon, painting, or image of any sort which is meant to be a representation of God can only detract from His glory. God does not want His people to worship a picture of "what He might look like," He wants all our worship for Himself alone.   **20:5** *a jealous God.* In other words, He has a zeal for the truth that He alone is God, and He is jealous of any rivals.   **20:6** *shewing mercy unto thousands.* The contrasting of the phrases "third and fourth generation" (v. 5) with "thousands" demonstrates that God's mercy is greater than His wrath. The lingering effects of righteousness will last far longer than the lingering effects of wrath.   **20:7** *in vain.* Using God's name in vain is trivializing His name by regarding it as insignificant, trying to advance evil purposes by coaxing God to violate His character and purposes, or even simply using it thoughtlessly, without any attempt to realize of whom we are speaking.

8 ᴿRemember the sabbath day, to keep it holy.   Le 26:2; De 5:12

9 ᴿSix days shalt thou labour, and do all thy work: Lk 13:14

10 But the ᴿseventh day *is* the sabbath of the Lᴏʀᴅ thy God: *in it* thou shalt not do any work, thou, nor thy son, nor thy daughter, thy manservant, nor thy maidservant, nor thy cattle, nor thy stranger that *is* within thy gates: Ge 2:2, 3

11 For ᴿ*in* six days the Lᴏʀᴅ made heaven and earth, the sea, and all that in them *is,* and rested the seventh day: wherefore the Lᴏʀᴅ blessed the sabbath day, and hallowed it.   31:17

12 Honour thy father and thy mother: that thy days may be long upon the land which the Lᴏʀᴅ thy God giveth thee.

13 ᴿThou shalt not kill.   Ro 13:9

14 ᴿThou shalt not commit adultery.   Ro 13:9; Jam 2:11

15 ᴿThou shalt not steal.   Le 19:11

16 Thou shalt not bear false witness against thy neighbour.

17 Thou shalt not covet thy neighbour's house, thou shalt not covet thy neighbour's wife, nor his manservant, nor his maidservant, nor his ox, nor his ass, nor any thing that *is* thy neighbour's.

18 And all the people saw the thunderings, and the lightnings, and the noise of the trumpet, and the mountain smoking: and when the people saw *it,* they removed, and stood afar off.

19 And they said unto Moses, ᴿSpeak thou with us, and we will hear: but let not God speak with us, lest we die.   Ga 3:19; He 12:19

20 And Moses said unto the people, ᴿFear not: ᴿfor God is come to prove you, and ᴿthat his fear may be before your faces, that ye sin not.   [Is 41:10, 13] · [De 13:3] · Is 8:13

21 And the people stood afar off, and Moses drew near unto the thick darkness where God *was.*

22 And the Lᴏʀᴅ said unto Moses, Thus thou shalt say unto the children of Israel, Ye have seen that I have talked with you ᴿfrom heaven.   De 4:36; 5:24, 26; Ne 9:13

23 Ye shall not make ᴿwith me gods of silver, neither shall ye make unto you gods of gold.   32:1

24 An altar of earth thou shalt make unto me, and shalt sacrifice thereon thy burnt offerings, and thy peace offerings, thy sheep, and thine oxen: in all ᴿplaces where I record my name I will come unto thee, and I will bless thee.   De 12:5; 16:6, 11; 2 Ch 6:6

25 And ᴿif thou wilt make me an altar of stone, thou shalt not build it of hewn stone: for if thou ᴿlift up thy tool upon it, thou hast polluted it.   De 27:5 · Jos 8:30, 31

26 Neither shalt thou go up by

20:12   20:14   20:16–17

20:8–11 *Remember the sabbath day.* The word Sabbath means "rest." The command to rest and remember the Lord on the seventh day goes back to the pattern set at the time of creation (Ge 2:2–3). **20:12** *Honour thy father and thy mother.* The term "honor" means "to treat with significance." Many times we equate "honor" with "obey," but in fact the two are not synonyms. Adult children, or children of ungodly parents can find ways to honor when they cannot in good conscience obey. **20:14** *adultery.* God regards the sanctity of marriage as a sacred trust similar to the sanctity of life (v. 13). The marriage relationship is a symbol of God's faithfulness to us. **20:16** *false witness.* This command is an essential foundation for a just and effective judicial system. **20:20** *his fear.* God did not want His people to live in terror of Him, as though He were an irrational, uncontrolled, violent force, ready to be unleashed on innocent people without provocation. Rather, God wanted His people to respect the obvious hazards of wanton sin. Appropriate fear of God in this sense would make them circumspect, reverent, obedient, and worshipful, so that they might not sin. **20:26** *thy nakedness.* The pagan worship of the Canaanites involved sexually perverse acts. Nothing obscene or unseemly was permitted in the pure worship of the living God.

steps unto mine altar, that thy ᴿ nakedness be not discovered thereon. 28:42, 43

21 Now these *are* the ᵀjudgments which thou shalt ᴿset before them. *ordinances* · De 4:14; 6:1

2　ᴿIf thou buy an Hebrew servant, six years he shall serve: and in the seventh he shall go out free for nothing. Le 25:39–43; Je 34:14

3　If he came in by himself, he shall go out by himself: if he were married, then his wife shall go out with him.

4　If his master have given him a wife, and she have born him sons or daughters; the wife and her children shall be her master's, and he shall go out by himself.

5　ᴿAnd if the servant shall plainly say, I love my master, my wife, and my children; I will not go out free: De 15:16, 17

6　Then his master shall bring him unto the judges; he shall also bring him to the door, or unto the door post; and his master shall bore his ear through with an aul; and he shall serve him for ever.

7　And if a man sell his daughter to be a maidservant, she shall not go out as the menservants do.

8　If she please not her master, who hath betrothed her to himself, then shall he let her be redeemed: to sell her unto a ᵀstrange nation he shall have no power, seeing he hath dealt deceitfully with her. *foreign people*

9　And if he have betrothed her unto his son, he shall deal with her after the manner of daughters.

10　If he take him another *wife*; her food, her raiment, ᴿand her duty of marriage, shall he not diminish. [1 Co 7:3, 5]

11　And if he do not these three unto her, then shall she go out free without money.

12　ᴿHe that smiteth a man, so that he die, shall be surely put to death. Ge 9:6; Le 24:17; Nu 35:30

13　And if a man lie not in wait, but God deliver *him* into his hand; then ᴿI will appoint thee a place whither he shall flee. Nu 35:11

14　But if a man come ᵀpresumptuously upon his neighbour, to slay him with guile; thou shalt take him from mine altar, that he may die. *with premeditation*

15　And he that smiteth his father, or his mother, shall be surely put to death.

16　And ᴿhe that ᵀstealeth a man, and ᴿselleth him, or if he be found in his hand, he shall surely be put to death. De 24:7 · *kidnaps* · Ge 37:28

17　And ᴿhe that curseth his father, or his mother, shall surely be put to death. Le 20:9; Pr 20:20

18　And if men strive together, and one smite another with a stone, or with *his* fist, and he die not, but keepeth *his* bed:

19　If he rise again, and walk abroad upon his staff, then shall he that smote *him* be ᵀquit: only he shall pay *for* the loss of his time, and shall cause *him* to be thoroughly healed. *acquitted*

20　And if a man smite his servant, or his maid, with a rod, and he die under his hand; he shall be surely punished.

21　Notwithstanding, if he continue a day or two, he shall not be punished: for he *is* his money.

22　If men strive, and hurt a woman with child, so that her fruit depart *from her,* and yet no mischief follow: he shall be surely punished, according as the woman's husband will lay upon him; and he shall pay as the judges *determine.*

21:22

21:1 *the judgments.* Also translated "ordinances," this word describes God's response to a specific action, something like an umpire's call. The judgments of God set forth here are responses to specific situations; the Ten Commandments are more general laws, a code for living rather than a response to a certain problem.

23 And if *any* mischief follow, then thou shalt give life for life,

24 Eye for eye, tooth for tooth, hand for hand, foot for foot,

25 Burning for burning, wound for wound, stripe for stripe.

26 And if a man smite the eye of his servant, or the eye of his maid, that it perish; he shall let him go free for his eye's sake.

27 And if he smite out his manservant's tooth, or his maidservant's tooth; he shall let him go free for his tooth's sake.

28 If an ox gore a man or a woman, that they die: then the ox shall be surely stoned, and his flesh shall not be eaten; but the owner of the ox *shall be* quit.

29 But if the ox ᵀwere wont to push with his horn in time past, and it hath been ᵀtestified to his owner, and he hath not kept him in, but that he hath killed a man or a woman; the ox shall be stoned, and his owner also shall be put to death.   *tended · made known*

30 If there be laid on him a sum of money, then he shall give for ᴿthe ransom of his life whatsoever is laid upon him.   v. 22; Nu 35:31

31 Whether he have gored a son, or have gored a daughter, according to this judgment shall it be done unto him.

32 If the ox shall push a manservant or a maidservant; he shall give unto their master ᴿthirty shek'els of silver, and the ox shall be stoned.   Ze 11:12, 13; Ma 26:15

33 And if a man shall open a pit, or if a man shall dig a pit, and not cover it, and an ox or an ass fall therein;

34 The owner of the pit shall make *it* good, *and* give money unto the owner of them; and the dead *beast* shall be his.

35 And if one man's ox hurt another's, that he die; then they shall sell the live ox, and divide the money of it; and the dead ox also they shall divide.

36 Or if it be known that the ox hath used to push in time past, and his owner hath not kept him in; he shall surely pay ox for ox; and the dead shall be his own.

22 If a man shall steal an ox, or a sheep, and kill it, or sell it; he shall restore five oxen for an ox, and four sheep for a sheep.

2 If a thief be found ᴿbreaking ᵀup, and be smitten that he die, *there shall* ᴿno blood *be shed* for him.   Ma 6:19; 1 Pe 4:15 · *in* · Nu 35:27

3 If the sun be risen upon him, *there shall be* blood *shed* for him; *for* he should make full restitution; if he have nothing, then he shall be ᴿsold for his theft.   21:2

4 If the theft be certainly ᴿfound in his hand alive, whether it be ox, or ass, or sheep; he shall ᴿrestore double.   21:16 · Pr 6:31

5 If a man shall cause a field or vineyard to be eaten, and shall put in his beast, and shall feed in another man's field; of the best of his own field, and of the best of his own vineyard, shall he make restitution.

6 If fire break out, and catch in thorns, so that the stacks of corn, or the standing corn, or the field, be consumed *therewith;* he that kindled the fire shall surely make restitution.

7 If a man shall ᴿdeliver unto his neighbour money or stuff to keep, and it be stolen out of the man's

---

21:24 Eye for eye, tooth for tooth. Here we encounter the best known statement of the "law of retaliation." The idea here is not to foster revenge, but to curtail it. The natural, sinful human response is "a head for an eye, a jaw for a tooth, an arm for a hand." This law says *"no more than* eye for eye, tooth for tooth." **22:1–4 the sun be risen upon him.** There is a difference between struggling with an intruder at the moment when he is caught red-handed, and hunting him up in order to kill him later on. The law made a distinction between self-defense and murder as retaliation.

house; if the thief be found, let him pay double. Le 6:1–7

8   If the thief be not found, then the master of the house shall be brought unto the ᴿjudges, *to see* whether he have put his hand unto his neighbour's goods. 21:6, 22

9   For all manner of trespass, *whether it be* for ox, for ass, for sheep, for raiment, *or* for any manner of lost thing, which *another* challengeth to be his, the cause of both parties shall come before the judges; *and* whom the judges shall condemn, he shall pay double unto his neighbour.

10   If a man deliver unto his neighbour an ass, or an ox, or a sheep, or any beast, to keep; and it die, or be hurt, or driven away, no man seeing *it:*

11   *Then* shall an ᴿoath of the Lᴏʀᴅ be between them both, that he hath not put his hand unto his neighbour's goods; and the owner of it shall accept *thereof*, and he shall not make *it* good. He 6:16

12   And ᴿif it be stolen from him, he shall make restitution unto the owner thereof. Ge 31:39

13   If it be torn in pieces, *then* let him bring it *for* witness, *and* he shall not make good that which was torn.

14   And if a man borrow ᵀought of his neighbour, and it be hurt, or die, the owner thereof *being* not with it, he shall surely make *it* good. *anything*

15   *But* if the owner thereof *be* with it, he shall not make *it* good: if it *be* an hired *thing*, it came for his hire.

16   And ᴿif a man entice a maid that is not betrothed, and lie with her, he shall surely endow her to be his wife. De 22:28, 29

17   If her father utterly refuse to give her unto him, he shall pay money according to the ᴿdowry of virgins. Ge 34:12; 1 Sa 18:25

18   ᴿThou shalt not suffer a witch to live. Le 19:31; 20:6, 27; De 18:10, 11

19   Whosoever lieth with a beast shall surely be put to death.

20   ᴿHe that sacrificeth unto *any* god, save unto the Lᴏʀᴅ only, he shall be utterly destroyed. Le 17:7

21   ᴿThou shalt neither vex a stranger, nor oppress him: for ye were strangers in the land of Egypt. 23:9; De 10:19; Ze 7:10

22   ᴿYe shall not afflict any widow, or fatherless child. Je 7:6

23   If thou afflict them in any wise, and they cry at all unto me, I will surely hear their cry;

24   And my ᴿwrath shall wax hot, and I will kill you with the sword; and ᴿyour wives shall be widows, and your children fatherless. Ps 69:24 · Ps 109:9

25   If thou lend money to *any of* my people *that is* poor by thee, thou shalt not be to him as an usurer, neither shalt thou lay upon him ᴿusury.ᵀ Ps 15:5 · *interest*

26   ᴿIf thou at all take thy neighbour's raiment to pledge, thou shalt deliver it unto him by that the sun goeth down: Pr 20:16

27   For that *is* his covering only, it *is* his raiment for his skin: wherein shall he sleep? and it shall come to pass, when he crieth unto me, that I will hear; for I *am* ᴿgracious. 34:6, 7

28   ᴿThou shalt not revile the ᵀgods, nor curse the ᴿruler of thy people. Ec 10:20 · *God* · Ac 23:5

29   Thou shalt not delay *to offer* the first of thy ripe fruits, and of thy liquors: ᴿthe firstborn of thy sons shalt thou give unto me. 13:2

30   ᴿLikewise shalt thou do with thine oxen, *and* with thy sheep: ᴿseven days it shall be with his dam; on the eighth day thou shalt give it me. De 15:19 · Le 22:27

22:18 *Thou shalt not suffer a witch to live.* The Bible does not record any executions of sorcerers or sorceresses, but it does recount the deadly consequences of false worship (ch. 32; Nu 25).

31 And ye shall be holy men unto me: neither shall ye eat *any* flesh *that is* torn of beasts in the field; ye shall cast it to the dogs.

23 Thou shalt not raise a false report: put not thine hand with the wicked to be an ᴿunrighteous witness.   Ps 35:11; Ac 6:11

2 ᴿThou shalt not follow a multitude to *do* evil; neither shalt thou speak in a cause to decline after many to wrest *judgment:*   Ge 7:1

3 Neither shalt thou countenance a poor man in his cause.

4 ᴿIf thou meet thine enemy's ox or his ass going astray, thou shalt surely bring it back to him again.   [Ro 12:20]

5 ᴿIf thou see the ass of him that hateth thee lying under his burden, and wouldest forbear to help him, thou shalt surely help with him.   De 22:4

6 Thou shalt not wrest the judgment of thy poor in his cause.

7 Keep thee far from a false matter; and the innocent and righteous slay thou not: for ᴿI will not justify the wicked.   Ro 1:18

8 And ᴿthou shalt take no ᵀgift: for the gift blindeth the wise, and perverteth the words of the righteous.   Pr 15:27; 17:8; Is 5:22, 23 · *bribe*

9 Also thou shalt not oppress a stranger: for ye know the heart of a stranger, seeing ye were strangers in the land of Egypt.

10 And ᴿsix years thou shalt sow thy land, and shalt gather in the fruits thereof: Le 25:1-7

11 But the seventh *year* thou shalt let it rest and lie still; that the poor of thy people may eat: and what they leave the beasts of the field shall eat. In like manner thou shalt deal with thy vineyard, *and* with thy ᵀoliveyard.   *olive grove*

12 ᴿSix days thou shalt do thy work, and on the seventh day thou shalt rest: that thine ox and thine ass may rest, and the son of thy handmaid, and the stranger, may be refreshed.   Lk 13:14

13 And in all *things* that I have said unto you be circumspect: and ᴿmake no mention of the name of other gods, neither let it be heard out of thy mouth.   Jos 23:7; Ps 16:4

14 ᴿThree times thou shalt keep a feast unto me in the year.   34:22

15 ᴿThou shalt keep the feast of unleavened bread: (thou shalt eat unleavened bread seven days, as I commanded thee, in the time appointed of the month A'-bib; for in it thou camest out from Egypt: ᴿand none shall appear before me empty:)   Le 23:6-8 · 22:29; 34:20

16 ᴿAnd the feast of harvest, the firstfruits of thy labours, which thou hast sown in the field: and ᴿthe feast of ingathering, *which is* in the end of the year, when thou hast gathered in thy labours out of the field.   Nu 28:26 · De 16:13

17 ᴿThree times in the year all thy males shall appear before the Lord GOD.   v. 14; 34:23; De 16:16

18 ᴿThou shalt not offer the blood of my sacrifice with leavened bread; ᴿneither shall the fat of my sacrifice remain until the morning.   Le 2:11 · Le 7:15; De 16:4

19 ᴿThe first of the firstfruits of thy land thou shalt bring into the house of the LORD thy God. ᴿThou shalt not seethe a kid in his mother's milk.   De 26:2 · De 14:21

23:1 *false report.* Malicious talk is everywhere condemned in Scripture (see James 3:1–12). **23:3** *countenance a poor man.* God's support of the poor did not overrule His justice. Here God anticipated that some would use poverty as an excuse for greedy, even criminal activity. **23:11** *rest and lie still.* Letting the land rest allowed the poor to glean any produce that might grow during the fallow year. It also gave the land time to rejuvenate for greater productivity in subsequent years. The year of rest was an act of faith, for the Israelites would have to trust God to meet their needs. **23:17** *Lord GOD.* Here two names for God, Adonai (translated as Lord), and Yahweh (translated as GOD), are used together. This expression emphasizes God's sovereignty.

20 ^RBehold, I send an Angel before thee, to keep thee in the way, and to bring thee into the place which I have prepared.   3:2
21 Beware of him, and obey his voice, provoke him not; for he will not pardon your transgressions: for ^Rmy name *is* in him.   Je 23:6
✠22 But if thou shalt indeed obey his voice, and do all that I speak; then ^RI will be an enemy unto thine enemies, and an adversary unto thine adversaries. Ge 12:3
23 ^RFor mine Angel shall go before thee, and ^Rbring thee in unto the Am'-or-ites, and the Hit'-tites, and the Per'-iz-zites, and the Ca'-naan-ites, the Hi'-vites, and the Jeb'-u-sites: and I will cut them off.   v. 20 · Jos 24:8, 11
24 Thou shalt not bow down to their gods, nor serve them, nor do after their works: ^Rbut thou shalt utterly overthrow them, and quite break down their images.   2 Ki 18:4
✠25 And ye shall ^Rserve the LORD your God, and he shall bless thy bread, and thy water; and I will take sickness away from the midst of thee.   De 6:13
26 ^RThere shall nothing cast their young, nor be barren, in thy land: the number of thy days I will ^Rfulfil.   De 28:4; Mal 3:11 · 1 Ch 23:1
27 I will send ^Rmy fear before thee, and will destroy all the people to whom thou shalt come, and I will make all thine enemies turn their backs unto thee.   Jos 2:9
28 And I will send hornets before thee, which shall drive out the Hi'-vite, the Ca'-naan-ite, and the Hit'-tite, from before thee.
29 ^RI will not drive them out from before thee in one year; lest the

land become desolate, and the beast of the field multiply against thee.   De 7:22
30 By little and little I will drive them out from before thee, until thou be increased, and inherit the land.
31 And I will set thy bounds from the Red sea even unto the sea of the Phi-lis'-tines, and from the desert unto the river: for I will deliver the inhabitants of the land into your hand; and thou shalt drive them out before thee.
32 ^RThou shalt make no ^Tcovenant with them, nor with their gods.   34:12, 15; De 7:2 · *treaty*
33 They shall not dwell in thy land, lest they make thee sin against me: for if thou serve their gods, ^Rit will surely be a snare unto thee.   De 12:30; Jos 23:13; Ju 2:3

24 And he said unto Moses, Come up unto the LORD, thou, and Aaron, Na'-dab, and A-bi'-hu, and seventy of the elders of Israel; and worship ye afar off.
2 And Moses alone shall come near the LORD: but they shall not come nigh; neither shall the people go up with him.
3 And Moses came and told the people all the words of the LORD, and all the judgments: and all the people answered with one voice, and said, ^RAll the words which the LORD hath said will we do.   19:8
4 And Moses ^Rwrote all the words of the LORD, and rose up early in the morning, and builded an altar under the hill, and twelve ^Rpillars, according to the twelve tribes of Israel.   De 31:9 · Ge 28:18

✠ 23:22   ✠ 23:25

23:20 Angel. The statement "My name is in him" (v. 21) shows that this messenger is the Angel of the Lord, who is none other than God Himself; with the promise of His presence and protection comes the warning "Obey His voice," for the Lord is a holy God who cannot dwell in the presence of sin. Obedience is the evidence of reality of the covenant relationship. The Angel of the Lord "encampeth round about them that fear him" (Ps 34:7). **23:26 cast their young, nor be barren.** God reminded His people that He was the one who controlled reproduction—not the fertility cults of the pagan Canaanites.

5   And he sent young men of the children of Israel, which offered ᴿburnt offerings, and sacrificed peace offerings of oxen unto the LORD.   18:12; 20:24
6   And Moses ᴿtook half of the blood, and put *it* in basons; and half of the blood he sprinkled on the altar.   29:16, 20; He 9:18
7   And he ᴿtook the book of the covenant, and read in the audience of the people: and they said, All that the LORD hath said will we do, and be obedient.   He 9:19
8   And Moses took the blood, and sprinkled *it* on the people, and said, Behold ᴿthe blood of the covenant, which the LORD hath made with you concerning all these words.   Ze 9:11; [Lk 22:20]
9   Then went up Moses, and Aaron, Na'-dab, and A-bi'-hu, and seventy of the elders of Israel:
10   And they saw the God of Israel: and *there was* under his feet as it were a paved work of a sapphire stone, and as it were the body of heaven in *his* clearness.
11   And upon the nobles of the children of Israel he laid not his hand: also ᴿthey saw God, and did ᴿeat and drink.   Ju 13:22 · 1 Co 10:18
12   And the LORD said unto Moses, Come up to me into the mount, and be there: and I will give thee ᴿtables of stone, and a law, and commandments which

I have written; that thou mayest teach them.   31:18; 32:15; De 5:22
13   And Moses rose up, and ᴿhis minister Joshua: and Moses went up into the mount of God.   32:17
14   And he said unto the elders, Tarry ye here for us, until we come again unto you: and, behold, Aaron and ᴿHur *are* with you: if any man have any matters to do, let him come unto them.   17:10, 12
15   And Moses went up into the mount, and ᴿa cloud covered the mount.   19:9; Ma 17:5
16   And ᴿthe glory of the LORD abode upon mount Si'-nai, and the cloud covered it six days: and the seventh day he called unto Moses out of the midst of the cloud.   16:10; 33:18; Nu 14:10
17   And the sight of the glory of the LORD *was* like ᴿdevouring fire on the top of the mount in the eyes of the children of Israel.   3:2
18   And Moses went into the midst of the cloud, and gat him up into the mount: and ᴿMoses was in the mount forty days and forty nights.   34:28; De 9:9; 10:10

25 And the LORD spake unto Moses, saying,
2   Speak unto the children of Israel, that they bring me an offering: ᴿof every man that giveth it willingly with his heart ye shall take my offering.   Ez 2:68; Ne 11:2
3   And this *is* the offering which

24:6 blood. This blood anticipated the death of the coming Messiah, Jesus. His blood could do what the blood of bulls and goats could never accomplish; His death opened the way for direct communication with God (12:7; Ro 3:23–26; He 10:4,10).   **24:8 the blood of the covenant.** Just as their houses were protected from the Passover by the sign of blood (ch. 12), now the people were brought into a covenant relationship with the Lord with a sign of blood. This is a picture of our own relationship with God, brought about by the blood of Jesus (1 Pe 1:2).   **24:9–17 God of Israel.** This vision of God was a great privilege. The elders of the people saw God standing on a structure resembling a transparent sapphire platform, which emphasized His grandeur. Blue was one of the colors favored by some members of ancient Near Eastern royalty. God's glory is the manifestation of all His divine characteristics, including power and holiness, which for Israel were represented by the billowing consuming fire (He 12:29).   **24:12 Come up to me.** Only Moses could draw near to God at that time. Today, we are all called to draw near to God through Jesus (see He 4:14–16).   **25:2 of every man that giveth it willingly.** God does not need the gifts of His people, but He desires us to give to Him as an expression of true worship.

ye shall take of them; gold, and silver, and brass,

4 And blue, and purple, and scarlet, and fine linen, and goats' *hair,*

5 And rams' skins dyed red, and [T]badgers' skins, and shit'-tim wood,   Or *dolphin*

6 [R]Oil for the light, [R]spices for anointing oil, and for sweet incense,   27:20 · 30:23

7 Onyx stones, and stones to be set in the [R]e'-phod, and in the breastplate.   28:4, 6–14

8 And let them make me a sanctuary; that [R]I may dwell among them.   1 Ki 6:13; [He 3:6]

9 According to all that I shew thee, *after* the pattern of the tabernacle, and the pattern of all the instruments thereof, even so shall ye make *it.*

10 [R]And they shall make an ark *of* shit'-tim wood: two cubits and a half *shall be* the length thereof, and a cubit and a half the breadth thereof, and a cubit and a half the height thereof.   De 10:3; He 9:4

11 And thou shalt overlay it with pure gold, within and without shalt thou overlay it, and shalt make upon it a crown of [R]gold round about.   37:2; He 9:4

12 And thou shalt cast four rings of gold for it, and put *them* in the four corners thereof; and two rings *shall be* in the one side of it, and two rings in the other side of it.

13 And thou shalt make staves *of* shit'-tim wood, and overlay them with gold.

14 And thou shalt put the staves into the rings by the sides of the ark, that the ark may be borne with them.

15 [R]The staves shall be in the rings of the ark: they shall not be taken from it.   Nu 4:6; 1 Ki 8:8

16 And thou shalt put into the ark [R]the testimony which I shall give thee.   De 31:26; 1 Ki 8:9; He 9:4

17 And [R]thou shalt make a mercy seat *of* pure gold: two cubits and a half *shall be* the length thereof, and a cubit and a half the breadth thereof.   37:6; He 9:5

18 And thou shalt make two cher'-u-bims *of* gold, *of* beaten work shalt thou make them, in the two ends of the mercy seat.

19 And make one cherub on the one end, and the other cherub on the other end: *even* of the mercy seat shall ye make the cher'-u-bims on the two ends thereof.

20 And [R]the cher'-u-bims shall stretch forth *their* wings on high, covering the mercy seat with their wings, and their faces *shall look* one to another; toward the mercy seat shall the faces of the cher'-u-bims be.   1 Ki 8:7; 1 Ch 28:18; He 9:5

21 [R]And thou shalt put the mercy seat above upon the ark; and in the ark thou shalt put the testimony that I shall give thee.   26:34; 40:20

22 And there I will meet with thee, and I will commune with thee from above the mercy seat, from [R]between the two cher'-u-bims which *are* upon the ark of the testimony,

---

25:9 *the pattern.* The language of these verses suggests that there is a heavenly pattern that the earthly tabernacle was designed to resemble (see v. 40; 26:30; 27:8; Ac 7:44; He 8:5). **25:10 *ark.*** In contrast to the idolatry of Israel's neighbors, the shrine of the living God had no likeness or idol of any sort (20:2–6). ***cubit.*** This measurement was represented by the length of a man's arm from elbow to extended middle finger. The commonly accepted estimate for the cubit is eighteen inches. Therefore, the ark was about four feet long and two and one quarter feet wide and high. **25:17 *mercy seat.*** This English phrase translates a Hebrew noun derived from the verb meaning "atone for," "to cover over," or "to make propitiation." The mercy seat was the lid of the ark, the place where God's spirit rested. **25:22 *I will commune with thee.*** God dwells with His people in the space-time reality in which He created them, and communes with them in the language with which He endowed them. He is not aloof and He is not silent. His words are an extension of Himself and reflect His nature. They are altogether pure

Continued on the next page

of all *things* which I will give thee in commandment unto the children of Israel.   Ps 80:1

23 Thou shalt also make a table *of* shit'-tim wood: two cubits *shall be* the length thereof, and a cubit the breadth thereof, and a cubit and a half the height thereof.

24 And thou shalt overlay it with pure gold, and make thereto a crown of gold round about.

25 And thou shalt make unto it a border of an hand breadth round about, and thou shalt make a golden crown to the border thereof round about.

26 And thou shalt make for it four rings of gold, and put the rings in the four corners that *are* on the four feet thereof.

27 Over against the border shall the rings be for places of the staves to bear the table.

28 And thou shalt make the staves *of* shit'-tim wood, and overlay them with gold, that the table may be borne with them.

29 And thou shalt make [R] the dishes thereof, and spoons thereof, and covers thereof, and bowls thereof, to cover withal: *of* pure gold shalt thou make them. 37:16

30 And thou shalt set upon the table [R] shewbread before me alway.   39:36; 40:23; Le 24:5-9

31 [R] And thou shalt make a candlestick *of* pure gold: *of* beaten work shall the candlestick be made: his shaft, and his branches, his bowls, his knops, and his flowers, shall be of the same.   Ze 4:2

32 And six branches shall come out of the sides of it; three branches of the candlestick out of the one side, and three branches of the candlestick out of the other side:

33 [R] Three bowls made like unto almonds, *with* a knop and a flower in one branch; and three bowls made like almonds in the other branch, *with* a knop and a flower: so in the six branches that come out of the candlestick.   37:19

34 And [R] in the candlestick *shall be* four bowls made like unto almonds, *with* their knops and their flowers.   37:20-22

35 And *there shall be* a knop under two branches of the same, and a knop under two branches of the same, and a knop under two branches of the same, according to the six branches that proceed out of the candlestick.

36 Their knops and their branches shall be of the same: all it *shall be* one beaten work *of* pure gold.

37 And thou shalt make the seven lamps thereof: and [R] they shall [T] light the lamps thereof, that they may [R] give light over against it.   Le 24:3, 4 · *arrange* · Nu 8:2

38 And the tongs thereof, and the snuffdishes thereof, *shall be of* pure gold.

39 *Of* a talent of pure gold shall he make it, with all these vessels.

40 And look that thou make *them* after their pattern, which was shewed thee in the mount.

26 Moreover thou shalt make the tabernacle *with* ten curtains *of* fine twined linen, and blue, and purple, and scarlet: *with* cher'-

---

and without blemish, and they are fully authoritative. At the same time, His words reach out to man and are rooted in love, issued from the mercy seat. He speaks them Himself or has them spoken by His authority. He preserves them. He writes them or has them written under His superintendence. God is the ultimate Author of His own Word. This Word is and remains His living and abiding Voice. **25:29 *pure gold.*** All of the implements for making bread were also to be costly and wonderfully designed to physically represent their holiness. They were "set apart" to God. **25:30 *shewbread.*** Twelve loaves representing the twelve tribes of Israel were placed in two rows with six loaves in each row (Le 24:5-9). It was called showbread because it was placed symbolically before the face of God. **25:39 *talent.*** A talent weighed about 75 pounds. **26:1 *tabernacle.*** The word tabernacle simply means "tent."

u-bims of cunning work shalt thou make them.

2   The length of one curtain *shall be* eight and twenty cubits, and the breadth of one curtain four cubits: and every one of the curtains shall have one measure.

3   The five curtains shall be coupled together one to another; and *other* five curtains *shall be* coupled one to another.

4   And thou shalt make loops of blue upon the edge of the one curtain from the selvedge in the coupling; and likewise shalt thou make in the uttermost edge of *another* curtain, in the coupling of the second.

5   Fifty loops shalt thou make in the one curtain, and fifty loops shalt thou make in the edge of the curtain that *is* in the coupling of the second; that the loops may take hold one of another.

6   And thou shalt make fifty taches of gold, and couple the curtains together with the taches: and it shall be one tabernacle.

7   And ᴿthou shalt make curtains *of* goats' *hair* to be a covering upon the tabernacle: eleven curtains shalt thou make.   36:14

8   The length of one curtain *shall be* thirty cubits, and the breadth of one curtain four cubits: and the eleven curtains *shall be all* of one measure.

9   And thou shalt couple five curtains by themselves, and six curtains by themselves, and shalt double the sixth curtain in the forefront of the tabernacle.

10   And thou shalt make fifty loops on the edge of the one curtain *that is* outmost in the coupling, and fifty loops in the edge of the curtain which coupleth the second.

11   And thou shalt make fifty taches of brass, and put the taches into the loops, and couple the tent together, that it may be one.

12   And the remnant that remaineth of the curtains of the tent, the half curtain that remaineth, shall

hang over the backside of the tabernacle.

13   And a cubit on the one side, and a cubit on the other side of that which remaineth in the length of the curtains of the tent, it shall hang over the sides of the tabernacle on this side and on that side, to cover it.

14   And ᴿthou shalt make a covering for the tent *of* rams' skins dyed red, and a covering above *of* badgers' skins.   35:7, 23; 36:19

15   And thou shalt ᴿmake boards for the tabernacle *of* shit'-tim wood standing up.   36:20–34

16   Ten cubits *shall be* the length of a board, and a cubit and a half *shall be* the breadth of one board.

17   Two ᵀtenons *shall there be* in one board, set in order one against another: thus shalt thou make for all the boards of the tabernacle.   *projections for joining*

18   And thou shalt make the boards for the tabernacle, twenty boards on the south side southward.

19   And thou shalt make forty sockets of silver under the twenty boards; two sockets under one board for his two tenons, and two sockets under another board for his two tenons.

20   And for the second side of the tabernacle on the north side *there shall be* twenty boards:

21   And their forty sockets *of* silver; two sockets under one board, and two sockets under another board.

22   And for the sides of the tabernacle westward thou shalt make six boards.

23   And two boards shalt thou make for the corners of the tabernacle in the two sides.

24   And they shall be ᵀcoupled together beneath, and they shall be coupled together above the head of it unto one ring: thus shall it be for them both; they shall be for the two corners.   Lit. *doubled*

25   And they shall be eight boards, and their sockets *of* silver, sixteen

sockets; two sockets under one board, and two sockets under another board.

26 And thou shalt make bars *of* shit'-tim wood; five for the boards of the one side of the tabernacle,

27 And five bars for the boards of the other side of the tabernacle, and five bars for the boards of the side of the tabernacle, for the two sides westward.

28 And the [R]middle bar in the midst of the boards shall reach from end to end. 36:33

29 And thou shalt overlay the boards with gold, and make their rings *of* gold *for* places for the bars: and thou shalt overlay the bars with gold.

30 And thou shalt [T]rear up the tabernacle [R]according to the fashion thereof which was shewed thee in the mount. *raise* · Ac 7:44

31 And [R]thou shalt make a vail *of* blue, and purple, and scarlet, and fine twined linen of cunning work: with cher'-u-bims shall it be made: Ma 27:51; He 9:3; 10:20

32 And thou shalt hang it upon four pillars of shit'-tim *wood* overlaid with gold: their hooks *shall be of* gold, upon the four sockets of silver.

33 And thou shalt hang up the vail under the taches, that thou mayest bring in thither within the vail [R]the ark of the testimony: and the vail shall divide unto you between [R]the holy *place* and the most holy. 40:21 · Le 16:2; He 9:2, 3

34 And thou shalt put the mercy seat upon the ark of the testimony in the most holy *place*.

35 And [R]thou shalt set the table [T]without the vail, and the candlestick over against the table on the side of the tabernacle toward the south: and thou shalt put the table on the north side. He 9:2 · *outside*

36 And [R]thou shalt make an hang-ing for the door of the tent, *of* blue, and purple, and scarlet, and fine twined linen, wrought with needlework. 36:37

37 And thou shalt make for the hanging [R]five pillars *of* shit'-tim *wood,* and overlay them with gold, *and* their hooks *shall be of* gold: and thou shalt cast five sockets of brass for them. 36:38

27 And thou shalt make [R]an altar *of* shit'-tim wood, five cubits long, and five cubits broad; the altar shall be foursquare: and the height thereof *shall be* three cubits. 38:1; Eze 43:13

2 And thou shalt make the horns of it upon the four corners thereof: his horns shall be of the same: and thou shalt overlay it with brass.

3 And thou shalt make his pans to receive his ashes, and his shovels, and his basons, and his fleshhooks, and his firepans: all the vessels thereof thou shalt make *of* brass.

4 And thou shalt make for it a grate of network *of* brass; and upon the net shalt thou make four brasen rings in the four corners thereof.

5 And thou shalt put it under the compass of the altar beneath, that the net may be even to the midst of the altar.

6 And thou shalt make staves for the altar, staves *of* shit'-tim wood, and overlay them with brass.

7 And the staves shall be put into the rings, and the staves shall be upon the two sides of the altar, to bear it.

8 Hollow with boards shalt thou make it: [R]as it was shewed thee in the mount, so shall they make it. 26:30; Ac 7:44; [He 8:5]

9 And [R]thou shalt make the court of the tabernacle: for the south side southward *there shall be* hangings for the court *of* fine twined linen

---

27:9–18 court of the tabernacle. The courtyard separated the ceremonies of worship from common areas. It was arranged to keep people and stray animals from wandering into the tabernacle. Entering the tent could only be a deliberate act.

of an hundred cubits long for one side: 38:9–20
10 And the twenty pillars thereof and their twenty sockets *shall be of* brass; the hooks of the pillars and their fillets *shall be of* silver.
11 And likewise for the north side in length *there shall be* hangings of an hundred *cubits* long, and his twenty pillars and their twenty sockets *of* brass; the hooks of the pillars and their fillets *of* silver.
12 And *for* the breadth of the court on the west side *shall be* hangings of fifty cubits: their pillars ten, and their sockets ten.
13 And the breadth of the court on the east side eastward *shall be* fifty cubits.
14 The hangings of one side *of the gate shall be* fifteen cubits: their pillars three, and their sockets three.
15 And on the other side *shall be* hangings fifteen *cubits:* their pillars three, and their sockets three.
16 And for the gate of the court *shall be* an hanging of twenty cubits, *of* blue, and purple, and scarlet, and fine twined linen, wrought with needlework: *and* their pillars *shall be* four, and their sockets four.
17 All the pillars round about the court *shall be* filleted with silver; their [R] hooks *shall be of* silver, and their sockets *of* brass. 38:19
18 The length of the court *shall be* an hundred cubits, and the breadth fifty [T] every where, and the height five cubits *of* fine twined linen, and their sockets *of* brass. *throughout*
19 All the vessels of the tabernacle in all the service thereof, and all the pins thereof, and all the pins of the court, *shall be of* brass.
20 And [R] thou shalt command the children of Israel, that they bring thee pure oil olive beaten for the light, to cause the lamp to [T] burn always. Le 24:1–4 · Lit. *ascend*
21 In the tabernacle of the congregation without the vail, which *is* before the testimony, Aaron and his sons shall order it from evening to morning before the LORD: [R] *it shall be* a statute for ever unto their generations on the behalf of the children of Israel. Le 3:17; 16:34

28 And take thou unto thee Aaron thy brother, and his sons with him, from among the children of Israel, that he may minister unto me in the priest's [R] office, *even* Aaron, Na'-dab and A-bi'-hu, E-le-a'-zar and Ith'-a-mar, Aaron's sons. Ps 99:6; He 5:4
2 And [R] thou shalt make holy garments for Aaron thy brother for glory and for beauty. Le 8:7–9
3 And thou shalt speak unto all *that are* wise hearted, [R] whom I have filled with the spirit of wisdom, that they may make Aaron's garments to consecrate him, that he may minister unto me in the priest's office. Is 11:2; Ep 1:17
4 And these *are* the garments which they shall make; a breastplate, and an e'-phod, and a robe, and a broidered coat, a [T] mitre, and [R] a [T] girdle: and they shall make holy garments for Aaron thy brother, and his sons, that he may minister unto me in the priest's office. *turban* · Le 8:7 · *sash*
5 And they shall take gold, and

27:20 *pure oil olive beaten.* All that was used in the tabernacle and sacrifices must be pure and without blemish in order to honor God's holiness. ***the lamp to burn always.*** The oil for the lampstand was the gift of the children of Israel. It had to be pure oil, as a symbol of our need to call upon the Lord from a pure heart (2 Ti 2:22). The lamps were to burn continuously, a reminder of the perpetual need of the sinner for the light of God's word, "a lamp unto my feet, and a light unto my path" (Ps 119:105). **28:3 *all that are wise hearted.*** This expression literally means "those who are wise at heart." The same expression is used of the skillful women who did the weaving (35:25). **28:5–14 *e-phod.*** The ephod has been described as a cape or vest made of fine linen with brilliant colors. Its

Continued on the next page

blue, and purple, and scarlet, and fine linen.

6 And they shall make the e'-phod *of* gold, *of* blue, and *of* purple, *of* scarlet, and fine twined linen, with ᵀcunning work.   *artistic*

7 It shall have the two shoulderpieces thereof joined at the two edges thereof; and *so* it shall be joined together.

8 And the ᵀcurious girdle of the e'-phod, which *is* upon it, shall be of the same, according to the work thereof; *even of* gold, *of* blue, and purple, and scarlet, and fine twined linen.   *intricately woven*

9 And thou shalt take two onyx stones, and grave on them the names of the children of Israel:

10 Six of their names on one stone, and *the other* six names of the rest on the other stone, according to their ᴿbirth.   Ge 35:16

11 With the work of an ᴿengraver in stone, *like* the engravings of a signet, shalt thou engrave the two stones with the names of the children of Israel: thou shalt make them to be set in ᵀouches of gold.   35:35 · *settings*

12 And thou shalt put the two stones upon the shoulders of the e'-phod *for* stones of memorial unto the children of Israel: and ᴿAaron shall bear their names before the LORD upon his two shoulders for a memorial.   39:6, 7

13 And thou shalt make ouches *of* gold;

14 And two chains *of* pure gold at the ends; *of* wreathen work shalt thou make them, and fasten the wreathen chains to the ouches.

15 And ᴿthou shalt make the breastplate of judgment with cunning work; after the work of the e'-phod thou shalt make it; *of* gold, *of* blue, and *of* purple, and *of* scar-

let, and *of* fine twined linen, shalt thou make it.   39:8–21

16 Foursquare it shall be *being* doubled; a span *shall be* the length thereof, and a span *shall be* the breadth thereof.

17 And thou shalt set in it settings of stones, *even* four rows of stones: *the first* row *shall be* a sardius, a topaz, and a ᵀcarbuncle: *this shall be* the first row.   *emerald*

18 And the second row *shall be* an ᵀemerald, a sapphire, and a ᵀdiamond.   *turquoise · sapphire*

19 And the third row a ᵀligure, an agate, and an amethyst. *jacinth*

20 And the fourth row a ᵀberyl, and an ᵀonyx, and a jasper: they shall be set in gold in their inclosings.   *yellow jasper · onyx* or *carnelian*

21 And the stones shall be with the names of the children of Israel, twelve, according to their names, *like* the engravings of a signet; every one with his name shall they be according to the twelve tribes.

22 And thou shalt make upon the breastplate chains at the ends *of* wreathen work *of* pure gold.

23 And thou shalt make upon the breastplate two rings of gold, and shalt put the two rings on the two ends of the breastplate.

24 And thou shalt put the two wreathen *chains* of gold in the two rings *which are* on the ends of the breastplate.

25 And *the other* two ends of the two wreathen *chains* thou shalt fasten in the two ouches, and put *them* on the shoulderpieces of the e'-phod before it.

26 And thou shalt make two rings of gold, and thou shalt put them upon the two ends of the breastplate in the border thereof, which *is* in the side of the e'-phod inward.

27 And two *other* rings of gold thou shalt make, and shalt put them

two main sections covered the chest and back, with seams at the shoulders and a band at the waist.   **28:16 *span.*** The span was determined as the length from the tip of the thumb to the tip of the small finger on an outstretched hand. It is generally estimated as nine inches, or half a cubit.

on the two sides of the e'-phod underneath, toward the forepart thereof, over against the *other* coupling thereof, above the curious girdle of the e'-phod.

28 And they shall bind the breastplate by the rings thereof unto the rings of the e'-phod with a lace of blue, that *it* may be above the curious girdle of the e'-phod, and that the breastplate be not loosed from the e'-phod.

29 And Aaron shall [R]bear the names of the children of Israel in the breastplate of judgment upon his heart, when he goeth in unto the holy *place*, for a memorial before the LORD continually.   v. 12

30 And thou shalt put in the breastplate of judgment the [T]U'-rim and the Thum'-mim; and they shall be upon Aaron's heart, when he goeth in before the LORD: and Aaron shall bear the judgment of the children of Israel upon his heart before the LORD continually.   Lit. *Lights and the Perfections*

31 And thou shalt make the robe of the e'-phod all *of* blue.

32 And there shall be an hole in the top of it, in the midst thereof: it shall have a binding of woven work round about the hole of it, as it were the hole of an habergeon, that it be not rent.

33 And *beneath* upon the hem of it thou shalt make pomegranates *of* blue, and *of* purple, and *of* scarlet, round about the hem thereof; and bells of gold between them round about:

34 A golden bell and a pomegranate, a golden bell and a pomegranate, upon the hem of the robe round about.

35 And it shall be upon Aaron to minister: and his sound shall be heard when he goeth in unto the holy *place* before the LORD, and when he cometh out, that he die not.

36 And [R]thou shalt make a plate *of* pure gold, and grave upon it, *like* the engravings of a signet, HOLINESS TO THE LORD.   39:30

37 And thou shalt put it on a blue lace, that it may be upon the mitre; upon the forefront of the mitre it shall be.

38 And it shall be upon Aaron's forehead, that Aaron may [R]bear the iniquity of the holy things, which the children of Israel shall hallow in all their holy gifts; and it shall be always upon his forehead, that they may be [R]accepted before the LORD.   [Is 53:11] · Is 56:7

39 And thou shalt [R]embroider the coat of fine linen, and thou shalt make the mitre *of* fine linen, and thou shalt make the girdle *of* needlework.   35:35; 39:27–29

40 And for Aaron's sons thou shalt make coats, and thou shalt make for them girdles, and [T]bonnets shalt thou make for them, for glory and for [R]beauty.   hats · v. 2

41 And thou shalt put them upon Aaron thy brother, and his sons with him; and shalt anoint them, and consecrate them, and sanctify them, that they may minister unto me in the priest's office.

42 And thou shalt make them linen breeches to cover their nakedness; from the loins even unto the thighs they shall reach:

43 And they shall be upon Aaron, and upon his sons, when they come in unto the tabernacle of the congregation, or when they come near unto the altar to minister in the holy *place*; that they [R]bear not iniquity, and die: [R]*it shall be* a stat-

---

28:30 the Urim and the Thummim. These translated Hebrew words mean "Lights" and "Perfections." Together their names may mean "perfect knowledge" or a similar idea. It is not known exactly what the Urim and Thummim were, or how they were used. Some have suggested that they were two stones used for the casting of lots. **28:42 breeches.** The command to wear trousers protected the modesty of the priests. Given the sexually preoccupied worship of Israel's neighbors, this provision was decidedly countercultural.

ute for ever unto him and his seed after him. Le 5:1, 17 · Le 17:7

29 And this *is* the thing that thou shalt do unto them to hallow them, to minister unto me in the priest's office: ^RTake one young bullock, and two rams without blemish, [He 7:26–28]

2 And ^Runleavened bread, and cakes unleavened tempered with oil, and wafers unleavened anointed with oil: *of* wheaten flour shalt thou make them. Le 2:4; 6:19–23

3 And thou shalt put them into one basket, and bring them in the basket, with the bullock and the two rams.

4 And Aaron and his sons thou shalt bring unto the door of the tabernacle of the congregation, and shalt wash them with water.

5 ^RAnd thou shalt take the garments, and put upon Aaron the coat, and the robe of the e′-phod, and the e′-phod, and the breastplate, and gird him with the curious girdle of the e′-phod: Le 8:7

6 ^RAnd thou shalt put the mitre upon his head, and put the holy crown upon the mitre. 28:36, 37

7 Then shalt thou take the anointing ^Roil, and pour *it* upon his head, and anoint him. Ps 133:2

8 And thou shalt bring his sons, and put coats upon them.

9 And thou shalt gird them with girdles, Aaron and his sons, and put the bonnets on them: and ^Rthe priest's office shall be theirs for a perpetual statute: and thou shalt ^Rconsecrate Aaron and his sons. Nu 3:10; 18:7; 25:13 · 28:41

10 And thou shalt cause a bullock to be brought before the tabernacle of the congregation: and ^RAaron and his sons shall put their hands upon the head of the bullock. Le 1:4; 8:14

11 And thou shalt kill the bullock before the LORD, *by* the door of the tabernacle of the congregation.

12 And thou shalt take of the blood of the bullock, and put *it* upon the horns of the altar with thy finger, and ^Rpour all the blood beside the bottom of the altar. 27:2

13 And ^Rthou shalt take all the fat that covereth the inwards, and the caul *that is* above the liver, and the two kidneys, and the fat that *is* upon them, and burn *them* upon the altar. Le 1:8; 3:3, 4

14 But the flesh of the bullock, and his skin, and his dung, shalt thou burn with fire ^Twithout the camp: it *is* a sin offering. *outside*

15 ^RThou shalt also take one ram; and Aaron and his sons shall ^Rput their hands upon the head of the ram. Le 8:18 · Le 1:4–9

16 And thou shalt slay the ram, and thou shalt take his blood, and ^Rsprinkle *it* round about upon the altar. 24:6; Le 1:5, 11

17 And thou shalt cut the ram in pieces, and wash the inwards of him, and his legs, and put *them* unto his pieces, and ^Tunto his head. *with*

18 And thou shalt burn the whole

29:1 hallow. The priests' actions should mark them as distinct, holy, set aside for God's purposes. **29:9 consecrate.** The verb translated *consecrate* in this verse literally means "to fill one's hand." A king was handed a rod as the symbol of his political power; so the hand of the priest was filled with spiritual power. **29:1–9 hallow them.** The outward purification process was used to symbolize the inward purity which was demanded of the priests of Israel, the intermediaries between the people and their holy God. Obviously the priests were not perfectly pure; it was only God's gracious act of accepting blood sacrifices that allowed the priests to stand in His presence on behalf of the people. The outward washings of the priests showed that they were doing everything possible to live their lives in the way they had been commanded by God. Likewise, in the New Testament era, the only reason that Christians can stand before God as believer-priests is because God graciously accepts Christ's sacrifice on behalf of our sins. **29:18 burnt offering.** Aaron and his sons needed to offer sacrifices for themselves as much as for their fellow Israelites (He 5:1–4).

ram upon the altar: it *is* a ᴿburnt offering unto the LORD: it *is* a sweet ᵀsavour, an offering made by fire unto the LORD.   20:24 · *aroma*

19 ᴿAnd thou shalt take the other ram; and Aaron and his sons shall put their hands upon the head of the ram.   Le 8:22

20 Then shalt thou kill the ram, and take of his blood, and put *it* upon the tip of the right ear of Aaron, and upon the tip of the right ear of his sons, and upon the thumb of their right hand, and upon the great toe of their right foot, and sprinkle the blood upon the altar round about.

21 And thou shalt take of the blood that *is* upon the altar, and of the anointing oil, and sprinkle *it* upon Aaron, and upon his garments, and upon his sons, and upon the garments of his sons with him: and ᴿhe shall be hallowed, and his garments, and his sons, and his sons' garments with him.   v. 1; 28:41; [He 9:22]

22 Also thou shalt take of the ram the fat and the rump, and the fat that covereth the inwards, and the caul *above* the liver, and the two kidneys, and the fat that *is* upon them, and the right shoulder; for it *is* a ram of consecration:

23 ᴿAnd one loaf of bread, and one cake of oiled bread, and one wafer out of the basket of the unleavened bread that *is* before the LORD: Le 8:26

24 And thou shalt put all in the hands of Aaron, and in the hands of his sons; and shalt ᴿwave them *for* a wave offering before the LORD.   Le 7:30; 10:14

25 ᴿAnd thou shalt receive them of their hands, and burn *them* upon the altar for a burnt offering, for a sweet savour before the LORD: it *is* an offering made by fire unto the LORD.   Le 8:28

26 And thou shalt take ᴿthe breast of the ram of Aaron's consecration, and wave it *for* a wave offering before the LORD: and it shall be thy part.   Le 7:31, 34; 8:29

27 And thou shalt sanctify ᴿthe breast of the wave offering, and the shoulder of the heave offering, which is waved, and which is ᵀheaved up, of the ram of the consecration, *even* of *that* which *is* for Aaron, and of *that* which is for his sons: Le 7:31, 34; De 18:3 · *raised*

28 And it shall be Aaron's and his sons' by a statute for ever from the children of Israel: for it *is* an heave offering: and ᴿit shall be an heave offering from the children of Israel of the sacrifice of their peace offerings, *even* their heave offering unto the LORD. Le 3:1; 7:34

29 And the holy garments of Aaron ᴿshall be his sons' after him, to be anointed therein, and to be consecrated in them.   Nu 20:26

30 *And* that son that is priest in his stead shall put them on ᴿseven days, when he cometh into the tabernacle of the congregation to minister in the holy *place.* Le 8:35

31 And thou shalt take the ram of the consecration, and ᴿseethe his flesh in the holy place.   Le 8:31

32 And Aaron and his sons shall eat the flesh of the ram, and the ᴿbread that *is* in the basket, *by* the door of the tabernacle of the congregation.   Ma 12:4

33 And ᴿthey shall eat those things wherewith the atonement was made, to consecrate *and* to sanctify them: ᴿbut a stranger shall not eat *thereof,* because they *are* holy.   Le 10:14, 15 · 12:43; Le 22:10

34 And if ought of the flesh of the consecrations, or of the bread, remain unto the morning, then ᴿthou shalt burn the remainder with fire: it shall not be eaten, because it *is* holy.   34:25; Le 7:18; 8:32

35 And thus shalt thou do unto Aaron, and to his sons, according

---

29:24 *wave offering.* This offering made it clear that everything was owed to God, but some was received back as God's gift (Le 7:30; 10:14).

to all *things* which I have commanded thee: [R]seven days shalt thou consecrate them.   Le 8:33–35
36 And thou [R]shalt offer every day a bullock *for* a sin offering for atonement: and thou shalt cleanse the altar, when thou hast made an atonement for it, and thou shalt anoint it, to sanctify it.   He 10:11
37 Seven days thou shalt make an atonement for the altar, and sanctify it; and it shall be an altar most holy: [R]whatsoever toucheth the altar shall be holy.   Ma 23:19
38 Now this *is that* which thou shalt offer upon the altar; [R]two lambs of the first year [R]day by day continually.   1 Ch 16:40 · Da 12:11
39 The one lamb thou shalt offer in the morning; and the other lamb thou shalt offer at even:
40 And with the one lamb a tenth deal of flour mingled with the fourth part of an hin of beaten oil; and the fourth part of an hin of wine *for* a drink offering.
41 And the other lamb thou shalt [R]offer [T]at even, and shalt do thereto according to the meat offering of the morning, and according to the drink offering thereof, for a sweet savour, an offering made by fire unto the LORD.   Ez 9:4, 5; Ps 141:2 · *at twilight*
42 *This shall be* [R]a continual burnt offering throughout your generations *at* the door of the tabernacle of the congregation before the LORD: where I will meet you, to speak there unto thee.   30:8
43 And there I will meet with the children of Israel, and *the tabernacle* [R]shall be sanctified by my glory.   1 Ki 8:11; Eze 43:5; Hag 2:7, 9
44 And I will sanctify the taber-

nacle of the congregation, and the altar: I will [R]sanctify also both Aaron and his sons, to minister to me in the priest's office.   Le 21:15
45 And [R]I will dwell among the children of Israel, and will be their God.   [Jo 14:17, 23; Re 21:3]
46 And they shall know that [R]I *am* the LORD their God, that [R]brought them forth out of the land of Egypt, that I may dwell among them: I *am* the LORD their God.   16:12; 20:2; De 4:35 · Le 11:45

30 And thou shalt make [R]an altar to burn incense upon: *of* shit'-tim wood shalt thou make it.   37:25–29
2 A cubit *shall be* the length thereof, and a cubit the breadth thereof; foursquare shall it be: and two cubits *shall be* the height thereof: the horns thereof *shall be* of the same.
3 And thou shalt overlay it with pure gold, the top thereof, and the sides thereof round about, and the horns thereof; and thou shalt make unto it a [T]crown of gold round about.   *moulding*
4 And two golden rings shalt thou make to it under the crown of it, by the two corners thereof, upon the two sides of it shalt thou make *it*; and they shall be for places for the staves to bear it withal.
5 And thou shalt make the staves *of* shit'-tim wood, and overlay them with gold.
6 And thou shalt put it before the [R]vail that *is* by the ark of the testimony, before the mercy seat that *is* over the testimony, where I will meet with thee.   26:31–35
7 And Aaron shall burn thereon

29:40 *tenth deal . . . hin.* One tenth of an deal was about two quarts; one fourth of a hin was about one quart. **29:45** *dwell among the children.* Man is God's special creation, created in His image and likeness. A part of that image and likeness is the uniqueness of personality that allows communion with God. He did not create a race of robots but rather endowed man with a will so that he might choose fellowship with God. In Israel, fellowship with God centered in the tabernacle and especially in the mercy seat which symbolized His presence. Today, believers have fellowship with God through the indwelling of the Holy Spirit. In eternity He will dwell in the midst of His people more fully than ever before. **30:7** *sweet incense.* Burning incense was a privilege restricted to those who were allowed to approach God.

[R]sweet incense every morning: when he dresseth the lamps, he shall burn incense upon it. Lk 1:9

8   And when Aaron lighteth the lamps [T]at even, he shall burn incense upon it, a perpetual incense before the LORD throughout your generations.   *at twilight*

9   Ye shall offer no [R]strange incense thereon, nor burnt sacrifice, nor meat offering; neither shall ye pour drink offering thereon.   Le 10:1

10   And [R]Aaron shall make an atonement upon the horns of it once in a year with the blood of the sin offering of atonements: once in the year shall he make atonement upon it throughout your generations: it *is* most holy unto the LORD.   Le 16:3–34

11   And the LORD spake unto Moses, saying,

12   When thou takest the sum of the children of Israel after their number, then shall they give every man [R]a ransom for his soul unto the LORD, when thou numberest them; that there be no plague among them, when *thou* numberest them.   [Ma 20:28; 1 Pe 1:18, 19]

13   [R]This they shall give, every one that passeth among them that are numbered, half a shek'-el after the shek'-el of the sanctuary: ([R]a shek'-el *is* twenty ge'-rahs:) an half shek'-el *shall be* the offering of the LORD.   Ma 17:24 · Le 27:25

14   Every one that passeth among them that are numbered, from twenty years old and above,

shall give an [T]offering unto the LORD.   *contribution*

15   The [R]rich shall not give more, and the poor shall not give less than half a shek'-el, when *they* give an offering unto the LORD, to make an atonement for your souls.   Job 34:19; Pr 22:2; [Ep 6:9]

16   And thou shalt take the atonement money of the children of Israel, and [R]shalt appoint it for the service of the tabernacle of the congregation; that it may be a memorial unto the children of Israel before the LORD, to make an atonement for your souls.   38:25–31

17   And the LORD spake unto Moses, saying,

18   [R]Thou shalt also make a [T]laver *of* brass, and his foot *also of* brass, to wash *withal:* and thou shalt [R]put it between the tabernacle of the congregation and the altar, and thou shalt put water therein.   38:8; 1 Ki 7:38 · *basin* · 40:30

19   For Aaron and his sons [R]shall wash their hands and their feet thereat: Is 52:11; Jo 13:8, 10; He 10:22

20   When they go into the tabernacle of the congregation, they shall wash with water, that they die not; or when they come near to the altar to minister, to burn offering made by fire unto the LORD:

21   So they shall wash their hands and their feet, that they die not: and [R]it shall be a [T]statute for ever to them, *even* to him and to his [T]seed throughout their generations. 28:43 · *requirement* · *descendants*

30:9 strange incense. The incense offered to God was to be made from a special recipe consecrated to be used only in the worship at the tabernacle. No other incense was acceptable.   **30:10 atonement.** The sacrificial blood of the sin offering (Le 16:18) was applied to the incense altar to indicate that even this article needed cleansing to preserve its ideal holiness because of man's willful or accidental sin. The Hebrew word for "atonement" involves the covering or canceling of sin, resulting in the offender being reconciled to God. Without blood being shed there can be no forgiveness (He 9:22). The atonement made annually for this small altar is a reminder that everything in God's service must be holy to the Lord (Ze 14:20).   **30:12 ransom.** The idea is to pay a price for one's life. The Israelites had to acknowledge that their lives were from God and governed by Him by giving Him an offering of money.   **30:19 wash their hands and their feet.** The continual washing was symbolic of the need to be cleansed from sin regularly.

22 Moreover the LORD spake unto Moses, saying,
23 Take thou also unto thee principal spices, of pure myrrh five hundred *shek'-els,* and of sweet cinnamon half so much, *even* two hundred and fifty *shek'-els,* and of sweet calamus two hundred and fifty *shek'-els,*
24 And of cassia five hundred *shek'-els,* after the shek'-el of the sanctuary, and of oil olive an hin:
25 And thou shalt make it an oil of holy ointment, an ointment compound after the art of the ᵀapothecary: it shall be ᴿan holy anointing oil.   *perfumer* · Ps 89:20; 133:2
26 ᴿAnd thou shalt anoint the tabernacle of the congregation therewith, and the ark of the testimony,   40:9; Le 8:10; Nu 7:1
27 And the table and all his vessels, and the candlestick and his vessels, and the altar of incense,
28 And the altar of burnt offering with all his vessels, and the laver and ᵀhis foot.   *its base*
29 And thou shalt sanctify them, that they may be most holy: ᴿwhatsoever toucheth them shall be holy.   29:37; Nu 4:15; Hag 2:11–13
30 ᴿAnd thou shalt anoint Aaron and his sons, and consecrate them, that *they* may minister unto me in the priest's office.   Le 8:12
31 And thou shalt speak unto the children of Israel, saying, This shall be an holy anointing oil unto me throughout your generations.
32 Upon man's flesh shall it not be poured, neither shall ye make *any other* like it, after the composition of it: ᴿit *is* holy, *and* it shall be holy unto you.   vv. 25, 37
33 Whosoever compoundeth *any* like it, or whosoever putteth *any* of it upon a stranger, shall even be cut off from his people.

34 And the LORD said unto Moses, ᴿTake unto thee sweet spices, stac'-te, and on'-y-cha, and gal'-banum; *these* sweet spices with pure frankincense: of each shall there be a like *weight:*   25:6; 37:29
35 And thou shalt make it a perfume, a confection after the art of the ᵀapothecary, ᵀtempered together, pure *and* holy: *perfumer · salted*
36 And thou shalt beat *some* of it very small, and put of it before the testimony in the tabernacle of the congregation, ᴿwhere I will meet with thee: ᴿit shall be unto you most holy.   Le 16:2 · Le 2:3
37 And *as for* the perfume which thou shalt make, ᴿye shall not make to yourselves according to ᵀthe composition thereof: it shall be unto thee holy for the LORD.   v. 32 · Lit. *its proportion*
38 Whosoever shall make like unto that, to smell thereto, shall even be cut off from his people.

31 And the LORD spake unto Moses, saying,
2 See, I have called by name Be-zal'-e-el the son of U'-ri, the son of Hur, of the tribe of Judah:
3 And I have ᴿfilled him with the spirit of God, in wisdom, and in understanding, and in knowledge, and in all manner of workmanship,   35:31; 1 Ki 7:14; Ep 1:17
4 To devise ᵀcunning works, to work in gold, and in silver, and in brass,   *artistic*
5 And in cutting of stones, to set *them,* and in carving of timber, to work in all manner of workmanship.
6 And I, behold, I have given with him A-ho'-li-ab, the son of A-his'-a-mach, of the tribe of Dan: and in the hearts of all that are ᵀwise hearted I have put wisdom,

31:3 *filled him with the spirit of God.* We often think of the "filling of the Spirit" only in connection with Acts 2, but passages such as this one help us to see the continuity of God's work among His people through the ages. In this case, the Spirit empowered uniquely gifted people to design and build a tabernacle befitting a holy and magnificent God.

that they may make all that I have commanded thee;   *gifted artisans*
7   ᴿThe tabernacle of the congregation, and ᴿthe ark of the testimony, and ᴿthe mercy seat that *is* thereupon, and all the furniture of the tabernacle,   36:8 · 37:1–5 · 37:6–9
8   And ᴿthe table and his furniture, and ᴿthe pure candlestick with all his furniture, and the altar of incense,   37:10–16 · 37:17–24
9   And ᴿthe altar of burnt offering with all his furniture, and ᴿthe laver and his foot,   38:1–7 · 38:8
10   And ᴿthe ᵀcloths of service, and the holy garments for Aaron the priest, and the garments of his sons, to minister in the priest's office,   39:1, 41 · *woven garments*
11   ᴿAnd the anointing oil, and sweet incense for the holy *place:* according to all that I have commanded thee shall they do.   30:23–38
12   And the Lᴏʀᴅ spake unto Moses, saying,
13   Speak thou also unto the children of Israel, saying, ᴿVerily my sabbaths ye shall keep: for it *is* a sign between me and you throughout your generations; that *ye* may know that I *am* the Lᴏʀᴅ that doth sanctify you.   Le 19:3, 30
14   Ye shall keep the sabbath therefore; for it *is* holy unto you: every one that defileth it shall surely be put to death: for ᴿwhosoever doeth *any* work therein, that soul shall be cut off from among his people.   Jo 7:23
15   ᴿSix days may work be done; but in the seventh *is* the sabbath

of rest, holy to the Lᴏʀᴅ: whosoever doeth *any* work in the sabbath day, he shall surely be put to death.   20:9–11; Le 23:3; De 5:12–14
16   Wherefore the children of Israel shall keep the sabbath, to observe the sabbath throughout their generations, *for* a perpetual covenant.
17   It *is* a sign between me and the children of Israel for ever: for *in* six days the Lᴏʀᴅ made heaven and earth, and on the seventh day he rested, and was refreshed.
18   And he gave unto Moses, when he had made an end of communing with him upon mount Si'-nai, ᴿtwo tables of testimony, tables of stone, written with the finger of God.   [De 4:13; 2 Co 3:3]

32 And when the people saw that Moses delayed to come down out of the mount, the people gathered themselves together unto Aaron, and said unto him, Up, make us gods, which shall ᴿgo before us; for *as for* this Moses, the man that ᴿbrought us up out of the land of Egypt, we wot not what is become of him.   13:21 · v. 8
2   And Aaron said unto them, Break off the ᴿgolden earrings, which *are* in the ears of your wives, of your sons, and of your daughters, and bring *them* unto me.   11:2; 35:22; Ju 8:24–27
3   And all the people brake off the golden earrings which *were* in their ears, and brought *them* unto Aaron.
4   ᴿAnd he received *them* at

31:18 *the finger of God.* This verse underscores the divine origin of the law. Scholars of religion have long spoken of Israel's religious ideas as its unique contribution to civilization, much as the Greeks developed philosophy and the Romans displayed a genius for organization and empire-building. Yet such a comparison misses the point of Scripture. The Bible speaks not of the genius of Israel, but of the finger of God. The Ten Commandments were not the product of man, but the revelation of the Lord. **32:1– 35 The Golden Calf**—The story of the Israelites' worship of the golden calf reveals both the unfaithfulness of the Israelites and God's great mercy. Even though the people had so quickly broken their promise to obey Him, God forgave their sin and began again with them. **32:2–3 *golden earrings.*** These were part of the treasure from Egypt that should have been used for building the tabernacle (35:20–29). **32:4 *a molten calf.*** This was an ominous worship symbol. Not only were the cow and the bull worshipped

Continued on the next page

their hand, and fashioned it with a graving tool, after he had made it a molten calf: and they said, These *be* thy gods, O Israel, which brought thee up out of the land of Egypt.   Ne 9:18; Ps 106:19; Ac 7:41

5   And when Aaron saw *it,* he built an altar before it; and Aaron made proclamation, and said, To morrow *is* a feast to the LORD.

6   And they rose up early on the morrow, and offered burnt offerings, and brought peace offerings; and the people sat down to eat and to drink, and rose up to play.

7   And the LORD said unto Moses, Go, get thee down; for thy people, which thou broughtest out of the land of Egypt, ^Rhave corrupted *themselves:*   Ge 6:11, 12

8   They have turned aside quickly out of the way which ^RI commanded them: they have made them a molten calf, and have worshipped it, and have sacrificed thereunto, and said, ^RThese *be* thy gods, O Israel, which have brought thee up out of the land of Egypt.   20:3, 4; De 32:17 · 1 Ki 12:28

9   And the LORD said unto Moses, I have seen this people, and, behold, it *is* a stiffnecked people:

10   Now therefore ^Rlet me alone, that my wrath may wax hot against them, and that I may consume them: and I will make of thee a great nation.   De 9:14, 19

11   ^RAnd Moses besought the LORD his God, and said, LORD, why doth thy wrath wax hot against thy people, which thou hast brought forth out of the land of Egypt with great power, and with a mighty hand?   De 9:18, 26–29

12   Wherefore should the Egyptians speak, and say, For mischief did he bring them out, to slay them

in the mountains, and to consume them from the face of the earth? Turn from thy fierce wrath, and ^Rrepent of this evil against thy people.   v. 14

13   Remember Abraham, Isaac, and Israel, thy servants, to whom thou ^Rswarest by thine own self, and saidst unto them, I will multiply your seed as the stars of heaven, and all this land that I have spoken of will I give unto your seed, and they shall inherit *it* for ever.   Ge 22:16–18; [He 6:13]

14   And the LORD ^Trepented of the ^Tevil which he thought to do unto his people.   *relented from · harm*

15   And ^RMoses turned, and went down from the mount, and the two tables of the testimony *were* in his hand: the tables *were* written on both their sides; on the one side and on the other *were* they written.   De 9:15

16   And the ^Rtables *were* the work of God, and the writing *was* the writing of God, graven upon the tables.   31:18

17   And when Joshua heard the noise of the people as they shouted, he said unto Moses, *There is* a noise of war in the camp.

18   And he said, *It is* not the voice of *them that* shout for mastery, neither *is it* the voice of *them that* cry for being overcome: *but* the ^Tnoise of *them that* sing do I hear.   *voice*

19   And it came to pass, as soon as he came nigh unto the camp, that ^Rhe saw the calf, and the dancing: and Moses' anger waxed hot, and he cast the tables out of his hands, and brake them beneath the mount.   De 9:16, 17

20   ^RAnd he took the calf which they had made, and burnt *it* in the

---

in Egypt, but the bull was a familiar embodiment of Baal seen in Canaan. It appears that the worship of the Lord had been blended with the symbols of Baal and other fertility gods. In this one scene, the people broke the first three of God's commandments.
32:14 the LORD repented. Here is a wonderful example of the interaction of faithful intercessory prayer and the purpose of the Lord. He uses our prayer combined with His own determination to make His will come to pass.

fire, and ground *it* to powder, and [T]strawed *it* upon the water, and made the children of Israel drink *of it.*   Nu 5:17, 24; De 9:21 · *scattered*

21 And Moses said unto Aaron, [R]What did this people unto thee, that thou hast brought so great a sin upon them?   Ge 26:10

22 And Aaron said, Let not the anger of my lord wax hot: [R]thou knowest the people, that they *are* set on [T]mischief.   14:11; De 9:24 · *evil*

23 For they said unto me, Make us gods, which shall go before us: for *as for* this Moses, the man that brought us up out of the land of Egypt, we [T]wot not what is become of him.   *know*

24 And I said unto them, Whosoever hath any gold, let them break *it* off. So they gave *it* me: then I cast it into the fire, and there came out this calf.

25 And when Moses saw that the people *were* [R]naked; (for Aaron [R]had made them naked unto *their* shame among their enemies:)   33:4, 5 · 2 Ch 28:19

26 Then Moses stood in the gate of the camp, and said, Who *is* on the LORD's side? *let him come* unto me. And all the sons of Levi gathered themselves together unto him.

27 And he said unto them, Thus saith the LORD God of Israel, Put every man his sword by his side, *and* go in and out from gate to gate throughout the camp, and slay every man his brother, and every

man his companion, and every man his neighbour.

28 And the children of Levi did according to the word of Moses: and there fell of the people that day about three thousand men.

29 [R]For Moses had said, Consecrate yourselves to day to the LORD, even every man upon his son, and upon his brother; that he may bestow upon you a blessing this day.   1 Sa 15:18, 22; Ze 13:3

30 And it came to pass on the morrow, that Moses said unto the people, Ye have sinned a great sin: and now I will go up unto the LORD; peradventure I shall make an atonement for your sin.

31 And Moses returned unto the LORD, and said, Oh, this people have sinned a great sin, and have [R]made them gods of gold.   20:23

32 Yet now, if thou wilt forgive their sin—; and if not, [R]blot me, I pray thee, [R]out of thy book which thou hast written.   Is 4:3 · Ph 4:3

33 And the LORD said unto Moses, [R]Whosoever hath sinned against me, him will I [R]blot out of my book.   Le 23:30 · Ps 9:5; Re 3:5

34 Therefore now go, lead the people unto *the place* of which I have spoken unto thee: [R]behold, mine Angel shall go before thee: nevertheless [R]in the day when I [R]visit I will visit their sin upon them.   Jos 5:14 · Ro 2:5, 6 · Ps 89:32

35 And the LORD plagued the peo-

32:25–26 were naked. Obedience to God is many times just the opposite of "what everybody else is doing." Humans are very prone to giving in to peer pressure at the crucial moment. We often care more about what those around us think than about what God thinks. Aaron and the other Levites fell into this trap initially, but when Moses gave them another chance to say where their loyalties really lay, they chose the path of obedience. Even though almost "everybody was doing it," they were willing to say, "No, this is wrong. We were wrong." The Levites were not innocent, but God blessed them for their repentance and their obedience. **32:27–28 his brother . . . his companion . . . his neighbour.** This terrible massacre is hard for us to reconcile with our feelings, but we must realize that sin is loathsome, and deserving of death. The Levites were used by God to execute His judgment in this instance, but they were not given general authority to kill sinners. **32:32–33 blot me . . . out of thy book.** Like Paul many centuries later, Moses could almost wish himself to be cursed, if by being so he could secure the salvation of his people (Ro 9:3). **32:34 in the day.** This may refer to the day of the Lord, proclaimed by later prophets (Joel 2; Zep 1).

ple, because [R]they made the calf, which Aaron made.   Ne 9:18

33 And the LORD said unto Moses, Depart, *and* go up hence, thou and the people which thou hast brought up out of the land of Egypt, unto the land which I sware unto Abraham, to Isaac, and to Jacob, saying, [R]Unto thy seed will I give it: Ge 12:7

2   [R]And I will send an angel before thee; [R]and I will drive out the Ca′-naan-ite, the Am′-or-ite, and the Hit′-tite, and the Per′-iz-zite, the Hi′-vite, and the Jeb′-u-site: Jos 5:14 · Jos 24:11

3   [R]Unto a land flowing with milk and honey: for I will not go up in the midst of thee; for thou *art* a stiffnecked people: lest I consume thee in the way.   3:8

4   And when the people heard these evil tidings, [R]they mourned: and no man did put on him his ornaments.   Nu 14:1, 39

5   For the LORD had said unto Moses, Say unto the children of Israel, Ye *are* a stiffnecked people: I will come up into the midst of thee in a moment, and consume thee: therefore now put off thy [T]ornaments from thee, that I may know what to do unto thee. *jewels*

6   And the children of Israel stripped themselves of their ornaments by the mount Ho′-reb.

7   And Moses took the tabernacle, and pitched it without the camp, afar off from the camp, and called it the Tabernacle of the congregation. And it came to pass, *that* every one which sought the LORD went out unto the tabernacle of the congregation, which *was* without the camp.

8   And it came to pass, when Moses went out unto the tabernacle, *that* all the people rose up, and stood every man [R]*at* his tent door, and looked after Moses, until he was gone into the tabernacle.   Nu 16:27

9   And it came to pass, as Moses entered into the tabernacle, the cloudy pillar descended, and stood *at* the door of the tabernacle, and *the* [T]LORD [R]talked with Moses. Lit. *He* · 25:22; 31:18; Ps 99:7

10   And all the people saw the cloudy pillar stand *at* the tabernacle door: and all the people rose up and [R]worshipped, every man *in* his tent door.   4:31

11   And [R]the LORD spake unto Moses face to face, as a man speaketh unto his friend. And he turned again into the camp: but his servant Joshua, the son of Nun, a young man, departed not out of the tabernacle.   De 34:10

12 And Moses said unto the LORD, See, [R]thou sayest unto me, Bring up this people: and thou hast not let me know whom thou wilt send with me. Yet thou hast said, [R]I know thee by name, and thou hast also found grace in my sight. 32:34 · Jo 10:14, 15; 2 Ti 2:19

13   Now therefore, I pray thee, if I have found grace in thy sight, [R]shew me now thy way, that I may know thee, that I may find grace

---

33:5 *stiffnecked.* Contrary to popular belief, God did not choose the Hebrew people because of their righteousness or willingness to serve Him (De 9:7). In fact, one of Israel's besetting sins was obstinacy (vv. 3,5), and God saw them as a rebellious and stiff-necked people. The opposite of being obstinate is to have a "circumcised heart" (De 10:16). Such a heart is inclined to obey the Word of God. God's presence with His people was in response to His covenantal promise: if they obeyed Him they would be His "peculiar treasure" (Ex 19:5). **33:6 *stripped themselves of their ornaments.*** These ornaments were probably associated with the idolatrous worship of the golden calf. Their removal was a mark of genuine repentance and renewal. **33:8 *all the people rose up, and stood.*** In contrast to their former wickedness, the people now responded reverently to the living God. **33:11 *his servant Joshua.*** The word translated *servant* here does not mean slave, but rather a minister, one who does spiritual service.

in thy sight: and consider that this nation *is* thy people.   Ps 25:4; 27:11

↗14 And he said, ᴿMy presence shall go *with thee,* and I will give thee ᴿrest. Is 63:9 · De 12:10

15 And he said unto him, ᴿIf thy presence go not *with me,* carry us not up hence.   v. 3

16 For wherein shall it be known here that I and thy people have found grace in thy sight? ᴿ*is it* not in that thou goest with us? so ᴿshall we be separated, I and thy people, from all the people that *are* upon the face of the earth.   Nu 14:14 · 34:10; De 4:7, 34

↗17 And the Lᴏʀᴅ said unto Moses, ᴿI will do this thing also that thou hast spoken: for thou hast found grace in my sight, and I know thee by name.   [Jam 5:16]

18 And he said, I beseech thee, shew me ᴿthy glory.   24:16, 17

19 And he said, I will make all my ᴿgoodness pass before thee, and I will proclaim the name of the Lᴏʀᴅ before thee; and will be gracious to whom I will be gracious, and will shew mercy on whom I will shew mercy.   34:6, 7

20 And he said, Thou canst not see my face: for ᴿthere shall no man see me, and live.   [Ge 32:30]

21 And the Lᴏʀᴅ said, Behold, *there is* a place by me, and thou shalt stand upon a rock:

22 And it shall come to pass, while my glory passeth by, that I will put thee ᴿin a clift of the rock, and will ᴿcover thee with my hand while I pass by: Is 2:21 · Ps 91:1, 4

23 And I will take away mine

hand, and thou shalt see my back parts: but my face shall ᴿnot be seen.   v. 20; [Jo 1:18]

34 And the Lᴏʀᴅ said unto Moses, Hew thee two tables of stone like unto the first: and ᴿI will write upon *these* tables the words that were in the first tables, which thou brakest.   De 10:2, 4

2 And be ready in the morning, and come up in the morning unto mount Si'-nai, and present thyself there to me ᴿin the top of the mount.   19:11, 18, 20

3 And no man shall ᴿcome up with thee, neither let any man be seen throughout all the mount; neither let the flocks nor herds feed before that mount.   24:9–11

4 And he hewed two tables of stone like unto the first; and Moses rose up early in the morning, and went up unto mount Si'-nai, as the Lᴏʀᴅ had commanded him, and took in his hand the two tables of stone.

5 And the Lᴏʀᴅ descended in the ᴿcloud, and stood with him there, and ᴿproclaimed the name of the Lᴏʀᴅ.   19:9 · 33:19

6 And the Lᴏʀᴅ passed by before him, and proclaimed, The Lᴏʀᴅ, The Lᴏʀᴅ God, merciful and gracious, longsuffering, and abundant in goodness and truth,

7 Keeping mercy for thousands, forgiving iniquity and transgression and sin, and that will by no means clear *the guilty;* visiting the iniquity of the fathers upon the

↗ 33:14   ↗ 33:17–19

33:17 *I know thee by name.* God's grace was accompanied by His intimate knowledge of and care for Moses.   **33:22–23 *my hand.*** The use of words such as hand, back, and face is a way of describing God, who is Spirit, in terms familiar to humans. **34:6 *merciful and gracious . . . abundant in goodness and truth.*** God is overwhelmingly gracious. John's description of the coming of Jesus echoes this passage, describing the Messiah as "full of grace and truth" (Jo 1:14,17). To see Jesus is to see the Father (Jo 1:18).   **34:7 *forgiving iniquity.*** God is a God of unlimited grace, mercy, and forgiveness. But man is not automatically forgiven—"He will by no means leave the guilty unpunished." We receive forgiveness from God only when we repent and seek reconciliation with Him. The second covenant with Israel (34:10) included relief from the judgment of the people's sins to allow them to be taught their need and seek forgiveness.

children, and upon the children's
children, unto the third and to the
fourth *generation.*
8 And Moses made haste, and
[R]bowed his head toward the earth,
and worshipped. 4:31
9 And he said, If now I have
found grace in thy sight, O Lord,
[R]let my Lord, I pray thee, go among
us; for it *is* a [R]stiffnecked people;
and pardon our iniquity and our
sin, and take us for [R]thine inheritance. 33:12–16 · 33:3 · Ps 33:12
10 And he said, Behold, [R]I
make a covenant: before all thy
people I will [R]do marvels, such
as have not been done in all the
earth, nor in any nation: and all
the people among which thou *art*
shall see the work of the LORD: for
it *is* [R]a terrible thing that I will do
with thee. De 5:2 · Ps 77:14 · Ps 145:6
11 Observe thou that which I command thee this day: behold, I drive
out before thee the Am'-or-ite, and
the Ca'-naan-ite, and the Hit'-tite,
and the Per'-iz-zite, and the Hi'-
vite, and the Jeb'-u-site.
12 [R]Take heed to thyself, lest thou
make a covenant with the inhabitants of the land whither thou goest, lest it be for a snare in the
midst of thee: 23:32, 33
13 But ye shall [R]destroy their al-
tars, break their images, and [R]cut
down their groves: 23:24 · De 16:21
14 For thou shalt worship [R]no
other god: for the LORD, whose
[R]name *is* Jealous, *is* a [R]jealous
God: [20:3–5] · [Is 57:15] · [De 4:24]
15 Lest thou make a covenant
with the inhabitants of the land,
and they [R]go a whoring after their
gods, and do sacrifice unto their
gods, and *one* call thee, and thou
eat of his sacrifice; Ju 2:17
16 And thou take of their daughters unto thy sons, and their daughters go a whoring after their gods,
and make thy sons go a whoring
after their gods.
17 [R]Thou shalt make thee no molten gods. 32:8; Le 19:4; De 5:8
18 The feast of [R]unleavened bread
shalt thou keep. Seven days thou
shalt eat unleavened bread, as I
commanded thee, in the time of
the [R]month A'-bib: for in the
month A'-bib thou camest out from
Egypt. 12:15, 16 · 12:2; 13:4
19 [R]All that openeth the [T]matrix
is mine; and every firstling among
thy cattle, *whether* ox or sheep,
that is male. 13:2; 22:29 · *womb*
20 But [R]the firstling of an ass thou
shalt redeem with a lamb: and if
thou redeem *him* not, then shalt
thou break his neck. All the firstborn of thy sons thou shalt redeem.
And none shall appear before me
[R]empty. 13:13 · De 16:16
21 [R]Six days thou shalt work, but
on the seventh day thou shalt rest:
in [T]earing time and in harvest
thou shalt rest. 20:9 · *plowing*
22 And thou shalt observe the
feast of weeks, of the firstfruits of
wheat harvest, and the feast of ingathering at the year's end.
23 Thrice in the year shall all your
men children appear before the
Lord GOD, the God of Israel.
24 For I will cast out the nations
before thee, and enlarge thy borders: neither shall any man desire
thy land, when thou shalt go up to
appear before the LORD thy God
thrice in the year.
25 Thou shalt not offer the blood
of my sacrifice with leaven; [R]nei-
ther shall the sacrifice of the feast
of the passover be left unto the
morning. 12:10
26 [R]The first of the firstfruits of

34:10

34:15 ***go a whoring.*** This is probably more than a figure of speech. Unfaithfulness to the Lord was often manifested in sexual rites with temple prostitutes (male and female), acts of supposed union with Baal, Asherah, and other pagan deities. **34:16** ***take of their daughters unto thy sons.*** The quickest way for the Israelites to become corrupted with the false worship of the Canaanites would have been to marry into it.

thy land thou shalt bring unto the house of the LORD thy God. Thou shalt not seethe a kid in his mother's milk.   23:19; De 26:2

27 And the LORD said unto Moses, Write thou [R]these words: for after the tenor of these words I have made a covenant with thee and with Israel. 17:14; 24:4; De 31:9

28 And he was there with the LORD forty days and forty nights; he did neither eat bread, nor drink water. And he wrote upon the tables the words of the covenant, the ten commandments.

29 And it came to pass, when Moses came down from mount Si'-nai with the [R]two tables of testimony in Moses' hand, when he came down from the mount, that Moses wist not that [R]the skin of his face shone while he talked with him.   32:15 · Ma 17:2; 2 Co 3:7

30 And when Aaron and all the children of Israel saw Moses, behold, the skin of his face shone; and they were afraid to come nigh him.

31 And Moses called unto them; and Aaron and all the rulers of the congregation returned unto him: and Moses talked with them.

32 And afterward all the children of Israel came nigh: [R]and he gave them in commandment all that the LORD had spoken with him in mount Si'-nai.   24:3

33 And till Moses had done speaking with them, he put [R]a vail on his face.   [2 Co 3:13, 14]

34 But when Moses went in before the LORD to speak with him, he took the vail off, until he came out. And he came out, and spake unto the children of Israel that which he was commanded.

35 And the children of Israel saw the face of Moses, that the skin of Moses' face shone: and Moses put the vail upon his face again, until he went in to speak with him.

35 And Moses gathered all the congregation of the children of Israel together, and said unto them, [R]These are the words which the LORD hath commanded, that ye should do them.   34:32

2 [R]Six days shall work be done, but on the seventh day there shall be to you an holy day, a sabbath of rest to the LORD: whosoever doeth work therein shall be put to [R]death.   20:9, 10; Le 23:3 · Nu 15:32–36

3 [R]Ye shall kindle no fire throughout your habitations upon the sabbath day.   12:16; 16:23

4 And Moses spake unto all the congregation of the children of Israel, saying, [R]This is the thing which the LORD commanded, saying,   25:1, 2

5 Take ye from among you an offering unto the LORD: [R]whosoever is of a willing heart, let him bring it, an offering of the LORD; gold, and silver, and brass,   25:2

6 And [R]blue, and purple, and scarlet, and fine linen, and [R]goats' hair,   36:8 · 36:14

7 And rams' skins dyed red, and badgers' skins, and shit'-tim wood,

8 And oil for the light, [R]and spices for anointing oil, and for the sweet incense,   25:6; 30:23–25

9 And onyx stones, and stones to be set for the e'-phod, and for the breastplate.

10 And [R]every [T]wise hearted among you shall come, and make all that the LORD hath commanded;   31:2–6; 36:1, 2 · skilful

11 [R]The tabernacle, his tent, and his covering, his taches, and his

---

34:28 forty days and forty nights. A person can survive without food for weeks, but no one can go entirely without water for more than three or four days. This fact has been used to cast doubt on the truth of this passage, but we must recall that there is no reason to think that God could not keep His servant hydrated in any way He chose. **34:33 a vail on his face.** Paul taught that Moses wore the veil because the glow faded, a sign of imperfect glory (2 Co 3:7, 13).

boards, his bars, his pillars, and his sockets, 26:1, 2; 36:14

12 ᴿThe ark, and the staves thereof, *with* the mercy seat, and the vail of the covering, 25:10–22

13 The ᴿtable, and his staves, and all his vessels, ᴿand the shewbread, 25:23 · 25:30; Le 24:5, 6

14 The candlestick also for the light, and his furniture, and his lamps, with the oil for the light,

15 ᴿAnd the incense altar, and his staves, ᴿand the anointing oil, and the sweet incense, and the hanging for the door at the entering in of the tabernacle, 30:1 · 30:25

16 ᴿThe altar of burnt offering, with his brasen grate, his staves, and all his vessels, the laver and his foot, 27:1–8

17 ᴿThe hangings of the court, his pillars, and their sockets, and the hanging for the door of the court, 27:9–18

18 The pins of the tabernacle, and the pins of the court, and their cords,

19 ᴿThe cloths of service, to do service in the holy *place,* the holy garments for Aaron the priest, and the garments of his sons, to minister in the priest's office. 31:10

20 And all the congregation of the children of Israel departed from the presence of Moses.

21 And they came, every one whose heart ᵀstirred him up, and every one whom his spirit made willing, *and* they ᴿbrought the LORD's offering to the work of the tabernacle of the congregation, and for all his service, and for the holy garments. Lit. *lifted up* · v. 24

22 And they came, both men and women, as many as were willing hearted, *and* brought bracelets, and earrings, and rings, and tablets, all jewels of gold: and every man that offered *offered* an offering of gold unto the LORD.

23 And every man, with whom was found blue, and purple, and scarlet, and fine linen, and goats' *hair,* and red skins of rams, and badgers' skins, brought *them.*

24 Every one that did offer an offering of silver and brass brought the LORD's offering: and every man, with whom was found shit'-tim wood for any work of the service, brought *it.*

25 And all the women that were ᴿwise hearted did spin with their hands, and brought that which they had spun, *both* of blue, and of purple, *and* of scarlet, and of fine linen. 28:3; 31:6; 36:1

26 And all the women whose heart ᵀstirred them up in wisdom spun goats' *hair.* Lit. *lifted them up*

27 And ᴿthe rulers brought onyx stones, and stones to be set, for the e'-phod, and for the breastplate; 1 Ch 29:6; Ez 2:68

28 And ᴿspice, and oil for the light, and for the anointing oil, and for the sweet incense. 30:23

29 The children of Israel brought a willing offering unto the LORD, every man and woman, whose heart made them willing to bring for all manner of work, which the LORD had commanded to be made by the hand of Moses.

30 And Moses said unto the children of Israel, See, ᴿthe LORD hath called by name Be-zal'-e-el the son of U'-ri, the son of Hur, of the tribe of Judah; 31:1–6

31 And he hath filled him with the spirit of God, in wisdom, in un-

---

35:31–35 *spirit of God.* The work of the Holy Spirit is often thought to have begun at Pentecost (Ac 2), but in fact the Holy Spirit of God was at work long before that time. The Old Testament shows that He was active in creation (Ge 1:2; Job 33:4). The Spirit came upon men for prophetic utterance (1 Sa 10:10) and for all divine revelation (2 Sa 23:2). Men were endowed for special functions by the power of the Holy Spirit (Ex 31:3; Ju 11:29; 13:25; 14:6). Bezalel is a good example of a man indwelt by the Spirit of God in the Old Testament (37:1–9).

derstanding, and in knowledge, and in all manner of workmanship;

32 And to devise curious works, to work in gold, and in silver, and in brass,

33 And in the cutting of stones, to set *them,* and in carving of wood, to make any manner of [T]cunning work. *artistic workmanship*

34 And he hath put in his heart that he may teach, *both* he, and [R]A-ho'-li-ab, the son of A-his'-a-mach, of the tribe of Dan. 31:6

35 Them hath he filled with wisdom of heart, to work all manner of work, of the engraver, and of the cunning workman, and of the embroiderer, in blue, and in purple, in scarlet, and in fine linen, and of the weaver, *even* of them that do any work, and of those that devise cunning work.

36 Then wrought Be-zal'-e-el and A-ho'-li-ab, and every wise hearted man, in whom the LORD put wisdom and understanding to know how to work all manner of work for the service of the sanctuary, according to all that the LORD had commanded.

2 And Moses called Be-zal'-e-el and A-ho'-li-ab, and every wise hearted man, in whose heart the LORD had put wisdom, *even* every one whose heart stirred him up to come unto the work to do it:

3 And they received of Moses all the [R]offering, which the children of Israel [R]had brought for the work of the service of the sanctuary, to make it *withal.* And they brought yet unto him free offerings every morning. 35:5 · 35:27

4 And all the wise men, that wrought all the work of the sanctuary, came every man from his work which they made;

5 And they spake unto Moses, saying, [R]The people bring much more than enough for the service of the work, which the LORD commanded to make. 2 Ch 24:14; 31:6–10

6 And Moses gave commandment, and they caused it to be proclaimed throughout the camp, saying, Let neither man nor woman make any more work for the offering of the sanctuary. So the people were restrained from bringing.

7 For the stuff they had was sufficient for all the work to make it, and too [R]much. 1 Ki 8:64

8 [R]And every wise hearted man among them that wrought the work of the tabernacle made ten curtains *of* fine twined linen, and blue, and purple, and scarlet: *with* cher'-u-bims of cunning work made he them. 26:1–14

9 The length of one curtain *was* twenty and eight cubits, and the breadth of one curtain four cubits: the curtains *were* all of one size.

10 And he coupled the five curtains one unto another: and *the other* five curtains he coupled one unto another.

11 And he made loops of blue on the edge of one curtain [T]from the selvedge in the coupling: likewise he made in the uttermost side of *another* curtain, in the coupling of the second. *on the selvedge of one set*

12 Fifty loops made he in one curtain, and fifty loops made he in the edge of the curtain which *was* in the coupling of the second: the loops held one *curtain* to another.

13 And he made fifty [T]taches of gold, and coupled the curtains one unto another with the taches: so it became one tabernacle. *clasps*

14 [R]And he made curtains of goats' *hair* for the tent over the tab-

---

36:8–37:29 Servant—Not only ability was required for service in building the tabernacle. God also wanted willing hearts (36:2). Even if we do not feel that we are particularly good at anything, we must remember that every talent we possess, no matter how small, is a gift from God. He gives us these gifts so that we will have something to give back to Him. We should look at ourselves, not saying, "I don't have any great skill, I'll just sit and watch," but rather, "Here's what I have—where shall I start?"

ernacle: eleven curtains he made them.   26:7

15 The length of one curtain *was* thirty cubits, and four cubits *was* the breadth of one curtain: the eleven curtains *were* of one size.

16 And he coupled five curtains by themselves, and six curtains by themselves.

17 And he made fifty loops upon the uttermost edge of the curtain in the coupling, and fifty loops made he upon the edge of the curtain which coupleth the second.

18 And he made fifty taches *of* brass to couple the tent together, that it might be one.

19 ᴿAnd he made a covering for the tent *of* rams' skins dyed red, and a covering *of* ᵀbadgers' skins above *that.*   26:14 · Or *dolphin skins*

20 ᴿAnd he made boards for the tabernacle *of* shit'-tim wood, standing up.   26:15–29

21 The length of a board *was* ten cubits, and the breadth of a board one cubit and a half.

22 One board had two tenons, ᴿequally distant one from another: thus did he make for all the boards of the tabernacle.   26:17

23 And he made boards for the tabernacle; twenty boards for the south side southward:

24 And forty sockets of silver he made under the twenty boards; two sockets under one board for his two tenons, and two sockets under another board for his two tenons.

25 And for the other side of the tabernacle, *which is* toward the north corner, he made twenty boards,

26 And their forty sockets of silver; two sockets under one board, and two sockets under another board.

27 And for the sides of the tabernacle westward he made six boards.

28 And two boards made he for the corners of the tabernacle in the two sides.

29 And they were ᵀcoupled beneath, and coupled together at the head thereof, to one ring: thus he did to both of them in both the corners.   *twined*

30 And there were eight boards; and their sockets *were* sixteen sockets of silver, under every board two sockets.

31 And he made bars of shit'-tim wood; five for the boards of the one side of the tabernacle,

32 And five bars for the boards of the other side of the tabernacle, and five bars for the boards of the tabernacle for the sides westward.

33 And he made the middle bar to ᵀshoot through the boards from the one end to the other.   *pass*

34 And he overlaid the boards with gold, and made their rings *of* gold *to be* places for the bars, and overlaid the bars with gold.

35 And he made a vail *of* blue, and purple, and scarlet, and fine twined linen: *with* cher'-u-bims made he it of cunning work.

36 And he made thereunto four pillars *of* shit'-tim *wood,* and overlaid them with gold: their hooks *were of* gold; and he cast for them four sockets of silver.

37 And he made an ᴿhanging for the tabernacle door *of* blue, and purple, and scarlet, and fine twined linen, of needlework;   26:36

38 And the five pillars of it with their hooks: and he overlaid their ᵀchapiters and their fillets with gold: but their five sockets *were* of brass.   *capitals*

37 And ᴿBe-zal'-e-el made ᴿthe ark *of* shit'-tim wood: two cubits and a half *was* the length of it, and a cubit and a half the

---

37:1–9 Bezaleel. Bezalel carefully reproduced the pattern given to Moses (25:10–22). Obviously this pattern wasn't just a "design suggestion" from God. Each detail had to be just like the plan because each part was a symbol or reminder of their relationship with God, His character, and His holiness.

breadth of it, and a cubit and a half the height of it: 36:1 · 25:10–20

2 And he overlaid it with pure gold ᵀwithin and without, and made a ᵀcrown of gold to it round about. *inside* and *outside* · *moulding*

3 And he cast for it four rings of gold, *to be set* by the four corners of it; even two rings upon the one side of it, and two rings upon the other side of it.

4 And he made staves *of* shit'-tim wood, and overlaid them with gold.

5 And he put the staves into the rings by the sides of the ark, to bear the ark.

6 And he made the ᴿmercy seat *of* pure gold: two cubits and a half *was* the length thereof, and one cubit and a half the breadth thereof. 25:17

7 And he made two cher'-u-bims *of* gold, beaten out of one piece made he them, on the two ends of the mercy seat;

8 One cherub on the end on this side, and another cherub on the *other* end on that side: out of the mercy seat made he the cher'-u-bims on the two ends thereof.

9 ᴿAnd the cher'-u-bims spread out *their* wings on high, *and* covered with their wings over the mercy seat, with their faces one to another; *even* to the mercy seatward were the faces of the cher'-u-bims. 25:20

10 And he made ᴿthe table *of* shit'-tim wood: two cubits *was* the length thereof, and a cubit the breadth thereof, and a cubit and a half the height thereof: 25:23–29

11 And he overlaid it with pure gold, and made thereunto a crown of gold round about.

12 Also he made thereunto a border of an handbreadth round about; and made a crown of gold for the border thereof round about.

13 And he cast for it four rings of gold, and put the rings upon the four corners that *were* in the four feet thereof.

14 Over against the border were the rings, the places for the staves to bear the table.

15 And he made the staves *of* shit'-tim wood, and overlaid them with gold, to bear the table.

16 And he made the vessels which *were* upon the table, his dishes, and his spoons, and his bowls, and his covers to cover ᵀwithal, *of* pure gold. *with them*

17 And he made the ᴿcandlestick *of* pure gold: *of* beaten work made he the candlestick; his shaft, and his branch, his bowls, his knops, and his flowers, were of the same: 25:31–39

18 And six branches going out of the sides thereof; three branches of the candlestick out of the one side thereof, and three branches of the candlestick out of the other side thereof:

19 Three bowls made after the fashion of almonds in one branch, a knop and a flower; and three bowls made like almonds in another branch, a knop and a flower: so throughout the six branches going out of the candlestick.

20 And in the candlestick *were* four bowls made like almonds, his knops, and his flowers:

21 And a knop under two branches of the same, and a knop under two branches of the same, and a knop under two branches of the same, according to the six branches going out of it.

22 Their knops and their branches were of the same: all of it *was* one beaten work *of* pure gold.

23 And he made his seven lamps, and his ᴿsnuffers, and his snuffdishes, *of* pure gold. Nu 4:9

24 *Of* a talent of pure gold made he it, and all the vessels thereof.

25 ᴿAnd he made the incense altar *of* shit'-tim wood: the length of it *was* a cubit, and the breadth of it a cubit; *it was* foursquare; and two cubits *was* the height of it; the horns thereof were of the same. 30:1–5

26 And he overlaid it with pure gold, *both* the top of it, and the sides thereof round about, and the horns of it: also he made unto it a crown of gold round about.

27 And he made two rings of gold for it under the crown thereof, by the two corners of it, upon the two sides thereof, to be places for the staves to bear it withal.

28 And he ᴿmade the staves *of* shit'-tim wood, and overlaid them with gold.   30:5

29 And he made the holy anointing oil, and the pure incense of sweet spices, according to the work of the apothecary.

38 And ᴿhe made the altar of burnt offering *of* shit'-tim wood: five cubits *was* the length thereof, and five cubits the breadth thereof; *it was* four-square; and three cubits the height thereof. 27:1–8

2 And he made the horns thereof on the four corners of it; the horns thereof were of the same: and he overlaid it with brass.

3 And he made all the vessels of the altar, the pots, and the shovels, and the basons, *and* the fleshhooks, and the firepans: all the vessels thereof made he *of* brass.

4 And he made for the altar a brasen grate of network under the compass thereof beneath unto the midst of it.

5 And he cast four rings for the four ends of the grate of brass, *to be* places for the staves.

6 And he made the staves *of* shit'-tim wood, and overlaid them with brass.

7 And he put the staves into the rings on the sides of the altar, to bear it withal; he made the altar hollow with boards.

8 And he made ᴿthe laver *of* brass, and the foot of it *of* brass, of the ᵀlookingglasses of *the women* assembling, which assembled *at* the door of the tabernacle of the congregation.   30:18 · *mirrors*

9 And he made the court: on the south side southward the hangings of the court *were of* fine twined linen, an hundred cubits:

10 Their pillars *were* twenty, and their brasen sockets twenty; the hooks of the pillars and their fillets *were of* silver.

11 And for the north side *the hangings were* an hundred cubits, their pillars *were* twenty, and their sockets of brass twenty; the hooks of the pillars and their fillets *of* silver.

12 And for the west side *were* hangings of fifty cubits, their pillars ten, and their sockets ten; the hooks of the pillars and their fillets *of* silver.

13 And for the east side eastward fifty cubits.

14 The hangings of the one side *of the gate were* fifteen cubits; their pillars three, and their sockets three.

15 And for the other side of the court gate, on this hand and that hand, *were* hangings of fifteen cubits; their pillars three, and their sockets three.

16 All the hangings of the court round about *were* of fine twined linen.

17 And the sockets for the pillars *were of* brass; the hooks of the pillars and their fillets *of* silver; and the overlaying of their ᵀchapiters *of* silver; and all the pillars of the court *were* filleted with silver.   *capitals*

18 And the hanging for the gate of the court *was* needlework, *of* blue, and purple, and scarlet, and fine twined linen: and twenty cubits *was* the length, and the height in the breadth *was* five cubits, ᵀanswerable to the hangings of the court.   *corresponding*

19 And their pillars *were* four, and their sockets *of* brass four; their hooks *of* silver, and the overlaying of their ᵀchapiters and their fillets *of* silver.   *capitals*

20 And all the ᴿpins of the tabernacle, and of the court round about, *were of* brass.   27:19

21 This is the sum of the taber-

nacle, *even* of ^Rthe tabernacle of testimony, as it was counted, according to the commandment of Moses, *for* the service of the Levites, by the hand of Ith'-a-mar, son to Aaron the priest.   Ac 7:44

22   And ^RBe-zal'-e-el the son of U'-ri, the son of Hur, of the tribe of Judah, made all that the LORD commanded Moses.   1 Ch 2:18–20

23   And with him *was* A-ho'-li-ab, son of A-his'-a-mach, of the tribe of Dan, an engraver, and a cunning workman, and an embroiderer in blue, and in purple, and in scarlet, and fine linen.

24   All the gold that was occupied for the work in all the work of the holy *place*, even the gold of the offering, was twenty and nine talents, and seven hundred and thirty shek'-els, after ^Rthe shek'-el of the sanctuary.   30:13, 24; Le 5:15

25   And the silver of them that were numbered of the congregation *was* an hundred talents, and a thousand seven hundred and threescore and fifteen shek'-els, after the shek'-el of the sanctuary:

26   ^RA be'-kah for every man, *that is*, half a shek'-el, after the shek'-el of the sanctuary, for every one that went to be numbered, from twenty years old and upward, for six hundred thousand and three thousand and five hundred and fifty *men*.   30:13, 15

27   And of the hundred talents of silver were cast ^Rthe sockets of the sanctuary, and the sockets of the vail; an hundred sockets of the hundred talents, a talent for a socket.   26:19, 21, 25, 32

28   And of the thousand seven hundred seventy and five *shek'-els* he made hooks for the pillars, and overlaid their ^Tchapiters, and ^Rfilleted them.   *capitals* · 27:17

29   And the brass of the offering *was* seventy talents, and two thousand and four hundred shek'-els.

30   And therewith he made the sockets to the door of the tabernacle of the congregation, and the brasen altar, and the brasen grate for it, and all the vessels of the altar,

31   And the sockets of the court round about, and the sockets of the court gate, and all the pins of the tabernacle, and all the pins of the court round about.

39 And of the ^Rblue, and purple, and scarlet, they made ^Rcloths of service, to do service in the holy *place*, and made the holy garments for Aaron; as the LORD commanded Moses.   25:4; 35:23 · 31:10

2   And he made the ^Re'-phod *of* gold, blue, and purple, and scarlet, and fine twined linen.   Le 8:7

3   And they did beat the gold into thin plates, and cut *it into* wires, to work *it* in the blue, and in the purple, and in the scarlet,

---

38:22–23 Responsibility—No higher tribute can be paid than "Well done—you've finished." Bezalel and his assistant, Oholiab, were called, Spirit endowed, and commissioned for one work and one work alone. Neither of these individuals ever became celebrities, but God does not measure our effectiveness in His kingdom work by how many times we make the headlines in the local media. God cares about whether we obey Him faithfully, not whether other people approve of us. It is easy to make verbal commitments that sound really good, but God isn't looking for fine words. He complimented Bezalel and Oholiab on finishing their assignment, not on their fine start or their good intentions (39:43). **38:24 All the gold.** The weight of all the gold used in the work may have been about a ton. The talent weighed about 75 pounds, and equaled 3,000 shekels. **38:25 the silver.** The quantity of silver was enormous, about 7,000 pounds. **38:26 A bekah for every man.** The census of Numbers 14:6 puts the number of men over the age of 20 at 603,550. **38:27–28 the sanctuary.** Although the tabernacle was a tent, it was not a makeshift dwelling. It was a glorious shrine that symbolized the presence of the living God in the midst of the people. **38:29 brass.** About 5,000 pounds of brass were used.

and in the fine linen, *with* [T]cunning work.   *artistic designs*

4   They made shoulderpieces for it, to couple *it* together: by the two edges was it coupled together.

5   And the curious girdle of his e′-phod, that *was* upon it, *was* of the same, according to the work thereof; *of* gold, blue, and purple, and scarlet, and fine twined linen; as the LORD commanded Moses.

6   [R]And they wrought onyx stones inclosed in [T]ouches of gold, graven, as signets are graven, with the names of the children of Israel.   *28:9–11 · settings*

7   And he put them on the shoulders of the e′-phod, *that they should be* stones for a [R]memorial to the children of Israel; as the LORD commanded Moses.   *28:12, 29; Jos 4:7*

8   [R]And he made the breastplate *of* cunning work, like the work of the e′-phod; *of* gold, blue, and purple, and scarlet, and fine twined linen.   *28:15–30*

9   It was foursquare; they made the breastplate double: a span *was* the length thereof, and a span the breadth thereof, *being* doubled.

10   [R]And they set in it four rows of stones: *the first* row *was* a [T]sardius, a topaz, and a carbuncle: this *was* the first row.   *28:17 · ruby*

11   And the second row, an emerald, a sapphire, and a diamond.

12   And the third row, a ligure, an agate, and an amethyst.

13   And the fourth row, a beryl, an onyx, and a jasper: *they were* inclosed in [T]ouches of gold in their inclosings.   *settings*

14   And the stones *were* according to the names of the children of Israel, twelve, according to their names, *like* the engravings of a signet, every one with his name, according to the twelve tribes.

15   And they made upon the breastplate chains at the ends, *of* wreathen work *of* pure gold.

16   And they made two [T]ouches *of* gold, and two gold rings; and

put the two rings in the two ends of the breastplate.   *settings*

17   And they put the two wreathen chains of gold in the two rings on the ends of the breastplate.

18   And the two ends of the two wreathen chains they fastened in the two [T]ouches, and put them on the shoulderpieces of the e′-phod, before it.   *settings*

19   And they made two rings of gold, and put *them* on the two ends of the breastplate, upon the border of it, which *was* on the side of the e′-phod inward.

20   And they made two *other* golden rings, and put them on the two sides of the e′-phod underneath, toward the forepart of it, over against the *other* coupling thereof, above the [T]curious girdle of the e′-phod.   *intricately woven band*

21   And they did bind the breastplate by his rings unto the rings of the e′-phod with a lace of blue, that it might be above the curious girdle of the e′-phod, and that the breastplate might not be loosed from the e′-phod; as the LORD commanded Moses.

22   [R]And he made the [R]robe of the e′-phod *of* woven work, all *of* blue.   *28:31–35 · 29:5; Le 8:7*

23   And *there was* an hole in the midst of the robe, as the hole of an habergeon, *with* a band round about the hole, that it should not rend.

24   And they made upon the hems of the robe pomegranates *of* blue, and purple, and scarlet, *and* twined *linen.*

25   And they made [R]bells *of* pure gold, and put the bells between the pomegranates upon the hem of the robe, round about between the pomegranates;   *28:33*

26   A bell and a pomegranate, a bell and a pomegranate, round about the hem of the robe to [T]minister *in;* as the LORD commanded Moses.   *serve*

27   [R]And they made coats *of* fine

linen *of* woven work for Aaron, and for his sons, 28:39, 40

28 [R] And a mitre *of* fine linen, and goodly bonnets *of* fine linen, and [R] linen breeches *of* fine twined linen,   Le 8:9; Eze 44:18 · Le 6:10

29 [R] And a girdle *of* fine twined linen, and blue, and purple, and scarlet, *of* needlework; as the LORD commanded Moses.   28:39

30 And they made the plate of the holy crown *of* pure gold, and wrote upon it a writing, *like to* the engravings of a signet, [R] HOLINESS TO THE LORD.   Ze 14:20

31 And they tied unto it a lace of blue, to fasten *it* on high upon the mitre; as the LORD commanded Moses.

32 Thus was all the work of the tabernacle of the tent of the congregation [R] finished: and the children of Israel did [R] according to all that the LORD commanded Moses, so did they.   40:17 · vv. 42, 43; 25:40

33 And they brought the tabernacle unto Moses, the tent, and all his furniture, his taches, his boards, his bars, and his pillars, and his sockets,

34 And the covering of rams' skins dyed red, and the covering of badgers' skins, and the vail of the covering,

35 The ark of the testimony, and the staves thereof, and the mercy seat,

36 The table, *and* all the vessels thereof, and the shewbread,

37 The pure candlestick, *with* the lamps thereof, *even with* the lamps to be set in order, and all the vessels thereof, and the oil for light,

38 And the golden altar, and the anointing oil, and the sweet incense, and the hanging for the tabernacle door,

39 The brasen altar, and his grate of brass, his staves, and all his vessels, the laver and his foot,

40 The hangings of the court, his pillars, and his sockets, and the hanging for the court gate, his cords, and his pins, and all the vessels of the service of the tabernacle, for the tent of the congregation,

41 The cloths of service to do service in the holy *place,* and the holy garments for Aaron the priest, and his sons' garments, to minister in the priest's office.

42 According to all that the LORD commanded Moses, so the children of Israel [R] made all the work.   35:10

43 And Moses did look upon all the work, and, behold, they had done it as the LORD had commanded, even so had they done it: and Moses [R] blessed them.   Le 9:22

40 And the LORD [R] spake unto Moses, saying,   25:1—31:18

2 On the first day of the [R] first month shalt thou set up [R] the tabernacle of the tent of the congregation.   12:2; 13:4 · v. 17; 26:1, 30

3 And [R] thou shalt put therein the ark of the testimony, and cover the ark with the vail.   v. 21

4 And [R] thou shalt bring in the table, and set in order the things that are to be set in order upon it; and thou shalt bring in the candlestick, and light the lamps thereof.   vv. 22–25

5 [R] And thou shalt set the altar of gold for the incense before the

---

39:32–43 *so did they.* Because it was so important in God's plan for His people, both in the wilderness and today, the tabernacle had to be constructed in exact accordance with the divine pattern. It was the place where His glory would actually dwell and where they could meet Him. Because they had done just as the Lord had commanded, "Moses blessed them." A mood of celebration pervades these verses. One can sense the pride of accomplishment coupled with the reverence for all of these holy objects. **40:2** *first month.* This was the month of Abib, also called Nisan (12:2; 13:4). The tabernacle was completed nine months after the arrival of the people at Mount Sinai (19:1) and two weeks before the second celebration of the Passover (v. 17).

ark of the testimony, and put the hanging of the door to the tabernacle.   v. 26

6   And thou shalt set the ^Raltar of the burnt offering before the door of the tabernacle of the tent of the congregation.   39:39

7   And ^Rthou shalt set the laver between the tent of the congregation and the altar, and shalt put water therein.   v. 30; 30:18

8   And thou shalt set up the court round about, and hang up the hanging at the court gate.

9   And thou shalt take the anointing oil, and ^Ranoint the tabernacle, and all that *is* therein, and shalt hallow it, and all the vessels thereof: and it shall be holy.   30:26; Le 8:10

10   And thou shalt anoint the altar of the burnt offering, and all his vessels, and sanctify the altar: and it shall be an altar most holy.

11   And thou shalt anoint the laver and his foot, and sanctify it.

12   ^RAnd thou shalt bring Aaron and his sons unto the door of the tabernacle of the congregation, and wash them with water.   29:4–9

13   And thou shalt put upon Aaron the holy ^Rgarments, ^Rand anoint him, and sanctify him; that he may minister unto me in the priest's office.   29:5; 39:1, 41 · Le 8:12

14   And thou shalt bring his sons, and clothe them with coats:

15   And thou shalt anoint them, as thou didst anoint their father, that they may minister unto me in the priest's office: for their anointing shall surely be ^Ran everlasting priesthood throughout their generations.   29:9; Nu 25:13

16   Thus did Moses: according to all that the LORD commanded him, so did he.

17   And it came to pass in the first month in the second year, on the first *day* of the month, *that* the tabernacle was reared up.

18   And Moses reared up the tab-

ernacle, and fastened his sockets, and set up the boards thereof, and put in the bars thereof, and reared up his pillars.

19   And he spread abroad the tent over the tabernacle, and put the covering of the tent above upon it; as the LORD commanded Moses.

20   And he took and put the testimony into the ark, and set the staves on the ark, and put the mercy seat above upon the ark:

21   And he brought the ark into the tabernacle, and ^Rset up the vail of the covering, and covered the ark of the testimony; as the LORD commanded Moses.   26:33

22   ^RAnd he put the table in the tent of the congregation, upon the side of the tabernacle northward, without the vail.   26:35

23   And he set the bread in order upon it before the LORD; as the LORD had commanded Moses.

24   ^RAnd he put the candlestick in the tent of the congregation, over against the table, on the side of the tabernacle southward.   26:35

25   And ^Rhe lighted the lamps before the LORD; as the LORD commanded Moses.   30:7, 8; Le 24:3, 4

26   ^RAnd he put the golden altar in the tent of the congregation before the vail: v. 5; 30:1, 6

27   ^RAnd he burnt sweet incense thereon; as the LORD commanded Moses.   30:7

28   ^RAnd he set up the hanging *at* the door of the tabernacle.   26:36

29   ^RAnd he put the altar of burnt offering *by* the door of the tabernacle of the tent of the congregation, and ^Roffered upon it the burnt offering and the meat offering; as the LORD commanded Moses.   v. 6 · 29:38–42

30   ^RAnd he set the laver between the tent of the congregation and the altar, and put water there, to wash *withal*.   v. 7; 30:18

40:20–21 *the testimony . . . the mercy seat.* The Testimony was the stone tablets of the Ten Commandments (25:16). The mercy seat was the cover of the ark (25:17–22).

31   And Moses and Aaron and his sons [R] washed their hands and their feet thereat: 30:19, 20; Jo 13:8
32   When they went into the tent of the congregation, and when they came near unto the altar, they washed; [R] as the LORD commanded Moses.   30:19
33   [R] And he reared up the court round about the tabernacle and the altar, and set up the hanging of the court gate. So Moses [R] finished the work.   v. 8 · [He 3:2–5]
34   [R] Then a cloud covered the tent of the congregation, and the glory of the LORD filled the tabernacle.   Nu 9:15; 2 Ch 5:13; Is 6:4

35   And Moses [R] was not able to enter into the tent of the congregation, because the cloud abode thereon, and the glory of the LORD filled the tabernacle.   [Le 16:2]
36   [R] And when the cloud was taken up from over the tabernacle, the children of Israel went onward in all their journeys: 13:21, 22
37   But if the cloud were not taken up, then they journeyed not till the day that it was taken up.
38   For the cloud of the LORD was upon the tabernacle by day, and fire was on it by night, in the sight of all the house of Israel, throughout all their journeys.

The Third Book of Moses Called
LEVITICUS

AUTHOR: Moses is declared to be the author of Leviticus fifty-six times within the book. External evidence supporting the authorship of Moses includes 1) A uniform ancient testimony. 2) Parallels found in the Ras Shamra Tablets dating from 1400 B.C. 3) The testimony of Christ (Ma 8:2–4 and Le 14:1–4; Ma 12:4 and Le 24:9; Lk 2:22).

KEY VERSE: Le 20:7–8

TIME: C. 1405 B.C.

THEME: Leviticus is God's guidebook for His newly redeemed people. It shows them how to worship and live holy lives. The instructions for the sacrificial system point to a holy God and what he requires from people who would serve him. The laws of holiness and sanctification provide basic instructions for living in a community. Together the two groups of laws are a framework for relationship between God and man. Blessings result from obedience to these laws and discipline is the result of disobedience.

A ND the LORD [R] called unto Moses, and spake unto him [R] out of the tabernacle of the congregation, saying,   Ex 19:3; 25:22 · Ex 40:34
2   Speak unto the children of Israel, and say unto them, [R] If any man of you bring an offering unto the LORD, ye shall bring your offering of the cattle, even of the herd, and of the flock.   22:18, 19

40:34 cloud . . . glory. When the Lord came near in 19:20, the people were terrified, but this time they were overjoyed. The glory of the Lord filling the tabernacle demonstrated His presence with the Israelites, His significance to them, and His awe-inspiring wonder.   **40:35 the cloud abode thereon.** God is not "far away in heaven," occasionally looking at the earth through binoculars. He lives among His people, and He desires to communicate with them (Jo 1:14).   **40:38 the cloud of the LORD.** The Book of Exodus ends with the picture of the gracious God hovering protectively over His people. He allowed His presence to be felt and seen.   **1:1–17 offering unto the LORD.** Leviticus continues the Exodus narrative of the dedication of the tabernacle by indicating how the liberated Israelites are to worship their God. This book deals with the voluntary sacrifices for thanksgiving, communion, or cleansing from sin. These offerings from the herd or flock

Continued on the next page

3   If his offering *be* a burnt sacrifice of the herd, let him offer a male without blemish: he shall offer it of his own voluntary will at the door of the tabernacle of the congregation before the LORD.

4   And he shall put his hand upon the head of the burnt offering; and it shall be accepted for him to make atonement for him.

5   And he shall kill the [R]bullock before the LORD: and the priests, Aaron's sons, shall bring the blood, and sprinkle the blood round about upon the altar that *is by* the door of the tabernacle of the congregation.   Mi 6:6

6   And he shall flay the burnt offering, and cut it into his pieces.

7   And the sons of Aaron the priest shall put [R]fire upon the altar, and [R]lay the wood in order upon the fire: Mal 1:10 · Ge 22:9

8   And the priests, Aaron's sons, shall lay the parts, the head, and the fat, in order upon the wood that *is* on the fire which *is* upon the altar:

9   But his inwards and his legs shall he wash in water: and the priest shall burn all on the altar, *to be* a burnt sacrifice, an offering made by fire, of a [R]sweet savour unto the LORD.   Ge 8:21; [2 Co 2:15]

10   And if his offering *be* of the flocks, *namely,* of the sheep, or of the goats, for a burnt sacrifice; he

shall bring it a male [R]without blemish.   Eze 43:22; [1 Pet. 1:19]

11   [R]And he shall kill it on the side of the altar northward before the LORD: and the priests, Aaron's sons, shall sprinkle his blood round about upon the altar.   v. 5

12   And he shall cut it into his pieces, with his head and his fat: and the priest shall lay them in order on the wood that *is* on the fire which *is* upon the altar:

13   But he shall wash the inwards and the legs with water: and the priest shall bring *it* all, and burn *it* upon the altar: it *is* a burnt sacrifice, an [R]offering made by fire, of a sweet savour unto the LORD.   Nu 15:4–7; 28:12–14

14   And if the burnt sacrifice for his offering to the LORD *be* of fowls, then he shall bring his offering of [R]turtledoves, or of young pigeons.   Ge 15:9; Lk 2:24

15   And the priest shall bring it unto the altar, and wring off his head, and burn *it* on the altar; and the blood thereof shall be wrung out at the side of the altar:

16   And he shall pluck away his crop with his feathers, and cast it [R]beside the altar on the east part, by the place of the ashes: 6:10

17   And he shall cleave it with the wings thereof, *but* [R]shall not divide *it* asunder: and the priest shall burn it upon the altar, upon the

---

represented the labor and financial investment of the owner, and were a continual reminder that a price always has to be paid for sin. **1:3 *burnt sacrifice.*** The "burnt sacrifice" was the only offering that was entirely consumed on the altar. It foreshadows the total sacrifice of Christ on the cross, as well as representing wholehearted, unreserved worship where nothing is withheld or left over. It reminds us that nothing must be held back for ourselves; it all belongs to Him. ***male without blemish.*** Offering a perfect animal was a real sacrifice, not just "something they didn't really need or want." These perfect animals were valuable for breeding or for sale. The principle still holds. God's people are to offer their best, of their own free will, and with joy. **1:4 *he shall put his hand upon the head of the burnt offering.*** Each worshipper brought his or her own offering and laid his own hand on the animal's head. No one could send another to act on his behalf. In the same way, no one today can send someone else to accept Christ's atonement for him; we must each come to Christ ourselves, acknowledging our own sin before Him. **1:9 *sweet savour.*** Never does Scripture represent God as eating the offerings brought to Him, as the pagan gods were thought to do. When a sacrifice was done in faith with a free will, it was accepted by the Lord as desirable, or sweet.

wood that *is* upon the fire: [R]it *is* a burnt sacrifice, an offering made by fire, of a sweet savour unto the LORD.　　　　　Ge 15:10 · vv. 9, 13

2 And when any will offer a [T]meat offering unto the LORD, his offering shall be *of* fine flour; and he shall pour oil upon it, and put frankincense thereon:　*grain*

2　And he shall bring it to Aaron's sons the priests: and he shall take thereout his handful of the flour thereof, and of the oil thereof, with all the frankincense thereof; and the priest shall burn [R]the memorial of it upon the altar, *to be* an offering made by fire, of a sweet savour unto the LORD:　　　　2:9

3　And [R]the remnant of the meat offering *shall be* Aaron's and his [R]sons': *it is* a thing most holy of the offerings of the LORD made by fire.　　7:9 · 6:6; 10:12, 13

4　And if thou bring an oblation of a meat offering baken in the oven, *it shall be* unleavened cakes of fine flour mingled with oil, or unleavened wafers [R]anointed[T] with oil.　　Ex 29:2 · *spread*

5　And if thy oblation *be* a meat offering *baken* in a [T]pan, it shall be *of* fine flour unleavened, mingled with oil.　*flat plate* or *griddle*

6　Thou shalt part it in pieces, and pour oil thereon: it *is* a meat offering.

7　And if thy oblation *be* a meat offering *baken* in the [R]fryingpan, it shall be made *of* fine flour with oil.　　　　　　7:9

8　And thou shalt bring the meat offering that is made of these things unto the LORD: and when it is presented unto the priest, he shall bring it unto the altar.

9　And the priest shall take from the meat offering [R]a memorial thereof, and shall burn *it* upon the altar: *it is* an [R]offering made by fire, of a sweet savour unto the LORD.　5:12; 6:15 · Ex 29:18

10　And [R]that which is left of the meat offering *shall be* Aaron's and his sons': *it is* a thing most holy of the offerings of the LORD made by fire.　　　　v. 3; 6:16

11　No meat offering, which ye shall bring unto the LORD, shall be made with [R]leaven: for ye shall burn no leaven, nor any honey, in any offering of the LORD made by fire.　　Ex 23:18; [1 Co 5:8; Ga 5:9]

12　[R]As for the [T]oblation of the firstfruits, ye shall offer them unto the LORD: but they shall not be burnt on the altar for a sweet savour.　　Ex 22:29; 34:22 · *offering*

13　And every oblation of thy meat offering [R]shalt thou season with

2:1 oil . . . frankincense. Olive oil was a primary part of the diet and a prominent symbol of blessing and prosperity. Frankincense was a costly incense from South Arabia and East Africa, an imported luxury that would have to be bought with money. By including frankincense, as well as the animals and grain they could raise on their land, every aspect of Israel's wealth was made a part of the offerings to God.　**2:3 shall be Aaron's and his sons.'** A significant portion of the priest's daily food came from this part of the grain offering. Only the consecrated priests were allowed to eat it, and only within the tabernacle.　**2:8–9 priest.** There were always two individuals involved when the ancient Hebrew brought his sacrifice to God. One was the offerer himself and the other was the officiating priest, who was the "bridge builder" between men and God. Jesus, as a better priest and a better sacrifice, once for all time bridged the gap between God and man, and through Him we can have direct access to God, to confess our sins and receive forgiveness.　**2:11 leaven.** Leaven and honey were prohibited because both cause fermentation, which represents corruption.　**2:13 salt of the covenant of thy God.** Salt was to be used in every grain offering. This was a reminder of the covenant that God had made with Israel at Sinai, and was a symbol of faithfulness to God and His covenant. There is an old saying, "he has eaten my salt," which means that you have taken someone into your home, given them shelter, food, and hospitality. The idea of the "salt" of God's covenant was a well understood concept.

salt; neither shalt thou suffer the salt of the covenant of thy God to be lacking from thy meat offering: with all thine offerings thou shalt offer salt.   [Mk 9:49, 50; Col 4:6]

14   And if thou offer a meat offering of thy firstfruits unto the LORD, ^Rthou shalt offer for the meat offering of thy firstfruits green ears of corn dried by the fire, *even* corn beaten out of ^Rfull ears.   23:10, 14 · 2 Ki 4:42

15   And ^Rthou shalt put oil upon it, and lay frankincense thereon: it *is* a meat offering.   v. 1

16   And the priest shall burn ^Rthe memorial of it, *part* of the beaten corn thereof, and *part* of the oil thereof, with all the frankincense thereof: *it is* an offering made by fire unto the LORD.   v. 2

3 And if his oblation *be* a ^Rsacrifice of peace offering, if he offer *it* of the herd; whether *it be* a male or female, he shall offer it ^Rwithout blemish before the LORD.   7:11, 29 · 1:3; 22:20–24

2   And ^Rhe shall lay his hand upon the head of his offering, and kill it *at* the door of the tabernacle of the congregation: and Aaron's sons the priests shall ^Rsprinkle the blood upon the altar round about.   16:21; Ex 29:10, 11, 16, 20 · 1:5

3   And he shall offer of the sacrifice of the peace offering an offering made by fire unto the LORD; ^Rthe fat that covereth the inwards, and all the fat that *is* upon the inwards,   1:8; Ex 29:13, 22

4   And the two kidneys, and the fat that *is* on them, which *is* by the flanks, and the ^Tcaul above the liver, with the kidneys, it shall he take away.   *fatty lobe attached to*

5   And Aaron's sons ^Rshall burn it on the altar upon the ^Rburnt sacrifice, which *is* upon the wood that *is* on the fire: *it is* an offering made by fire, of a sweet savour unto the LORD.   Ex 29:13 · 2 Ch 35:14

6   And if his offering for a sacrifice of peace offering unto the LORD *be* of the flock; male or female, ^Rhe shall offer it without blemish.   v. 1; 22:20–24

7   If he offer a lamb for his offering, then shall he ^Roffer it before the LORD.   1 Ki 8:62

8   And he shall lay his hand upon the head of his offering, and kill it before the tabernacle of the congregation: and Aaron's sons shall sprinkle the blood thereof round about upon the altar.

9   And he shall offer of the sacrifice of the peace offering an offering made by fire unto the LORD; the fat thereof, *and* the whole rump, it shall he take off hard by the backbone; and the fat that covereth the

3:1 *peace offering.* The Hebrew word for "peace" means "wholeness, completeness, soundness, health." When a person possesses all of these attributes, he is at peace. The peace offerings were a time of celebrating and enjoying the gift of peace with God. Yet it was only after Christ's death and resurrection, when He became our perfect peace offering (Col 1:20) that we could really have perfect peace with God. The sacrifices had to be made over and over, but Christ's death was once, for all time. **3:3–4** *two kidneys, and the fat that is on them . . . caul above the liver.* The fat was one of the most prized portions of the meat, and the kidneys were considered the seat of the emotions. The liver was an essential organ for telling the future in the pagan cultures surrounding Israel. Giving all of these things to God symbolized giving Him the best, giving Him the hopes, dreams, and desires of life; recognizing that He alone has control of the future, and that He will reveal it in His own way, at His own time. **3:5** *upon the burnt sacrifice.* The peace offering normally followed the burnt offering, which was entirely consumed on the altar. Being reconciled to God through the burnt offering, the worshiper was in a position to fellowship with God. Repentance and reconciliation must always come before genuine fellowship. **3:9** *the whole rump.* The tail of the Palestinian broad-tailed sheep is almost entirely fat and can weigh more than 16 pounds. This explains its special mention in the regulations for offering the fat of the sheep.

inwards, and all the fat that *is* upon the inwards,

10   And the two kidneys, and the fat that *is* upon them, which *is* by the flanks, and the caul above the liver, with the kidneys, it shall he take away.

11   And the priest shall burn it upon the altar: *it is* ^Rthe food of the offering made by fire unto the LORD.   Nu 28:2; [Eze 44:7; Mal 1:7, 12]

12   And if his ^Roffering *be* a goat, then ^Rhe shall offer it before the LORD.   Nu 15:6–11 · v. 1, 7

13   And he shall lay his hand upon the head of it, and kill it before the tabernacle of the congregation: and the sons of Aaron shall sprinkle the blood thereof upon the altar round about.

14   And he shall offer thereof his offering, *even* an offering made by fire unto the LORD; the fat that covereth the inwards, and all the fat that *is* upon the inwards,

15   And the two kidneys, and the fat that *is* upon them, which *is* by the flanks, and the caul above the liver, with the kidneys, it shall he take away.

16   And the priest shall burn them upon the altar: *it is* the food of the offering made by fire for a sweet savour: ^Rall the fat *is* the LORD'S.   7:23–25; 1 Sa 2:15; 2 Ch 7:7

17   *It shall be* a ^Rperpetual statute for your generations throughout all your dwellings, that ye eat neither fat nor ^Rblood.   6:18 · 7:23, 26

4 And the LORD spake unto Moses, saying,

2   Speak unto the children of Israel, saying, ^RIf a soul shall sin through ignorance against any of the commandments of the LORD *concerning things* which ought not to be done, and shall do against any of them: Ac 3:17

3   If the priest that is anointed do sin according to the sin of the people; then let him bring for his sin, which he hath sinned, a young bullock without blemish unto the LORD for a sin offering.

4   And he shall bring the bullock ^Runto the door of the tabernacle of the congregation before the LORD; and shall lay his hand upon the bullock's head, and kill the bullock before the LORD.   1:3, 4

5   And the priest that is anointed ^Rshall take of the bullock's blood, and bring it to the tabernacle of the congregation: Nu 19:4

6   And the priest shall dip his finger in the blood, and sprinkle of the blood seven times before the LORD, before the ^Rvail of the sanctuary.   Ex 40:21, 26

7   And the priest shall ^Rput *some* of the blood upon the horns of the altar of sweet incense before the LORD, which *is* in the tabernacle of the congregation; and shall pour ^Rall the blood of the bullock at the bottom of the altar of the burnt offering, which *is at* the door of the tabernacle of the congregation.   8:15; 9:9 · Ex 40:5, 6

8   And he shall take off from it all the fat of the bullock for the sin offering; the fat that covereth the inwards, and all the fat that *is* upon the inwards,

9   And the two kidneys, and the fat that *is* upon them, which *is* by the flanks, and the caul above the liver, with the kidneys, it shall he take away,

10   ^RAs it was taken off from the bullock of the sacrifice of peace offerings: and the priest shall burn them upon the altar of the burnt offering.   3:3–5

11   ^RAnd the skin of the bullock, and all his flesh, with his head, and with his legs, and his inwards, and his dung,   Ex 29:14

12   Even the whole bullock shall he carry forth ^Twithout the camp

---

4:11–12 *Even the whole bullock.* Burning the whole bull ensured that the priest did not profit in any way from his own sin or the atonement for his sin. Carrying it outside the camp was another way of symbolizing the seriousness and pollution of sin.

unto a clean place, where the ashes are poured out, and ^Rburn him on the wood with fire: where the ashes are poured out shall he be burnt.   *outside* · [He 13:11, 12]

13 And ^Rif the whole congregation of Israel sin through ignorance, ^Rand the thing be hid from the eyes of the assembly, and they have done *somewhat against* any of the commandments of the LORD *concerning things* which should not be done, and are guilty;   Nu 15:24–26; Jos 7:11 · 5:2–4

14 When the sin, which they have sinned against it, is known, then the congregation shall offer a young bullock for the sin, and bring him before the tabernacle of the congregation.

15 And the elders of the congregation ^Rshall lay their hands upon the head of the bullock before the LORD: and the bullock shall be killed before the LORD.   1:3, 4

16 ^RAnd the priest that is anointed shall bring of the bullock's blood to the tabernacle of the congregation: v. 5; [He 9:12–14]

17 And the priest shall dip his finger *in some* of the blood, and sprinkle *it* seven times before the LORD, *even* before the vail.

18 And he shall put *some* of the blood upon the horns of the altar which *is* before the LORD, that *is* in the tabernacle of the congregation, and shall pour out all the blood at the bottom of the altar of the burnt offering, which *is at* the door of the tabernacle of the congregation.

19 And he shall take all his fat from him, and burn *it* upon the altar.

20 And he shall do with the bullock as he did ^Rwith the bullock for a sin offering, so shall he do with this: ^Rand the priest shall make an atonement for them, and it shall be forgiven them.   v. 3 · 1:4

21 And he shall carry forth the bullock ^Twithout the camp, and burn him as he burned the first bullock: it *is* a sin offering for the congregation.   *outside*

22 When a ruler hath sinned, and ^Rdone *somewhat* through ignorance *against* any of the commandments of the LORD his God *concerning things* which should not be done, and is guilty;   vv. 2, 13

23 Or ^Rif his sin, wherein he hath sinned, come to his knowledge; he shall bring his offering, a kid of the goats, a male without blemish: v. 14; 5:4

24 And ^Rhe shall lay his hand upon the head of the goat, and kill it in the place where they kill the burnt offering before the LORD: it *is* a sin offering.   v. 4; [Is 53:6]

25 ^RAnd the priest shall take of the blood of the sin offering with his finger, and put *it* upon the horns of the altar of burnt offering, and shall pour out his blood at the bottom of the altar of burnt offering.   vv. 7, 18, 30, 34

26 And he shall burn all his fat upon the altar, as the fat of the sacrifice of peace offerings: and the priest shall make an atonement for him as concerning his sin, and it shall be forgiven him.

27 And ^Rif any one of the common people sin through ignorance,

---

4:13–21 the whole congregation. Interestingly, not only individuals bring a sin offering to God, but the whole congregation as well. We are used to thinking of individuals coming under conviction and repenting, but how can a whole community come to this way of thinking? A congregation or community can begin to realize that they have misrepresented God, or fallen short of their God-given responsibilities, and together repent and ask for forgiveness, even though the members repenting may not have been the actual people who made the bad decisions that created the problem. Groups need to turn around and redirect their actions, just as much as individuals do, and this is one of the ways that God changes whole societies.

while he doeth *somewhat against* any of the commandments of the LORD *concerning things* which ought not to be done, and be guilty; v. 2; Nu 15:27

28 Or ^Rif his sin, which he hath sinned, come to his knowledge: then he shall bring his offering, a kid of the goats, a female without blemish, for his sin which he hath sinned. v. 23

29 ^RAnd he shall lay his hand upon the head of the sin offering, and slay the sin offering in the place of the burnt offering. vv. 4, 24

30 And the priest shall take of the blood thereof with his finger, and put *it* upon the horns of the altar of burnt offering, and shall pour out all the blood thereof at the bottom of the altar.

31 And he shall take away all the fat thereof, as the fat is taken away from off the sacrifice of peace offerings; and the priest shall burn *it* upon the altar for a ^Rsweet savour unto the LORD; ^Rand the priest shall make an atonement for him, and it shall be forgiven him. Ge 8:21; Ex 29:18 · v. 26

32 And if he bring a lamb for a sin offering, ^Rhe shall bring it a female without blemish. v. 28

33 And he shall ^Rlay his hand upon the head of the sin offering, and slay it for a sin offering in the place where they kill the burnt offering. 1:4; Nu 8:12

34 And the priest shall take of the blood of the sin offering with his finger, and put *it* upon the horns of the altar of burnt offering, and shall pour out all the blood thereof at the bottom of the altar:

35 And he shall take away all the fat thereof, as the fat of the lamb is taken away from the sacrifice of the peace offerings; and the priest shall burn them upon the altar, ^Raccording to the offerings made by fire unto the LORD: ^Rand the priest shall make an atonement for his sin that he hath committed, and it shall be forgiven him. 3:5 · vv. 26, 31

5 And if a soul sin, and hear the voice of swearing, and *is* a witness, whether he hath seen or known *of it*; if he do not utter *it*, then he shall bear his iniquity.

2 Or if a soul touch any unclean thing, whether *it be* a carcase of an unclean beast, or a carcase of unclean cattle, or the carcase of unclean creeping things, and *if* it be hidden from him; he also shall be unclean, and guilty.

3 Or if he touch ^Rthe uncleanness of man, whatsoever uncleanness *it be* that a man shall be defiled withal, and it be hid from him; when he knoweth *of it*, then he shall be guilty. vv. 12, 13, 15

4 Or if a soul swear, pronouncing with *his* lips to do evil, or ^Rto do good, whatsoever *it be* that a man shall pronounce with an oath, and it be hid from him; when he knoweth *of it*, then he shall be guilty in one of these. Mk 6:23

5 And it shall be, when he shall be guilty in one of these *things*, that he shall ^Rconfess that he hath sinned in that *thing*: Ps 32:5

6 And he shall bring his trespass offering unto the LORD for his sin which he hath sinned, a female from the flock, a lamb or a kid of

---

5:3 uncleanness of man. Body fluids, a person's waste, and contact with a corpse were all causes of uncleanness. The ancient Israelites knew nothing about microbiology, but God, who knows everything, gave them laws that prevented disease and made them distinct from their neighbors. **5:4 swear . . . and it be hid from him.** Certainly a person would know when he makes a vow, but he might not be immediately aware of how rash his vow is, or that the long term consequences are undesirable. Whether the vow was made with good intentions, but not carried out, or made with wicked intentions, but not carried out, the person who made the vow is still responsible to repent of his foolishness when he becomes aware of it.

the goats, for a sin offering; and the priest shall make an atonement for him concerning his sin.

7 And if he be not able to bring a lamb, then he shall bring for his trespass, which he hath committed, two ᴿturtledoves, or two young pigeons, unto the Lᴏʀᴅ; one for a sin offering, and the other for a burnt offering.   1:14

8 And he shall bring them unto the priest, who shall offer *that* which *is* for the sin offering first, and ᴿwring off his head from his neck, but shall not divide *it* ᵀasunder: 1:15–17 · *apart*

9 And he shall sprinkle of the blood of the sin offering upon the side of the altar; and the ᴿrest of the blood shall be wrung out at the bottom of the altar: it *is* a sin offering.   4:7, 18, 30, 34

10 And he shall offer the second *for* a burnt offering, according to the ᴿmanner: and the priest shall make an atonement for him for his sin which he hath sinned, and it shall be forgiven him.   1:14–17

11 But if he be ᴿnot able to bring two turtledoves, or two young pigeons, then he that sinned shall bring for his offering the tenth part of an e′-phah of fine flour for a sin offering; ᴿhe shall put no oil upon it, neither shall he put *any* frankincense thereon: for it *is* a sin offering. 14:21–32 · 2:1, 2; Nu 5:15

12 Then shall he bring it to the priest, and the priest shall take his handful of it, ᴿ*even* a ᵀmemorial thereof, and burn *it* on the altar, ᴿaccording to the offerings made by fire unto the Lᴏʀᴅ: it *is* a sin offering.   2:2 · *memorial portion* · 4:35

13 And the priest shall make an atonement for him as touching his sin that he hath sinned in one of these, and it shall be forgiven him: and *the remnant* shall be the priest's, as a meat offering.

14 And the Lᴏʀᴅ spake unto Moses, saying,

15 If a soul commit a trespass, and sin through ignorance, in the holy things of the Lᴏʀᴅ; then he shall bring for his trespass unto the Lᴏʀᴅ a ram without blemish out of the flocks, with thy estimation by shek′-els of silver, after ᴿthe shek′-el of the sanctuary, for a trespass offering: Ex 30:13

16 And he shall make amends for the harm that he hath done in the holy thing, and ᴿshall add the fifth part thereto, and give it unto the priest: and the priest shall make an atonement for him with the ram of the trespass offering, and it shall be forgiven him.   22:14

17 And if a soul sin, and commit any of these things which are forbidden to be done by the commandments of the Lᴏʀᴅ; ᴿthough

---

5:7 *two turtledoves.* Part of the purification offering was burned on the altar, and part was not burned. When offering birds, the worshipper brought two in order to accomplish this. **5:11 *tenth part of an e-phah.*** This was approximately two quarts. **5:13 *the remnant shall be the priest's.*** Part of the offering was burned on the altar, as was part of the animal sacrifices. The rest belonged to the priests, as did the remainder of the animal sacrifices brought by ordinary citizens, except for their burnt offerings. **5:15 *commit a trespass, and sin through ignorance . . . . . trespass offering.*** This refers both to the objective responsibility of a sinner for his or her actions and the subjective feeling of guilt experienced by the sinner. The offering righted the wrong of the offense and cleared the conscience of the sinner. **5:15–6:7 *soul commit a trespass.*** The trespass offering covers both offenses against God (5:15–19) and against people (6:1–7). The offense may be unintentional, or quite deliberate, but regardless of the motive, such actions make the perpetrator guilty. The quickest way to mend relationships with God and with fellow human beings is to honestly admit our guilt and wrongdoing, pay back or repair where we can, and ask forgiveness of those we have sinned against. This responsibility cannot be sidestepped. **5:17 *though he wist it not, yet is he guilty.*** Ignorance does not make an offense harmless. The offender was

he wist *it* not, yet is he guilty, and shall bear his iniquity. 4:2, 13, 22, 27

18 ᴿAnd he shall bring a ram without blemish out of the flock, with thy estimation, for a trespass offering, unto the priest: and the priest shall make an atonement for him concerning his ignorance wherein he erred and wist *it* not, and it shall be forgiven him. v. 15

19 It *is* a trespass offering: ᴿhe hath certainly trespassed against the LORD.   Ez 10:2

6 And the LORD spake unto Moses, saying,

2 If a soul sin, and commit a trespass against the LORD, and ᴿlie unto his neighbour in that which was delivered him to keep, or in fellowship, or in a thing taken away by violence, or hath deceived his neighbour;   Col 3:9

3 Or ᴿhave found that which was lost, and lieth concerning it, and ᴿsweareth falsely; in any of all these that a man doeth, sinning therein: Ex 23:4 · Ex 22:11; Ze 5:4

4 Then it shall be, because he hath sinned, and is guilty, that he shall restore that which he took violently away, or the thing which he hath deceitfully gotten, or that

which was delivered him to keep, or the lost thing which he found,

5 Or all that about which he hath sworn falsely; he shall even ᴿrestore it in the principal, and shall add the fifth part more thereto, *and* give it unto him to whom it appertaineth, in the day of his trespass offering.   Nu 5:7, 8

6 And he shall bring his trespass offering unto the LORD, a ram without blemish out of the flock, with thy estimation, for a trespass offering, unto the priest:

7 ᴿAnd the priest shall make an atonement for him before the LORD: and it shall be forgiven him for any thing of all that he hath done in trespassing therein.   4:26

8 And the LORD spake unto Moses, saying,

9 Command Aaron and his sons, saying, This *is* the ᴿlaw of the burnt offering: It *is* the burnt offering, because of the burning upon the altar all night unto the morning, and the fire of the altar shall be burning in it.   Ex 29:38–42

10 And the priest shall put on his linen garment, and his linen breeches shall he put upon his flesh, and take up the ashes which

still guilty and bore responsibility for his sin. He might also be troubled in conscience, though he might never learn the exact nature of his offense. This raises the concept that a person can be aware of a break in his fellowship with God, without being sure what caused this break. **5:18 *erred and wist it not.*** This was not a sin of rebellion, but one for which the offender earnestly desired to atone, though he did not know what it was. **5:19 *he hath certainly trespassed against the LORD.*** The fact that the priest declared him forgiven, and the peace of conscience that the worshipper had, declares that he was indeed guilty of some trespass; it was not his imagination. It is possible for a Christian to have an overactive conscience that keeps the believer in a constant state of anxiety about unknown sins. It is good to remember that God knows all about this, and if we confess our feelings of guilt, He will either show us our true guilt and grant us forgiveness and a clear conscience, or show us the error in our thinking regarding what He expects from us. **6:5–6 *even restore it.*** Restitution and a one fifth fine were evidence of genuine repentance. Then the offender could bring the ram for the trespass offering and be forgiven for the sin of swearing falsely in God's name. Jesus preserved this order for the person who remembered at the altar that he had offended his brother (Ma 5:23). **6:10 *breeches.*** The breeches were linen trousers that prevented immodest exposure as the priest ascended and descended the altar ramp. This modesty communicated to the Israelites that human sexuality could not influence God. That idea was a central feature of Baal worship, which continually tempted the Israelites. The priests of Baal would use obscene gestures and actions in the pagan worship of their depraved god.

the fire hath consumed with the burnt offering on the altar, and he shall put them beside the altar.

11 And ^Rhe shall put off his garments, and put on other garments, and carry forth the ashes ^Twithout the camp ^Runto a clean place.   Eze 44:19 · *outside* · 4:12

12 And the fire upon the altar shall be burning in it; it shall not be put out: and the priest shall burn wood on it every morning, and lay the burnt offering in order upon it; and he shall burn thereon ^Rthe fat of the peace offerings.   3:3

13 The fire shall ever be burning upon the ^Raltar; it shall never go out.   1:7

14 And this *is* the law of the ^Tmeat offering: the sons of Aaron shall offer it before the LORD, before the altar.   *grain* or *meal*

15 And he shall take of it his handful, of the flour of the meat offering, and of the oil thereof, and all the frankincense which *is* upon the meat offering, and shall burn *it* upon the altar *for* a ^Tsweet savour, *even* the memorial of it, unto the LORD.   *pleasing aroma*

16 And the remainder thereof shall Aaron and his sons eat: with unleavened bread shall it be eaten in the holy place; in the court of the tabernacle of the congregation they shall eat it.

17 It shall not be baken with leaven. I have given it *unto them* for their ^Tportion of my offerings made by fire; it *is* most holy, as *is* the sin offering, and as the ^Rtrespass offering.   *share* · 7:7

18 All the males among the children of Aaron shall eat of it. *It shall be* a statute for ever in your generations concerning the offerings of the LORD made by fire: ^Revery one that toucheth them shall be holy.   Nu 4:15; Hag 2:11–13

19 And the LORD spake unto Moses, saying,

20 ^RThis *is* the offering of Aaron and of his sons, which they shall offer unto the LORD in the day when he is anointed; the tenth part of an ^Re'-phah of fine flour for a meat offering perpetual, half of it in the morning, and half thereof at night.   Ex 29:2 · Ex 16:36

21 In a ^Rpan it shall be made with oil; *and when it is* baken, thou shalt bring it in: *and* the baken pieces of the meat offering shalt thou offer *for* a sweet savour unto the LORD.   2:5; 7:9

22 And the priest of his sons ^Rthat is anointed in his stead shall offer it: *it is* a statute for ever unto the LORD; ^Rit shall be ^Twholly burnt.   4:3 · Ex 29:25 · *completely*

23 For every meat offering for the priest shall be wholly burnt: it shall not be eaten.

24 And the LORD spake unto Moses, saying,

25 Speak unto Aaron and to his sons, saying, This *is* the law of the sin offering: ^RIn the place where the burnt offering is killed shall the sin offering be killed before the LORD: it *is* most holy.   1:1, 3, 5, 11

26 ^RThe priest that offereth it for sin shall eat it: in the holy place shall it be eaten, in the court of

---

6:13 fire shall ever be burning. There are at least three reasons the priests are instructed to keep the fire burning. The original fire on the altar came from God, perpetual fire symbolized perpetual worship, and perpetual fire was a reminder of the continual need for atonement and reconciliation with God. **6:20 half of it in the morning . . . half thereof at night.** The idea of a morning and evening appointment with God is ancient. It is a precious privilege, open to every believer because Jesus opened the door into the presence of God when He died on the cross for our sins. **6:22 a statute for ever.** This grain offering and the burnt offering were sacrificed daily—with some interruptions, most notably during the exile—until the destruction of the temple in A.D. 70. Even in the periods of Judah's worst apostasy, the evidence suggests that the daily offerings continued, though often for incorrect or inadequate reasons. (Is 1:10–17; Je 7:8–15; Mi 6:6–8).

the tabernacle of the congregation. [10:17, 18]; Nu 18:9, 10
27 Whatsoever shall touch the
flesh thereof shall be holy: and
when there is sprinkled of the blood
thereof upon any garment, thou
shalt wash that whereon it was
sprinkled in the holy place.
28 But the earthen vessel wherein
it is ᵀsodden ᴿshall be broken: and
if it be sodden in a brasen pot, it
shall be both scoured, and rinsed
in water. boiled · 11:33; 15:12
29 All the males among the priests
shall eat thereof: it is most holy.
30 ᴿAnd no sin offering, whereof
any of the blood is brought into
the tabernacle of the congregation
to reconcile withal in the holy place,
shall be eaten: it shall be burnt in
the fire. [He 13:11, 12]

7 Likewise ᴿthis is the ᵀlaw of
the trespass offering: it is most
holy. 5:14—6:7 · He torah
2 In the place where they kill
the burnt offering shall they kill the
trespass offering: and the blood
thereof shall he sprinkle round
about upon the altar.
3 And he shall offer of it all the
fat thereof; the rump, and the fat
that covereth the inwards,
4 And the two kidneys, and the
fat that is on them, which is by the
flanks, and the caul that is above
the liver, with the kidneys, it shall
he take away:
5 And the priest shall burn them
upon the altar for an offering made
by fire unto the LORD: it is a trespass offering.
6 ᴿEvery male among the priests
shall eat thereof: it shall be
eaten in the holy place: ᴿit is most
holy. 6:16–18, 29; Nu 18:9 · 2:3
7 As the sin offering is, so is ᴿthe
trespass offering: there is one law
for ᵀthem: the priest that maketh

atonement therewith shall have
it. 6:24–30; 14:13 · them both
8 And the priest that offereth
any man's burnt offering, even the
priest shall have ᵀto himself the
skin of the burnt offering which
he hath offered. for
9 And ᴿall the meat offering that
is baken in the oven, and all that
is dressed in the fryingpan, and in
the pan, shall be the priest's that
offereth it. Nu 18:9
10 And every meat offering, mingled with oil, and dry, shall all the
sons of Aaron have, one as much
as another.
11 And ᴿthis is the law of the sacrifice of peace offerings, which he
shall offer unto the LORD. 3:1
12 If he offer it for a thanksgiving, then he shall offer with the
sacrifice of thanksgiving unleavened cakes mingled with oil, and
unleavened wafers ᴿanointed with
oil, and cakes mingled with oil, of
fine flour, fried. 2:4; Nu 6:15
13 Besides the cakes, he shall offer for his offering ᴿleavened bread
with the sacrifice of thanksgiving
of his peace offerings. 2:12
14 And of it he shall offer one out
of the whole oblation for an heave
offering unto the LORD, ᴿand it
shall be the priest's that sprin-
kleth the blood of the peace offerings. Nu 18:8, 11, 19
15 ᴿAnd the flesh of the sacrifice
of his peace offerings for thanksgiving shall be eaten the same day
that it is offered; he shall not leave
any of it until the morning. 22:29
16 But ᴿif the sacrifice of his offering be a vow, or a voluntary offering, it shall be eaten the same
day that he offereth his sacrifice:
and on the morrow also the remainder of it shall be eaten: 19:5–8
17 But the remainder of the flesh

7:1–7 trespass offering. The guilt or trespass offering was "most holy," showing how
seriously and carefully God considers the acts of reparation made by His people. The
priest was to eat it in a holy place. It was his to eat, as part of God's provision for him,
but he was to remember where it came from. The price of atonement has never been
cheap in God's eyes, even when it was as incomplete as the offering of a goat or lamb.

of the sacrifice on the third day shall be burnt with fire.

18 And if *any* of the flesh of the sacrifice of his peace offerings be eaten at all on the third day, it shall not be accepted, neither shall it be [R]imputed unto him that offereth it: it shall be an abomination, and the soul that eateth of it shall bear his iniquity.   Nu 18:27

19 And the flesh that toucheth any unclean *thing* shall not be eaten; it shall be burnt with fire: and as for the flesh, all that be [T]clean shall eat thereof.   *pure*

20 But the soul that eateth *of* the flesh of the sacrifice of peace offerings, that *pertain* unto the [R]LORD, having his uncleanness upon him, even that soul shall be cut off from his people.   [He 2:17]

21 Moreover the soul that shall touch any unclean *thing*, *as* [R]the uncleanness of man, or *any* [R]unclean beast, or any [R]abominable unclean *thing*, and eat of the flesh of the sacrifice of peace offerings, which *pertain* unto the LORD, even that soul shall be cut off from his people.   5:2, 3, 5 · 11:24, 28 · Eze 4:14

22 And the LORD spake unto Moses, saying,

23 Speak unto the children of Israel, saying, [R]Ye shall eat no manner of fat, of ox, or of sheep, or of goat.   De 14:21; Eze 4:14; 44:31

24 And the fat of the beast that dieth of itself, and the fat of that which is torn with beasts, may be used in any other use: but ye shall in no wise eat of it.

25 For whosoever eateth the fat of the beast, of which men offer an offering made by fire unto the LORD, even the soul that eateth *it* shall be cut off from his people.

26 [R]Moreover ye shall eat no manner of blood, *whether it be* of fowl or of beast, in any of your dwellings.   Ge 9:4; 1 Sa 14:33

27 Whatsoever [T]soul *it be* that eateth any manner of blood, even that soul shall be cut off from his people.   *person*

28 And the LORD spake unto Moses, saying,

29 Speak unto the children of Israel, saying, [R]He that offereth the sacrifice of his peace offerings unto the LORD shall bring his oblation unto the LORD of the sacrifice of his peace offerings.   22:21

30 [R]His own hands shall bring the offerings of the LORD made by fire, the fat with the breast, it shall he bring, that the [R]breast may be waved *for* a wave offering before the LORD.   3:3, 4, 9, 14 · Ex 29:24, 27

31 [R]And the priest shall burn the fat upon the altar: but the breast shall be Aaron's and his sons'. 3:5

32 And [R]the right shoulder shall ye give unto the priest *for* an heave offering of the sacrifices of your peace offerings.   Nu 6:20

33 He among the sons of Aaron, that offereth the blood of the peace offerings, and the fat, shall have the right shoulder for *his* part.

34 For [R]the wave breast and the heave shoulder have I taken of the children of Israel from off the sacrifices of their peace offerings, and have given them unto Aaron the priest and unto his sons by a statute for ever from among the children of Israel.   Ex 29:28; De 18:3

35 This *is the portion* of the anointing of Aaron, and of the anointing of his sons, out of the offerings of the LORD made by fire, in the day *when* he presented them to minister unto the LORD in the priest's office;

36 Which the LORD commanded to be given them of the children of Israel, [R]in the day that he anointed them, *by* a statute for ever throughout their generations.   8:12

37 This *is* the law [R]of the burnt

7:34 *the wave breast and the heave shoulder.* This present was a contribution to the officiating priest as his portion of the peace offerings for thanksgiving. The offering was waved before the Lord as an acknowledgment that He is the giver of all gifts.

offering, of the meat offering, and of the sin offering, and of the trespass offering, [R]and of the consecrations, and of the sacrifice of the peace offerings;   6:9 · Ex 29:1
38 Which the LORD commanded Moses in mount Si'-nai, in the day that he commanded the children of Israel [R]to offer their oblations unto the LORD, in the wilderness of Si'-nai.   1:1, 2; De 4:5

8 And the LORD spake unto Moses, saying,
2   Take Aaron and his sons with him, and the garments, and the anointing oil, and a bullock for the sin offering, and two rams, and a basket of unleavened bread;
3   And gather thou all the congregation together [T]unto the door of the tabernacle of the [T]congregation.   at · meeting
4   And Moses did as the LORD commanded him; and the assembly was gathered together unto the door of the tabernacle of the congregation.
5   And Moses said unto the congregation, This is the thing which the LORD commanded to be done.
6   And Moses brought Aaron and his sons, and [R]washed them with water.   Ex 30:20; He 10:22
7   And he put upon him the coat, and girded him with the girdle, and clothed him with the robe, and put the e'-phod upon him, and he girded him with the curious girdle of the e'-phod, and bound it unto him therewith.
8   And he put the breastplate

upon him: also he [R]put in the breastplate the U'-rim and the Thum'-mim.   De 33:8; 1 Sa 28:6
9   [R]And he put the mitre upon his head; also upon the mitre, even upon his forefront, did he put the golden plate, the holy crown; as the LORD commanded Moses.   Ex 28:36, 37; 29:6
10   [R]And Moses took the anointing oil, and anointed the tabernacle and all that was therein, and sanctified them. Ex 30:26–29; 40:10, 11
11   And he sprinkled thereof upon the altar seven times, and anointed the altar and all his vessels, both the laver and his foot, to sanctify them.
12   And he poured of the anointing oil upon Aaron's head, and anointed him, to sanctify him.
13   [R]And Moses brought Aaron's sons, and put coats upon them, and girded them with girdles, and put bonnets upon them; as the LORD commanded Moses.   Ex 29:8, 9
14   [R]And he brought the bullock for the sin offering: and Aaron and his sons laid their hands upon the head of the bullock for the sin offering.   Ex 29:10; Ps 66:15; Eze 43:19
15   And he slew it; and Moses took the blood, and put it upon the horns of the altar round about with his finger, and purified the altar, and poured the blood at the bottom of the altar, and sanctified it, to make reconciliation upon it.
16   [R]And he took all the fat that was upon the inwards, and the caul above the liver, and the two kidneys,

8:6–13 Purification—Moses carried out the Lord's command (Ex 29:4) by purifying Aaron and his sons for the priesthood. The purification process began with an outward washing of water which symbolized an inward purity. The believer today also shows his inward reality (his acceptance of Christ and the presence of the Holy Spirit) with his outward actions. These acts of obedience do not create the inward reality, but they confirm it. **8:8 *the Urim and the Thummim.*** These were the sacred lots used to determine the will of God. What they looked like and how they were used is not known. Apparently, the high priest phrased questions so the answers would be yes, or no, depending on how the lots came up. **8:12 *anointed him.*** The high priests of Israel, beginning here with Aaron, were anointed, as were the kings of Israel (1 Sa 10:1; 16:13) and at least one of the prophets (1 Ki 19:16). Jesus combines in His person the offices of High Priest, King, and Prophet, so He is *the* Anointed One, which is the meaning of the names Messiah (Hebrew) and Christ (Greek).

and their fat, and Moses burned *it* upon the altar.   Ex 29:13
17   But the bullock, and his hide, his flesh, and his dung, he burnt with fire without the camp; as the LORD [R] commanded Moses. Ex 29:14
18 [R] And he brought the ram for the burnt offering: and Aaron and his sons laid their hands upon the head of the ram.   Ex 29:15
19   And he killed *it*; and Moses sprinkled the blood upon the altar round about.
20   And he cut the ram into pieces; and Moses [R] burnt the head, and the pieces, and the fat.   1:8
21   And he washed the inwards and the legs in water; and Moses burnt the whole ram upon the altar: it *was* a burnt sacrifice for a sweet savour, *and* an offering made by fire unto the LORD; as the LORD commanded Moses.
22   And he brought the other ram, the ram of consecration: and Aaron and his sons laid their hands upon the head of the ram.
23   And he slew *it*; and Moses took of the [R] blood of it, and put *it* upon the tip of Aaron's right ear, and upon the thumb of his right hand, and upon the great toe of his right foot.   14:14; Ex 29:20, 21
24   And he brought Aaron's sons, and Moses put of the [R] blood upon the tip of their right ear, and upon the thumbs of their right hands, and upon the great toes of their right feet: and Moses sprinkled the blood upon the altar round about.   [He 9:13, 14, 18–23]
25 [R] And he took the fat, and the rump, and all the fat that *was* upon the inwards, and the caul *above* the liver, and the two kidneys, and their fat, and the right shoulder: Ex 29:22
26 [R] And out of the basket of unleavened bread, that *was* before the LORD, he took one unleavened cake, and a cake of oiled bread, and one wafer, and put *them* on the fat, and upon the right shoulder: Ex 29:23
27   And he put all [R] upon Aaron's hands, and upon his sons' hands, and waved them *for* a wave offering before the LORD.   Ex 29:24
28   And Moses took them from off their hands, and burnt *them* on the altar upon the burnt offering: they *were* consecrations for a sweet savour: it *is* an offering made by fire unto the LORD.
29   And Moses took the breast, and waved it *for* a wave offering before the LORD: *for* of the ram of consecration it was Moses' part; as the LORD commanded Moses.
30   And Moses took of the anointing oil, and of the blood which *was* upon the altar, and sprinkled *it* upon Aaron, *and* upon his garments, and upon his sons, and upon his sons' garments with him; and sanctified Aaron, *and* his garments, and his sons, and his sons' garments with him.
31   And Moses said unto Aaron and to his sons, [R] Boil the flesh *at* the door of the tabernacle of the congregation: and there eat it with the bread that *is* in the basket of consecrations, as I commanded, saying, Aaron and his sons shall eat it.   Ex 29:31, 32
32 [R] And that which remaineth of the flesh and of the bread shall ye burn with fire.   Ex 29:34
33   And ye shall not go out of the door of the tabernacle of the congregation *in* seven days, until the days of your consecration be at an end: for [R] seven days shall he consecrate you.   Ex 29:30, 35; Eze 43:25
34   As he hath done this day, *so* the LORD hath commanded to do, to make an atonement for you.
35   Therefore shall ye abide *at* the door of the tabernacle of the con-

---

8:35 *that ye die not.* This statement was a reminder that it is dangerous to approach God carelessly, without reverence, or ignore His instructions. Two of Aaron's sons failed to heed this warning and died (ch. 10).

gregation day and night seven days, and ᴿkeep the charge of the Lᴏʀᴅ, that ye die not: for so I am commanded.   1 Ki 2:3; Eze 48:11

36 So Aaron and his sons did all things which the Lᴏʀᴅ commanded by the hand of Moses.

9 And ᴿit came to pass on the eighth day, *that* Moses called Aaron and his sons, and the elders of Israel;   Eze 43:27

2 And he said unto Aaron, Take thee a young ᴿcalf for a sin offering, and a ram for a burnt offering, without blemish, and offer *them* before the Lᴏʀᴅ.   Ex 29:21

3 And unto the children of Israel thou shalt speak, saying, Take ye a kid of the goats for a sin offering; and a calf and a lamb, *both* of the first year, without blemish, for a burnt offering;

4 Also a bullock and a ram for peace offerings, to sacrifice before the Lᴏʀᴅ; and ᴿa meat offering mingled with oil: for to day the Lᴏʀᴅ will appear unto you.   2:4

5 And they brought *that* which Moses commanded before the tabernacle of the congregation: and all the congregation drew near and stood before the Lᴏʀᴅ.

6 And Moses said, This *is* the thing which the Lᴏʀᴅ commanded that ye should do: and the glory of the Lᴏʀᴅ shall appear unto you.

7 And Moses said unto Aaron, Go unto the altar, and offer thy sin offering, and thy burnt offering, and make an atonement for thyself, and for the people: and ᴿoffer the offering of the people, and make an atonement for them; as the Lᴏʀᴅ commanded.   4:16; He 5:1

8 Aaron therefore went unto the altar, and slew the calf of the sin offering, which *was* for himself.

9 And the sons of Aaron brought the blood unto him: and he dipped his finger in the blood, and put *it* upon the horns of the altar, and poured out the blood at the bottom of the altar:

10 ᴿBut the fat, and the kidneys, and the caul above the liver of the sin offering, he burnt upon the altar; as the Lᴏʀᴅ commanded Moses.   8:16; Ex 23:18

11 ᴿAnd the flesh and the hide he burnt with fire ᵀwithout the camp.   4:11, 12; 8:17 · *outside*

12 And he slew the burnt offering; and Aaron's sons presented unto him the blood, ᴿwhich he sprinkled round about upon the altar.   1:5; 8:19

13 ᴿAnd they presented the burnt offering unto him, with the pieces thereof, and the head: and he burnt *them* upon the altar.   8:20

14 ᴿAnd he did wash the inwards and the legs, and burnt *them* upon the burnt offering on the altar.   8:21

15 ᴿAnd he brought the people's offering, and took the goat, which *was* the sin offering for the people, and slew it, and offered it for sin, as the first.   [Is 53:10; He 2:17]

16 And he brought the burnt offering, and offered it ᴿaccording to the manner.   1:1–13

17 And he brought the meat offering, and took an handful thereof, and burnt *it* upon the altar, ᴿbeside the burnt sacrifice of the morning.   Ex 29:38, 39

18 He slew also the bullock and

9:4 *the Lᴏʀᴅ will appear unto you.* The purpose of all worship is to fellowship with God. The sacrifices were not an end in themselves; they allowed the worshiper to meet with God without being destroyed. The Israelites looked forward and we look back to Christ's atonement, which made the way for us to come freely into God's presence.
9:15 *the goat, which was the sin offering.* This goat was offered for atonement of the people as a general acknowledgment that they would always need to make things right with God before they could worship Him, and is referred to again in ch. 16. The bull for the sin offering (4:14) was for a specific sin, rather than dealing with sin nature (that is, our ability to sin).

the ram *for* [R] a sacrifice of peace of-ferings, which *was* for the people: and Aaron's sons presented unto him the blood, which he sprinkled upon the altar round about,   3:1–11
19 And the fat of the bullock and of the ram, the rump, and that which covereth *the inwards*, and the kidneys, and the caul *above* the liver:
20 And they put the fat upon the breasts, [R] and he burnt the fat upon the altar: 3:5, 16
21 And the breasts and the right shoulder Aaron waved [R] *for* a wave offering before the LORD; as Mo-ses commanded.   Ex 29:24, 26, 27
22 And Aaron lifted up his hand toward the people, and [R] blessed them, and came down from offer-ing of the sin offering, and the burnt offering, and peace offer-ings.   Nu 6:22–26; De 21:5; Lk 24:50
23 And Moses and Aaron went into the tabernacle of the congre-gation, and came out, and blessed the people: and the glory of the LORD appeared unto all the people.
24 And [R] there came a fire out from before the LORD, and con-sumed upon the altar the burnt offering and the fat: *which* when all the people saw, they shouted, and fell on their faces.   Ju 6:21

10 And Na'-dab and A-bi'-hu, the sons of Aaron, took either of them his censer, and put fire therein, and put incense there-on, and offered strange fire before the LORD, which he commanded them not.

2 And there [R] went out fire from the LORD, and devoured them, and they died before the LORD. Re 20:9
3 Then Moses said unto Aaron, This *is it* that the LORD spake, say-ing, I will be sanctified in them [R] that come nigh me, and before all the people I will be glorified. And Aaron held his peace.   Eze 20:41
4 And Moses called Mish'-a-el and El'-za-phan, and the sons of Uz-zi'-el the uncle of Aaron, and said unto them, Come near, [R] carry your brethren from before the sanc-tuary out of the camp.   Ac 5:6
5 So they went near, and car-ried them in their coats out of the camp; as Moses had said.
6 And Moses said unto Aaron, and unto E-le-a'-zar and unto Ith'-a-mar, his sons, Uncover not your heads, neither rend your clothes; lest ye die, and [R] lest wrath come upon all the people: but let your brethren, the whole house of Is-rael, bewail the burning which the LORD hath kindled.   2 Sa 24:1
7 [R] And ye shall not go out from the door of the tabernacle of the congregation, lest ye die: [R] for the anointing oil of the LORD *is* upon you. And they did according to the word of Moses.   8:33; 21:12 · 8:30
8 And the LORD spake unto Aaron, saying,
9 Do not drink wine nor strong drink, thou, nor thy sons with thee, when ye go into the tabernacle of the congregation, lest ye die: *it shall*

🕯️ 10:1–3

9:22 Aaron . . . blessed them. The ultimate function of the priests was to bless the people. The purpose of the priest's sacrifices was to cleanse the priests so they could bless the people, and the purpose of the people's sacrifices was to cleanse the people to receive this blessing from God. **10:1–2 strange fire.** Aaron and his sons served the Lord as high priests in the worship of the tabernacle. They had been properly appointed, purified, clothed, anointed, and ordained. Initially they did everything that the Lord commanded through Moses. But when Nadab and Abihu disobeyed God in the very performance of their duties, the Lord swiftly punished them with a consuming fire. Being blessed with a thriving ministry, is no excuse to go off and do things our own way. God doesn't take such actions lightly, and neither should we. **10:3 in them that come nigh me . . . I will be glorified.** Although this passage refers specifically to the priests of Israel, it is still a good concept for all believers. We are close to God, we remember that He is holy, that He paid a great price to redeem us, and it is our purpose to glorify Him.

be a statute for ever throughout your generations:

10 And that ye may put difference between holy and unholy, and between unclean and clean;

11 And that ye may teach the children of Israel all the statutes which the LORD hath spoken unto them by the hand of Moses.

12 And Moses spake unto Aaron, and unto E-le-a'-zar and unto Ith'-a-mar, his sons that were left, Take ᴿthe meat offering that remaineth of the offerings of the LORD made by fire, and eat it without leaven beside the altar: for ᴿit *is* most holy: Nu 18:9 · 21:22

13 And ye shall eat it in the ᴿholy place, because it *is* thy due, and thy sons' due, of the sacrifices of the LORD made by fire: for ᴿso I am commanded.   Nu 18:10 · 2:3; 6:16

14 And the wave breast and heave shoulder shall ye eat in a clean place; thou, and thy sons, and thy ᴿdaughters with thee: for *they be* thy due, and thy sons' ᴿdue, *which* are given out of the sacrifices of peace offerings of the children of Israel.   22:13 · Nu 18:10

15 ᴿThe heave shoulder and the wave breast shall they bring with the offerings made by fire of the fat, to wave *it for* a wave offering before the LORD; and it shall be thine, and thy sons' with thee, by a statute for ever; as the LORD hath commanded.   7:29, 30, 34

16 And Moses diligently sought ᴿthe goat of the sin offering, and, behold, it was burnt: and he was angry with E-le-a'-zar and Ith'-a-mar, the sons of Aaron *which were* left *alive,* saying,   9:3, 15

17 ᴿWherefore have ye not eaten the sin offering in the holy place, seeing it *is* most holy, and *God* hath given it you to bear ᴿthe iniquity of the congregation, to make atonement for them before the LORD?   6:24–30 · 22:16; Ex 28:38; Nu 18:1

18 Behold, ᴿthe blood of it was not brought in within the holy *place:* ye should indeed have eaten it in the holy *place,* ᴿas I commanded.   6:30 · 6:26, 30

19 And Aaron said unto Moses, Behold, this day have they offered their sin offering and their burnt offering before the LORD; and such things have befallen me: and *if* I had eaten the sin offering to day, ᴿshould it have been accepted in the sight of the LORD?   [Is 1:11–15]

20 And when Moses heard *that,* he was content.

11 And the LORD spake unto Moses and to Aaron, saying unto them,

2 Speak unto the children of Israel, saying, These *are* the beasts which ye shall eat among all the beasts that *are* on the earth.

3 Whatsoever parteth the hoof, and is clovenfooted, *and* cheweth the cud, among the beasts, that shall ye eat.

4 Nevertheless these shall ye not eat of them that chew the cud, or of them that divide the hoof: *as* the camel, because he cheweth the cud, but divideth not the hoof; he *is* unclean unto you.

5 And the coney, because he cheweth the cud, but divideth not the hoof; he *is* unclean unto you.

6 And the hare, because he cheweth the cud, but divideth not the hoof; he *is* unclean unto you.

7 And the swine, though he divide the hoof, and be clovenfooted,

---

11:3 *cheweth the cud.* Ruminants, like cows, sheep, goats, deer, and antelope, eat only plants, mainly grasses and grains. No meat-eating animal chews the cud. **11:4 *the camel.*** Some of Israel's neighbors considered the camel a great delicacy. **11:5–6 *coney . . . hare.*** The coney, or rock hyrax, lives in colonies among the rocks. It is about the size of the rabbit, and like the rabbit, appears to chew constantly, but it is not a true ruminant, nor does it have a hoof. **11:7 *the swine.*** The swine is the best known of the unclean

Continued on the next page

yet he cheweth not the cud; [R]he *is* unclean to you.   Is 65:4

8   Of their flesh shall ye not eat, and their carcase shall ye not touch; they *are* unclean to you.

9   [R]These shall ye eat of all that *are* in the waters: whatsoever hath fins and scales in the waters, in the seas, and in the rivers, them shall ye eat.   De 14:9

10   And all that have not fins and scales in the seas, and in the rivers, of all that move in the waters, and of any living thing which *is* in the waters, they *shall be* an [R]abomination unto you: De 14:3

11   They shall be even an abomination unto you; ye shall not eat of their flesh, but ye shall have their carcases in abomination.

12   Whatsoever hath no fins nor scales in the waters, that *shall be* an abomination unto you.

13   [R]And these *are they which* ye shall have in abomination among the fowls; they shall not be eaten, they *are* an abomination: the eagle, and the [T]ossifrage, and the [T]ospray,   Is 66:17 · *vulture* · *buzzard*

14   And the [T]vulture, and the kite after his kind;   *kite, and falcon*

15   Every raven after his kind;

16   And the owl, and the night hawk, and the cuckow, and the hawk after his kind,

17   And the little owl, and the cormorant, and the great owl,

18   And the swan, and the pelican, and the gier eagle,

19   And the stork, the heron after her kind, and the lapwing, and the bat.

20   All fowls that creep, going upon *all* four, *shall be* an abomination unto you.

21   Yet these may ye eat of every flying creeping thing that goeth upon *all* four, which have legs above their feet, to leap withal upon the earth;

22   *Even* these of them ye may eat; the locust after his kind, and the bald locust after his kind, and the beetle after his kind, and the grasshopper after his kind.

23   But all *other* flying creeping things, which have four feet, *shall be* an abomination unto you.

24   And for these ye shall be unclean: whosoever toucheth the carcase of them shall be unclean until the even.

25   And whosoever beareth *ought* of the carcase of them [R]shall wash his clothes, and be unclean until the even.   Ze 13:1

26   *The carcases* of every beast which divideth the hoof, and *is* not clovenfooted, nor cheweth the cud, *are* unclean unto you: every one that toucheth them shall be unclean.

27   And whatsoever goeth upon his paws, among all manner of beasts that go on *all* four, those *are* unclean unto you: whoso toucheth their carcase shall be unclean until the even.

28   And he that beareth the carcase of them shall wash his clothes,

animals. We know now that pigs can pass some diseases to humans, and that inadequately cooked meat is one way these diseases are transferred. Pigs were sacrificed to pagan deities, and God was carefully steering His people away from these corrupted cultures. **11:8 *their carcase shall ye not touch.*** In the case of these unclean aminals, eating their meat or touching their dead bodies caused the Israelite to be unclean, or ritually impure. However, touching a live animal did not make the Israelites unclean, and they were allowed to use camels and donkeys as beasts of burden. **11:11–12 *abomination.*** The phrasing is careful, deliberate, and repetitive to remove any possibility of finding any exception anywhere. Abhorrent is a stronger word than "unclean," and implies not just avoidance, but repulsion. **11:20 *going upon all four.*** This phrase is an idiom for crawling on the ground, as insects do on their six legs. Many insects move about in filth and eat refuse. **11:21 *legs above their feet.*** The joints are the enlarged third legs of locusts and grasshoppers that enable them to leap. Locusts and grasshoppers do not live in filth or eat dung; they eat only plants.

and be unclean until the even: they *are* unclean unto you.

29 These also *shall be* unclean unto you among the creeping things that creep upon the earth; the weasel, and ᴿthe mouse, and the tortoise after his kind,   Is 66:17

30 And the ferret, and the chameleon, and the lizard, and the snail, and the mole.

31 These *are* unclean to you among all that creep: whosoever doth ᴿtouch them, when they be dead, shall be unclean until the even.   Hag 2:13

32 And upon whatsoever *any* of them, when they are dead, doth fall, it shall be unclean; whether *it be* any vessel of wood, or raiment, or skin, or sack, whatsoever vessel *it be,* wherein *any* work is done, ᴿit must be put into water, and it shall be unclean until the even; so it shall be cleansed.   15:12

33 And every ᴿearthen vessel, whereinto *any* of them falleth, whatsoever *is* in it shall be unclean; and ye shall break it.   6:28

34 Of all meat which may be eaten, *that* on which *such* water cometh shall be unclean: and all drink that may be drunk in every *such* vessel shall be unclean.

35 And every *thing* whereupon *any part* of their carcase falleth shall be unclean; *whether it be* oven, or ranges for pots, they shall be broken down: *for* they *are* unclean, and shall be unclean unto you.

36 Nevertheless a ᵀfountain or ᵀpit, *wherein there is* plenty of water, shall be clean: but that which toucheth their carcase shall be unclean.   *spring · cistern*

37 And if *any part* of their carcase fall upon any sowing seed which is to be sown, it *shall be* clean.

38 But if *any* water be put upon the seed, and *any part* of their carcase fall thereon, it *shall be* ᵀunclean unto you.   *impure*

39 And if any beast, of which ye may eat, die; he that toucheth the carcase thereof shall be ᴿunclean until the even.   Hag 2:11–13

40 And ᴿhe that eateth of the carcase of it shall wash his clothes, and be unclean until the even: he also that beareth the carcase of it shall wash his clothes, and be unclean until the even.   22:8

41 And every creeping thing that creepeth upon the earth *shall be* ᵀan abomination; it shall not be eaten.   *detestable*

42 Whatsoever goeth upon the belly, and whatsoever goeth upon *all* four, or whatsoever hath more feet among all creeping things that creep upon the earth, them ye shall not eat; for they *are* an abomination.

43 ᴿYe shall not make your selves abominable with any creeping thing that creepeth, neither shall ye make yourselves unclean with them, that ye should be defiled thereby.   20:25

44 For I *am* the LORD your God: ye shall therefore sanctify yourselves, and ᴿye shall be holy; for I *am* holy: neither shall ye defile yourselves with any manner of creeping thing that creepeth upon the earth.   [Am 3:3]; Ma 5:48

45 For I *am* the LORD that bringeth you up out of the land of Egypt, to be your God: ye shall therefore be holy, for I *am* holy.

46 This *is* the law ᵀof the beasts, and of the fowl, and of every living creature that moveth in the waters,

---

11:44–45 be holy. Our Lord calls us to personal holiness, and holy living can only come from a life which spends time with the Lord, meditating on who He is, seeking His power to be like Him. We will make mistakes and sin all of our lives, which God never does; when He asks us to be holy because He is holy, it is a goal that we grow toward. Even though we never finish, we still overcome many, many areas of sin, and this growth shows others that we serve a holy God, because they see His characteristics in us.

and of every creature that creepeth upon the earth: *concerning*
47   ^RTo make a difference between the unclean and the clean, and between the beast that may be eaten and the beast that may not be eaten.   Eze 44:23; Mal 3:18

12 And the LORD spake unto Moses, saying,
2   Speak unto the children of Israel, saying, If a woman have conceived seed, and born a man child: then ^Rshe shall be unclean seven days; according to the days of the separation for her infirmity shall she be unclean.   8:33; Lk 2:22
3   And in the ^Reighth day the flesh of his foreskin shall be circumcised.   Ge 17:12; Jo 7:22, 23
4   And she shall then continue in the blood of her purifying three and thirty days; she shall touch no hallowed thing, nor come into the sanctuary, until the days of her purifying be fulfilled.
5   But if she bear a maid child, then she shall be unclean two weeks, as in her separation: and she shall continue in the blood of her purifying threescore and six days.
6   And ^Rwhen the days of her purifying are fulfilled, for a son, or for a daughter, she shall bring a ^Rlamb of the first year for a

burnt offering, and a young pigeon, or a turtledove, for a sin offering, unto the door of the tabernacle of the congregation, unto the priest: Lk 2:22 · [Jo 1:29]
7   Who shall offer it before the LORD, and make ^Tan atonement for her; and she shall be cleansed from the issue of her blood. This *is* the law for her that hath born a male or a female.   *a propitiation*
8   ^RAnd if she be not able to bring a lamb, then she shall bring two turtles, or two young pigeons; the one for the burnt offering, and the other for a sin offering: ^Rand the priest shall make an atonement for her, and she shall be ^Tclean.   5:7; Lk 2:22–24 · 4:26 · *pure*

13 And the LORD spake unto Moses and Aaron, saying,
2   When a man shall have in the skin of his flesh a rising, a scab, or bright spot, and it be in the skin of his flesh *like* the plague of leprosy; ^Rthen he shall be brought unto Aaron the priest, or unto one of his sons the priests: Lk 17:14
3   And the priest shall look on the ^Tplague in the skin of the flesh: and *when* the hair in the plague is turned white, and the plague in sight *be* deeper than the skin of his flesh, it *is* a plague of leprosy: and the

---

12:2 *conceived seed, and born a . . . child . . . unclean.* The child did not cause the mother to be unclean. God had ordained and blessed childbirth from the beginning, even before the sin in the garden (Ge 1:28). It was the blood and other fluids in childbirth that made the mother ritually unclean for a period of time, just as other bodily fluids caused people to be unclean. **12:4** *blood of her purifying three and thirty days.* There is a practical as well as a ceremonial aspect to these instructions. The eighth day marked the end of the mother's uncleanness with regard to everyday objects and activities; she would no longer make them unclean by touching them. But her personal uncleanness continued. This corresponds with the medical characteristics of childbirth, and the need for special care and rest for the mother. (There is no reason given why this period is double with the birth of a female child.) **12:8** *if she be not able to bring a lamb.* Mary, following the birth of Jesus and the days of her purification, went to the temple in Jerusalem and offered a pair of doves because she was poor. *be clean.* The law of purification after childbirth demonstrates that all aspects of human existence are touched by sin. Childbirth itself is not sinful, and having children was one of the good commands that the Lord gave Adam and Eve in the garden. Yet pain in childbirth was one of the curses of the fall, and this time of purification can be viewed as a reminder that humans are still dealing with a sin nature that needs God's mercy and purification. **13:2** *a man.* The Hebrew word for "a man" means "human being," that is, anyone.

priest shall look on him, and pronounce him ᵀunclean. sore · defiled
4   If the bright spot *be* white in the skin of his flesh, and in sight *be* not deeper than the skin, and the hair thereof be not turned white; then the priest shall ᵀshut up *him that hath* the plague ᴿseven days: isolate · 14:8
5   And the priest shall look on him the seventh day: and, behold, *if* the plague in his sight be at a stay, *and* the plague spread not in the skin; then the priest shall shut him up seven days more:
6   And the priest shall look on him again the seventh day: and, behold, *if* the plague *be* somewhat dark, *and* the plague spread not in the skin, the priest shall pronounce him clean: it *is but* a scab: and he ᴿshall wash his clothes, and be clean.   11:25; 14:8; [Jo 13:8, 10]
7   But if the scab spread much abroad in the skin, after that he hath been seen of the priest for his cleansing, he shall be seen of the priest again:
8   And *if* the priest see that, behold, the scab spreadeth in the skin, then the priest shall pronounce him ᵀunclean: it *is* a leprosy.   defiled
9   When the plague of leprosy is in a man, then he shall be brought unto the priest;
10 ᴿAnd the priest shall see *him:* and, behold, *if* the rising *be* white in the skin, and it have turned the hair white, and *there be* quick raw flesh in the rising;   2 Ki 5:27
11 It *is* an old leprosy in the skin of his flesh, and the priest shall pronounce him unclean, and shall not shut him up: for he *is* unclean.
12 And if a leprosy break out abroad in the skin, and the leprosy cover all the skin of *him that hath* the plague from his head even to his foot, wheresoever the priest looketh;

13 Then the priest shall consider: and, behold, *if* the leprosy have covered all his flesh, he shall pronounce *him* clean *that hath* the plague: it is all turned ᴿwhite: he *is* clean.   Ex 4:6
14 But when raw flesh appeareth in him, he shall be unclean.
15 And the priest shall see the raw flesh, and pronounce him to be unclean: *for* the raw flesh *is* unclean: it *is* a leprosy.
16 Or if the raw flesh turn again, and be changed unto white, he shall come unto the priest;
17 And the priest shall see him: and, behold, *if* the plague be turned into white; then the priest shall pronounce *him* clean *that hath* the plague: he *is* clean.
18 The flesh also, in which, *even* in the skin thereof, was a ᴿboil, and is healed,   Ex 9:9; 15:26
19 And in the place of the boil there be a white rising, or a bright spot, white, and somewhat reddish, and it be shewed to the priest;
20 And if, when the priest seeth it, behold, it *be* in sight ᵀlower than the skin, and the hair thereof be turned white; the priest shall pronounce him unclean: it *is* a plague of leprosy broken out of the boil.   deeper
21 But if the priest look on it, and, behold, *there be* no white hairs therein, and *if* it *be* not lower than the skin, but *be* somewhat dark; then the priest shall ᵀshut him up seven days: isolate
22 And if it spread much abroad in the skin, then the priest shall pronounce him unclean: it *is* a ᵀplague.   infection or *leprous sore*
23 But if the bright spot ᵀstay in his place, *and* spread not, it *is* a burning boil; and the priest shall pronounce him clean.   remains
24 Or if there be *any* flesh, in the skin whereof *there is* a hot burn-

---

13:11 *shall not shut him up.* Isolation, or quarantine, was for the purpose of protecting the community until a diagnosis was reached. In this case, the patient was already diagnosed as "unclean," which meant he had to live outside the camp (v.46).

ing, and the quick *flesh* that burneth have a white bright spot, somewhat reddish, or white;

25 Then the priest shall look upon it: and, behold, *if* the hair in the bright spot be turned white, and it *be in* sight deeper than the skin; it *is* a leprosy broken out of the burning: wherefore the priest shall pronounce him unclean: it *is* the ᵀplague of leprosy. *infection*

26 But if the priest look on it, and, behold, *there be* no white hair in the bright spot, and it *be* no lower than the *other* skin, but *be* somewhat dark; then the priest shall shut him up seven days:

27 And the priest shall look upon him the seventh day: *and* if it be spread much abroad in the skin, then the priest shall pronounce him unclean: it *is* the plague of leprosy.

28 And if the bright spot stay in his place, *and* spread not in the skin, but it *be* somewhat dark; it *is* a rising of the burning, and the priest shall pronounce him clean: for it *is* an inflammation of the burning.

29 If a man or woman have a plague upon the head or the beard;

30 Then the priest shall see the plague: and, behold, if it *be* in sight deeper than the skin; *and there be* in it a yellow thin hair; then the priest shall pronounce him unclean: it *is* a dry scall, *even* a leprosy upon the head or beard.

31 And if the priest look on the plague of the scall, and, behold, it *be* not in sight deeper than the skin, and *that there is* no black hair in it; then the priest shall shut up *him that hath* the plague of the scall seven days:

32 And in the seventh day the priest shall look on the plague: and, behold, *if* the scall spread not, and there be in it no yellow hair, and the scall *be* not in sight deeper than the skin;

33 He shall be shaven, but the scall shall he not shave; and the priest shall shut up *him that hath* the scall seven days more:

34 And in the seventh day the priest shall look on the scall: and, behold, *if* the scall be not spread in the skin, nor *be* in sight deeper than the skin; then the priest shall pronounce him clean: and he shall wash his clothes, and be clean.

35 But if the scall spread much in the skin after his cleansing;

36 Then the priest shall look on him: and, behold, if the scall be spread in the skin, the priest shall not seek for yellow hair; he *is* unclean.

37 But if the scall be in his sight at a stay, and *that* there is black hair grown up therein; the scall is healed, he *is* clean: and the priest shall pronounce him clean.

38 If a man also or a woman have in the skin of their flesh bright spots, *even* white bright spots;

39 Then the priest shall look: and, behold, *if* the bright spots in the skin of their flesh *be* darkish white; it *is* a freckled spot *that* groweth in the skin; he *is* clean.

40 And the man whose hair is fallen off his head, he *is* bald; *yet is* he clean.

41 And he that hath his hair fallen off from the part of his head toward his face, he *is* forehead bald: *yet is* he clean.

42 And if there be in the bald head, or bald ᴿforehead, a white reddish sore; it *is* a leprosy sprung up in his bald head, or his bald forehead. 2 Ch 26:19

43 Then the priest shall look upon it: and, behold, *if* the rising of the sore *be* white reddish in his bald head, or in his bald forehead, as the leprosy appeareth in the skin of the flesh;

44 He is a leprous man, he *is* unclean: the priest shall pronounce him utterly unclean; his plague *is* in his ᴿhead. Is 1:5

45 And the leper in whom the plague *is,* his clothes shall be rent, and his head bare, and he shall